"Wendy Lesser has ingeniously organized her book . . . Her research . . . approaches the monumentality of Kahn's best buildings. Biographers who write about architects sometimes err when it comes to the treatment of the work but not Lesser." —Jack Quinan, *The Buffalo News*

"If [*You Say to Brick*] inspires us to do more, whether to seek out deeper study of [Louis Kahn's] works on our own or to see the world with wider, more curious eyes, then Lesser has done something that the best biographers can hope to do but which only a portion of them achieve. That she does so with a voice that can appeal to the uninitiated as well as the scholar makes *You Say to Brick* all the more impressive, and a deep source of inspiration." —Jedd Beaudoin, *Spectrum Culture*

"[*You Say to Brick* is] a riveting account of Kahn's life . . . Lesser's biography, at once reverential and bracingly candid, serves as a powerful epitaph to Kahn's achievements." —Julia M. Klein, *Forward*

"[Wendy Lesser is] a critic of unusual scope . . . [*You Say to Brick* is an] intriguing speculation about the inner drives that propelled [Louis Kahn] to brilliant design and to numerous affairs, illegitimate children, and chaotic business practices." —*Harvard Magazine*

"Stellar . . . Extensively researched . . . A splendid biography that penetrates the inner lives of Kahn's buildings as well as the inner life of their creator." —*Kirkus Reviews* (starred review)

"[A] supremely enlightening and involving chronicle of an avid and complicated creative life . . . Lesser tracks with clarity and drama each demanding phase in Kahn's evolution as an ardent and magnetic architect and teacher." —*Booklist* (starred review)

"Exhaustively researched and poetically written, [*You Say to Brick*] offers a fitting and eminently accessible tribute to an architect who so ardently sought to bring beauty to the public square." —*Publishers Weekly*

"Louis Kahn has long eluded serious attention. He needed careful, fierce, and passionate study to bring alive his remarkable life and work. In

Wendy Lesser he has found the perfect interlocutor. This book is a triumph."

—Edmund de Waal

"We are always intrigued, with great artists we respect, to learn how and what about their personal lives inspired their work. Wendy Lesser's *You Say to Brick* succeeds in realizing Louis Kahn's long journey from his youth in Europe to his late recognition as one of the great architects of the twentieth century."

—Moshe Safdie

"The American architect Louis Kahn was a luminous man, full of secrets, who made some of the most beautiful buildings of the modern era. He was powerfully drawn to the romance of beginnings (in his love affairs no less than in his art), but he also understood modern concrete. In *You Say to Brick: The Life of Louis Kahn*, Wendy Lesser knows that she has an important but also wonderfully tricky subject on her hands. She brings to life the public art and the private man in ways that do admirable justice to both."

—Mark Stevens and Annalyn Swan

"I was very pleased to read this wonderfully written book. It took me back to the memories of my time and conversation with Lou. I must add that this book has indeed recorded and documented his life very well, and it brings the history of Kahn's work and life alive."

—Balkrishna Doshi

RICHARD RIZZO

WENDY LESSER

YOU SAY TO BRICK

Wendy Lesser is the founder and editor of *The Threepenny Review* and the author of one novel and nine previous books of nonfiction, including *Music for Silenced Voices* and *Why I Read*, which garnered rave reviews from coast to coast. She has written for *The New York Times Book Review*, the *London Review of Books*, *The Times Literary Supplement*, and other publications. To complete this biography, she received one of the first National Endowment for the Humanities Public Scholar awards.

ALSO BY WENDY LESSER

YOU SAY TO BRICK

YOU SAY TO BRICK

THE LIFE OF LOUIS KAHN

WENDY LESSER

FARRAR, STRAUS AND GIROUX   NEW YORK

Farrar, Straus and Giroux
175 Varick Street, New York 10014

Copyright © 2017 by Wendy Lesser
All rights reserved
Published in 2017 by Farrar, Straus and Giroux
First paperback edition, 2018

The Library of Congress has cataloged the hardcover edition as follows:
Names: Lesser, Wendy, author.
Title: You say to brick : the life of Louis Kahn / Wendy Lesser.
Description: First edition. | New York : Farrar, Straus and Giroux, 2017.
Identifiers: LCCN 2016025613 | ISBN 9780374279974 (hardback) |
    ISBN 9780374713317 (e-book)
Subjects: LCSH: Kahn, Louis I., 1901–1974. | Architects—United States—
    Biography. | BISAC: BIOGRAPHY & AUTOBIOGRAPHY / Artists, Architects,
    Photographers. | ARCHITECTURE / Individual Architects & Firms / General. |
    ARCHITECTURE / History / Contemporary (1945–).
Classification: LCC NA737.K32 L48 2017 | DDC 720.92 [B]—dc23
LC record available at https://lccn.loc.gov/2016025613

ISBN: 978-0-374-53763-0

Designed by Jonathan D. Lippincott

Our books may be purchased in bulk for promotional, educational, or business
use. Please contact your local bookseller or the Macmillan Corporate and
Premium Sales Department at 1-800-221-7945, extension 5442, or by e-mail
at MacmillanSpecialMarkets@macmillan.com.

www.fsgbooks.com
www.twitter.com/fsgbooks • www.facebook.com/fsgbooks

Cover photographs: Portrait of Louis Kahn © Keith de Lellis. Trenton Jewish
Community Center, plan of bathhouse (detail), 1955, pencil on vellum, courtesy
of the Louis I. Kahn Collection, University of Pennsylvania and the Pennsylvania
Historical and Museum Commission; housed in the Harvey and Irwin Kroiz Gallery,
the resources of the Kahn Collection are used with the permission of The Architectural Archives, University of Pennsylvania School of Design. Textures © Daniel
Kaesler / EyeEm / Getty Images; iStock.com / PAPStock

P1

For Ileene Smith

I honor beginnings. Of all things, I honor beginnings. I believe that what was has always been, and what is has always been, and what will be has always been.

—Louis Kahn

CONTENTS

PROLOGUE

PROLOGUE

There was much to praise in his work, his colleagues felt, and they would not have hesitated to call him one of the greatest architects of the twentieth century. Just about everybody in the profession, across a broad range of architectural schools and styles, admired what he did. They thought of him as the artist among them. His output over the course of a lifetime was small, but his best buildings were uniquely his, and they were beautiful in a surprising new way.

If he inspired any feelings of envy, they were rare and strangely muted. Perhaps that was because he was such a bad businessman, so hopeless at the financial side of the practice that no one worried about having to compete with him. Or perhaps it was his soft, disarming manner. Through some combination of his poverty-stricken childhood, his unsuccessful school days, and his generally unprepossessing appearance, he had acquired a personality that was completely unthreatening. Even among people who knew how good his work was, the character he radiated was affable, conciliatory, and a bit self-mocking.

Louis Kahn was a warm, captivating man, beloved by students, colleagues, and friends, enduringly attractive to strangers and intimates alike. But he was also a secretive man hiding under a series of masks. There was the physical mask he wore permanently on his face, a layer of heavy scars produced by a childhood accident. Then there was the mask of conventionality he wore in his private life—the forty-four-year marriage to Esther Kahn, mother of his oldest daughter and partner in his Philadelphia social life—which covered over his intense romantic liaisons with two other women, Anne Tyng and Harriet Pattison, each of whom bore him a child outside of wedlock. There was also his name, which was not really his name at all, but a convenient invention devised by Kahn's father and subsequently imposed on his whole family when they immigrated to America. The boy who had been born Leiser-Itze Schmulowsky in Estonia became Louis Isadore Kahn in America: not an escape from Jewish identity itself, but a purposeful elevation from the lowly Eastern European category to the more respectable and established ranks of German Jews. And even Jewishness, for Kahn, may have been another kind of mask, defining him in the eyes of WASP Philadelphia, not to mention the echt-Protestant architecture world, but less fully defining him to himself. If he received more commissions to build synagogues than churches or mosques, it is nonetheless the case that among his built masterpieces only a mosque (in Dhaka's Parliament Building) and a church (First Unitarian in Rochester) emerged triumphant; the synagogues, for the most part, foundered in the design phase. "I'm too religious to be religious," he once told a friend, after a major Philadelphia synagogue commission had disappointingly died on the drafting board following years of conflict with, and within, the congregation.

Perhaps he also meant that his sole religion was architecture. This was what everyone who knew him sensed about him. His wife, his lovers, and his three children—Sue Ann, Alexandra, and Nathaniel—came to understand sooner or later that his work was his one great love. His fellow architects often voiced their respect for his tremendous integrity, repeatedly noting (perhaps with a combination of schadenfreude and chagrin) the way he emphasized the artistic side of the profession over the business side. Even his clients, who sometimes wanted to tear their hair out at his refusal to let a project out of his hands, perceived that his constant revisions resulted from a deep-seated perfectionism, not just orneriness or bad judgment.

His father had wanted him to be a painter, and his mother had wanted him to be a musician. They saw these talents in him as a child, and these remained important aspects of himself that he was to cultivate all his life. But even his parents recognized that once he had discovered architecture, there was no turning back. It became his life. It would not be quite accurate to say it was a life he never regretted, for even to contemplate regret implies the awareness of a path not taken, and for Louis Kahn there was no other path. He had always been meant to be an architect, or so he believed, and such convictions were at the core of his way of thinking. "You say to brick, 'What do you want, brick?'" Kahn remarked in one of his famously gnomic talks. "Brick says to you, 'I like an arch.' If you say to brick, 'Arches are expensive, and I can use a concrete lintel over an opening. What do you think of that, brick?' Brick says, 'I like an arch.'" For Kahn, there was no going against the inherent nature of the materials—and that included himself.

This is not to say that Louis Kahn was the kind of egotistical, overbearing, power-mad architect routinely handed to us by fiction and drama, in characters like Ibsen's manipulative Halvard Solness or Ayn Rand's appalling Howard Roark. The authors of such imaginary architects may nervously disown them, as Ibsen tries to do, or jealously adore them, in Rand's heavy-handed mode, but either way this character is always a galvanizing central figure who wields tremendous force in his own realm. He doesn't just control the physical environment other people inhabit. He also seems to control the people themselves. Women are violently attracted to him, and he exploits this to the full. He is the master of all fates, his own and others', and whether things turn out well or badly for him, he is viewed by both his author and himself as the prime mover in his life.

That caricature does not describe Louis Kahn. (Perhaps it does not describe anybody, including Baron Haussmann and Albert Speer: reality, even at its most grotesque, rarely lives up to the overheated imaginings of writers.) If Kahn was an egotist, it was of a very different sort. He was a generous egotist, who wanted others to get as much pleasure out of life and work as he did. He was a communally minded egotist, who depended heavily on his collaborators and made them feel the value of their contribution, whether it was a single visual element or the knowledge of a specific building material. He was an egotist who supported and inspired the careers of his students. He was the kind of egotist who saw and acknowledged the corresponding ego in every other living thing, and even in some things—like brick—that were not living. Perhaps, in the normal sense of the word, he was not an egotist at all, except in the way children are. But he certainly knew his own worth, he trusted his own instincts, and he was, in his own way, ruthless. It was these qualities that allowed him, in the face of the enormous opposition that life puts up against new ideas, to produce his architectural wonders.

An architect is a strange kind of artist. Compared to a painter or a writer, he stands at a rather distant remove from his finished work. The course of his artistic project, the shape of its ultimate outcome, even whether there will *be* an ultimate outcome are all subject to factors far beyond his control. Money is one of these factors; so are client tastes. Local climate conditions, building regulations, and availability of materials will also come into play. Even history—political or religious or cultural developments about which the architect has no say and possibly even no knowledge—can interfere with his project, and the larger the project, the more likely this is to happen.

Serendipity plays a role in all art, but in architecture it plays an even greater role than usual. Like a filmmaker or an opera director, the architect must depend on many other people to execute his work. These people not only need to know what *they* are doing; they must also have some affinity with, or at least understanding of, the architect's own private vision. When you contemplate all the things that can go wrong and need to go right for a building to end up as its designer imagined it, it is remarkable that any of them succeed.

With many architects—and Louis Kahn was certainly among them— the interplay between these constantly arising difficulties and the architect's own fertility of imagination is an essential part of the process. Kahn was not an isolated genius who came up with perfect ideas and then supervised their exact construction. He was a collaborator of extraordinary abilities. He knew how to inspire people to do their best work, and how to infect his associates with his own enthusiasms. Whether contemplating his own ideas or those of others, he was always relentlessly picking and choosing, tinkering and rejecting, until he finally got what he wanted. Faced with the demands of clients—which were often economic demands for a reduction in scale or at least cost—he would repeatedly go back to the drawing board to find a new approach. He was not a prima donna; in this respect, at any rate, he was a practical builder. At the same time, he was not a pushover, and he could not be forced, especially later in his career, to sign off on a project he wasn't satisfied with.

Yet that desire to have his way, that personal sense of involvement, did not result in anything as specific as a definite architectural style. When you see a building by Robert Venturi or Frank Gehry, even if it's one you've never seen before, you are likely to recognize it as a Venturi or a Gehry because of its trademark stylistic qualities: its postmodern symmetry and fanciful façade, say, or its billowing skin of titanium. Louis Kahn's great buildings, by contrast, often look quite different from each other, and when viewed from the outside, some of them may not even look particularly distinctive. You cannot necessarily recognize a Kahn project by the way it looks. What you can recognize is the feeling it gives you to be inside it, to wander around it. That feeling—a combination of exhilaration and repose, a sense of being intimately contained and at the same time offered access to grand, expansive possibilities—may well be what defines a Kahn work, for us and for him. It doesn't happen every time: he had some failures, just as every artist does. But it happens often enough to make a difference.

What kind of difference *does* architecture make in our lives? This is not a rhetorical question, and it is not just a matter of beauty (though beauty, considered in its widest sense, is bound to play a role). Rome is without a doubt more beautiful than Rochester or Dhaka, but for most of us Rome is not an option. Architecture needs to come to us—and unlike most other art forms, architecture comes to us whether we want it to or not. You have to go to a museum to look at paintings, attend a concert to hear live music, pick up a novel if you intend to read it. These art forms are, in that respect, relatively passive. Architecture, on the other hand, is aggressive: it surrounds us all the time, not just in our homes and offices but in public places. It is ever-present and often forgettable, but even when we aren't particularly focused on it, it can make us feel better or worse, depending on its quality.

Consider, for example, two pieces of public architecture that Louis Kahn did not design but that he used frequently. Both are train stations: 30th Street Station in Philadelphia, built in the early 1930s, and Penn Station in New York, constructed in the late 1960s. Between them, they pretty much define the full spectrum of architectural quality, from best to worst.

If you approach 30th Street Station from the east by driving along Philadelphia's JFK Boulevard, it presents itself from quite a distance as a visible destination. Standing on its own by the bank of the Schuylkill River, this huge symmetrical structure rises eight stories high at its center, with lower matching wings on either side. As your car or taxi pulls up to the station, you step out under a grand portico which, with its tall columns and massive roof, reflects the whole width and height of the main central structure. You are in no doubt that you have arrived somewhere.

Even if you come by subway and approach from the other direction, entering the building sideways through one of its lower wings, you will soon find yourself in the enormous main concourse that occupies the central structure. This room (and it does come across as a single room, despite its vast size) measures nearly three hundred feet lengthwise and about half that in width, with an intricately painted coffered ceiling hanging ninety feet above your head. Natural light floods in from all four sides—so much light that in the daytime the thirty-two tall windows surrounding the main concourse have to be veiled with gauzy curtains. These multistory, multipaned windows, which extend from below mid-wall up to the rim of the high ceiling, are evenly distributed around the pleasingly proportioned rectangle of the room, so that five occupy each of the narrower ends and eleven line the longer sides. Even if you don't consciously count the windows on each wall, there is something intuitively reassuring in the combination of their odd numbers and the regular, even spacing between them—a kind of grand symmetry that allows you to locate yourself within the space, physically, visually, and psychologically. From any point in this immense room, you can have a sense of exactly where you are.

The emptiness above your head is by no means wasted space. Though it cannot be used commercially—perhaps *because* it cannot be used commercially—that seven-story gap of pure light and air feels like a crown on your head, a symbol of your own worth as a valued traveler passing through. Far from diminishing you or making you feel antlike, the grandeur elevates you to its own level. (It's a phenomenon Kahn himself remarked on in a different context, when he said of the ancient Baths of Caracalla: "We know that we can bathe just as well under an 8-foot ceiling as we can under a 150-foot ceiling, but I believe there's something about a 150-foot ceiling that makes a man a different kind of man.") And though there is a faint echoing effect produced by all that empty space, this does not in any way interfere with the audibility of the murmured conversations taking place on the comfortable wooden benches grouped intermittently around the edges of the 30th Street concourse. If you eavesdrop on these passengers, you will hear a surprising number of them commenting on what a nice train station it is. People notice such things.

Even at night, when this grand room needs to be lit artificially, a sense of light and warmth remains. Ten large and beautifully designed Art Deco chandeliers hang from the coffered ceiling, five to each side of the long rectangle, well set in from the walls. They descend low enough to cast a clear light but remain high enough to leave plenty of space between their bottommost metal-banded rim and the unobtrusive information booth, complete with destination boards, that occupies the center of the room. The chandeliers cast a warm light that picks up the golden tone of the stone walls, the rosy gray of the marble floors, the polished glow of the old wooden benches, and the gilded ornamentation on the tall Corinthian columns that separate the end windows from each other. Nothing can quite match the glory of the room's daylight appearance, but even after dark, 30th Street Station is a comfortable, pleasant place to sit and wait. And though you do have to migrate downstairs when the time comes to catch your train, you have been so generously accommodated in this elegantly humane waiting room that you don't really mind the brief descent.

If you are taking the train from Philadelphia to New York, you emerge ninety minutes later into something like a living hell. At first you hurry along narrow platforms between grimy trains, anxious to get out of this subterranean region that feels even deeper and darker than the one you left behind in Philadelphia. But then, after you climb the crowded steps from the track level to the so-called main concourse of Penn Station, you discover that you are *still* underground. No natural light has ever entered this relentlessly oppressive space, and the artificial lighting, which emerges from various indistinct sources, is cold and harsh without being bright.

The main room of the station is long and narrow, but it seems to have no particular size or even shape because its edges are for the most part indecipherable. The floor beneath your feet is made up of large gray and beige squares that look as if they were designed for the sole purpose of bearing heavy traffic. The ceiling feels so low that it seems to press down on your head. What makes the space feel even more cramped is the gigantic destination board that hangs down from the ceiling midway along the concourse, taking up over half the vertical space and about three-quarters of the room's width. There is no seating in this entire concourse (a couple of spartanly furnished waiting rooms, divided by class and set aside for ticket holders only, are cloistered off to the side), so the people who are waiting for their train's announcement stand like clustered zombies in front of the giant notice board. As you weave your way through these unhappy shades, you thank your stars that your journey is almost over, even if that means you must now choose between the dingy subway and the frantic mess that is Eighth Avenue.

The experience of present-day Penn Station is made worse by the knowledge that something marvelous once stood in its place. Even for those who never saw the grandly classical Pennsylvania Station that existed before 1963—and most of the many millions who now use this station did not—something of its memory still clings to the place, like a long-lost childhood dream underlying a painful adult reality. If you search online for images of Penn Station in New York, fully half the pictures that come up will be photos of that triumphantly arched stone, glass, and steel interior. It makes you wonder about your fellow humans, the ones who allowed that beautiful building to be torn down and this monstrosity put up instead. It also makes you understand, in a distressingly visceral way, why architecture might matter to us.

▪

One of the things Louis Kahn realized, and repeatedly emphasized in his thinking and his writing as well as in his design process, was that architecture exists in time, not just in space. Goethe's phrase about architecture being "frozen music" has been misused so many times that it no longer has much meaning. But for Kahn architecture was like music precisely because it was *not* frozen. He often compared the architect's plan to a musical score: the drawings were not an artwork in themselves, but a set of written instructions that would ultimately give rise to an artwork in unpredictable and unduplicatable ways. And this same unexpectedness, this sense of movement, fluidity, and narrative excitement, characterizes his completed projects. Kahn's best buildings are works of art that, to be fully appreciated, need to be experienced by a body moving through space. Only by walking around and through one of his finished structures can you perceive how many different pathways to discovery it offers, how many observations about light and shadow and weight and transcendence it is making.

That is why this account of Kahn's life and career, as it unfolds in the following pages, is punctuated by a series of "in situ" descriptions of what it feels like to move through his built structures. The five selected locations—the Salk Institute for Biological Studies, the Kimbell Art Museum, the Phillips Exeter Library, the National Assembly Building of Bangladesh, and the Indian Institute of Management—are all masterpieces Kahn created in his last fifteen years. That was the nature of this slowly developing career: the notable achievements were all bunched up toward the end. The buildings themselves, though, are both timeless and of our time, eternally located in their own present tense, and for this reason they have been lifted out of the chronology of his life and presented in these five sections as discrete dramatic experiences.

That almost choreographic sensation—of one's own movement in relation to the stillness of the structures—is notoriously difficult to convey in printed form, whether in architectural descriptions or in photographs. One of the few places where it comes across at all, in fact, is in the filmmaker Nathaniel Kahn's wonderful movie about his father, *My Architect*. Yet even within the limitations imposed by a book, the attempt to describe this dynamic seems repeatedly worth making, since it lies at the heart of Kahn's accomplishment. Louis Kahn's buildings are not pretty pictures beheld against a skyline, but events that happen to those who encounter them, and this is partly why people in general, and not just his fellow architects, love and value his work.

Architecture, as Kahn knew, also exists in time in another way. Buildings can be destroyed, but some of them will persist, coming down to us from centuries and millennia in the past. If we are lucky, they come down to us whole, or at least whole enough to convey a strong sense of their original nature. The ancient works that Kahn himself loved most, like the Pantheon in Rome or the Greek temples at Paestum, have this strange quality of existing both in their own era and in ours. They directly address our sense of mortality, and at the same time they persuade us that something made by humans—something larger than ourselves but nonetheless partaking of ourselves—can lastingly endure. Great buildings, great structures, sometimes allow us to feel that what is dead can come to life again. One might almost say that architecture, at its best, has the power to make time flow backwards.

ENDING

He was tired, and he was not accustomed to being tired. He had always been famous for his energy. He could work all night, make a presentation in the morning, take off on an airplane in the afternoon, chat to his seatmate about architecture for five hours straight, and make up for it all with a quick catnap. He did not feel seventy-three, not at all. Although his body had thickened somewhat with age, his arms and chest still showed the strength of the wrestler he had been at college. He could still split an apple with his bare hands. He could still run up the four flights of stairs that led to his Philadelphia office. And he could still charm young women—or at least the occasional young woman— with his sparkling blue eyes. He was used to pushing himself to the limits of his capacity, of all his capacities. It was the only way he knew how to live.

Still, the last few months had been hard. Since November of 1973 he had made at least eight quick trips to visit clients overseas. At home, there had been times when he definitely felt ill. Esther called it "indigestion" and worried about what he ate. Sue Ann, the few times she had come down from New York, had commented to her mother that he did not look well. One night, when he was visiting Harriet and Nathaniel on the occasion of Nathaniel's violin recital, there was an episode that frightened Harriet so much she drove him to the emergency room. But the hospital doctor had checked him out and said he was fine: false alarm. So he continued his heavy travel schedule. In January of 1974 he had flown to Dacca to sign some additional contracts for the work his firm was doing in the Bangladeshi capital. In February he had gone to Iran, where he was to collaborate with Kenzo Tange on a 12,000-acre new town in the heart of Tehran. In April he was due to visit Teddy Kollek, the mayor of Jerusalem, to consult about the garden for the Hurva Synagogue. "I find that I must visit Jerusalem to spend time on the site of the Hurva, to be in your company, and think about the whole thing in the presence of everything around it," he had written to Kollek earlier that year. "A garden is a very special thing . . . Please expect me in Jerusalem, within two months or so."

And now, taking advantage of his weeklong spring break from teaching at Penn, he was in Ahmedabad, giving a talk for the Ford Foundation, taking a look at the Institute buildings with an eye toward making some additions, and spending time with his dear friend Balkrishna V. Doshi. He and Doshi had first met in 1958 or 1959, and they had been working together since 1962, when he was invited to design the Indian Institute of Management in Doshi's home city, Ahmedabad. From the Indian architect's point of view, this American colleague had proven to be something quite out of the ordinary. "Every time he talked about the people of India," Doshi would later remark, "I got more and more interested. Somehow he found there was a much closer affinity between him and the people of India. I really feel that he was more Eastern, more Indian than a lot of Indians are . . . Temperamentally, he was like a sage; he was like a yogi. Always thinking about things beyond, thinking about the spirit."

During this March trip, as on most of his previous trips to Ahmedabad, he made sure to leave time to visit with Doshi's family. He was particularly fond of the youngest child, Maneesha. "He thought she was the most remarkable because she had the talent of Picasso. He liked to think this," Doshi noted wryly. On this occasion Doshi and his wife brought out all of Maneesha's drawings and showed them to him. "And mind you," Doshi continued, "more than forty to fifty minutes, he is going through each drawing, watching them carefully, satisfying himself of every intricacy that she was drawing. And then once he explained why this was good and why this was not good. In fact to me it was a revelation. I had never felt that this man saw so well and in such detail."

Though he had been scheduled to fly back on Friday the 15th, intending to reach Philadelphia on Saturday so as to be rested and ready for his Monday class, he delayed his return by a day so that he could see Kasturbhai Lalbhai. The venerable old mill-owner, one of the master-minds behind the Indian Institute of Management, was nearing ninety now, and given his age, one couldn't help but be aware that each visit could be the last. "I must see Kasturbhai," he said to Doshi, "and I don't mind leaving on Saturday." So on his last afternoon in Ahmedabad, they went to Kasturbhai's house for tea. The three of them chatted about the additions he was designing for the IIM, and he promised to return with drawings in May or June, immediately after a further trip to Tehran.

"You will bring me cashew nuts from there, from Tehran, when you come?" said Kasturbhai.

"Of course," he answered, according to Doshi, "I will bring for you not only one box, I will bring for you two boxes, Kasturbhai. If you like something, I must do it for you."

At some point before Doshi drove him to the airport for the flight to Bombay, the two of them had a long talk about art. Doshi didn't write anything down at the time, but later he thought about their conversation and tried to remember some of his friend's exact phrases so as to note them in his diary. All that he could recapture with certainty, though, were a few words about "the process of discovery, the fountain of joy and the spirit of light."

■

The flight from Ahmedabad got him to Bombay's Santacruz Airport in plenty of time to catch his usual Air India flight to London, which left late at night. Before boarding, he went through passport control, where the immigration official stamped his passport with the airport's characteristic oval mark and wrote the date—March 16, 1974—in the center. Once aboard, he endured a seemingly endless journey as the plane stopped in Kuwait, Rome, and Paris before finally reaching London, where he was supposed to connect with a TWA flight that would bring him straight to Philadelphia. But by the time he reached Heathrow on Sunday, he had missed his scheduled flight, so he had to rebook on an Air India flight that would instead take him to New York.

At the London airport, by complete chance, he met a fellow architect, Stanley Tigerman, who was on his way to Bangladesh. "I'm at the airport and I see this old man, who looks like he has detached retinas, is really raggy and looks like a bum. It was Lou," Tigerman later reported. "If I had not known he was Lou Kahn, I would have thought he was a homeless person."

Louis Kahn had been a teacher of Tigerman's at Yale in the 1950s. Years later they had run into each other in Dacca, where they both started working on architectural projects at about the same time. Tigerman, however, had withdrawn from his projects during the nine-month war that turned East Pakistan into Bangladesh, whereas Kahn had retained his ties to the capital, quietly working on his plans throughout the war and then being welcomed back as the architect of the new country's government center. They hadn't seen much of each other in the years since, but now the two men greeted each other cordially, sat down together in the airport, and talked for a while—mainly about architecture, Kahn's eternal subject.

"We were reminiscing. We had a nice talk," Tigerman recalled, and then went on: "He seemed exhausted, depressed. He looked like hell."

One of the things Tigerman remembered from his time at Yale was that Paul Rudolph, who eventually became dean of the architecture school, was "kind of not nice" to Kahn. (In fact, what Rudolph did was to remodel the interior of Louis Kahn's first major project, the Yale University Art Gallery, without asking his permission or advice.) But on that Sunday at Heathrow, after he had said goodbye to his former student, Kahn suddenly turned and called out, "Tigerman, come here. I want to tell you something." As the younger man later described it, "He said, 'I know you are close to Paul, and I haven't seen him in such a long time. Tell him when you see him that I miss him and I think he is really a terrific architect.' I was really touched by that," Tigerman added.

Kahn caught his Air India flight out of London and got to JFK around 6:00 p.m. on Sunday the 17th, nearly three hours after he had originally been due to arrive at Philadelphia's airport. Instead of trying to catch a connecting flight, though, he made his way to New York's Penn Station so as to travel by train to 30th Street Station—always his preferred mode of arriving in Philadelphia. He was unable to get a ticket on the 7:30 Metroliner, so he bought one for the 8:30 train. Since he had over an hour before his train boarded, he bought a newspaper and checked his overcoat and suitcase in a locker. Although he had been away for a whole week, he was traveling with just one suitcase, the somewhat battered old leather case, barely larger than a briefcase, that he liked to take on all his trips. Attached to its worn handle was a permanent luggage tag on which were typed the words "Prof. Louis I. Kahn, 921 Clinton Street, Philadelphia, PA, USA."

A woman who knew Kahn by sight, an artist from Philadelphia, saw him go up to a pay phone and try to make a call, but apparently no one picked up at the other end. She watched as he headed off toward the men's room, which was on the lower level of the station. This would have been sometime after seven.

Just before eight o'clock, a man who didn't know Louis Kahn—but who happened, as it later turned out, to be the brother of a friend of Esther Kahn's—encountered Kahn in the men's room. He noticed this small white-haired guy with thick glasses and a heavily scarred face walking around with his jacket off and his shirt collar open, and he thought the guy looked very pale. So he went over to him and asked, "Is there anything I can do for you?" Kahn told him he didn't feel well, and asked him to find the bathroom attendant and send him for a doctor. The man did this, and the attendant left immediately—and then the bystander left too, because he had to meet his wife upstairs and he didn't think the old guy looked dangerously ill. He had looked "gray," this man later reported, but he also looked in complete control of himself and he was walking around. As the man got up to the main concourse and was about to tell his wife what had happened, he spotted the attendant returning with the police.

■

When her husband failed to show up that Sunday afternoon, Esther was not too concerned, because the Air India flight to London was often late and Lou frequently missed his connecting flight. And when he didn't come home that evening, she assumed he might have gone straight to the office, as he had a habit of doing. Or he could have been at Harriet's, for all she knew. So, aside from the fact that he hadn't called her when he landed—which was odd, because he always did, even after a short trip—she didn't think there was anything much to worry about.

By midnight, though, she had begun to feel anxious, and when he still hadn't been heard from on Monday morning, she had his office call India. Kathy Condé, Kahn's secretary, placed calls to both Doshi and Kasturbhai Lalbhai, and then waited for the response. In the meantime Kathy called the airlines and discovered that Kahn was not on the passenger lists for any of the flights coming into Philadelphia from London, nor on any of the other available manifests. (Air India, she learned, did not maintain a passenger manifest for security reasons.) Later that day she heard back from Doshi that Kahn had boarded the plane from Ahmedabad to Bombay in time to catch the Saturday flight. Kathy continued to make calls all evening—to Western Union in order to see whether any cables had been sent either to the office or to Esther; to the Arrivals number at Kennedy Airport; to Pan Am; and again to Air India. By the time she left the office at 12:30 that night, she had begun to keep a log documenting each step taken during the emergency. "It was feared that he had reached London and something happened to him there or he was too tired to call" was her last entry for Monday night.

On Tuesday morning Kathy returned to the office at 7:30 and called the London police and Scotland Yard. Meanwhile, Esther managed to ascertain, through a contact who had an office in London, that Kahn had indeed been on the Air India flight to Heathrow, had missed his TWA connection, and had rebooked on the Air India flight to New York. Esther called Air India and got a supervisor named Mr. Magee, whom she asked to find out anything he could; when he called her back, he was able to tell her that Louis Kahn had gone through Customs and Immigration in New York at 6:20 p.m. on Sunday. On Kathy's advice, Esther then called Mayor Rizzo's office, and two Philadelphia detectives were sent out, first to Kahn's office and then to the Kahn residence. At one point the two detectives, Mr. Magee, and Kathy Condé were all independently checking to see if Kahn might have boarded a helicopter which Air India had made available on Sunday night to those seeking to connect with an Eastern Airways flight from LaGuardia to Philadelphia. They found he had not.

Kathy then called Gracie Mansion and asked for any help the New York City mayor's office could give. Less than half an hour later she got a call back from a woman who told her that Kahn was not in any New York hospital or city morgue. The woman said she was still checking with the police department, though, and she promised to call back if she learned anything.

■

The two New York City policemen who had returned with the men's room attendant on that Sunday night at Penn Station were Officer Allen and Officer Folmer. According to the police report that Folmer later filed at the Fourteenth Precinct, they arrived on the scene to find Louis Kahn "lying face up next to the men's room." Officer Allen tried to administer oxygen to the fallen man, but with no effect. The terse, practical report does not say whether Kahn was conscious or unconscious when the two policemen found him, but no mention is made of any speech or movement on his part. He was probably already dead.

Officer Folmer accompanied the body to St. Clare's Hospital in nearby Hell's Kitchen, where Kahn was pronounced DOA by a Dr. Vidal. The police officer then proceeded to go through the deceased's pockets in the presence of the morgue attendant. There he must have found the locker key, because the leather suitcase, the coat, Kahn's passport, and his train ticket all eventually showed up with the body. Folmer's assumption in the police report he wrote later that night—that it was a natural death caused by cardiac arrest—was confirmed the next day when Dr. John Furey, deputy chief medical examiner for New York City, concluded that Louis Kahn had died of occlusive coronary arteriosclerosis.

In the meantime, though, something strange had happened. Though their report correctly identified the body as that of Louis I. Kahn, the policemen somehow got the idea that Kahn's office address, 1501 Walnut Street, was where he lived. That was the home address they put into their report, and that was the address they cabled to the Philadelphia police at 9:50 p.m. "Notify Esther Kahn, 1501 Walnut St., your city, that a white male, 72 years, tentatively identified as her husband Louis Kahn of the same address, is deceased this city," read the teletype that arrived that Sunday night in the operations room of Philadelphia's Ninth District headquarters. Unlike the error in his age, which could have been a mere subtraction mistake (the passport stated that Louis Isadore Kahn had been born on February 20, 1901, in Estonia), this error was not easily explained. There was no address at all listed in the passport itself, but Kahn's vaccination certificate, which was firmly attached to the passport, gave 921 Clinton Street as his home address. Besides, his leather suitcase—logged in by the New York police, and labeled with a strip of masking tape that had "DOA" written across it—bore that permanent tag with his home address typed on it. Perhaps the police, in their first search of his pockets, found a business card or a piece of letterhead with the Walnut Street office address printed on it. Perhaps they looked him up in the Philadelphia phone book, where he was listed at 1501 Walnut rather than at his home address. No matter. The damage was done, and the wrong address was included in the teletype to Philadelphia.

When this cable arrived, it was already late on a Sunday night—and not just any Sunday night, but Saint Patrick's Day. A police car was dispatched to the Walnut Street address, where the officers found only a closed office building. They returned to the station and proceeded to forget about the notification. The cable from New York was left lying in the wrong box, and nobody paid any further attention to it for two full days. By the time the missing teletype was finally rediscovered, it had become obsolete.

About twenty minutes after hearing that Kahn was not in any hospital or morgue in New York City, Kathy Condé got another call from a different woman in New York, who informed her that Louis Kahn was dead. Kathy was told that the body had been taken to Missing Persons, located in a blue-brick building next to the Medical Examiner's Office on First Avenue, and she was given a number to call. She called the number and gave Kahn's description to the man at the other end; he confirmed that the body was there and that a telegram stating this would be sent to Mrs. Kahn, but he also said someone would have to come in person to make a positive identification. The office, he told her, would be open until 5:00 p.m.

"Of course I went to New York to get Lou and here it was again confusion compounded upon confusion," Esther wrote in a letter several months later, describing this series of events to an Italian friend of

Kahn's, "but I was assured he suffered only a very short time and he looked simply wonderful. If anyone can be said to look wonderful in death, he did." She also noted in the letter that "Lou died in the arms of two policemen who were members of the rescue squad"—possibly Missing Persons' kindhearted elaboration of the police report's bare facts, or perhaps just Esther's own version of the death as she pictured it.

That Tuesday evening, Esther called her daughter at Bennington, where Sue Ann spent one night each week so as to teach a regular music class. Sue Ann was about to turn thirty-four. She was a professional flutist, married, living in New York, well aware of at least some of the difficulties in her parents' marriage—an adult, in other words, not in immediate need of a father's care. But the news was so upsetting and so unexpected that she barely retained a sense of the surrounding circumstances. "It was quite a shock," she recalled nearly four decades later. "It was a long time before I came to grips with the fact that he was really dead." Later, upon reflection, she modified her recollection: "I had a premonition. I remember at Christmas dinner he had turned very red"—but then she reversed herself again, adding, "It was a shock because everyone thought he was so vigorous."

There were still two other children to be notified, and Esther naturally did not consider this her job. Late that Tuesday afternoon, Kathy Condé called Harriet Pattison's house. Calls had been going back and forth between Kathy and Harriet since Monday, because Harriet Pattison, in addition to being a landscape architect who worked with Louis Kahn's firm, was known by everyone in the office to be the mother of his eleven-year-old son. The fact that Lou went out to Chestnut Hill practically every week to see the two of them, have dinner, and maybe spend part of the night was an accepted part of his routine; even Esther knew about the relationship, and would report to Sue Ann that Nathaniel was now taking violin lessons, for instance, or that Harriet was driving Lou crazy. So when Kahn didn't show up at the office that Monday morning, Harriet's was one of the first places Kathy had called. Now, however, she had to make a different and much harder call.

Nathaniel was standing in the kitchen with his mother when she picked up the ringing telephone. "Is he dead?" Harriet asked. Then she quietly put the receiver back in its cradle. "She didn't need to tell me," Nathaniel said many years later. "I knew he was dead." The two of them went outside and stood on the lawn near their neighbors' house. It was almost spring, and the days were getting longer, but they could still feel a chill in the air as they watched the sun go down over the hill. "Will happy times ever come again?" Nathaniel asked.

Nobody at Kahn's office thought to call Anne Tyng. She hadn't, after all, been working there regularly since the early 1960s. But Anne and Lou had stayed in close touch long after their sexual relationship had ended—in part because their daughter, Alexandra, brought them together, but also because they liked and respected each other. Even after Alex went away to college, they would occasionally see each other. Just recently, for instance, they had been looking at something together on the Penn campus, where both of them taught in the architecture school, and Lou had patted her affectionately and commented, not for the first time, "You never stop loving someone."

Now, on that Tuesday night, Anne got a phone call from the news director at a major Philadelphia radio station, a man who was the father of one of Alex's high-school friends. News of Louis Kahn's death had gone out over the wires, and this man, knowing of the family connection, wanted to make sure that Anne Tyng heard about it from him before she saw it on the television news or read about it in the next day's paper. As soon as Anne got off the phone, she called Alex, who was a junior at Harvard. "My mother called me and I rushed home," said the grown-up Alex Tyng, a painter, thinking back on these events nearly forty years later. "I just remember lying on my bed and thinking: Your father isn't sick a day in his life and now he's dead."

The March 20 edition of *The New York Times* carried a front-page obituary by Paul Goldberger as well as an appreciation of Louis Kahn's work written by Ada Louise Huxtable. Headlined "Kahn, a Blender of Logic, Power, Grace," the Huxtable article singled out the Phillips Exeter Library, the capital buildings in Bangladesh, the Richards Medical Laboratories at Penn, and the Kimbell Art Museum in Fort Worth as examples of Kahn's "strong and subtle" spaces. The *Philadelphia Inquirer* obituary that appeared that same Wednesday focused more on the strange circumstances surrounding his death, with a follow-up article on

March 21 headed "Police Here Failed to Notify Wife of Kahn's Death"; but the *Inquirer* also published an elegiac editorial in Thursday's edition entitled "Louis Kahn, Fundamental Genius." The *Times* obit listed only Esther and Sue Ann as Kahn's survivors, while the *Inquirer* added in Lou's sister, Sarah. Nowhere were the other two children mentioned.

The office was deluged with phone calls, while telegrams addressed to Esther Kahn began to pour in at both the home and work addresses. Among them was a cable from the White House that began "It is with the deepest sense of grief that I learned of the passing of your husband Louis I. Kahn, one of America's truly great architects" and ended with the signature "Richard Nixon." Teddy Kollek wrote from Israel ("Deeply shocked. Louis' death a tremendous loss to Jerusalem and the world") and Isamu Noguchi from Japan ("The world shares your great loss"). Telegrams came from Nancy Hanks, chair of the National Endowment for the Arts, and from Aaron Copland and John Hersey, in their roles as president and secretary of the American Academy of Arts and Letters, as well as from a wide range of Kahn's fellow architects, including I. M. Pei, Kevin Roche, Carlo Scarpa, José Luis Sert, and Bob and Denise Venturi. The lengthiest and most detailed cable was from Buckminster Fuller, who wrote, among other things: "I first knew him when he was struggling through Depression days designing homes for the ILGWU. I watched him grow and grow as an architect and a philosopher . . . So long as any of his buildings stand, and most will stand for a long, long time, Lou will be speaking directly to the living humans whom he loved and who all loved him."

Meanwhile, plans went forward for the funeral, which had been announced for 10:00 a.m. on Friday the 22nd. Traditional Jewish law requires that the body be buried as soon as possible, preferably within twenty-four hours of death, but such speed is rare in the modern world, and Judaism allows its adherents to adapt to unusual circumstances. In this case, Louis Kahn was to receive a Jewish burial five days after he had died and three days after his body had been identified. He had never been a practicing Jew, but he had been married by a rabbi, and both his parents had been buried by rabbis; it was assumed he would have wanted the same for himself. So a Society Hill rabbi who had never even met Lou was enlisted to conduct the service. A small list of pallbearers and a much longer list of honorary pallbearers were

drawn up, and invitations were issued to the great and good of Philadelphia and beyond.

The funeral was held at the Oliver Bair Funeral Home, a large neo-
clàssical building located at 1820 Chestnut Street in the heart of old
Philadelphia. The service itself was on the second floor, in the largest
available chapel, with a side chapel reserved for the overflow crowd.
Over a thousand people showed up at Bair's on that Friday morning and
mounted the grand staircase that led to the second floor. Most of them
managed to crowd into the big main room, where Rabbi Ivan Caine—
assisted by a Roman Catholic pastor, Monsignor John McFadden, who
had actually known Lou—presided over the service. At the front of the
room, the simple oak coffin rested on a pedestal covered with red
velvet. Esther and Sue Ann sat in the first row. Around and just behind
them were relatives and close friends, followed by the people who
had worked at Kahn's office and his colleagues from Penn. Dignitaries
and architects from all over the world had arrived to pay their respects.
But there were also numerous other guests who had no official standing
and were simply drawn by their affection for Lou and his work. "There
was this group of conservative old Jewish people and then there was
a huge crowd of students, sort of hippie-ish, and they weren't exactly
dressed to the nines," observed Ed Richards, a man who had worked in
Kahn's office for a few years in the early 1960s. "It was a very big crowd.
I thought it was great, all the students."

Another of Kahn's former employees, David Slovic, also remembered how crowded it was, and he even thought he recalled a slight
scuffle—but whether that resulted from an attempt to keep someone
out, or was simply due to competition for scarce seats, he couldn't be
sure. "I was kind of an outsider, no longer in the office," he said. "I was
not aware of the tensions: Esther trying to prevent them coming, and all
the things I found out later." But Jack MacAllister, a longer-term employee who had managed the Salk project for Kahn and had remained
close to him even after starting his own practice in La Jolla, knew of
the potential difficulties. "I was asked to go to the funeral, and I wisely
did not go," he remarked. "I saw it as a place where the vultures would be
descending—all the people who wanted a part of him, or a part of the
business. I heard that various members of the family didn't want other
members there."

A close friend of Esther's named Anne Meyers—who was not only the wife of Kahn's colleague Marshall Meyers, but also Esther Kahn's informal financial advisor—said that Esther gave her rather explicit instructions in this regard. The other two children and their mothers were to be treated with respect if they insisted on coming to the funeral, but she did not want them sitting "in her line of sight." So Angel Meyers, as she was called, tried to make sure that these unwanted guests were steered to the side chapel, from which the coffin was not visible but to which the speakers' voices could be piped in.

"I remember seeing a number of people seated up front, and knowing we were not going to be sitting there," said the grown-up Nathaniel Kahn, reflecting back on the eleven-year-old self who had been through these experiences. "When you have these different families, there's this sense that everyone is isolated in their own particular grief. And there's this awkward sense that you're being watched, that you're not really supposed to be there. Somehow there's this memory I have of being told to go into the side room. I remember not being able to see. There was a loudspeaker, a kind of walnut-cased cloth-covered speaker, through which I was hearing the proceedings. So there was this really disconnected sense—there was this random rabbi, who was saying really nice things but that didn't seem to have anything to do with the father I knew."

Much more pertinent, from the young Nathaniel's point of view, was the comment of the taxi driver who had brought his uncle Willy from the airport to the funeral home. When Willy Pattison (who, according to Nathaniel, "was definitely no fan of Lou's") met his sister and nephew at the top of the staircase inside Oliver Bair's, he told them about the conversation he'd had in the cab. "Oh, you're going to the funeral of the professor," said the driver, adding: "We all knew him. He was a great man." Nathaniel felt this opinion was confirmed by the line of taxis he had seen waiting outside the funeral home. They were "paying their respects," he recalled, "like they wanted to be part of it: the taxi drivers all knew Lou, because he didn't drive." Inside the chapel, by contrast, there was only the disembodied voice of Rabbi Caine, telling anecdotes about the famous man he had never met. "It was like the voice of God coming through the speaker. It was surreal," Nathaniel reflected. "It was kind of the beginning of having him taken away."

Alex Tyng, who was nearly nine years older than Nathaniel, handled the situation differently. Alex had always possessed a strong personality. It was she who, at the age of sixteen, had sought out both her younger half-brother and her older half-sister, forging enduring connections between the previously isolated families. Alex had also insisted on being present at various public occasions involving Lou, often bringing her little brother with her, as if to demonstrate that they too were part of Kahn's life, despite all the subterfuges and concealments. And now, at her father's funeral, she was not going to submit to being put in her place.

"The funeral was actually on my birthday—I was twenty," recalled Alex. "The same woman who was always trying to make us go to the back—she was the wife of someone who worked for him—tried to usher us into the side room. Actually, let me back up: she called our house before the funeral. I heard my mother talking to her and saying, 'How could you tell us not to come?' She was furious. So that kind of set up this anxious feeling in my stomach, since I knew I would have to contend with this force that would try to prevent us from sitting where we wanted to sit."

When Angel Meyers was unable to persuade Alex and Anne Tyng to go to the side room, she sat them at the very back of the main room—"even though my mother had worked in the office for years," Alex pointed out. Anne Tyng remained at the back for the duration of the service. But Alex marched up to the front, where she was hailed by Harry Saltzman, Sue Ann's husband, who was sitting in the second row.

"When my sister came in, she came up to the front," Sue Ann observed. "She's not one to take any guff. My husband said to her, 'Come sit with me—this is where all the good people are sitting.' I went to find Harriet and she was in a side chapel." Alex, too, went looking for Nathaniel at the same time.

"Alex said did I want to come sit up front with her, but I wanted to stay with my mother," Nathaniel recollected, and Alex remembered the same thing: "He felt he wanted to comfort his mother, which was really sweet. I felt a little guilty that I wasn't sitting next to my mother and comforting her, but I knew she could take care of herself. I knew I would be really angry if I sat in the back, so I didn't."

None of this family drama impinged in any noticeable way on the stately proceedings. "Rabbi Caine drew a similarity between Louis Kahn and the prophet Moses," ran the fulsome report in that Friday's *Evening Bulletin*, while "Kahn's wife, the former Esther Israeli, sat in the front row in the ornate funeral parlor . . . surrounded by friends and relatives." ("Esther was there as if she should have gotten an Academy Award" was Ed Richards' unkinder take.) When the eulogies by Rabbi Caine, Monsignor McFadden, and Kahn's old friend and fellow architect Norman Rice had been delivered, the coffin was solemnly carried out by the official pallbearers. The young Nathaniel was very impressed by the sight: "I remember seeing all the men from his office carry the casket down the steps on their shoulders"—though in fact only one of the pallbearers, David Wisdom, actually worked in Kahn's firm. The others included Dr. Bernard Alpers, the neurologist who had employed Esther as his medical technician for most of her working life; David Zoob, Lou's lawyer; Norman Rice, who had known Lou since their boyhood; Charles Madden, a Philadelphia artist; and four other local dignitaries. Together they carried the plain wooden box down the sweeping staircase and out to the waiting hearse.

About fifty cars followed the hearse to the Montefiore Cemetery in northeast Philadelphia. *The Evening Bulletin* was impressed not only by the number of vehicles, but by their variety: "Immediately behind a shiny black Mercedes was a well-used Volkswagen bus," the reporter noted. Sue Ann and Alex rode separately but met up at the graveyard. "I remember Sue being upset," said Alex. "She was holding my hand. I don't know who was comforting who." They didn't let go even when they reached the grave itself. "We were supposed to put earth on the casket," Alex recalled. "I had never been to a Jewish funeral before, so I didn't know what to do, but she kind of showed me. We held hands and did it together."

Nathaniel didn't go to the cemetery to see his father buried. He watched as the coffin was lifted into the hearse, and then he and Harriet left town immediately, going straight from the funeral home to stay with relatives in Boston. "My mother had decided that she didn't want to go to the graveside," he said. "I remember several years later wishing that I had."

He was not the only one left with a feeling of incompletion. Sue Ann had chosen not to look at her father's body in its coffin, though her mother had offered to open the casket so she could do so. "I wish I had," she said many years later. "Then I would have known he was dead in a way that took me months to realize. Normally I wouldn't see him for months, and it just seemed like that at first."

■

It was not just the suddenness of his death that made it hard to realize Louis Kahn was gone. Something about the way he disappeared from the world—irregularly, mysteriously, with that strange two-day gap when nobody he knew could find him—left many people unable to take in the facts of his death.

For the California relatives, who learned about Lou's death through a series of relayed phone calls, there was a persistent confusion about where and how he had died. Decades later, Kahn's niece, nephew, grandnephew, and two grandnieces all thought he had suffered a heart attack on the way back from Bangladesh; their memories, that is, selected his much-celebrated Dhaka project over the rarely discussed Ahmedabad campus. They knew he had died in a train station, but at least two of them remembered it as Grand Central—again, a more appropriately monumental choice. (These erroneous details proved to be so persuasive that they even entered the historical record, for in a 1993 *Toledo Blade* article listing the highlights of Louis Kahn's life, the Ohio newspaper included the line: "1974 – Dies of heart attack in Grand Central Station, New York City, en route from Bangladesh to Philadelphia.") The West Coast Kahns believed, moreover, that Lou's body, with its characteristically messy hair and rumpled clothing, had been taken for that of a transient for two days, until somebody finally realized who it was. Part of their distress had to do with this idea of unrecognizability: they could hardly credit that someone as famous as Louis I. Kahn could go unidentified for two days.

Among at least some of the East Coast relatives, a different story prevailed. According to this view, the New York police had included the wrong address in their initial cable because Kahn, for reasons unknown, had obliterated his home address in his passport. Harriet Pattison, a firm believer in this version, was convinced that he was finally intending to leave his wife and come live with her and their son. Nathaniel

Kahn, who incorporated this story into his movie about his father, called his mother's interpretation "a nice myth," though he believed that the address had indeed been crossed out. Anne Tyng felt that Lou would never have changed his domestic arrangements, but she too credited the altered-passport idea, as did her daughter. "There is no doubt in my mind that the home address was crossed off," Alex Tyng said, "but why, or what he intended to do, I don't know. Maybe he had chest pains on the plane and wanted to make some kind of gesture or statement that would be found if he died before he got home. We'll never know."

But American passports, then as now, did not have the bearer's home address printed on them. There was a space at the front where one could, if one wished, write in a home address, but the passport Louis Kahn was carrying on that last trip—the one with the March 16 exit stamp from Bombay's Santacruz Airport—had nothing written in the home address space. The only address in the passport was on the vaccination certificate attached at the back, and it was completely uncrossed out. "I heard the passport in question has disappeared," said Alex, but all the while it was in her older sister's possession. Yet even Sue Ann had not bothered to dig out the document until she was pressed to do so many decades after her father's death. Some mysteries apparently beg not to be solved.

The myth of the crossed-out passport persisted over the years, surfacing anew with each discussion of Kahn's death. For outsiders, it was merely a curious feature of an incompletely resolved case. But for the women and children who had been officially excluded from the obituaries and posthumous commemorations, the story seemed to offer the consolation of a private, secret affirmation of their role in Lou's life. And this is understandable. Whenever people die unexpectedly, away from those who knew and loved them, the survivors will long for a final message from their dead, and when it is not forthcoming, they may have trouble believing it was never sent. With someone like Louis Kahn, who meant so many different things to so many different people, the usual sense of loss and uncertainty would have been compounded by the mysterious circumstances of his death. Lou's habit of secretly slipping off from one place to another, of being routinely unlocatable for an indeterminate period of time, had gone from temporary to permanent. It was as if he had simply slid through a hole in reality, moved from existence to nonexistence when no one was noticing. Yet if his absence was hard to grasp, it was nonetheless the only fact that could be agreed upon. He was no longer around, bodily, to hold everything together. He was no longer physically present to persuade each friend or loved one, each client or employee, that he was exactly the person they knew and wanted him to be.

This had practical consequences as well as emotional ones. When the funeral was over and the accountants finally had a chance to examine the books, it was determined that his architectural firm, Louis I. Kahn Architect, owed $464,423.83 to its creditors—mostly to engineers and staff, but some of it to outside suppliers and institutions as well. No one had ever considered Lou a good businessman; on the other hand, no one had realized that his financial balancing act was this precarious. Esther had no way of paying off the debt on her own, but after nearly two years of effort by David Zoob and a few other devoted friends, the Pennsylvania legislature passed a bill authorizing the state to purchase the Louis I. Kahn Collection for exactly the sum needed to pay the creditors. The Kahn Collection, including not only his personal and professional records but also 6,363 drawings he had made over the course of his career, was placed at the University of Pennsylvania, which had agreed to house it in the same building where Kahn had taught.

There still remained the question of his unfinished building projects. Several of Louis Kahn's trusted associates, led by David Wisdom and Henry Wilcots, kept working on the massive Bangladesh capital project for nine more years, until it was at long last brought to completion in 1983 (the same year, incidentally, that Dacca became Dhaka). Marshall Meyers and his firm, Pellecchia & Meyers, supervised the final design and construction phases of the Yale Center for British Art, which was finished in 1977. Eventually, other architects would do the actual drawings for the Graduate Theological Union's library in Berkeley, California, the Bishop Field Estate in Lenox, Massachusetts, and a second version of the music barge for the American Wind Symphony Orchestra, all based on initial plans sketched out by Kahn. And nearly four decades after his death, in the wake of numerous arguments, negotiations, and revisions, the FDR Four Freedoms Park would open on Roosevelt Island, in a form very much like the design Lou had unveiled in 1973. But all the other ambitious projects he had undertaken—

including the Palazzo dei Congressi in Venice and the Hurva Synagogue in Jerusalem—came to an abrupt end. There was no one who could complete them as Kahn would have done. There was not even enough of a design, in most cases, for others to attempt to carry on his work. Those grand pieces of architecture, to the extent they existed, existed ònly in the mind of Louis Kahn, and they died with him.

Still, enough magnificent work remained to justify the storm of acclaim that arrived after his death. It had taken him a long time and a great deal of effort to create his few masterpieces, but their importance to the world—not only the world of architecture, but the world of ordinary people who occupy and use architecture—was never in doubt. Jonas Salk, whom Lou always described as his favorite client because of their fruitful work together on the Salk Institute, gave expression to this general feeling in a poem he wrote shortly after Kahn's death and read aloud at a memorial event on April 2, 1974. "Out of the mind of a tiny whimsical man," Salk's poem began,

> who happened by chance,
> great forms have come,
> great structures, great spaces that function.

Salk praised his lost friend for possessing the words of a poet and the cadences of a musician, as well as "the vision of an artist, / the understanding of a philosopher, / the knowledge of a metaphysician, / the reason of a logician." Yet even as it commended Louis Kahn's natural talents, the poem also pointed out how lengthy the road was that led up to his final achievements:

> For five decades he prepared himself
> and did in two
> what others wish they could do in five.

IN SITU:
SALK INSTITUTE FOR
BIOLOGICAL STUDIES

Plaza of Salk Institute at sunset
(Anonymous photograph from the author's collection)

A few miles north of San Diego, off a winding tree-lined road called North Torrey Pines, lies the structure that Louis Kahn designed for Jonas Salk in the early 1960s. You arrive by car, as one so often does in Southern California, but you can really only see the complex as a pedestrian, so you park in the eastern lot and walk in through the high front gates that remain open from six a.m. to six p.m. This is the first noticeable oddity: a major research center that is open to the public all day long. Some people are obviously coming for science-related reasons, but many, it seems, are here just to admire and relax in and take heart from Kahn's buildings—a symmetrical set of study towers and lab buildings mirroring each other across a remarkable central plaza.

To get to this plaza, you have to pass between two newer buildings built in imitation Kahn style to house the more recent labs and offices. In Kahn's own time, the approach would have been through a grove of eucalyptus trees, only a few of which remain standing as emblems of what was lost. You do not pay much attention to this diminished approach, though, because you are drawn forward by the promise of something magical lurking beyond the rust-colored oxidized steel fence that marks the beginning of the original site. And that promise is soon fulfilled.

Reaching the near side of the ninety-yard-long, pale-travertine-paved plaza, you see in the distance a band of blue, the Pacific Ocean, glinting at you from beyond the open end of the rectangular space. The long stone bench set perpendicularly in your path forces you to pause. Nearly as wide as the plaza itself, the bench asks you to stop and take in the view from this position, where sea and sky have been placed within a frame created by the tall, saw-toothed edges of the surrounding buildings. A foot-wide shallow stream, encased in a travertine channel, runs in a straight line from a small, square fountain directly in front of you and guides your eye westward, almost to the horizon. Twice a year, at the vernal and autumnal equinoxes, the sun sets directly over that shining runnel of water: not so much an allusion to Stonehenge and its ancient cousins as a confirmation that this building, too, marks its history on an astronomical scale of time. Now, however, it is high summer, and the whole plaza is bathed in bright August daylight, so that the shadows—the gaps between the buildings that line the north and south sides of the plaza, the open entrances at the ground level, the recesses under the travertine benches, the slight spaces where one block of matter meets another—show up as almost black. It's a bit like being in an architectural rendering or a black-and-white photo come to life, except that your sense of your own presence in this three-dimensional space is so powerful.

In order to move forward, which the view compels you to do, you must first move to the side to get around the bench. Whichever way you choose to go, whether north or south, to the right or to the left, you end up facing the jagged buildings that form the front line of the structures on either side of the plaza. Focusing on them now for the first time, you realize that these four-story concrete towers—in which the second and fourth floors hold scientists' studies, with a covered steel-railed terrace sandwiched between them on the third floor—must provide all their occupants with marvelous views. Every one of the studies has a large, protruding window on the western, Pacific-facing side of its acutely angled wedge, as well as another window, set within narrow, vertical teak boards, that overlooks the mirror-image studies on the opposite side.

That transverse view is what you see now: a composition in concrete, metal, glass, and teak, all put together in a way that complements the rigorous geometric design of the plaza while softening it with something more human. Is the human element provided by the hand-milled teak, which has weathered to a soft, variegated grayish brown, giving a sense of time's passage to this otherwise timeless place? Or does it stem from the concrete itself, which is warmer, smoother, and more personable— more person-*sized*, even—than anything you have previously associated with this material? Despite the feeling of weight and mass that inflects the structure as a whole, there is a tangible delicacy to the construction, with its numerous separate panels of concrete each the size and shape of a large door. These panels are doubly scored at their meeting points, as if to frame each pale gray rectangle individually. They are also pocked at regular intervals with round, symmetrically arranged holes. The holes, visibly plugged with a darker gray lead, are like the belly buttons of the concrete: they emphasize its origins, marking the places at which it was originally tied into its plywood forms. And because they puncture the concrete panels in such an orderly, balanced fashion, they reinforce the eye's sense of pleasure, and hence the brain's repose. *Nothing is random here*, they imply, *and what is done for practical reasons can also be supremely beautiful.* This applies to the science practiced within these walls, one presumes, as well as to the walls themselves.

On a very hot day, or a very rainy one, you might seek protection under the concrete, passing through the heavily shadowed, obliquely sunlit arcades that run at ground level along the full length of the study structures. But on a normally sunny day you will want to remain out in the plaza, hewing close to the central channel of water even as you follow its course toward the ocean. As you approach the stream's western endpoint, you discover a previously invisible rectangular pool (a ha-ha, in farmer's or landscape architect's terms) into which the runnel empties. Like the long bench at the eastern end, this pool initially halts your progress until you move around to its northern or southern side. From here you can see what lies beyond the plaza—the ground level of the Salk complex, accessible by a stairway—and now it becomes apparent that the true horizon is far away, past a series of low hills that continue to block your view of all but the thinnest strip of ocean. What you saw when you first entered the plaza was merely an illusion of infinity, created by the framing device of the building itself; having now reached that infinite point, you find it has disappeared, and what you are left with is a much more prosaic if still pretty view of the ocean.

■

Behind the rows of studies lie two matching lab buildings, the north wing and the south wing. Each is six stories high, but they appear to be the same height as the study buildings because two of the stories are sunk belowground, though even these are naturally lit by courtyards functioning as light-wells. It turns out there are actually only three floors of labs, alternating with three "interstitial" floors where all the maintenance, storage, electrical, ventilation, and structural functions of the building reside. If you are with an official guide, you may be allowed to peek into one of these dark, cluttered, in-between floors, where you can spot the famous Vierendeel trusses that Kahn's brilliant engineer, August Komendant, used to solve one of the project's key technical problems. These catenary-curved, steel-reinforced concrete beams, each nine feet by sixty-five feet, are strong enough and yet flexible enough to allow the lab floors to remain open from end to end, without supporting walls or columns interrupting the lab space.

If you are lucky, your guide will also take you into the open labs themselves, which are lit for the most part with daylight pouring in through the huge glass curtain walls on either side, though there are also fluorescent lights hanging from the eleven-foot ceilings. As you look up at those ceilings, you notice rectangular incisions every five feet or so— covered-over access points through which all maintenance functions can be performed from the interstitial floors. These precut openings serve the same function as the cinder blocks that form one whole wall of the largely underground eastern maintenance wing: they allow ceilings or walls to be opened panel by panel, stone by stone, so that no major structure ever has to be taken down or compromised. You had decided, out in the plaza, that Louis Kahn was a highly imaginative visionary; now you see that he also had the practical soul of a maintenance man.

"This is the cat's meow of a facility manager's deal," says Tim Ball, the current Salk maintenance director, as he takes you on his own personal tour of Kahn's ingenious design. "This gives us the capacity to maintain, repair, clean, without interrupting the occupant. It's expensive to build this way in the first place, with full-height interstitials, but the Institute has probably paid for itself six times over since it was built." Ball tells you he recently spent fourteen months replacing all the outmoded infrastructure that heated, cooled, cleaned, and powered the labs, but without altering the architecture or disturbing the scientists in any way. "I don't know of another scientific building in the country where that could be done," he says.

Everything about the design that you thought was done for aesthetic reasons turns out, according to Ball, to have its practical side. Positioning the plaza directly in line with the equinoctial sun creates maximum access to natural light—"daylight harvesting," Ball calls it. Angling the western-facing windows toward the Pacific, with a setback between each pair in the double bays, doesn't just enable every scientist to have a beautiful view; it also allows each study to be cooled by the prevailing ocean breezes. The lovely travertine-enclosed central stream may recall the Spanish Alhambra or a Persian palace, but it too has a function, for all the water in it (along with any rainwater in the plaza) gets channeled via the rectangular pool into an underground cistern, from which it is eventually recycled back into the fountain. And even the "shadow joints" that are everywhere in Kahn's design—those one-inch gaps that separate concrete from wood or wood from metal—are not just a pleasing way for the eye to mark a change in material. They also, Ball tells you, help to preserve the wood, by protecting it from the condensation, expansion, and contraction caused by the variable heating and cooling of these three different substances.

At the conclusion to his tour, Tim Ball insists on taking you down to the lowest level of the maintenance wing, where all the central mechanical, electrical, and system-monitoring functions are housed. (Even down here, surprisingly, there is a light-well that brings in natural light.) Here in the basement, on one of the concrete walls, he shows you a couple of penciled notations in Louis Kahn's own hand. They were still trying out the concrete when they poured this part, Ball says, still experimenting with what it should look like in terms of texture, color, joins, and form markings. So right here, as the building was beginning to take shape, is where Kahn indicated the spots that had come out exactly the way he wanted them to, and his legible, hastily scrawled handwriting, accompanied by two rapid sketches of joints and forms, preserves his ghostly presence in those two places.

Like the facilities director, many of the scientists and administrators who work at the Salk Institute have a visceral sense of gratitude for both the beauty and the practicality of the space. A youthful immunologist who is lecturing to a crowd of visitors in front of the building mentions the fun of leaning back in her chair and waving down the full length of the lab to her colleague at the other end. A seasoned administrator crossing the plaza tells you that her favorite time to be there is in the rain, when the wet concrete walls turn a darker, slatier gray, and the drenched travertine gives off a sheen. When asked what associations she has with the plaza, she answers, "Salk. Jonas Salk." Then she pats the concrete post next to her and says, "This is known as 'Salkcrete.'" She is alluding to the fact that Salk and Kahn both stood by watching as the early, experimental concrete came out of its forms; together, they chose the final color and texture.

There are, of course, occasional naysayers among the site's regular users. A young neuroscientist, caught on his brief break, describes himself as "jaded." He no longer sees the pretty view, and he is tired of working in an open lab, where it can be difficult to collect one's own thoughts. When you gesture toward the studies in which the Nobel Prize winners and other eminences have their private offices, he nods in envious acknowledgment: that is the kind of space he could be happy in.

One such happy occupant is Greg Lemke, a prominent research scientist who has been at the Salk for about fifteen years. He invites you to take a look inside his study, which is perched on the second floor of one of the easternmost bays in the north wing. There are no bad views from any of these studies, but his is particularly good because he gets the ocean view framed, in classic Kahnian fashion, by the buildings to the west of his. He also prefers the way the light falls on the north wing, so he has kept his study here even though his lab is now located in the southern half of the complex. He comments on the fact that the light changes dramatically with the seasons, while also noting wryly that "Kahn didn't know about the fogs or the winter; he was designing for a tropical climate." In the summer, Lemke's study can be sheltered from the direct sun and cooled entirely by breezes—he demonstrates how this works by pulling the glass window sideways until it is entirely open, and then sliding a teakwood slatted blind into its place.

Mostly, Greg Lemke uses this luminous, spare, beautiful room when he wants to read papers or write grant proposals, though he has also been known to hold meetings here with up to a dozen people. Each occupant gets to arrange the room exactly as he wishes, and Lemke has his desk facing away from the largest concrete wall and toward the Pacific view; an L-shaped extension that holds his laptop faces out the other window toward the plaza. On one wall hangs a Picassoesque lithograph of a woman's head, done by one of the painter's longtime lovers, Françoise Gilot. (Gilot later became Mrs. Jonas Salk, and Lemke is the current holder of the Françoise Gilot-Salk Chair in Molecular Neurobiology and Immunology.) Otherwise the room is almost empty. Asked if he finds the concrete wall cold or impersonal, Lemke shakes his head. "If you look at the concrete, it has a lot going on. I like it a lot," he says.

■

Leaving the study towers, you find yourself back out on the plaza in the mid-afternoon light. You take a seat on one of the seven travertine benches lining three sides of the rectangle and try to figure out the source of this space's enormous appeal. While you are thinking, you notice that the jagged lines of mirror-image buildings edging toward the infinite view offer a transparently simple lesson in perspective: the sawtoothed pattern, which appears loose from close up, tightens as it extends away from you. In this sky-ceilinged, open-ended "room," the serrated walls are what give shape to the vastness, enclosing you in something recognizably man-made. And yet the exactness and symmetry of the construction are such that the place almost seems to partake of a mathematical, inherent order, something larger and more ancient than familiar architecture. What comes to mind are the Greek temples at Paestum, those grand, ruined buildings which Kahn loved, and which still strike awe into the heart of any visitor. But those monuments clearly belong to old, dead gods, whereas this one feels like a tribute to something living—science, perhaps, or human brains at work, or any kind of strenuous collaboration.

You are aware, in this plaza, of your own size and placement in the world. The rectangular space seems gigantic when it is empty, but as other people stroll across it, they look normal-sized, human-sized; the space does not diminish them. A feeling of calmness and repose prevails throughout, echoed in the constant plashing of the water. It is as if the sound of the water and the sight of the soothingly symmetrical buildings are two aspects of a single synaesthetic experience. Incorporated with these are an imagined sense of touch (the smoothness of the concrete, the intriguing texture of the pitted travertine, the gentle roughness of the weathered teak) and a potential or even actual sense of motion. The plaza invites you to move around it—in particular, to move toward the view—and in accepting the invitation, you become ever more firmly lodged in this particular place, at the western edge of the Western Hemisphere, overlooking the Pacific Ocean on a particular summer day.

If you are allowed to remain until sunset, you will witness all this warm beauty transformed into an eerie magic. The sun, which in August sets slightly to the north of the runnel, casts its early evening light on the southern row of studies, making their external faces stand out in gold, their receding faces hide in shadow. As the plaza dims, the shining strip of water at its center looks like a silver path laid down in a travertine plain. It leads you forward toward the sunset, and toward the western end of the building, where even the walls that are merely *facing* a sunlit wall seem to glow with reflected light. If you retreat to one of the benches and lift your face to the sky, you can see the clouds gently moving in your direction, emphasizing the archaic stillness of the dark buildings silhouetted beneath them. You may find yourself trying to capture each changing moment with your camera, but no camera is supple or delicate enough to catch all the elements at once—the sky and sea and framing concrete wedges, the paler travertine with its shiny ribbon of water. Only the human eye can perceive it in all its subtlety.

Now the sun, as it starts to sink rapidly through the clouds and toward the sea, turns immense, demonstrative, spectacular. It changes its shape second by second, visibly shifting from a cloud-sliced circle to a perfect half-circle to a flattened curve. And just before it disappears completely into the waves, it spreads itself along the horizon in a thin, lumpy layer of glowing orange-redness, like the last embers of a dying fire.

PREPARING

"I remember having come over with my mother and sister and brother on the boat from Estonia. I was five years old. Because I could draw, I made drawings of whatever happened . . . It was pointed out to me that the smoke from one boat was going the other way. It was a very slow boat and the smoke was faster than the movement of the boat, or the boat was arrested at that time. The captain called my attention to it. And because he liked the drawing so much, my mother thought we would give it to him. As a result we had oranges every day. And that was really something—oranges were a rare thing, and I was very proud."

That was how the little boy saw it, and later remembered it. But what would the captain himself have observed as his ship, the S.S. *Merion*, left Liverpool on June 13, 1906, bound for Philadelphia? If Lou's story is correct, the captain noticed and even spoke to the fatherless family who were up on deck as the ship wended its way along the River Mersey, heading toward the Irish Sea. The mother, in her early thirties, was not a conventionally pretty woman, but there was something in her face and carriage that radiated dignity, warmth, and calmness under difficult circumstances. It was a face that drew one to it, signaling a character that could be relied upon. The two younger children, the girl and especially the boy, were sweetly attractive in a manner typical of their age. But the oldest child, the one who was so good at drawing, clearly had something wrong with him. The entire lower half of his face and the backs of both hands were covered with red scar tissue that still looked raw—the result of a severe burning, perhaps, or some equally horrific accident. The poor little fellow didn't seem to mind it, himself. He was by far the most animated member of his little family, with his mop of auburn hair, his bright blue eyes taking everything in, and his pencil always at work on the page. The captain may have admiréd his talent, but he probably also felt sorry for him, and sorry for the mother who, in addition to all her other burdens, had to care for such a child. How could life ever be anything but difficult for a boy with a face like that?

According to the manifest of the "alien passengers" traveling on that voyage of the *Merion*, the woman was named Bertha Kahan; her three children were listed as Isidor, Jenie, and Oscher. They were Russian nationals, apparently, and passage for all four had been paid by their husband and father, Leopold, who was scheduled to meet them at the wharf in Philadelphia when the boat docked on June 25, 1906. That much, at least, proved to be true, and if just about everything else in the manifest entry was inaccurate or at any rate debatable, that did not differentiate it significantly from the many other lists of immigrants who in those decades were pouring into the United States.

It had been almost exactly two years since Bertha's husband had followed the same route from Liverpool to America. He too had started out in Èstonia (or rather Livonia, the Russian province which at the time included Latvia and southern Estonia), though his trip had originated in the mainland city of Pernau, rather than the island town of Arensburg, where Bertha's family all lived, and from which she and the children departed. Listed on the manifest as "Leib Schmulowsky" of the "Hebrew" race or nation, Lou's father had gotten off his ship in Wilmington, Delaware, where he was met by a cousin. From there he soon made his way to Philadelphia, and when he wrote to his wife, Beila-Rebeckah, back in Arensburg, he told her that since he was now called Leopold Kahn, she and the children should Americanize their names accordingly when it came time to join him. So their eldest, Leiser-Itze, became Louis Isadore. Schorre, who was just turning four, became Sarah—not Jenie, as the manifest inexplicably had it—and Oscher, the two-year-old baby of the family, became Oscar.

When he met their boat at the wharf, Leopold got his first real look at his younger son, who had been born just as he was preparing to leave for America. He had last seen his older son a few months after the accident, when many had feared (and Leib had almost hoped) that the badly damaged boy would not survive. But if Leopold was shocked at how scarred Lou's face still looked, he did not show it. Instead he gathered his family and took them home to 50 North 2nd Street in the Northern Liberties section of Philadelphia. This was the first of twelve residences, some of them lasting less than a year, that they were to occupy in that neighborhood over the subsequent quarter of a century.

They moved, for the most part, because they could not afford to stay where they were. This was not because rents were high—the Northern Liberties ward consisted mostly of poor immigrants, and much of the time the Kahns shared their dwellings with other renters—but because Leopold's income was low to nonexistent. Though he was described in his immigration papers as a shirtwaist maker, and though his children and grandchildren remembered him primarily as an artist in stained glass (as well as a talented linguist who knew five or six languages), he had apparently been employed as a laborer sometime during his first two years in America. An injury received at that time prevented him from working regularly, or so he always claimed. This meant that Bertha's small earnings, at first from her work in the garment industry and later from a family-run candy store, had to support all of them.

"We lived in poverty," Louis Kahn told an interviewer some fifty years later. "Very poor apartment—tenement type." Yet the family somehow rose above its surroundings, in part because they "had humor" and "were at ease about dire necessity." According to Lou, his parents "had no envy about money." They were different from the other poor immigrants around them, he felt: "They were happier, more intellectual. They were admired by the neighborhood, had wider horizons."

His father had a few relatives who had been in America longer and were noticeably better off—one was in real estate, another a wholesaler in the grocery business. Lou remembered, in particular, two uncles, one of whom "was really an s.o.b. He was enterprising. He married outside his religion, had handsome children. The other was a tailor. He was cheerful, did Russian dances, was entertaining." There were also relatives from Europe who came and stayed with them for short periods, making the cramped quarters even tighter. Lou always had to share a room with his brother, Oscar, and they squabbled a lot, sometimes even getting into physical fights, but in the end "we had no serious disputes. They were all settled casually." Throughout his childhood he felt that his parents and siblings "all were rooting for me. The family looked up to me. They sacrificed for me to some extent."

Whether that special attention was due to his prodigious talent or his poor health was impossible to say. Certainly he was a sickly child, and not just because of the accident. Soon after the family arrived in Philadelphia, Lou contracted scarlet fever so severely he had to go to the hospital, and his entry into primary school was delayed by a year as a result. When he did finally start school in the fall of 1907, he was teased by the other kids, who called him "scarface" and laughed at him. Art, he soon learned, offered the only available escape route. When his fellow students saw how well he could draw, they stopped mocking him and cultivated his friendship, and even the teachers who had previously criticized his poor academic performance began to praise him for his artistic skills.

"I was born into the consideration of art as a part of life, not something that's attached to life in a peripheral way," Kahn said as an adult. "My parents were in the middle of it. My mother had been a harpist and my father a stained glass worker, and we knew that art was in everyone's life."

Yet though he credited his parents for his immersion in art, Lou could also be resentful of their interference, especially if the instruction came from his father. "One day, I was copying a portrait of Napoleon," he recalled. "His left eye was giving me trouble. Already I had erased the drawing several times. My father lovingly corrected my work. I threw pencil and paper across the room, saying, *Now it's your drawing, not mine.*"

Such tantrums were rare, however, and for the most part the child was eager to learn the skills that others could teach him. When he was a little older, the woman in the apartment below theirs acquired a piano and hired a teacher to give her daughter lessons for twenty-five cents a session. Bertha Kahn offered to give the woman a nickel for every lesson that Lou could sit in on, but since the piano teacher certainly wouldn't have agreed to teach two children for the price of one, Lou was obliged to hide behind a large wingchair for the whole of each lesson, taking in everything by ear rather than by eye. After the teacher and the little girl had left the room, he would come out and practice at the piano, playing by heart what he had just heard. He never learned to read music, but he could reproduce almost any tune after hearing it once, and he could also improvise delightfully.

That skill was to prove financially useful a few years later, when Lou got a job playing the piano accompaniment to the silent films at the Poplar Cinema, just down the street from his family's home. The money he brought in was a substantial addition to Bertha's earnings, and it soon became essential to the family economy. At one point, though, he almost lost the job when the movie-house proprietor upgraded his instrument.

"Louis, I'm afraid your job is over because we're installing an organ," said his employer, according to Lou's account. "I guess you can't play the organ."

"Yes, I can," Lou insisted, though he had never seen one.

"That's great, that's wonderful," the man responded. "I was worried about it because I couldn't find a relief organist. They're pretty rare. No one knows how to play the thing."

The organ was installed over a Sunday (the one day the movie house was closed, in observance of Philadelphia's strict blue laws) and Lou watched the process, including the testing of the new organ by an expert player. After the installation was complete, Lou asked the organist if he would teach him to play it well enough so that he could perform the following evening. The man generously agreed, and they sat down for the next five or six hours, finishing the lesson at nine or ten that night. At that point Lou still hadn't mastered the foot pedals, but the organist told him, "If you can't use your feet, it'll be all right. It'll stand for the two hours you're playing, we can forget about the feet." Still, Lou resolved that he would try to use his feet as well, if he could figure out how to do it.

"Come Monday I was scared stiff," he recalled. "I got at the organ, and I was surprised—the thing was very responsive. It was electrical and no pain at all."

While they were changing the reels, the movie-house proprietor came to talk to him. "Lou, I didn't know you played so well, but you play too loudly," he said.

Lou realized it was the footwork that was causing the problem—he didn't know how to control it. "Suppose I lay off the feet," he suggested.

"That's a good idea," his employer agreed.

Lou managed to hold on to that job for years, all the way through high school and well into college. For a while he even played at *two* movie theaters, sprinting the eight blocks between them so as to cover both main features.

The boy may have been shy at school, but everywhere else he seemed willing to push the limits. The streets of the Northern Liberties, poor and rough as they were, became his playground. He was always out and about, listening to the sounds of the crowds and the traffic and the market hawkers, smelling the sharp odors of the tannery and brewery businesses, and taking in all the various kinds of buildings that lined the streets, from Victorian-era brick factories to the "Sawtooth Houses," a row of diagonally sited dwellings on St. John Neuman Way. In fact, that particular street of angular structures could have been one of the sources behind Kahn's eventual idea for the similarly angled Salk study towers. As Kahn said when he grew up, "A city should be a place where a little boy walking through its streets can sense what he would someday like to be." The Northern Liberties neighborhood was exactly that for him.

And if Bertha was overprotective in some ways (she would reportedly go to Lou's classroom and announce, "My son is a genius!" if she felt the teacher wasn't paying enough attention to him), she nevertheless allowed her son that necessary freedom of the streets. At times, unbeknownst to her, his adventurousness verged on the physically dangerous. "I was always trying to test my physical prowess," Lou observed, recalling a time when he had been sent to fetch some groceries. "There was a little street I had to pass, and I always tried to make it in one jump." This time, though, "I fell backwards and hit my head on the pavement. Somebody helped me to pick up the groceries." The crack on the head had somehow interfered with his vision: "I couldn't see anything around me. I knew where I was and I walked home thinking of what I would be if I lost my eyesight. I was ready to adjust to the whole thing right there and then. I walked up the three flights to where we lived, and I let on that everything was all right. I sat down in the corner, and my eyes cleared up."

During his brief period of blindness, he had decided that "the best thing was to try to become a musician, because it wasn't necessary to see everything. My mother always wanted me to be a musician, but my father thought I should be an artist because I used to draw all the time. That was my delight. In school days I never really studied, I just made drawings."

When Lou was eleven years old, in addition to attending the Wyoming Grammar School on Fairmount Avenue—where, by his own report, he earned consistently poor grades—he began going to the Public Industrial Art School to take drawing classes with J. Liberty Tadd. Tadd was a graduate of the Pennsylvania Academy of Fine Arts, where he had studied with Thomas Eakins, who emphasized drawing from nature and who recommended using photography, anatomy, and other new methods of discovery that could help further art's truthfulness and vitality. To these principles Tadd added his own version of Emersonian Transcendentalism, arguing that his techniques enabled young students not only to understand the wonders of nature, but also to bring out the divine light inherent in each one of them. He gave his students stuffed birds, fish, and animals to draw, as well as photographs and casts of these things, and he called his method "natural education." Tadd's teaching, which was firmly allied with the Progressive tradition in education, grew to be so highly regarded in Philadelphia that by the early years of the twentieth century any child in the public school system who demonstrated artistic talent was allowed to attend classes at the Public Industrial Art School for half a day each week.

Lou was recommended to J. Liberty Tadd's school by his fourth-grade teacher, and he took to the training as if it had been designed with him in mind. Fifty years later, Kahn was still putting into practice the things he had learned during his few years at the school. For example, Tadd repeatedly used ambidextrous exercises in his class: among other things, he would conduct double-handed blackboard drills during which his students had to draw oversized ornaments to scale, thus developing both their physical dexterity and their sense of proportion. Kahn, as an adult, would repeatedly demonstrate exactly this kind of ability, simultaneously drawing identical circles on a blackboard with his right hand and his left (often in front of a camera, so that several instances were captured on film). His lover and collaborator Anne Tyng felt that this talent of Kahn's illustrated a special connection between the right, "creative" side of his brain and the left, "rational" side. "Some people have better links in their brains between the two halves," she observed, and "the more you use it, the better it works." However he came by it, the ability had certainly been reinforced in Kahn by Tadd's training.

Tadd also stressed the relationship between three-dimensional sculpture and two-dimensional drawing. He frequently had his students make clay and wood models of a particular thing—working first in a soft material, then in a hard one—so that they would learn what he called "speaking through the finger tips." After this experience of creating something in three dimensions, he explained, "it is a very easy matter to draw it on paper or on the blackboard with the hand as firm and with a line as clean as though it were being made by a steel bar." This, too, became apparent in the adult Louis Kahn's drawings, which had not only vitality but "conviction," as Tyng put it. And Tyng was not the only one of Kahn's associates who noticed his special ability to think in three dimensions; in fact, it was to become one of the qualities that defined him as an architect. In a notebook entry from the 1940s, Kahn himself emphasized the importance of getting beyond the two-dimensional view. Observing that the standard architectural design was merely a "box with spaces in it," he concluded that this drafting-room attitude toward spaces "comes from viewing the space from above at small scale on a piece of paper or a board." The results, he wrote, were "drafting room visions 'sans situ.'"

Beyond the specific practical training, what the young Louis Kahn absorbed from Tadd was a semi-mystical and yet utterly concrete notion about the relationship between the natural and the man-made, the perceived and the created, the outer world and the inner one. "Drawing and manual training, properly taught," wrote Tadd in his 1899 book *New Methods of Education*, ". . . are modes of thought expression, just as speech and writing are modes of thought expression." And learning this "universal tongue" entailed not just copying, but also thinking. "I like my pupils and teachers to understand the distinction there is between sketching from nature and designing," Tadd noted. "In the one case we put down facts, and in the other, ideas. There is a tendency for many students to sketch only from nature. We get our ideas by thinking as well. More time should be given, then, to dwelling on our impressions . . . and to giving expression to these ideas constantly by designing and creative work." Something very much like these principles was to inform Kahn's distinction between Order (or its handmaiden, Form), which derived from nature, and Design, which was the specific human response. "Form encompasses a harmony of systems, a sense of Order . . . ," Kahn observed in a talk delivered more than sixty years after Tadd wrote his seminal book. "Form is 'what.' Design is 'how.' Form is impersonal. Design belongs to the designer." In both Tadd's and Kahn's cases, the link between the given world and the created one was necessarily organic and spontaneous as it was thoughtful and considered. The eye, the hand, and the mind were all engaged at once, bringing unconscious forms of knowledge—bodily sensation, dream thoughts, ancestral awareness—into conjunction with the rational brain. "One who accurately draws a bird, or a skeleton, or a flower, or a mathematical problem, has a more complete mastery of that special topic than could be gained in almost any other way," Tadd said.

It was a mode of thought that at any rate suited Lou. By the time he graduated from grammar school in 1916, he was noticeably better at drawing than at writing or studying. He was to embark on his four years at Central High School in Philadelphia with no firm idea of how to use the skills he had acquired from J. Liberty Tadd, and with all his academic difficulties still intact.

In the meantime, though, Lou had become officially American—and, for that matter, officially a Kahn. The onset of the war in Europe in August 1914 had triggered Leopold Kahn's delicate awareness of danger: he had left Livonia in 1904 in part to avoid being drafted into Russia's conflict with Japan, and he was not about to risk being clawed back now that a new war was starting. Within months he had resolved to join his fate permanently with that of his new country, thus severing the connection with the old. On January 29, 1915, a person described in the relevant documents as Leopold Schmulowsky—a tall, thin, light-complexioned white man, with brown hair and gray eyes, who had been born in 1875 in Wolmar, Russia, and now resided at 820 N. Marshall Street in Philadelphia—filed a petition for naturalization on behalf of all the members of his immediate family. At the same time he made an official request to change their last name from Schmulowsky to Kahn. This request was granted on May 4, 1915, the date on which Leopold Kahn swore his oath of allegiance before the clerk of the court, promising to "renounce forever all allegiance and fidelity . . . to Nicholas II, Emperor of All the Russias," and incidentally affirming that he was neither an anarchist nor a polygamist. By this means, Bertha, Louis, Sarah, and Oscar were all instantly converted into American citizens as well.

Lou continued to be a mediocre student throughout his first three years at the academically rigorous Central High. "Studying was something that never got through to me," he later remarked, and elsewhere he commented that he did "very poorly academically" in high school. "I'm not sure why," he said. "It was a wonderful school. I had an intense interest in art, drawing, piano . . . I could not remember formulae-experienced things like chemistry." By his own account, he rarely spoke up in class and spent a lot of his time daydreaming about things like knights on white chargers. "Fairy tales—I have read them all through my life," he noted, adding that his reading as an adolescent included "Horatio Alger, dime novels, Alexander Dumas." None of this helped him at school. As Lou's high-school classmate Norman Rice put it, "He was always on the verge of being flunked."

It wasn't until his final year, when he took a course in architecture offered by William F. Gray, the head of Central High School's excellent art department, that Lou's eyes were finally opened. "I was to be a painter, but he touched the very core of my expressive desires. How circumstantial, but how wonderful is the light thrown upon the threshold when the door is opened," Kahn recalled as an adult. "I wouldn't have been an architect if I hadn't gone to Central High School." When he was asked, on another occasion, whether any older person had influenced him in his high-school years, he answered, "My art teacher—an architect. He gave me direction and was very understanding." What Lou realized almost instantly, when he took Gray's class, was that "Architecture combined my love and desire for artistic creation, painting, and being able to express and stand out," and as a result "I was intensely dedicated."

Gray, like Tadd, had studied at the Pennysylvania Academy of Fine

Arts, and his training too was guided by the principles of Thomas Eakins, though in his case the transmission took place through an intermediary, Thomas Anshutz, who had been one of Eakins' students. William Gray's own theories were a combination of the Progressivism he had acquired at the Academy and an updated version of Romanticism he had gleaned through reading Ruskin. Resisting the neo-Baroque aesthetic that had recently been making its way into American architecture, Gray instead championed both the City Beautiful movement in Philadelphia and the Chicago-based development of "the skyscraper or cloudscratcher," as he termed the tall new buildings. What he borrowed from Ruskin was less an explicit affection for Gothic and other historic forms than a wider sense that architecture should above all be honest. Simplicity and clarity, in both design and materials, were key to his notion of architectural truth. "Any architectural feature which is not self-explanatory is wrong," he flatly stated.

Kahn evidently absorbed this principle at a very deep level, for it was to manifest itself repeatedly in his mature work. Yet what he remembered of Gray's teaching was not so much the underlying theories as the specifics of classroom work—and, in particular, the kindness shown by William Gray to him personally. The coursework, Lou recalled, "was a matter of listening to lectures and then making five plates of the various important styles: Renaissance, Roman, Greek, Egyptian, and Gothic. I helped half the class make those drawings and tried to disguise them in such a way that one wouldn't know I did them. But there was some evidence always that I did those drawings. When the teacher pointed it out to me and said, *Did you have a hand in this?* I said, *Yes, I did.* He said, *Well, I think that's all right.* He was a very nice guy."

His drawing skills had remained a lifeline for Lou all the way through high school, even before he discovered their practical use in Gray's class. Though he was no longer young enough to participate in Tadd's classes, art lessons remained a regular part of his week. On Saturdays he would walk from his home at 7th and Poplar Streets to the Graphic Sketch Club at 8th and Catharine, a distance of about twenty blocks. "I was given an easel, paper and charcoal in life class," he remembered. "All I could hear was the swishing of the strokes and the soft and privately directed voice of the critic." One Saturday morning he arrived early, when no one else was there. "The room to the right of the entrance was open. I walked in to see the work of the masters of the school on the walls. Someday, I hoped I would be selected too"—as in fact he was, more than a decade later.

Meanwhile, Lou was consistently receiving major art awards from other Philadelphia institutions. Just about every year, for instance, he would win the Wanamaker Prize, given annually by the Pennsylvania Academy of Fine Arts to the best watercolor by a Philadelphia high-school student. In May of 1919 the Academy awarded him first prize for the best original freehand drawing. And toward the end of high school he received the offer of a full scholarship to study art at the Pennsylvania Academy. (At around the same time, according to an oft-told family story which may or may not have been true, the young Louis Kahn was also awarded a composing scholarship by Samuel Fleisher, the Graphic Sketch Club's primary donor, who had heard him play an approximation of the Second Hungarian Rhapsody, by ear, at one of the Club's Sunday concerts. Lou said he had kept up his music by practicing on an old piano at home—an object which, once it was brought into the Kahn household, allegedly left so little room for other furniture that he had to sleep on top of it.)

The four-year art scholarship would have made Lou's entire course of higher education free, leaving his movie-house earnings to go straight into the family coffers and meanwhile satisfying his father's ambitions for him as an artist. But Lou had decided he wanted to be an architect. He had applied and been admitted to the architecture program at the University of Pennsylvania, considered at that point to be the best architecture school in America. But no scholarship money came with his admission, so he would have to pay his own way through college with a combination of his organ-playing at the cinema, summer jobs at architects' offices, and loans. "Every year for four years I borrowed the same amount of money. I paid it off and then I borrowed it again. My credit was very good," Kahn later remarked wryly, as if acknowledging the unlikelihood of such financial equilibrium in his life.

What this meant for the rest of the family, though, was that Lou could no longer be counted on as a source of household income. "The family could do nothing to dissuade him, not even his father, who was a very strict man," Esther Kahn recalled, basing her account on what her husband had told her. "Lou always used to listen to him but Lou kept affirming that he was going to be an architect and they had to give in because Lou was determined. But the situation was not easy because they were still very poor and Lou, though working like a dog, could never afford the tuition to go to college and support them too. One solution was that Lou's sister left school (this is the reason she couldn't finish her degree), and apprenticed herself to a milliner."

Sarah, Lou's younger sister, had shown many of the same talents he had as a child. "She could do anything with her hands," Esther Kahn noted, from painting, drawing, and sculpture to the fine sewing required of a milliner. Lou himself commented that "my sister had talent in the dance and craft things," and he also remarked on her early musical ability: after only a single piano lesson, he said, she had been able to fill in for him one day at his movie-house job. They had always been close, Lou and Sarah, and they remained close in the years to come. "She had all my mother's traits—was fine, unselfish," he said when he was in his late fifties. Yet at the age of nineteen he did not find it unreasonable that Sarah should give up her prospects in favor of his. And if he did have qualms, he learned to ignore them, lest they stand in the way of what he so desperately wanted.

Lou graduated from Central High School on June 25, 1920, and in September of that year he started classes at the University of Pennsylvania's School of Fine Arts. One of his fellow students there was his childhood friend Norman Rice, who had also taken William Gray's course at Central and felt similarly inspired to pursue architecture as a career. According to Rice, he and Lou "worked very hard for four years, often night and day, and gained the habit of working night and day that still persists." (Lou always worked, he interjected, "as if there were seventy-two hours in each day.") "In the senior year," he continued, "we attained our heart's desire, to study in the atelier of Paul Philippe Cret, the bright star of the faculty, a great architect and teacher." In fact the Cret course—called Architecture 6, Advanced Design—spanned three full semesters, with a fourth term devoted to competition for the Paris Prize, so it was actually the beginning of their junior year, in the fall of 1922, when they first started studying with this influential master teacher.

Cret, who was born and raised in France, was a product of the École des Beaux-Arts in Paris, and what he brought to Penn was an essentially classical Beaux-Arts vision as put forth by his own teacher, the rationalist Julien Guadet. In Cret's case this was modified not only by his encounter with the conflicting American traditions of neoclassicism and utopian modernism, but also by his own strenuously evolutionary beliefs. A disciple of Herbert Spencer and Hippolyte Taine, Cret believed that architecture should respond to its time and place. Twentieth-century American architects ought not to reach backward to a fake primitivism or a falsely embellished classicism, he felt, but nor could they leap forward with any kind of subjective, revolutionary, individually imposed ideal. Cret's version of classicism, often described as "modernized classicism" or "stripped classicism," involved a gradual, evolutionary response to the surrounding conditions, whether of techniques and materials or of society itself. "Modern architecture can then no longer aspire to the simplicity of the Antique or the Medieval," he wrote. "A modern plan provides a multitude of rooms for various uses distributed generally over several floors, and the external and internal appearance of the building faithfully renders this complexity by the number of openings, of stories, of reduplications of apartments on each floor, etc." One can hear in these sentences the seeds of Kahn's eventual definition of architecture as "the thoughtful making of spaces," and one can also sense at least one source of his belief that architecture should be *true*.

This advocacy of architectural truth—which included faithfulness to the site's demands as well as the client's needs, an emphasis on clarity of expression without any excess ornamentation, and a merging of utility with beauty—was at the heart of the program that Cret's teacher Guadet had elaborated in his *Éléments et théorie de l'architecture*. Guadet's underlying theory, as transmitted by Cret, also included a preference for axial relationships, symmetry, and proportional or balanced asymmetry—standard elements in classicism throughout the ages, as well as noticeable qualities in Louis Kahn's mature designs. Yet if Kahn responded to such teaching, it was not necessarily because he fell under the sway of the theories. As always, his access to learning was through the hand and the eye. What he remembered of the chief architecture textbook at Penn, Choisy's 1899 *Histoire de l'architecture*, was not so much the text itself as the 1,700 drawings of various historical buildings conveyed in both plan and section—that is, as cutaways seen both from above and from the side. And what he remembered from his own architectural training was the reliance on drawing itself.

"For beginning design problems Beaux-Arts training typically presented the student with a written program without comment from the instructor," Kahn told a historian many decades later. The student would then go off into a cubicle on his own for several hours, "during which he would make a quick sketch of his solution without consultation." This was the *esquisse*, or first idea, which then formed the basis for the entire elaboration of the design. "Once the sketch was made," Kahn explained, "we had to adhere to it during the time of study. So the sketch depended on our intuitive powers." That is to say, the student, closeted alone in his cubicle, had to forgo a reliance on known architectural precedents and come up instead with his own ideas about the nature of a library, or a legislative chamber, or whatever the assignment was. "You start as though a library had never been built," Kahn pointed out. "So I think the *esquisse* was valuable in giving a sense of what, out-of-the-blue, a library should be, as though we had never seen a library."

In pursuing this method, Kahn was helped a great deal by the excellence of his own drawing skills. He had been excused early on from the architecture school's four required semesters of freehand drawing, and he continued throughout his four years at Penn to do extremely well in watercolor, life drawing, and rendering; he was also notably good at art history. In his final semester he competed for the Paris Prize, as all Cret's students did, and finished in sixth place. Upon graduation in June of 1924 with a Bachelor in Architecture degree, he was awarded the Bronze Medal of the Arthur Spayd Brooke Memorial Prize, for "superior excellence." His days of academic underachievement were apparently over.

All through his college years Lou had lived with his family while commuting to Penn, and graduation brought no change in his address. There had been one change a year earlier: in the spring of 1923, toward the end of Lou's junior year, the Kahns had moved from a rental apartment to their own home at 2318 North 20th Street. (This was actually the second piece of property Leopold and Bertha had managed to purchase in Philadelphia; their earlier house, at 2019 North Franklin, had been bought in late 1919 but was sold only nine months later, when the city took over the land by eminent domain.) The house on North 20th Street was to remain in the family's hands for at least eight years, and it was listed as Lou's official address until he finally moved out in his very late twenties.

In 1925, Oscar Kahn, who had turned into something of a charmer, got married to Rosella, a lively, pretty girl from the neighborhood. Naturally Lou attended his younger brother's wedding, where he probably flirted with the bride, as was his habit whenever he, Oscar, and Rosella went out to the movies together. Whatever the specifics were, the Kahn boys' wedding-day behavior succeeded in bringing down their father's wrath, for Leopold reportedly slapped both his sons across the face on this very public occasion. Family gossip did not chronicle the precise nature of Lou and Oscar's offense (probably raunchy talk about sex or women, the relatives guessed), but what everyone remembered was that the patriarchal disciplinarian still felt entitled to hit his grown sons at the ages of twenty-four and twenty-one.

By this time Lou was certainly a grown-up in all outward respects. He had been given a position, right out of Penn, at the office of John Molitor, the City Architect of Philadelphia. Though hardly lucrative (it was technically considered part of his three-year apprenticeship in the architectural profession), the job gave Kahn a great deal of experience and, ultimately, responsibility. After one year as a lowly draftsman, he was appointed chief of design for the forthcoming Sesquicentennial International Exposition, to be held in Philadelphia in 1926 on the hundred and fiftieth anniversary of the signing of the Declaration of Independence. Lou used the opportunity to hire on a number of his Penn classmates. "He quickly recruited his young architect friends and we became the team," Norman Rice recalled. "Burning with our enthusiasms and with the ideals planted by our recent teachers, full of brash courage founded on naiveté, we did the Exposition and its many buildings within one year's time. For that era, some of the buildings were very creditable. It was an exhilarating and encouraging experience for all of us, and especially for Lou." The built structures were not, in fact, especially noteworthy, and they were all temporary. But the process did teach Kahn a great deal about industrial construction using lightweight steel and solid plaster infills—not methods or materials he would favor in his own later designs, but useful experience nonetheless.

This public display of his talents led, in turn, to a real, postapprenticeship job in the office of the Philadelphia architect William H. Lee, which Kahn took up in April of 1927. Lee, who at that time was designing buildings for Temple University, was best known for his sometimes outlandish cinemas, which ran the full Roaring Twenties gamut from Art Deco to Aztec style. Put to work on these high-paying projects while still living at home, Lou found he was able to save money out of his salary for a planned Grand Tour of Europe—the recommended cap to a Beaux-Arts architectural education, though one that rarely fell to young men of Kahn's social class.

And then, in June of 1927, Lou met a girl of his own. He had been brought by a friend of his to a graduation party given by some members of Philadelphia's "Russian intelligentsia." One of the honored guests was Esther Israeli, a twenty-one-year-old chemistry major who was about to graduate from Penn. Decades later, she was still able to recall specific details of the party—that the lights were turned down for the telling of ghost stories, for example, and that "when the lights went back on, there was someone playing the piano, and it was Lou." Esther didn't really meet him until the party was over, though. "Being an impatient person," she said, "I didn't want to wait for the elevator but ran down the stairs with my escort. Lou was waiting at the bottom, saw us coming down, and he told me later he wished he was running downstairs with that girl." Esther's escort, it turned out, knew Lou and lived near him, so he offered him a ride home in their car. Lou sat in the back seat, Esther and the other man in the front, and because it was a hot summer night, they decided to drive around for a while instead of going straight home.

"While we were driving Lou started to talk about a book he had just bought. It was a book about Rodin and he was absolutely fascinating though I didn't know anything about Rodin. He was just a spellbinder," Esther said of Lou. When they arrived at her house, the escort—who was not a boyfriend, simply a volunteer for this occasion—suggested to Lou that he should walk her up to the door, since she was evidently so taken by him. At the door Lou got up the courage to ask her for a date, but she told him she was still studying for her finals and couldn't go out. As a graduation present, he sent her a copy of the Rodin book.

Then Lou asked her out again, and this time she said yes, though her father, a Yale-educated lawyer, insisted on meeting the young man first. Family vetting dispensed with, the two of them spent their evening at the theater. On the way home they passed the window of a prominent flower shop, where Esther commented on how beautiful the dahlias were. "The next Friday, when I came home, my mother said that Lou must be crazy," Esther recalled, "since she never saw so many flowers in her life. Lou had never bought a girl flowers before, and he didn't know what I meant when I said that 'those dahlias' were beautiful, so he sent everything that was in the window."

"After that we saw each other all the time," said Esther, who felt they had probably fallen in love the minute they met. Her well-heeled parents must have thought it strange that their lovely, intelligent daughter, with her dramatic dark hair and her flashing eyes, should have fallen in love with this scarred, awkward fellow from the poorer side of Philadelphia. But they didn't try to interfere, and after nine months or so, fate appeared to relieve them of their problem. Lou announced to Esther that he had bought the ticket for his long-planned trip to Europe and "not even you are going to keep me back."

His ship, the S.S. *Île de France*, left the port of New York on April 26, 1928, bound for Plymouth, England. Lou was carrying a passport issued to him three weeks earlier in Washington, D.C. In this, his first American passport, he was described as being five foot seven, with brown hair, blue eyes, and the distinguishing marks of "scars on face." His occupation was given as "Architect," a self-description that would remain fixed for the rest of his life—unlike his birthplace, which would shift from Latvia (its listing here) to Estonia, as the new world order decided how to allocate the pieces of the former Livonia. In the photograph that was affixed to the passport, the unsmiling Lou, looking a bit fierce, sported a jaunty handkerchief in his suit pocket and appeared to defy anyone who might question his role as the elegant young gentleman abroad.

Kahn arrived in England on May 3 and spent a full month there, acquiring postcards from the British Museum, St. Paul's, and other London locations, sketching the castles at Windsor and Warwick, drawing

Oxford colleges and Stratford-on-Avon manor houses, and visiting a series of architectural monuments that included the Canterbury and Coventry cathedrals. Along the way he also managed, at the age of twenty-seven, to lose his virginity to a woman who owned one of the hotels he stayed in. "She made the advances," he told a psychologist some three decades later. "I felt incompetent."

On June 3 Lou left England and went, by way of Belgium, to the Netherlands, where his primary aim was to connect with the modernist architects he had begun to hear about in America. These included Hendrik Berlage, Piet Kramer, and particularly J. F. Staal, who spent a generous amount of time with the young American and then introduced him by letter to Willem Dudok, the City Architect of Hilversum. In an unsent postcard addressed to a Philadelphia friend named Rose, Lou wrote: "A very interesting and probably the most beneficial place visited was Amsterdam. There I met with the kind of architecture I was looking for and had an opportunity to interview the most famous architects of Holland. They invited me to their studios and drove me thru neighboring towns and Amsterdam to show me their work and explained to me their objectives in the past and future. Thru one of them I am getting a list of the most important publications on modern architecture. Very helpful." For his parents he bought a postcard with a picture of a windmill, and scribbled on the back: "Dear Mom & Pop, As you see Holland is very picturesque. I have seen a great deal here especially the modern work. Will write letter in few days. Love, Lou." This too remained unsent, as did many of the other cards he composed during the trip.

Toward the end of June, Kahn traveled by rail to Germany and spent a few days in the northern part of the country. On June 29 he embarked by boat from Hamburg to Scandinavia, stopping first in Denmark and then visiting Sweden and Finland. In Stockholm Lou met with the architect Ragnar Ostberg, designer of the new City Hall; in Helsinki he saw Eliel Saarinen's train station and Lars Sonck's Eira Hospital. At very much the last minute, on July 17, he obtained a visa to Estonia, then sailed from Helsinki to Tallinn on the 18th.

From the records of his transit, it would appear that Kahn only spent a single day in the country he would later claim as his birthplace. Upon arriving in Tallinn, he immediately boarded a train headed toward Riga, crossing the Estonian-Latvian border on July 19 and registering at a Riga hotel that same night. He was to remain in Latvia for almost a full month, until he crossed through Lithuania back to Germany on August 17. The lure of Riga was not architecture, though. It was family.

When Lou's mother left the Baltic island of Ösel in 1906, she left behind her father, her mother, and her six younger siblings, five of them born on the island. The family had been living in Arensburg, the only city on Ösel, since about 1880, though they had made frequent trips by ferry back to Riga (where Bertha herself, for example, was married in 1900). But when the First World War and then the Russian Revolution disrupted the island's connection with the mainland, they retreated back to their Latvian roots. Lou's grandfather, Mendel Mendelowitsch, died in Riga in 1916. Though his widow, Rocha-Lea, could have returned to Arensburg when the war was over, the family property on the island had been confiscated by then, and besides, five of her seven grown children now lived in Riga. Her Latvian passports, dated 1922 and 1927, were both issued at Riga, and she was to die in Riga in 1934; there was no evidence in any Arensburg records that she had ever lived there after the war. But in Lou's memories, at least as he recounted them in later life, she had stayed on alone in Arensburg.

"I went to visit my grandmother in 1928," Kahn told an interviewer when he was in his seventies. "She had a one-room house near the place where they kept fish. There was a sterno stove in one corner and two sacks of dried fish, a chair, a table and a bed. I slept on the floor, she slept on the bed. I lived there for months, and I used to see the fishermen bring in the catch. A frugal existence. She had nothing except what her children gave her. It was a time when the Russians had taken everything away."

The island was important to Lou because all his early childhood memories stemmed from there, and when he told this story, perhaps even he himself believed that this 1928 visit took place on Ösel. But that seems doubtful for a number of reasons. Ösel had by that time become part of Estonia, and Lou's passport records had him in Latvia during the whole of the month that he spent with his relatives. His name does not appear on the passenger lists for either of the steamships that occasionally brought tourists from Riga to Ösel that summer, and it's not clear how he could have made a quick, invisible trip in some other way. But even assuming he did manage to get to Ösel somehow, why is this fragment of a memory the only passage that survives from "months" spent there? Why is there no mention in any letters or notes, for instance, of a visit during his adulthood to the Arensburg castle, which was later to loom so powerfully behind his mature architecture? It seems more likely that this is a childhood memory brought forward in time to the period of his grown-up travels.

On the other hand, the visit to his grandmother *could* have taken place in Riga. The tiny house she and her husband had occupied when they lived in the Latvian capital—at 108 Maskavas Street, in the Jewish ghetto—was in a part of town very close to the harbor, so it could well have been the one-room hovel Lou described "near the place where they kept fish." Or perhaps he never saw his grandmother at all on this trip, and the poverty-stricken existence he envisioned in Arensburg somehow grew out of the accounts provided by his aunts and uncles.

"Her daughters and sons, my mother's brothers and sisters, went to Riga, where they were very well off and could send a few pennies to my grandmother," Kahn reported. "I visited the areas of Riga and saw my people. I was very much moved by it."

That they were actually "well off" might have been another of Lou's exaggerations, but certainly the Mendelowitsch children had done reasonably well for themselves in Riga. By the late 1920s they were all living within walking distance of one another in the newer art-nouveau area of the city, where numerous apartment blocks had gone up in the decade before the war. Lou's aunt Sara (also called Sora-Gita) and her husband, Leib Hirschberg, lived with their two sons, Leiser and Mischa, in a rather cheaply built six-story complex on Matisa Street. Less than five minutes' walk away, her older brother Abram and his family of seven had an apartment in a somewhat more substantial building on the same street. Ten minutes farther down Matisa and half a block to the right, one came to Benjamin's flat. Another ten-minute walk from there could have taken Lou to his other aunt, Haja-Mira, or else to his youngest uncle, Isak, who lived in a rather grand apartment building at the corner of Avotu and Gertrudes Streets. Lou had cousins in all five of these households, not to mention an aunt and uncle who were less than a dozen years older than he was; wherever he was staying, he would have seen a great deal of these relatives during his month in Riga.

He also wandered through the rest of the city. "I recalled the places my mother and father used to speak of," Lou said, and he no doubt visited the spots in the Old Town and elsewhere that had figured in Bertha's and Leopold's memories. But he also saw things that had sprung up in Riga since his parents' day. It would have been hard to miss the most remarkable new building project in town, the four-arched Central Market that had been under construction since 1924 and was almost finished when Lou arrived. Vaulted in the style of a steel-ribbed Victorian train station, but with a somewhat barer and more modern aesthetic, each of the four linked pavilions rose sixty feet or so from the ground, with massive semicircular windows lighting up the interior space from either end. This Central Market would, when completed, be an impressive riverside palace for shoppers, with separate pavilions devoted to fish, dairy, and other kinds of groceries, all boldly declaring Riga's architectural entrance into the modern age.

Architecture once again became Kahn's major concern when he left Latvia for Germany, Austria, and Czechoslovakia. By the end of September he had seen Berlin, Vienna, Prague, and Munich; he had also visited at least one Tyrolean village, for he collected a postcard on which he wrote (this time, apparently, to himself), "Typical mountain dwellings of Bayern and Tirol. The shutters, windows, balconies are painted in bright greens, white, and siennas. The stones on the roof are to retain the snow in winter and to prevent avalanches." On October 4, after indulging himself at Munich's Oktoberfest, Lou crossed the Brenner Pass into Italy, where the longest and perhaps most compelling part of his trip took place. "Compared to other countries, that is to the architect-artist, Italy certainly stands alone," he wrote in another unsent postcard, this one addressed to people named Laura and Goldie. "I am generalizing before I have seen all but from the first glimpse the rest I can summarize. Up until now I arranged my trip to take in the countries that are going in for the Modern—Now I am in the land that is the source of"

And there the note abruptly ended. The sudden break is startlingly true to the gap which at that point divided Lou's experiences of architecture. Emotionally and artistically, he found himself drawn to the ancient and medieval buildings he discovered in Europe, like the castles and cathedrals in England or the palaces, churches, and ruins of Italy. Yet what interested him on a conscious level were the experiments in modernism he found in places like Scandinavia, Germany, and the Netherlands; these were the things he intended to make use of when he returned to America.

For now, though, he reveled in the Italian landscape, traveling from Venice through Verona, Milan, Bologna, Florence, San Gimignano, Assisi, and Spoleto before arriving in Rome to spend Christmas Eve at St. Peter's Square. Then it was onward to Naples, Capri, Pompeii, Paestum, and the Amalfi Coast, sketching all the while. Finally, in early March of 1929, he tore himself away from Italy and went to Paris, where he spent the last five weeks of his trip exploring the city, his funds dwindling so low that he was obliged to trade his nightclubby piano-playing skills for a small room above a Left Bank restaurant. On April 12, having crossed to Dover the previous day, he left England aboard the merchant vessel S.S. *American Shipper*. After a notably unluxurious week at sea, he was back in New York, a bit thinner and much poorer, but richer in exactly the kinds of experiences he had set out to gain.

■

Before he left for Europe, Lou had worked out a plan for his re-entry into the Philadelphia architecture world. He would venture into private practice, he decided, with a Penn classmate who had also been employed at Molitor's office, a man named Sydney Jelinek. But Jelinek backed out while Kahn was away, leaving him without a partner and without the means to start up his own firm. Luckily he was able to land a job almost immediately upon his return with his old professor, Paul Cret. Kahn joined Cret's office in May of 1929, and in the subsequent seventeen months he worked on a number of large-scale projects, including the Chicago "Century of Progress" Exposition, the Folger Shakespeare Library, and some bridges for the Pennsylvania Railroad.

Stimulated by all the sketches and watercolors he had produced on his trip, Lou also decided to take his artwork more seriously than he had in recent years. In November of 1929 he exhibited four of the pencil drawings he had done in Europe at the annual exhibition put on by the Pennsylvania Academy of Fine Arts. Kahn was to continue showing his work there over the next three years, presenting the public with two landscapes, *Danube Country* and *A Coming Storm*, and a portrait of his father that he titled, with Whistlerian simplicity, *Black and White*. In 1931 he also published an article called "The Value and Aim of Sketching" in the journal put out by the T-Square Club. It was Kahn's first published piece of writing, and it made his mother proud. "The article interests me very much," Bertha wrote to him, "and according to my limited understanding of the technique of sketching, I think it is very good. The sketches themselves, I am particularly proud of, for in them I can see your own handiwork."

But by that time—a mere two years after his return from Europe—practically everything about Lou's life had changed. When he first came back to America, he had moved back in with his parents, expecting to resume his old existence as if nothing had altered in his absence. Esther Israeli, however, had moved on. "He didn't write (Kahns don't write letters)," she pointed out. "So when he came back I was engaged to someone else." Lou didn't find this out until he stopped by her house to see her, and when he heard the news, "he was furious. And I said, 'Well, how was I to know?' I didn't see him after that night," Esther added, "because Lou had a vicious temper, which he very seldom showed and he certainly showed it that night. He had brought many wonderful things for me from Europe but he gave everything away and naturally I got nothing."

But seeing Lou again had made her realize her fiancé's shortcomings. "You know, you bore me," she said to him one day, and that was the end of the engagement. Esther's mother was relieved it was over, since she had never much liked the young man. "But she didn't want me to marry Lou either," Esther observed. "That was something that both my parents felt because Lou had those scars, was poor, and his family was different from ours."

The Kahns were not just of a lower social class than the Israelis. They were also noticeably recent immigrants. They spoke German together at home, and perhaps even some Yiddish. There was "very little English," according to Esther (though Bertha's eloquent 1931 letter about the sketching article would suggest otherwise). "English only was spoken in my family," Esther pointed out. "My father was a lawyer, my mother did not come from indigent people. *His* family came from Russia," she said of Lou, managing to ignore the fact that her own parents had been born in Russia as well.

But unlike Leopold Kahn, Samuel Israeli had come to America as a child. His father, formerly in the grain business in Russia, did so well financially as a dry goods merchant in Hartford, Connecticut, that he was able to give all his children excellent educations. One of Samuel's brothers was a rabbi, another was an architect, and still another was a doctor; even his sister had an M.D., from the Women's Medical College of Pennsylvania. Samuel himself, after attending Mount Hermon Boys' School and Yale University, got a law degree at Penn and was practicing as a partner in his own Philadelphia firm by 1900. In 1902 he married a Philadelphia girl of Russian-Jewish origins, Annie Sinberg, with whom he had three daughters. Esther, born in 1905, was the oldest and in many ways the closest to both her parents.

Her family life, she felt, exemplified the best of professional-class comfort and civilization. "When you came to my family for dinner, dinner was ready," Esther observed, underlining the difference between the Israelis and the Kahns. "When you went to his house, they were running around, looking for bread or something." She praised certain things about Lou's parents—their "beautiful marriage," the fact that Bertha "spoke very beautiful German"—but even her admiration was couched in a degree of condescension. "Lou's mother was very quiet, very much in love with the father. She was not an attractive woman, and she thought he was just wonderful that he would marry her," she remarked. But apparently the disapproval ran both ways, or at least so Esther felt. "They didn't like me," she said of Lou's parents. "They wanted him to marry someone they could control."

Whether or not this was true, it was a moot point, since the wishes of the parental generation ultimately did not figure in this story. Nearly a year after Lou had stormed away from her house, and long after she had broken her own engagement, Esther found herself at a Philadelphia Orchestra concert featuring Beethoven's *Pastoral* Symphony. "I saw Lou there," Esther recalled. "Later I wrote him a note: 'I saw you at the concert. I was there with my father, and I thought it was a magnificent performance.'" Lou must have realized, from her purposeful reference to her father, that she was no longer engaged, because he called her the very next day. "We were married three months later," said Esther.

Planning the ceremony, though, posed its own problems. Esther wanted a secular wedding, but Lou insisted that for his parents' sake they needed to be married by a rabbi. This was a bit strange, as Judaism had not featured heavily in his childhood. In fact, he told an interviewer decades later that he had received no religious education, that he had spent a total of one day in Sunday school (family lore had it that his mother snatched him out when the rabbi smacked him), and that religion in his family was "secondary, completely routine." Yet the Kahns clearly thought of themselves as observant Jews, and they must have wanted to signal that allegiance at their son's wedding. Esther put up a small amount of resistance but then gave in—though, to judge from the number of times she mentioned this capitulation in later life, it must have continued to rankle.

About a week before the wedding, in early August of 1930, Esther had occasion to resort to her diary. "This is the first time since Lou and I decided to marry that I felt the need of writing," she began. "This evening, for the first time, all was not harmony." Apparently Esther had belatedly realized that there would be thirteen people at the wedding breakfast unless she invited two more, so she called up Lou to tell him of her choices. He was not immediately receptive to the idea; Esther figured he was "either hungry or tired or both and besides I don't like to talk to him on the phone—we always get into difficulties." He told her he had to consult someone else and would call her back, at which point she became deeply offended. "Lou is always telling me my faults—perhaps he doesn't realize that he has them also," she fumed to herself. He also seemed unaware that "in every instance I have given in to him—having a rabbi marry us, in the matter of the furniture, not getting 'at home' cards which is really a necessity and a thousand little things even to luggage and clothes. But I *won't* submerge my personality," she valiantly insisted, "and I won't change my feelings and actions. Afterall he loved me for them originally and now he wants me to change."

Yet this display of resistance was apparently made to herself alone. "Why haven't I the courage to tell him this?" she went on. "I agree with everything like a meek little lamb—that is what love does to you. I should think he would be happy to have a wife with a mind—not a very stupid one either." That she was far from stupid, and indeed somewhat unconventional, came through in the observation, "As next Thursday approaches he must feel very odd because marriage is something he wished to fight. I don't feel any better myself—I am an independent person also who never wanted to actually marry but love—and love makes you change your mind about things." Then she added wistfully, "I only hope we will not have any differences—they spoil everything and cause a very naked reaction in me—my whole body and mind freezes immediately toward anyone who is not treating me in a respectful way."

Louis I. Kahn and Esther Virginia Israeli were married on August 14, 1930, during one of the hottest Philadelphia summers on record. They left immediately on their honeymoon, which took them to the Adirondacks in upstate New York, Montreal and Quebec City in Canada, the White Mountains in New Hampshire, Gloucester and Boston in Massachusetts, and finally Atlantic City, New Jersey, where they met up with Lou's friends the Osers. Along the way Lou did a great deal of sketching, capturing landscapes he would later put into his paintings. They both relaxed, and Esther's faith in the marriage was restored: it was a "lovely honeymoon," she noted in her diary. (About Lou's feelings one cannot be sure. Years later he told a younger colleague that a week into his marriage, maybe even after the first night, he knew he'd made a mistake. But whether that was hindsight speaking, or possibly an effort to be convivially intimate—and whether even Lou fully believed it—is impossible to say.) On their honeymoon, Esther noticed that he seemed to be less self-conscious about his scars; in particular, he no longer tried to conceal them under a hat. "After we got married, Lou threw his hat away and never put it on again," she recalled in her old age. "The last time he ever wore a hat was when we got married. I was quite beautiful—you may not have thought it, but I was—and I guess he felt if it didn't bother me, it wouldn't bother anyone."

When they got back to Philadelphia, their plan was to move temporarily into Esther's parents' house, a gabled, brick-and-wood three-story row house at 5243 Chester Avenue in West Philadelphia. The place was spacious enough for them to have a bedroom, a bathroom, and a study all to themselves, plus a small studio for Lou. Esther was delighted to remain with her family, and her new husband got along well not only with her parents but also with her two younger sisters, Olivia and Regina, who were nineteen and sixteen at the time. The idea was that Lou and Esther would each continue working at their jobs for a year—he at Paul Cret's, she as a research assistant and administrator for the neurosurgeon Charles Frazier—all the while saving up money for an extended trip to Austria and Germany. Esther, who was interested in psychology, hoped to study with Anna Freud, while Lou wanted to work with Walter Gropius.

But the plan fell through less than a month after the honeymoon, when Lou came home one day in late September with the news that he was unemployed. The financial impact of the 1929 stock market crash had finally sifted down to the architecture profession, and even Cret's respected firm found itself unable to get new commissions. "Lou came home, as usual always late, and said to me that he was out of work; he could not stay at Cret's office and take money anymore because there was no work," Esther said. "Cret was exactly like Lou became; he never fired anybody. So Lou just walked out." The European trip was put on permanent hold and Esther stayed on at her job, while the newlyweds continued to live with her parents, now not in order to save money but because they couldn't afford anything else.

It wasn't as if they had no expenses at 5243 Chester. They had promised to pay her parents $100 a month for their board, and they continued to do this even in the months when Lou was out of work. Esther also set aside at least $20 a month, and sometimes much more, to give to Lou's parents. And then there were the other recurring costs—for clothes (including Esther's uniforms), concert and theater tickets, doctor visits, occasional gifts, small but regular "allowances" for herself and Lou, and other incidentals. Esther's detailed records of income and expenditure, which she kept from early 1931 onward, showed how carefully she had to monitor their financial situation, despite the fact that they were living with her parents.

Still, this living arrangement had the advantage of allowing Esther to pursue a master's degree in psychology even as she maintained her day job. "I could go to work and graduate school without thinking about anything else in the house; everything else was done for me," she observed. Annie Israeli, assisted by a maid, did all the housework, while

Samuel Israeli continued to bring in the bulk of the household income through his work as a lawyer. He cast no blame on his new son-in-law—after all, everyone was at risk of unemployment in those early Depression years—and in fact remained one of the staunchest believers in Lou's talent. "I say there were only two people in this world who knew what Lou was going to amount to, way back in 1927 when I met him," Esther later commented, "and that was my father, who Lou idolized, . . . and myself."

"Oh, and his mother thought he was great," Esther added. But Bertha could no longer serve as a source of local and immediate encouragement, for shortly after Lou lost his job, his parents left Philadelphia for good. The ostensible reason for the move was Leopold's health, which the doctors thought would improve in the warm, dry climate of Los Angeles. At least one family member—an Aunt Martha—already lived out there and could help smooth their way. A series of postcards in a slightly Anglicized German marked Bertha and Leopold's journey across the country ("We are just this Thursday *gekrost* into California State," they wrote, using a verb that combined the English *cross* with the German perfect tense), and then, in the winter of 1930–31, came a letter from Los Angeles itself. "When I saw the first palm trees I felt all excited," Bertha wrote to both Lou and Esther, though still in German. "You know, dear children, how much I love nature!" Then Leopold's tinier, more elegant script took over: "Apologies, but your mother couldn't write any more, it was already a bit much for her eyes." (Bertha's eyesight was beginning to worsen seriously, to such an extent that "during the day I go around with blue glasses," she said.) Leopold reported on their nighttime visit to a "wonderfully illuminated" Hollywood, commented on the city's wide commercial streets with their "magnificent and elegant stores," and in general praised the superiority of Los Angeles over Philadelphia. In May he sent another letter describing their new landlords, "elderly Christian people who love us and let us take everything from the kitchen garden; the garden is in front of our apartment." In an addendum to that letter, he asked Esther and Lou to "Please call Rosella and Sarah and ask them why they don't write!"

By June of 1931, when Bertha wrote to Lou about his sketching article, the language of communication had shifted permanently to English. But the concerns about being cut off from the family members in Philadelphia remained the same. "You refer to the house in your note, I am sorry, but I haven't been informed about any thing," Bertha said. "I haven't heard from Oscar or Rosala for a month. Has anything happened to them? I am quite worried." She had reason to be worried, for the family house at 2318 North 20th Street was in the process of being lost through a mortgage default. It was finally sold in a sheriff's sale in September, which meant that Oscar, Rosella, and Sarah all had to find housing elsewhere. Eventually Sarah moved to Brooklyn, New York, with her Canadian husband, Joe Freedman, and her little daughter, Gerry; from there she wrote piteous letters to Lou and Esther about how homesick she was. Oscar and Rosella—now with two small children, a boy named Alan and his baby sister, Rhoda—stayed on in Philadelphia, as Oscar tried out various unsuccessful business ventures. In the long run all of these Kahn family members, with the notable exception of Lou and Esther, would end up out in California with Leopold and Bertha.

Some of what kept Lou in Philadelphia was Esther's family, of which he had become an integral part, but most of it had to do with his architecture career. For he continued to have a career even in those periods when he had no job. He was not one to become easily discouraged, and soon after he left Cret's office he began making plans to go into private practice with another of the firm's laid-off architects, Solis Daniel Kopelan. Kahn got as far as designing the new firm's logo—a symmetrical, square-cut, blatantly modernist house—when he was rescued from this doomed venture by the offer of a job with the architectural practice of Zantzinger, Borie, and Medary. They had a contract to design the U.S. Department of Justice building in Washington, D.C., and since government work was practically the only guaranteed source of income for architects in the 1930s, it seemed advisable for Kahn to accept. He joined the firm at the end of December 1930, only three months after leaving Cret.

Thirteen months later, however, with the design process completed and the project set to go out to bid, the practice had no further need of Lou's services. The founding partner, Clarence Clark Zantzinger, let him go "with great regret" in January of 1932, and Lou was once again jobless. But if he couldn't get paid for his work, he nonetheless resolved to do something useful and interesting. In March of 1932 Kahn joined together with a number of other unemployed architects to found the Architectural Research Group, whose stated aim was to address problems of housing and slum clearance in the Philadelphia area. The ARG had about two dozen members, and though they were all officially equal, the charismatic, philosophically minded Kahn was generally viewed as their leader. It was through their joint membership in ARG that Lou first met David Wisdom, the stalwart employee who was to be the cornerstone of his private practice in the decades to come. During this period Kahn also grew friendly with George Howe, a leading progressive architect who, with his partner William Lescaze, had already designed the Philadelphia Savings Fund Building (often described as the first International Style skyscraper built in the United States). His connection to Lou was not so much through the Architectural Research Group—the fully employed Howe, widely known for his work on a series of elegant private residences, was not an ARG member, though he approved of the group's principles—as through the T-Square Club, which published Louis Kahn's first piece of writing. George Howe, as president of the club, was in charge of the club's journal, and it was he who had invited Lou to submit his article on sketching to its pages.

Over the course of its two-year existence (the group disbanded in 1934), ARG produced housing studies, made recommendations for rehabilitating slums, submitted proposals to local agencies, and engaged in heated group discussions about the role of architecture in the modern world. ARG also submitted entries to various national and international competitions (none of which won); among the more noteworthy of these was Kahn's 1932 design for a Lenin Memorial in Leningrad. The projects all came to nothing, in practical terms, and yet they both reflected and confirmed the intensity of Lou's engagement with his chosen profession. Though unremunerated, the work itself satisfied for a time his desire to be doing something new and self-determined in his field. It also brought him to the attention of people who would later be able to help him toward paid employment. As Esther put it in a July 1934 diary entry, "In the 2 years out of work Lou has formed A-R-G and did fine work in architecture—too bad that he has no income to continue studies. [He] has learned much in housing & made many connections."

As for herself, she noted that though she had managed to obtain her master's in psychology, she was "still working for Frazier at 125 a month." (By this time, though, the aging and somewhat difficult Dr. Frazier had been joined at Jefferson Medical College by the younger neurologist Bennie Alpers, whom Esther had included—along with his wife, Lillian—in a list of her and Lou's new friends.) That pretty much covered the 1934 updates devoted to "Lou" and "Me." Under the heading "Us," she wrote: "Quarrel a great deal because we are both on edge. Hard to get along financially which is bad & which helps us keep on edge. Both tired from hard work & neither doing the things we want."

This marked a severe contrast to her entry three years earlier, in July of 1931, when she had concluded after one year of marriage: "Our life together has been truly beautiful. Fortunately our likes and dislikes and more strongly our interests and ideals coincide. We find our pleasure in music & theatre & friends. Our days are filled with work we like and our evenings with work of our own and home. We love each other dearly and respect each other's wishes & desires. Lou is a perfect darling—considerate sweet quiet—gentle and extremely brilliant. I am sure neither of us would wish for a better life."

That this was not just Esther's rosy-tinted vision is suggested by some of the letters Lou wrote her during the summers in the 1930s, when she was vacationing up in Katonah with her friend Kit Sherman and he was hard at work in the city. "Dearestest:" begins one of these notes, written on a hot Monday night and filled with amusing, cartoon-like sketches, including one of himself naked at a drafting table. "Had meeting with Zantzinger this after noon. Everything coming along . . . I am slated to get a synagogue job—good opportunity . . . Bees Buzzin' But no honey produced yet. But we're young. Miss you! Miss me? Regards to Kit. Love, Lou." Another talks about an afternoon spent with several colleagues (though "It turned out to be a beer party instead of a serious cooperative architects office"), during which he engaged in a conversation about psychology with a woman named Sally Montgomery. "I was audacious enough to express myself in Psychological terms," Lou wrote, "racking my brain for all the terminology which you acquainted me with. The others joined in to unroot the metaphysical 'Human Nature' angle, the existance of which was not accepted by Sally nor myself on the basis of it not being definable." He reassured her that the subject of psychology only came up because "Sally inquired very affectionately about you and your work. I told her what a hell of a time you had accomplishing your aim and how you were waiting for my 1,000,000 job to clear the deck." After mentioning that he'd give her more details when he saw her over the coming weekend, Lou closed, "With love and kisses, Lou"—his name, in block capitals, composed entirely out of tiny x-kisses.

A more extended separation than these summer breaks began at the end of 1935, when Lou was offered a full-time job working under Alfred Kastner at the Resettlement Administration in Washington, D.C. Despite the lack of regular employment, 1935 had already been a good year for Kahn. He had passed his Architectural Registration Examination in May, allowing him to put at the head of the new stationery for his home-based practice: "Louis I. Kahn • Registered Architect • 5243 Chester Avenue Philadelphia Penna." Soon after this, in September, he received his first independent commission, for the Ahavath Israel synagogue in Philadelphia. It did not turn out to be a particularly distinguished building—completed in 1938, the functional brick-clad structure suffered from both the architect's inexperience and the congregation's insufficient funds—but it was certainly "nothing to be ashamed of," as one architecture critic was later to point out, and the commission itself marked a definite step in Kahn's progress toward having his own practice. Then, in late 1935, came the irresistible offer to work under the much-respected, Hamburg-trained Kastner on an entirely new workers' housing project. It was a dream job for Lou, even if it did require him to live in Washington during the week, and he accepted the position of "assistant principal architect" at the Resettlement Administration on December 23, 1935.

Jersey Homesteads—later renamed Roosevelt, New Jersey, after the president whose New Deal had financed its construction—was a utopian scheme designed to relocate impoverished garment workers from their cramped city tenements to a verdant, healthful community run along mildly socialist lines. Located a few miles south of Hightstown, the farming-and-factory cooperative occupied over a thousand acres of rolling pastureland and forested glens. The factory at its center was designed to employ 160 garment workers, all members of either the International Ladies Garment Workers Union or the Amalgamated City

Clothing Workers of America, and all paid at the union rate. The co-op village (which also included a school, a community center, and various other local facilities) was to be run on a one-member, one-vote basis, with the members buying into the system up front and paying only $18 to $24 per month for their housing over a thirty-year period. The initial plan was to house about 200 families, or 1,000 people, in three- and four-bedroom dwellings, with each house set in its own sizable garden. A communal farm of 500 acres would surround the houses, offering a buffer zone against encroaching growth and employing an additional six workers from the community.

Kahn's designs for the houses, which borrowed elements from both Le Corbusier and the Bauhaus, were simple yet pleasant, with concrete-block walls, overhanging flat roofs, and mainly white exteriors. The houses were set well back from the curving, sidewalk-free streets, lending a rural or perhaps semi-suburban air to the place. Driveways led up to small attached garages, and large windows looked out onto the front yards. Asymmetry was more prevalent than precise symmetry, but whether the front door was placed in the center or toward the side, each building had a sense of balance. Some of the houses were duplexes while others were single-family; some had two stories, some had one. There were twelve different housing styles, but all the buildings shared a similar look, lending the whole place a kind of forward-looking, egalitarian yet decidedly leafy feel, not at all what the words "factory town" might conjure up.

And in fact the factory element was to prove evanescent, for the unions in the end decided they didn't want their valuable workers exported to the countryside. Lou's contribution to the project was finished in early 1937, when the houses were completed to his specifications. Within two years, the utopian experiment had failed. Yet the low-priced homes remained, and in 1939 the artist Ben Shahn (who had earlier been brought in to do the mural in the community center) moved with his wife from their tiny New York apartment to one of the Jersey Homesteads houses. He was to remain there the rest of his life, and the place became something of an artists' colony as a result. The clean-lined houses Kahn had designed for workers were appealing enough, it turned out, to suit an aesthetically focused clientele.

In the meantime, though, life had changed significantly in the house that Lou himself occupied with Esther and her family. In February of 1936, less than two months into Lou's new Washington job, Samuel Israeli died of a heart arrhythmia. The family was devastated; even his in-laws "both cried like Babies, we loved him very much," as Leopold wrote in a condolence note to Lou. Esther herself was so shaken that a year later she could barely refer to the death. "So much has happened since the last entry that I haven't had the heart to write," she confided to her diary on January 28, 1937. "Feb 5 We lost our Daddy. No need to write about that since every detail will always be in my heart & mind and so will all the consequences. I cannot place on hard, unfeeling paper the agony, sorrow, and all that followed . . . Since then I have been only part a woman—part of me is gone and as a result I seem to be ill all the time."

One of the consequences was that the family finances instantly grew more straitened. Luckily Lou was fully employed for the whole of 1936, and the $4,599 he brought in from his Resettlement Administration job, when added to Esther's $1,500, more than made up for the extra expense of housing him in Washington. But Annie Israeli now depended more than ever on her oldest daughter, emotionally as well as financially, and Esther felt this as an additional source of pressure on her already weakened self. Meanwhile Annie continued, somewhat guilt-inducingly, to do all the housework: "She forgets that she is almost 60 and should let up on her activities but she doesn't," Esther wrote to Lou. Eventually the household's composition altered even further when Annie decided to rent out Olivia's now-empty room to a paying lodger, Catherine McMichael, a Catholic woman who was already known to the family as "Aunt Katie." All of this, combined with Lou's frequent work absences, made Esther feel slightly estranged at home, and she only seemed able to relax fully when she was with her friend Kit at Brookwood, their summer refuge in Katonah.

Nor did the needs of Lou's own family decline during this period; if anything, they increased. Over the course of 1936, Lou and Esther sent $500 to his parents and gave (or loaned) an additional $75 to his brother. Bertha Kahn came for a brief visit to Philadelphia in the middle of 1936, and shortly after she returned to Los Angeles, Oscar's and Sarah's families both moved out there as well. But life turned out to be far from easy in the Golden State, and in 1938 Leopold and Bertha were forced to file an application for state aid under the Old Age Security Law. In the letter Lou received from the County of Los Angeles, the Department of Charities representative informed him that under California law, "adult children are responsible for the care and support of their parents. We are, therefore, requesting that you give careful and serious consideration to the matter of your parents' care. What plan or suggestion can you offer for this care, either in your own home or elsewhere? To what extent are you now aiding your parents and to what extent will you be able to aid in the future?" Lou and Esther's response, after filling out the requisite "Statement of Responsible Relative," was to continue sending monthly checks, each of which was met with a grateful thank-you note from the elder Kahns.

After the Jersey Homesteads job ended, in February of 1937, there was again a lull on the employment front. But "Lou is not discouraged," as Esther noted in her diary. "I feel that he may soon begin to be recognized. He has such talent and ability, plus the enthusiasm & desire for his profession, that he will get ahead. But I hope it will be soon."

In 1937 and again in 1938, Lou finally had time to go with Esther on a couple of substantial vacations with Kit and Jay Sherman. The Shermans—he was a mathematician, she a medical researcher—were among the Kahns' closest friends. Esther had listed them, along with the Alperses and the Osers, as the people who were kindest to her in the terrible months after her father's death, and Kit had even helped Esther out financially during the periods of Lou's unemployment. The two couples had often vacationed together, and now, in the summer of 1937, they visited Gloucester, Massachusetts, and then drove north to the Gaspé region of Quebec, taking in parts of the Maine and Canadian coast on the way. The following year they went back to Canada and spent nearly two full weeks in Nova Scotia. Perhaps the northern coastal landscape reawakened Lou's childhood memories of the Baltic island where he had spent his first five years. What is certain is that, on both vacations, he eagerly recorded this fresh yet somehow familiar setting in numerous evocative sketches.

The lighthearted atmosphere of these summer trips was captured in two paintings that Lou made from his sketches when he returned to Philadelphia. In the partially abstract but recognizably figurative *Nude in a Doorway*, painted in tempera on paper, a tall, naked, faceless woman (her russet-colored nipples are her most distinct feature) strides past an open doorway as a much shorter, darker man sits or squats in the background. She is either outdoors or in a bright, sunny room; we, looking out at her, are definitely indoors, in a space that is paneled in green, yellow, and gray, with lively blue rectangular panels on the cinnamon-colored door that stands, ajar, between us and her. Esther Kahn felt that this painting commemorated the meager, squalid accommodations the Kahns shared with the Shermans on their trip to Halifax, Nova Scotia, where indoor plumbing and other niceties were sorely lacking. But the evident humor in this somewhat risqué picture suggests that even the deprivations were part of the fun.

The other painting, *In the Cabin, No. 2*, is a somewhat more serious undertaking, as its oil-on-canvas medium suggests. Within the cabin itself, obliquely facing us, sits a cross-legged man in a wooden chair, apparently reading a map or a newspaper; he and the chair are done entirely in shades of brown. His eyes are distinctly drawn, and he has the faint outline of an ear, but his lower face is blurred into invisibility. Around him is a room composed of planes, angles, and occasional curves, all in relatively solid blocks of color conveying domestic objects like a bureau (green), a mirror (dark blue), a pitcher (white), an armchair (olive-green front, electric-blue back), and the adjoining corners of a beige ceiling, a brown floor, and blue- and green-tinted walls. Outside the open doorway, practically in the center of the picture, is an abstract landscape that merges from white into yellow in a diagonal slash, and against that yellow ground, a tiny red figure, almost certainly a woman, appears in silhouette. The whole image is at once precise and dreamy, with thin lines of shape-sketching paint lending an almost cartoonish overlay to the gracefully abstract planes of color. It is a delicately balanced painting as well as an elegantly modern one, and Lou thought enough of it to hang it on the wall of his and Esther's sitting room, on the third floor of 5243 Chester.

Elsewhere in the house he had, over the years, put up other examples of his work. A watercolor called *Street in a Coastal Village, No. 4*, depicting the houses, cows, and people of Isle Madame, Nova Scotia, hung on the dining-room wall. So did a squiggly-lined oil painting of a scene in Rockport, Massachusetts, titled *The White Church*—a work whose bright yet threatening lighting effects gave it some of the eeriness of a de Chirico. Also in the dining room (which, of all the rooms in the house, had the best wall space for paintings) was *Danube Country*, the 1930 watercolor Lou had shown at the Pennsylvania Academy of Fine Arts, while on the wall of his and Esther's bedroom hung a 1929 water-color sketch of the Borghese Gardens in Rome. Not satisfied with the picture-hanging space the house offered, Lou even began to paint on the house itself: at one point he executed a series of Blake-like allegories, in oils, on the panels of the bedroom door.

All this created a welcome diversion from the joblessness of the late 1930s. There were fits and starts of professional activity, but much of it was unpaid. In 1938 Kahn collaborated with two other architects, Oscar Stonorov and Rudolf Mock, in creating a design for the Wheaton College Art Center competition. The result was never built, but it *was* selected for an architectural exhibit that traveled to seventeen venues, including New York's Museum of Modern Art. In response to a compe-tition announced by the new Philadelphia Housing Authority, Lou joined with George Howe, Kenneth Day, and others to submit plans for the Glenwood Housing Project. This too resulted in no actual build-ings, though a couple of additional Philadelphia-area housing studies were assigned to them over the next three years.

In early 1939 Lou was briefly hired as a technical advisor to the Information Services Division of the U.S. Housing Authority, and in that capacity he did the illustrations for a series of booklets with titles like *The Housing Shortage, Public Housing and the Negro*, and *Housing and Juvenile Delinquency*. He also designed the exhibition panels for the Authority's Rational City Plan, part of a show called *Art in Our Time* which was displayed at the Museum of Modern Art in May. In October of that year Kahn was introduced by a Housing Authority colleague to a fellow Philadelphian named Edmund Norwood Bacon, with whom he soon went on to organize a citywide housing protest and other activities focused on improving the city's dire conditions. Work-ing out of his home office, Lou also got tiny jobs doing alterations and additions to the local branch of the Battery Workers Union and a Phila-delphia dentist's building. And in 1940 his old friend Jesse Oser, whom he had known since Central High, hired him to design a single-family home in nearby Elkins Park—the first such commission that Kahn had ever received, and one that he faithfully and inventively completed within two years.

None of this, however, brought him anything like the success he was hoping for. He did not seem to be getting any closer at all to that million-dollar job he had jokingly mentioned to Esther. And meanwhile the need for such a job (or *any* job, for that matter) had become more pointed, for in the summer of 1939 Esther announced that she was pregnant. As if to underline both the tenderness and the anxiety of the occasion, Lou began painting a portrait of his pregnant wife, *Esther in Pink*, which turned out to be one of the most touchingly intimate pictures he had ever done.

Over the nine years they had been married, Lou had made a number of charcoal sketches of Esther: Esther framed in a window, Esther wearing a Matisse-like slanting hat, Esther holding a cat on her lap, and one isolated bust of Esther, large-eyed and serious and rather beautiful, gazing out at us with lowered chin. He had also painted at least one color picture of his wife, a 1935 watercolor that had the quick brush-strokes and vigorous, semi-abstract quality of the watercolors he had done on his Grand Tour. And then there were the composite drawings and paintings he called *Esther/Olivia*, one of which—*Esther/Olivia, No. 3*, from 1932—hung prominently in the living room at 5243 Chester.

For the sisters, too, had been drafted to pose for the artist. Olivia's reddish hair and clear, intelligent gaze, both of which inform the 1932 *Esther/Olivia*, come through on their own in the pastel-and-charcoal *Olivia*, a relatively realistic sketch made sometime in the 1930s. The same model appears in a slightly more abstract oil painting, done in 1939, called *Olivia with a Grape*. In the latter (which Lou gave to Olivia), the partially shadowed planes of the woman's face echo the joint at which the walls meet behind her, while the white hand delicately holding up a greenish grape against a red dress comes across as strangely detached and therefore pointedly symbolic. A different mood entirely characterizes the portraits of Regina, who in her late teens appears to have posed for Lou at least twice in the nude. Of these two charcoal-on-paper sketches (both of which ended up in Regina's possession), one is darker, more sultry, yet somehow more childish; the other, in a lighter style, emphasizes the curl of her hair, the arch of her eye and lip, and the soft swell of her breasts. Both resemble, to no small degree, certain of Picasso's female busts from his pre- and post-Cubist periods.

No one in the family seemed surprised or unnerved that in the course of his inveterate sketching the young artist should require the modeling services of his two young sisters-in-law as well as those of his wife. That Lou had captured something in these two women which they felt to be true to themselves was clear from the fact that they kept these portraits for the rest of their lives. They seemed willing and even pleased to be used repeatedly as his models—a kind of affirmation, they may have felt, of their relative importance in the household. Being Esther's younger sister had not, for either of them, been an easy role. Olivia, the tomboy and later the public-spirited intellectual, was convinced that her mother had always loved the other two more, while the pretty, fun-loving Regina, the baby of the family, felt that Esther was clearly their mother's favorite. So the alliance with their talented brother-in-law must have been balm to their injured feelings. Even as they grew older and graduated from college—Olivia from Temple, Regina from Penn—Lou continued to get along splendidly with both girls. He was especially close to Regina, who shared his love of music, and for whom he designed a pair of beautiful copper candlesticks on the occasion of her wedding.

By the end of the 1930s both sisters were married—Olivia to an economist named Milton Abelson, Regina to a dentist named Harold Fine (though she would later divorce him and marry a second husband, Morris Soopper, who ran a hardware store in Philadelphia). When they moved out, Olivia's third-floor bedroom was given over to the Catholic lady lodger, but Regina's second-floor room, which was always called "the baby's room," was left empty. Lou and Esther's own baby, it was decided, would occupy a new bedroom on the third floor of the house. This would place the infant on the same floor as the potentially anxious parents as well as only one flight up from the competent, knowledgeable grandmother.

The parents, as parents will, took pleasure in furnishing and decorating the room for the unknown visitor they were expecting. As the March 1940 due date approached, Lou hung his *Esther in Pink*—the last portrait, incidentally, that he was ever to paint of his wife—on the wall of the baby's bedroom. The painting, at once warm and cool, emotional and calm, was both an artistic expression and an amulet of sorts. Pregnant but not visibly so, her arms crossed on the table in front of her, her strong eyebrows, firm mouth, and prominent widow's peak softened by the expression in her liquid dark eyes, the mother-to-be stood out palely against the dark-blue geometries of the room-space surrounding her in the picture. This benign, watchful presence was presumably meant to offer round-the-clock reassurance to the child who was shortly to arrive.

IN SITU:
KIMBELL ART MUSEUM

Interior of Kimbell Art Museum
(Photograph by Robert LaPrelle, courtesy of the Kimbell Art Museum)

Like all art museums, the Kimbell is a place for looking and seeing. The relationship between the architecture and the art is intense and mutually reinforcing, and both are a delight to the eye. Great paintings look especially good on these walls—in part due to the light that is cast upon them, a perfect mixture of natural and artificial illumination, and in part because of the congenial textures and spaces that surround the works of art. Kahn's building never seems to overpower the paintings: it sees itself as their setting, their background, while nonetheless taking an active role in their display.

"The building does dictate the kind of art you can show," says Eric Lee, the Kimbell's current director. "You can't exhibit terribly large paintings, so we haven't acquired them. Also, strong paintings look better in this building, weaker paintings fall apart. So the building has helped dictate the quality of the collection." The spell the Kimbell casts apparently works on visiting paintings, too. Gesturing toward a large Matisse on loan from the Chicago Art Institute—the beautiful *Bathers by a River*, which here hangs alone on the central vault's travertine end wall—Lee repeats a comment made by his deputy director, George Shackelford, at the time this loan exhibition was installed: "He said this wall has waited its whole life for that painting, and that painting has waited its whole life to hang on that wall."

All this is true. The museum highlights and glorifies one sense above all, the sense of sight. And yet it also, curiously, emphasizes the limits of what can be seen. The building suggests that what your eyes tell you is truth of a kind, but not necessarily the whole truth, not an absolute and permanent truth. There are stories behind the stories, and scenes behind the scenes. The unseen, the unperceived, has its importance in this museum, as you only come to realize over time. Appearances can be deceptive—in a pleasurable way, granted, rather than a cruel one, but still in a way that misleads. And yet such deceptions are part of·the building's pursuit of truth, just as a novelist's inventions serve the truths that can only be told in fiction. The Kimbell Art Museum is Kahn's version of a Tolstoy novel: grand but contained, artful yet persuasively real, a blending of the physical world as we know it and something only the imagination can grasp.

Take, for instance, the most distinctive feature of the interior, the arched ceilings that curve over the individual galleries, each shedding its measure of natural light from above. Being inside these long, high rooms makes you feel utterly at peace: a bit like the sensation you get in England's Dulwich Picture Gallery, perhaps, except that here Sir John Soane's elegant nineteenth-century materials and structures have been replaced by something distinctly modern. The concrete vault over your head is high enough to give you a sense of grandeur, not so high as to intimidate, with a gentle, unspectacular curve that holds the facing walls and all the paintings on them in its tender embrace. Each gallery's ceiling seems composed of a single continuous piece of concrete, smooth and yet also faintly textured. The pearly gray surface appears to glow from within, especially as it reaches its peak, where the arch disappears under the winglike aluminum brackets—both spotlight holders and sunlight disseminators—that hang just beneath the ceiling. Somehow the harsh Texas sunlight which prevails outdoors has been converted into a cool, silver-tinted beam that bathes the concrete and the paintings and the people who stand in front of them, making everything seem as if it exactly belongs there.

"It has that feeling I have with really special buildings, like the· Pantheon," observes Nancy Edwards, a curator of European art who has been at the Kimbell for over twenty years. "The perfectness of the space, forever here. The perfect proportion, how it fits your body. And the light, different at every time of day. It has this durability and ephemerality at the same time." Elaborating on how this feeling is created by the particular curve and size of the arch, she points to "the ceiling height, but also the magic of the cycloid vault, because it's such a pleasing shape. The way it floats on top, and the clerestory gives you the idea of something above you. Part of it is the trick of the way the light bounces on that silvery surface. It acts as a sort of sky. That whole idea of a vault and a heaven: I'm sure Kahn thought about those things, because it's such an antique analogy."

Then Edwards pauses, as if thinking of some of the implications behind her words, especially terms like *magic* and *trick*. "Everything seems so simple, but when you look it's a little bit more complex," she goes on. "I was thinking: yes, but there's the slit down the middle."

She is referring to the fact that the vault's arch is not really a single continuous arch at all, but rather, two identically curved concrete shells that swoop upward toward each other and then fail to meet. That failure, that gap, is covered over by the aluminum reflector that diffuses the sunlight coming through the central slit and turns it into a silvery glow on the uppermost reaches of the finely textured concrete. The effect is glorious, but it is definitely an effect, a calculated invention to make you feel that light is being shed from an unseen source. And yet this is also the truth: the source *is* unseen, unless you manage to get to one of the few places in the building (the off-limits mezzanine library, for example) where you are close enough to the ceiling to spot the gap between the shells.

Nancy Edwards' sense that the concrete ceiling is floating over her head is shared by just about everyone who enters these rooms. But that too is a trick of sorts, an element of the "magic" created by Louis Kahn and his engineer August Komendant. As you look down the length of the vaulted gallery, it will seem as if the entire concrete structure is resting on quarter-inch glass: on the curved strip of clerestory window that surmounts the travertine arch at the end of the hall, and on the long, thin, horizontal window that runs along the top of the outermost gallery walls. But the ceiling only *seems* to rest on these slender bits of glass. In reality, it is supported not only by the metal post-tensioning cables buried invisibly within the four-inch-thick concrete shells, but also by four massive concrete columns standing in the corners of each vault. The seeming miracle is not a miracle, but a cunning feat of engineering.

It was, in fact, a purely technical engineering requirement that gave the building one of its most subtle visual effects, the elegant shape of the end-windows. Because Komendant insisted that the concrete arch sustaining each pair of shells had to thicken as it approached the top, the glass arc beneath it had to be thinned correspondingly, and the result is perhaps the most alluring "light joint" (as he called it) that Kahn ever created. It cannot help but remind you of church architecture, once you notice it; it definitely contributes to your sense that you are standing in a heavenly vault, or at least a cathedral nave. Yet the diminishment in the window's width is so gradual, so natural, that you may well sense the modulation before you see it. It, too, is at once visible and invisible.

■

Even from the outside, the Kimbell's apparent straightforwardness is somewhat deceptive. The building presents itself from the front as a piece of Palladian symmetry, with forward-thrusting outer wings—each containing five full vaults plus one hollow, vault-sized portico—flanking a center section of equal length that contains only four vaults. The extra space in front of the central part leaves room for a grand entrance, or *would* leave room for that, if this structure had actually been designed by Palladio. Instead, Kahn's entrance is obscured by a courtyard full of trees, and when you get close enough to see the doorway, you discover it is a simple glass door camouflaged within the surrounding curtain wall. Nor are the outer clusters of vaults readily visible or countable from the front. You really only get a sense of their shape, number, and connection from a sidelong view (a view that may remind you, if you have seen them, of the sequentially joined arched pavilions of Riga's Central Market).

"I think the Kahn building is most beautiful at these angles, and best approached from these angles," comments Eric Lee as he walks diagonally across the coarse, yellowing St. Augustine grass toward the southwest corner of the museum. When asked why he feels that way, he honestly admits, "I don't know." But he is certainly responding to something that is evident elsewhere in Kahn's practice—the sense that oblique approaches are the truest ones, and that entrances should be a bit hard to find.

Once you are inside the Kimbell, the feeling of symmetry quickly disappears, for the vaults are all divided up in different ways, giving each side of the building, and each story of it, an entirely different feeling. Downstairs lie the practical features of the museum: a loading dock to the north, curatorial offices and a conservation studio to the south, and a second entrance hall at the center. Each of these has its own size and shape, and each possesses its own unexpected facets. For instance, the conservation lab is a double-height room that looks out on its own double-height courtyard—a secret court extending up through the gallery level, where it is enclosed on all four sides and therefore invisible. A separate light-well, the size and length of the space between vaults, backs onto the curatorial offices and is disguised at the upper level by the portico wall. In both cases, an abundance of natural light is one of the special benefits Kahn conferred on the Kimbell's backstage workers. "It's just a concrete wall, but I always say it's the best view in North Texas: it's amazing watching the light changing, it's like a painting out there," Eric Lee remarks about the view out his back window. Claire Barry, the head of conservation, considers her double-height courtyard just one aspect of the building's brilliant design. "One thing I always notice: there's the same attention to detail in the behind-the-scenes places as there is in the public space," observes Barry. "It's not like that in other museums."

Up in the public galleries, too, there are a series of small eccentricities that break up the overall pattern. Each wing of the museum has an accessible interior courtyard, but they are not mirror images of each other. The grandest courtyard, centered in the North Wing, showcases one of the eight bronze and lead casts of Maillol's voluptuous figure *L'Air*, a sculpture Kahn had treasured ever since encountering the Yale Art Gallery's version. (He was apparently so fixated on its presence in Fort Worth that he even included the floating womanly shape in some of his earliest sketches for the Kimbell.) In the South Wing, the small "Penelope Courtyard," nicknamed after a sculpture in its midst, lurks between two galleries, accessible from either but gauzily curtained off from both. And to the east of this smallest courtyard, on the other side of the museum's central corridor, lies the walled-off middle-sized interior square leading down to the conservation studio. It is a feature that takes up space but is not, as a courtyard, present or even visible from the galleries. One doesn't miss it; one doesn't even know it is there.

Deceptions like this are possible not only because the galleries all have different shapes (most of the walls, with the exception of the travertine end walls, are movable), but also because most visitors will be focused on something other than the building. After all, if you have come to the Kimbell Art Museum, it is probably to see the art.

The paintings come alive in this place. According to the experts, the color temperature created by the Kimbell's precise combination of artificial and natural light is in the 3500K to 3800K range, the "sweet spot" for viewing color. But you don't need to have any scientific tools at your disposal to perceive that something special is going on in this museum.

Here, landscapes have the feel of being actually outdoors. Interiors and portraits glow. Pastel colors gain an added strength, and white highlights leap forward. Even a monochrome sketch like Degas's *After the Bath*, done in charcoal on yellow tracing paper, has a depth and intensity one wouldn't see elsewhere. And when paint comes into play, the specificity of color is remarkable. In Caillebotte's *On the Pont de l'Europe*, for instance, the gray-blue of the metal bridge is pocked by round metal studs in a slightly darker gray, while the men passing along the bridge wear coats and hats in other shades ranging from blue-gray through black-gray—all these different grays distinctly visible, as if for the first time, in the Kimbell's splendid illumination.

Because the paintings are for the most part small, or at any rate human-sized, they are fully graspable when viewed straight on from a couple of feet away. They allow you to form an intimate, one-on-one connection with them. The portraits, too, are hung so that the faces are just about at face height (if you are roughly five foot six, which was Kahn's height), and this increases the intimacy of the encounter. You may even get the feeling that some of these faces are leaning toward you, and that is not an optical illusion, for the paintings hanging on the travertine walls are actually suspended by nearly invisible threads that descend from above, causing the upper edge of each frame to jut out slightly while the bottom edge rests against the wall. This not only has the effect of making the image loom gently forward; it also makes the whole painting seem as if it were floating in air. And the travertine wall itself—which is set forward from the concrete ceiling above it, so that it again seems to bring the painting *toward* you—noticeably enriches the images placed against it. The warm, textured stone never competes with or distracts you from the pictures; on the contrary, it lends them added life.

◼

That is the Kimbell on a normal, sunny day. On a few evenings a month, though, visitors are allowed to remain in the galleries at night, and if you happen to be there then, you will witness a startling transformation. As the sun sinks below the horizon, the galleries darken unevenly, so that one side of the long vault briefly seems to be a slightly different color from the other. That last light coming through the reflectors onto the concrete ceiling appears almost blue in tone, compared to the silvery gray it was at midday, and the metal reflectors themselves—which are such a noticeable, winglike presence in the day—dull out and become much less visible against the ceiling. The concrete retains its texture, but more vaguely, more recessively. And the strong arcs of the clerestory windows, those subtly curved shapes which lent the vaults their churchlike appearance, are now muted to near-invisibility.

As evening approaches, the spotlights on the paintings and the shadows behind the frames become stronger and more noticeable. In place of the even, overall light of daytime, you now have a lot of smaller, more focused lights. The walls, fading into darkened areas around the paintings, have less of a forward presence. All the color and texture distinctions in the structure itself, so visible in the day—the transition from wood to travertine on the floor, say, or from concrete to metal on the ceiling—become much more blurred at sunset. The building seems more uniform in color, a mere background container for the spotlit art. And the paintings themselves are more like what you are used to in ordinary museums—less alive, more pointedly on display, not actively coming toward you. Color suffers, naturally, but monochrome suffers even more: the Degas nude has gone dead, so that it now looks more like a clinical analysis, a mere prep for a painting rather than an artwork in itself.

The twilight period at the Kimbell is all about loss—the disappearance of the natural light, the effacing of once-clear distinctions, the magical turning ordinary. But then, once darkness has fallen, the museum's other qualities take over. You become more aware of the intimacy of the small, linked galleries, the warm, inviting coziness of rooms glimpsed through other rooms. At the same time, you have a sense of something grand and monumental hanging overhead, a feeling of quiet awe that finds reinforcement in the shadows cast by the sculptures and the spot-lit beauty of individual paintings. The courtyards, too, acquire a new kind of allure, with the Penelope Courtyard darkened and only the Maillol lit up in the larger North Court; the museum's interior is now brighter than the enclosed exterior, and that produces its own kind of spell.

It is a different and a lesser place, the Kimbell viewed at night, but it is still a beautiful one, and if you had never seen the museum by daylight, you would take deep pleasure from your evening encounter with it. One imagines that to see it first by night, with its mysterious vaults above, and then to come back in the day, with sunlight diffusing through those vaults, would affect one as powerfully as the grandest of musical revelations. It would be like hearing the all-male King's College Choir first with its adult voices only, and only later with the unearthly sopranos of its boy choristers added in. Light, in Kahn's hands, becomes something almost audible—something that touches one through senses other than sight.

In the end, what is most special about the Kimbell is not only the light itself, but the way light enters and defines the room in which you are standing. That is not just an architectural experience. It also gets at the essence of art, where the visual becomes something tangible—where light itself becomes tangible. As the art critic T. J. Clark put it, alluding to the paintings of Vermeer and Pieter de Hooch: "It is no mean feat for painting to put objects in a room, and *describe* the room, and have light enter it . . . And it is even rarer to have light in the picture enter a room not as a mysterious effulgence but as an object among objects, attaching itself to things, vying with them for priority." In the same book, *Picasso and Truth*, he goes on to point out that

> there is one thing painting finds indispensable: namely, space—
> the making of an imaginatively habitable three dimensions, one
> having a specific character, offering itself as a surrounding
> whose shape and extent we can enter into . . . Being, for human
> beings—and how deep is the pathos of that recursive noun—

seems to have as its very precondition being "in": reaching out, really or imaginatively, and feeling the limits of a place.

Clark is talking specifically about Picasso here, that great modernist who was so much admired by his near-contemporary, Louis Kahn. But he could just as easily be speaking about the Kimbell Art Museum, where the experiences of "being" and "being in" are brought so forcibly together, and where the light cast *within* the paintings joins with the light cast upon them to give rise to a new kind of contemplation.

New, and yet always there; created, but also retrieved. When he finished the Kimbell Art Museum in 1972, Kahn said at the dedication ceremony, "This building feels—and it's a good feeling—as though I had nothing to do with it, that some other hand did it. Because it is a premise constructed." And what he meant by that curious remark is connected to another of his comments about the architectural process. "There's something that pulls on you," he said, "as though you were reaching out to something primordial, something that existed much before yourself. You realize when you are in the realm of architecture that you are touching the basic feelings of man and that architecture would never have been part of humanity if it weren't the truth to begin with."

BECOMING

At home, he was surrounded by females. Esther's mother, Annie, did all the cooking and cleaning and sewing and laundry, including ironing Lou's shirts, about which he was very particular. Shortly after the baby's birth, Esther had returned to her job with Dr. Alpers (who had become her sole employer after Dr. Frazier died in 1936), and she remained the steady breadwinner in the family, the only source of a regular paycheck. Another bit of household income came from their lodger, the widowed Catherine McMichael, whose honorary family title of "Aunt Katie" now gained additional meaning with her occasional babysitting responsibilities. And even the baby herself was a girl. Sue Ann, born on March 30, 1940, had become the main focus of attention for all the adults in the house; she too was part of the all-female atmosphere in which he comfortably dwelt.

But despite its comforts, it was not a complete life. Painting the door panels of the house with fanciful designs was hardly an occupation for a grown man. Neither was working on his landscapes and portraits, which he did upstairs in the bedroom he and Esther shared, the only room that got good enough light. Being a part-time painter, though he took it seriously enough, was a hobby, not a job. He was meant to be an architect, of that he was certain, and he just needed a chance to prove it to others. The occasional commissions he had received throughout the 1930s, his time-consuming entries into various competitions, all the consulting and volunteer organizing he had done in the field of architecture and urban planning—these were important, but they did not add up to real employment. He needed to get out of the house, to an office where other men worked too.

His wish was granted mainly because of changing conditions in the wider world. The Depression that had blighted most of his adult life was now nearing its close; the war in Europe, into which America would soon be drawn, had started to stimulate the economy, offering vastly expanded opportunities for new building. Responding to this, his friend George Howe, who had excellent connections in Washington, asked Lou to help him start an architecture practice specializing in government-sponsored housing construction. And so it was that in April of 1941, with two major commissions from the Federal Works Agency already in hand, the partnership of Howe & Kahn opened its offices on the ninth floor of the old *Evening Bulletin* building, just across the street from Philadelphia's City Hall. By the fall of 1941, when it became clear that Howe's increasing government consulting would prevent him from doing much work on the firm's projects, Oscar Stonorov was brought into the practice, and the name of the firm changed to Howe, Stonorov & Kahn.

Kahn's two partners could not have been more different. Howe was a Philadelphia aristocrat, born into the kind of wealthy Main Line family that prided itself on its connection to European culture. Like a figure out of Henry James, George had first been taken to the Paris Opera by his grandmother and his aunt when he was just six years old—a story that particularly appealed to Lou, and that seemed to him to define the kind of man Howe was. Tall and handsome, George Howe exuded a calm, easygoing self-assurance. He was also a thoughtful and intelligent man, and though he had access to old-money clients who could have supplied him with a lifetime of big, expensive housing commissions, he believed in architecture as a force for social change. As Esther Kahn observed, "Lou felt that Howe was one of the most civilized men he knew because he had an intellect as well as brilliancy and knowledge . . . He really adored him."

Oscar Stonorov also had European connections, but of a rather different sort. Born in 1905 in Frankfurt, Germany, Stonorov studied architecture in Florence and Zurich, then moved to Paris, where he helped edit the first volume of Le Corbusier's *Oeuvre complète* and briefly apprenticed himself to the sculptor Aristide Maillol. He came to

America in 1929 and met Kahn sometime in the 1930s, when they worked together on a few competition designs, all of which ultimately went unbuilt. In contrast to the elegant, good-looking Howe and the slender, shy Kahn, Stonorov was bald, a bit pudgy, and extremely out-going. Certain of his colleagues referred to him as "The Prince," in large part because of his pronounced Mitteleuropean accent but also, perhaps, because he had married an American heiress. Some people found him charming; others thought it a hollow charm. Peter Arfaa, a prominent Philadelphia architect who was himself an immigrant, and who briefly worked for Stonorov on his way up, confided, "Oscar was the rudest man I've ever met. He was a licker—what do you call it?—a kisser, a kiss-up. Lou," he added, "was not a kisser."

All three partners were interested in designing low-income hous-ing, and each had been involved in such work already: Howe and Kahn through a redevelopment plan they submitted to the Philadelphia Housing Authority in 1938 (though that project came to nothing in the end); Stonorov through the Carl Mackley Houses, a Philadelphia-area housing complex for hosiery workers which he and Alfred Kastner designed in the early 1930s; and Kahn through his Jersey Homesteads. Among the earliest commissions secured by their firm was the design of Carver Court, a hundred-unit cluster of steelworker dwellings, spe-cifically earmarked for black workers, that was located just outside Coatesville, Pennsylvania. This project was to receive a great deal of attention from other architects, especially after its inclusion in a 1944 show at the Museum of Modern Art called *Built in the USA*. The struc-ture was noteworthy mainly for the way the housing units were lifted up to the second story, leaving the ground-floor spaces free for parking, storage, and other functions—perhaps Kahn's earliest version of the "interstitial floors" or "servant spaces" that were later to become so use-ful to him.

When Howe left for Washington in 1942 to become the supervising architect at the Public Buildings Administration, the partnership was renamed Stonorov & Kahn, but its focus remained worker housing. Over the course of their six years in business together, Louis Kahn and Oscar Stonorov designed seven worker communities, of which five were ultimately built, yielding more than two thousand units of new housing. They also did an innovative if unbuilt hotel design for a project called

"194X," a series sponsored by *Architectural Forum* that put them in excellent company and brought them substantial attention. By all accounts, Oscar did the bulk of the promotion and client-getting while Lou concentrated on the actual designs. Despite their personality differences and the fact that, as Esther put it, "they were both too much of a primadonna," this arrangement worked for a time, because each was clearly better than the other at his assigned task. It was only when Kahn began to chafe under Stonorov's dubious approach to shared credit that the partnership finally broke up.

In design terms, the period with Stonorov did not lead to any spectacular work on Kahn's part. Though some of the projects received significant attention from within the architecture profession, none of the completed structures were more appealing or interesting than the wood-and-stone house Kahn had designed for his friends Jesse and Ruth Oser or the Jersey Homesteads housing he had done under Alfred Kastner. But the founding of the new partnership did allow him to bring in a real income for the first time since his Resettlement Administration job had ended. In 1941, the gross receipts of Howe, Stonorov & Kahn were $33,449.99, of which Kahn's equal partnership share (after $26,206.23 in expenses had been deducted) was $2,281.58. When added to the additional $2,020.84 he had made through Howe & Kahn, that year's income from his architecture practice was $4,302.42—a substantial addition to the annual $1,650 to $1,800 that Esther was regularly pulling in from Jefferson Medical College. Lou and Esther filed separate tax returns that year, as they generally did throughout the early 1940s, and he took Sue Ann as his dependent because he could better use the deduction. (In 1944, by contrast, they filed jointly, with Esther I. Kahn named as the primary taxpayer on the basis of her $1,800 salary, and with *both* Sue Ann *and* Lou listed as her dependents, since he had no partnership income at all that year. Apparently even the war-fueled construction of worker housing could be an up-and-down affair, with no guarantee of regular payment.)

But there were other benefits besides financial ones to working in a real office, and one of them was camaraderie. Peter Blake, one of the early employees of Stonorov & Kahn, recalled a particular Sunday in the summer of 1941 when he, Lou, and two of the other men from the firm drove out to New Jersey in an open convertible to inspect a construction site. Returning to the overly warm streets of Philadelphia at about six p.m., they decided they needed a few cold beers. "Well, in those days Philadelphia was closed down tight on Sundays," Blake reported, "and so, as we pulled up to a stop at a traffic light, I asked a guy in a car next to ours where you could get a drink in Philadelphia on a Sunday. 'No problem,' he said. 'Go to the 6th Ward Republican Club and tell them I sent you.'"

The address the man directed them to turned out to be a one-story house on Locust near Broad. "Who are you?" asked the manager of the club, and Lou loftily assured him, "We're all Harvard men." Temporarily abandoning their staunch Democratic principles, the four colleagues paid a dollar each to join the Republican Party. They then made their way into a long, dingy room and ordered a round of beers. An old upright piano was standing on a platform at one end, and according to Blake, "Lou went over to the piano, sat down on the stool, and started playing Gershwin's 'Rhapsody in Blue,' with enormous energy, enthusiasm and passion. The whole place began to shake—Lou had very large, very strong hands. He could crush your fingers in a handshake, and he could turn a piano into sawdust if he really tried. That night he was in great form." A few minutes later, though, the hotel across the street called to say they had a guest who was dying and could the pianist please tone it down. Lou complied instantly, but he continued to play the same tune softly and gently, as if to himself. When an ambulance eventually arrived, Lou called the hotel to see how the patient was. Receiving his answer, he returned to the piano and, to the delight of the other guys, played one last round of "Rhapsody in Blue" at full, rafter-shaking blast.

For Kahn, such moments of conviviality were an extension of the feeling he got from architecture work in general—the sense that it was a group effort, a pleasurable back-and-forth, with everyone putting in his two cents' worth. But there was another side to the work that was more solitary, more self-contained, and this too developed during his years with Stonorov & Kahn. For it was in this period, the early 1940s, that Lou established himself as a published writer, an architect who thought in terms of words on the page as well as buildings in space.

Kahn's first two publications, issued jointly with Oscar Stonorov, were pamphlets that the two men produced under the sponsorship of the

Revere Copper and Brass company. The earlier one, *Why City Planning Is Your Responsibility*, was a slim fourteen-page booklet that came out in 1943. Prefaced by a forward-looking wartime note from the president of Revere ("All of us are now working for Uncle Sam. No copper is available except for war. But in Revere's laboratories, research is hard at work in a dozen different directions so that we can bring better living to millions more after the war is won"), the pamphlet had a friendly yet insistent tone. "If city planning, of which everyone speaks, is ever going to become a reality and bring results, it must become the thing in which YOU—reader of this pamphlet—are vitally interested," it began. "Because city planning concerns *YOU* and *YOUR* neighborhood—and also the fellow that lives a little bit further away from your immediate vicinity . . . YOU, Mr. John Q. Public, should make yourself heard."

The booklet contained a number of anodyne if true generalizations (stressing, for instance, "the human values that are the most important of all in any city planning project"), but it also took issue with certain pieties of the time. It did not advocate annihilating all slums; on the contrary, it suggested that certain "not-quite blighted neighborhoods," though visibly in decline, should be protected and strengthened as "conservation areas" rather than destroyed wholesale. The authors had specific ideas for the ways in which life could be improved for city dwellers, which included converting unnecessary streets to playgrounds for children and adding real shopping areas in place of "inferior corner stores." They urged their imagined readers to "Take Action!" by forming their own neighborhood planning groups, and promised that if these methods succeeded, "You won't have to pull up stakes and seek for so-called better pastures in the suburbs."

At the end of the pamphlet, under the joint signatures of Oscar Stonorov and Louis Kahn, there was a photo of the two authors, identically dressed in white shirtsleeves and dark ties. Standing next to each other, they both looked out a nearby window, the bald one taller by at least a head, his hand on the shoulder of the smaller man, who was smiling gently and smoking thoughtfully on a pipe. Like figures in a Social Realist painting—though dressed in modern capitalist garb—Kahn and Stonorov appeared to be looking toward an enlightened future.

You and Your Neighborhood, which came out a year later, was a more sophisticated effort, though still worded "in terms that we hope make sense to average people," as Stonorov and Kahn put it in their brief introduction. Subtitled "A Primer for neighborhood planning," this larger pamphlet contained over eighty unnumbered pages, filled with various kinds of illustrations—from photos and cartoons to street diagrams and architectural plans—as well as punchy lists of common problems and their likely solutions. Under bold-faced headings like "Your house and your block," "Organize a neighborhood planning council," and "Alone you are powerless," the authors offered a series of very specific recommendations for how to organize a neighborhood, set up headquarters, and contact those with the power to do something. Their list of "neighborhood needs" included safe streets, playgrounds, a modern school, a place for teenagers to gather, and a shopping center. The underlying impulse was still an exhortation to communal action, but unlike the previous Revere booklet, this one rarely descended to abstract platitudes. Instead, it relied on a sequentially executable outline of plans and activities. It continued, though, to emphasize the core connection between the individual and the larger urban unit, between the family and the neighborhood. "The plan of a city should be as orderly as the plan of a house," the booklet concluded, noting in an almost poetic *envoi*:

> Cities have too few corridors
>> Cities have beds in their kitchens
>> Cities have their kitchens in all parts of the house
>> Cities have crammed living rooms or none at all
>> These are conditions you can help to change in your own
> city. From neighborhood, to community, to city—it's a big job,
> a long job, but by no means impossible if you will *help* to start
> it, and *stay* to finish it.

This was recognizably the same "you" that Stonorov and Kahn had been addressing all along, but the shrill enthusiasms of their first pamphlet had by now been toned down into somewhat more measured phrases.

More measured still, while also much more idiosyncratic and in many ways more impenetrable, was the sole piece of individual writing that Kahn produced during this time. Titled "Monumentality," this essay originally appeared in a 1944 collection called *New Architecture and City Planning: A Symposium*, edited by Paul Zucker. What was striking about it, in retrospect, was how many of Lou's mature architectural ideas appeared in embryonic form in this, his first major piece of writing.

"Monumentality in architecture may be defined as a quality, a spiritual quality inherent in a structure which conveys the feeling of its eternity, that it cannot be added to or changed," the essay began. While Kahn was explicitly referring to the Parthenon and other monumental works of the past, such notions also seem evocative of the monuments he himself would eventually produce, from the Salk Institute to the Kimbell Art Museum to the Bangladesh National Assembly. Even his specific comments about structure and materials at times appear to refer to these as-yet-unimagined buildings, as when he said, "Structural problems center about the roof. The permanence and beauty of its surfaces is a major problem confronting science," or observed, "The giant major skeleton of a structure can assert its rights to be seen. It need no longer be clothed for eye appeal," or singled out reinforced concrete as a material that was "emerging from infancy" and moving toward "its ultimate refinement." Yet even as he championed modern construction materials like concrete, steel, glass, and plastic along with the new engineering techniques available for shaping them, he insisted that ancient monuments still had value for twentieth-century architects. While arguing that old forms such as Gothic cathedrals and Greek temples should not merely be duplicated—that the past, in that sense, could not be appropriated or made to live again—Kahn still felt that "we dare not discard the lessons these buildings teach for they have the common characteristic of greatness upon which the buildings of our future must, in one sense or another, rely."

But the way to arrive at that greatness would by no means be obvious. Unlike the exhorting pamphlets he wrote with Oscar Stonorov, this essay of Kahn's had few if any specific recommendations, in part because the thing he was advocating in the Revere booklets—overt and conscious action—would not necessarily succeed in this other arena. "Monumentality is enigmatic," Kahn observed. "It cannot be intentionally created." What he seemed to be suggesting, even at this early stage, was that the architect could not simply impose his own egotistically ambitious, monument-seeking will on the material and the design. Instead, the modern designer or engineer needed to remain receptive to the kind of power that could only emerge organically from his chosen materials as he shaped them toward their specific functions. Such passive receptivity was the very opposite of the virile assertiveness that characterized contemporary architects in the popular imagination—in Ayn Rand's *The Fountainhead*, for instance, which had just come out the previous year. What Lou seemed to be advocating in his obscure little essay seemed, by contrast, positively feminine.

■

Busy as he was in these partnership years, Lou still had time for his daughter. Family photos from the 1940s show him standing on the porch or the sidewalk with the baby in his arms; sitting on the stoop in a casual T-shirt as he explained something to the attentive, pigtailed toddler; squatting down in swim trunks at the beach, a wide, closed-mouth grin on his face, as the dark-haired, serious-eyed little girl stood behind him and twined her arms around his neck. Though he was forty or more at the time, he still looked young and, despite the visible scars on his face, almost raffishly handsome, with a full head of tousled hair and a constant twinkle in his eyes.

"Whenever he came home, I was happy," said Sue Ann. "He was a lot of fun. He would draw me things. We played 'Chopsticks' on the piano together: I would play the simple left hand while he improvised. We used to read the funnies on Sunday morning, and then I would sit and watch him paint."

They shared a life in the neighborhood, too, beyond the confines of the old gabled house, which was filled with all the dark, heavy furniture purchased long ago by Esther's parents. "We would go on walks up 53rd Street to see if we could see the Northern Lights from the top of the slope. Then we'd get an ice cream," she recalled. "He took me to see my first movie, which was Mickey Mouse or something." And in the winter he took her sledding in Clark's Park, at the corner of 43rd and Chester. Lou would pull her in the sled all the way to the park and all the way up its hill, and then together they would swoop down the hill—"which petrified me," added Sue Ann.

Everyone in her family sometimes shortened her name to Sue or Susie, but her father had a lot of other nicknames for her: "Suessel, Picklepuss, whatever came to mind." And he had a wonderful way of holding her in his arms. He cared a lot about physical fitness, physical activity of any kind, and he was very strong and comfortable in his own body. "He would hold you and you knew you were completely safe," Sue remembered. This differentiated him not only from her stern-faced, gray-haired grandmother—who seemed to the little girl to be neither warm nor cold, just "solid" and reliable—but also from her mother, who was "more awkward as a hugger."

It was Esther, though, who maintained the family ties, not only with her own family but also with Lou's. She was the one who sent the Christmas presents out to California and then thanked Lou's parents for the Chanukah presents sent in return; it was she who wrote regularly with all the family news, despite the elder Kahns' repeated pleas to hear from Lou personally. In a letter addressed to Lou, Esther, and Sue Ann in early January of 1942, Leopold actually interjected a few lines aimed specifically at getting Lou to write. Having detailed Bertha's recent ill health and her "longingness for you children," he pleaded, "Dear Son, you can fix it up a lot by writing more often, we are very much satisfied with Esther's attention in writing to us in which we are very thankful, but *you* dear Son, leave it be a few lines, but for Mothers sake please do it." Leopold also wanted Lou to promise that he would "try to come out with your little family for a visit, I'm telling you she is worried sick and she worries me too, like last night she said to me. 'You know, Leopold: I'm going on my seventyeth year and I don't know if I'll live very much longer. I was never longing for my children back east so much as I'm longing for them now . . .'" And then, after signing off on behalf of the entire West Coast branch ("The best regards from Sara Joe & Geraldine, from Oscar, Rosella, Alan, and Rhoda") and concluding with the usual "Lots of love and best wishes, Mother & Dad," Leopold couldn't help adding: "P.S. Please write soon."

Two weeks later, he—or Bertha, or both of them speaking in chorus—sent another letter in a less beseeching mode. "Your letter was so sweet and amusing," this one began, "we enjoyed every word of it.

Especially the part telling us all about little darling Sue Ann. She must be adorable, we can just see Sue Ann at Christmas, with all her pretty toys and gifts. We would give anything to have been there—and believe us, we were there in spirit. You write that she sings so beautifully and want to know if Alan sang at her age." (Alan, the most obviously musical of the grandchildren, was already a skilled pianist.) "Well dear Esther, you dont have to go so far. Her Daddy was the one that sang. At her age he sang complete German songs and soldier marches. He could carry a tune and remember every note. So your dearest Sue Ann takes after her Daddy."

Like the previous letter, this one referred to wartime anxieties and expressed the hope that the war would end soon. Unlike the other, it also alluded to the financial relations between the elder and younger Kahns: it brought up the fact that Leopold and Bertha's regular government check was being reduced as of February, and warmly thanked Lou and Esther for pledging to send them an additional $15 a month to help make up the difference. The tone, on the whole, was cheerier than in the earlier letter—the Los Angeles weather was gorgeous, they were both feeling reasonably well—and though both missives were composed in Leopold's elegant script, it is tempting to imagine Bertha's calmer voice dominating the later one. In any event, the letter is signed as usual by both parents, and contains the usual fruitless request: "Tell Lou to drop us a few lines when he can. It seems ages since we heard from him."

Part of this was standard adult-son behavior—or at any rate standard doted-upon-Jewish-adult-son behavior, the result of an understandable desire to cut the notoriously binding maternal apron strings—but part of it was just Lou. He had always been and would always be a terrible correspondent. Years later, when one of his lovers complained about how infrequently he wrote to her, he was to answer, "I have never written as much to anyone as to you. I haven't written to my parents for over a year now but there is no excuse for that nor is there an excuse for not trying to write more often to you." He knew it was one of his shortcomings, and yet he couldn't do anything about it, or at least he felt he couldn't. Other things were more important to him. Other things took up his attention, and his time. Loving and intimate as he could be with those close by, he was not good at maintaining ties over a distance, especially if any substantial effort was involved. And perhaps he was particularly remiss in keeping up with the family into which he had been born—precisely those people whose unconditional love he took for granted, without feeling a need to earn it or respond to it.

Certainly his brother thought this was the case, and told him so in a remarkable letter Lou received in April of 1945. Written on Oscar's business stationery (headed "Advertising Ideas by Oscar Kahn," with a return address at the Bank of America Building in Stockton, California), the handwritten letter sprawled across four full pages, each sentence filled with the dashes and dots that characterized Oscar's flowing, expressive, if not always grammatical style. As a keen psychological view into Lou's character and his relation to his family, it is unmatched. Here it is in full:

> Dear Lou,
>
> I know that even though I haven't had word from you in many years that sometime or other you must think of me—and wonder how I am—what I'm doing and so many, many more other "question thoughts" that might associate our natural relationship with the past and present. Certainly I do—and when I hear indirectly a smattering of your activities I listen with keen interest. It just occurred to me—how distant (the fact that you are a brother of mine) is imbedded in the memory cells of my brain. I can only remember vaguely what you look like—and your swagger-walk—and although the smaller details that I associate with you and our youth are more vivid, still—it seems to flash by too rapidly for me to hold onto it. However they are identifications—beyond doubt. If you were to ask—what brought me to writing to you now—I couldn't answer it with a feeling of certainty—chalk it up to the likelyhood of the animal deserting to it's natural instincts after a strange environment— whatever it is—it is an inner unexplainable urge to rub closer to you—even in this short span—The period in which I know—I write this—+ travel time—+ your receiving this—reading it and I am sure feeling just as I do at this moment, precisely back about 20 years. Twenty years is a heck of a long time.

During your quest for Idealism's realization you too placed in the background the very things I talk about—you too have put aside—shall I say—the cloak of relationship or kinship to gain the greener pastures of other's favor. It's likely that you have been so enthused with your steady rise that the change wasn't hard to take—and in time you could almost throw off the yoke of it at will. It's very funny—now that I mention it—doesn't it strike as strange? If you were to try and put that inner reaction into words you would find—an unbearable smallness—one that is so minute that simplifying an explanation to anyone else in words would be folly. Just can't be done—anymore than you can say in words what Love is—or hate or describe pain—it's yours when you feel it—and mine when I do—to have and to hold—

Frankly this wasn't what I intended writing about. All I wanted to express was a wonderment toward your apparent disappearance. I could very easily express in poetic phrases the way I feel—but you might get the impression that this is all forethought, or an intentional plot to yank you back into the past. I don't relive the past with any genuine delight—other than the moments I can remember (or I should say, those that were important enough to warrant remembrance).

Look what years have done. I your younger brother am 40—Rosella 39—Alan 18—Rhoda 12. I charge the fact that the list isn't longer to Lady Luck (and the fact that she was a *lady*). These are my accomplishments. What I do to make my way has always been 2nd in importance—only because I realize that you don't have to divorce yourself from yourself to gain an objective. One must have the extream delight of Love—the immeasurable warmth of parental closeness—the *certain quality* kinship he must possess this in fact, before he can get the full pleasure of success. (*I don't mean measure*) I can't see how *your home* and wonderful family can benefit from your love and devotion to them without the former values.

Watch Sue Ann, Lou, watch how you feel when she grows, grows and grows, ever taller and more beautiful, more girlish, then suddenly you have a young lady. Then you will know what I mean regarding achievement.

Certainly you will build the *first* Breathing wall, you'll watch buildings erected under your supervision, or your plans materialize—but things don't stop long enough for you to fully enjoy them. Even skyscrapers have a height limitation. Just as our careers do—but you'll find that while all this is going on, your family is going on too. You'll find too how much more the achievements reflected in the timely growth of Sue Ann will mean to you—later—when material things show their true value—You'll suddenly reach out for even a splinter of the Family Tree—I hope I make sense.

Much Love,

Oscar

Addressed to Lou, quite unusually, at his work address in the Bulletin Building, the letter was mailed from California on April 9, 1945, and thus would have arrived in Philadelphia soon after the April 12 death of Franklin Delano Roosevelt. Nationally, locally, and within the Kahn household, this presidential death caused an intense degree of mourning: even Sue Ann, who was only five at the time, noticed how upset her parents were. So it's possible that Lou did not give the letter his full attention when it came. It's equally possible that, coming as it did when he was already softened by the national tragedy, it brought him even greater emotional pain than it would have otherwise. He left no record of his response to the document; he never, to anyone's knowledge, answered it. But he clearly felt the letter was important, because he kept it by him for the rest of his life.

One reason he may not have answered it—and one reason, too, for its special importance to him—was that within nine months of writing it, Oscar was dead. Lou's youngest sibling was only forty-one when he died of a heart attack on the last day of 1945. Oscar had been showing some symptoms of angina since the age of thirty-eight, and just the previous day, as he and his family were traveling by train from Stockton to Los Angeles, he had suffered what seemed to be a mild heart attack. Upon arriving in Los Angeles he went to the emergency room, where the doctors gave him a shot; then he went home to his parents' house, convinced the danger was over. No one in the family seemed very worried, because no one imagined that such a young man, on the verge of making a success of his own business, could be so close to death. He was a lively, bright fellow, and family stories suggested that even Lou thought Oscar might have turned out to be the more talented of the two, if only he had been able to focus. "Oscar was interested in many shiny things," said one of his granddaughters, speaking decades later about this man she never met. Like Lou, he had inherited artistic skill from his father and musical ability from his mother. "Oscar was naturally musical," his son, Alan, remarked. "He was a composer, he could play all sorts of instruments—piano, saxophone, xylophone, clarinet. He only played on the black keys on the piano; he liked the sound." Neither Lou nor Oscar had been trained on the piano, as Alan had, but "Dad used his hands differently. He never had that jerky, strong thing Lou did." According to Alan, Lou himself "felt that my dad was more intelligent and more skilled and more creative in every way, but he never reached the pinnacles because he was too anxious to touch all the bases in life."

His death, when it came, caught him unawares. At three in the morning on December 31, Rosella Kahn awoke to the sound of her husband's labored breathing. He had wet the bed, too, she noticed, but in her distress she paid it no mind. Understanding that it was the real thing this time, she put her arms around him and held him until he died.

Lou immediately flew out to Los Angeles for the funeral, which was attended by all the local relatives except Alan, who was in the navy and couldn't, or didn't, get leave. Oscar's daughter, Rhoda, who was thirteen at the time, recalled how important her uncle's presence had been to her. "When my father died—my father and I were very close—it was a tremendous loss for me," she said. "My uncle Lou came to the funeral, and his physical presence was so much like my father's—it was like a physical feeling, that he was transformed into my father." Reflecting on the physical similarity between them, Rhoda added, "It was his stature. The way he walked. His body type was very much like my dad's: broad shoulders tapering into a smaller waist. Short but not too short. And they were very strong."

Rhoda of course noticed her uncle's scars, but "I never recoiled. The minute you start talking to him, it fades out entirely." But she realized that the experience that caused them "must have been profound when it happened, because it completely disfigured his face." Later, she got up the nerve to ask her grandmother about it. She had stayed on with Bertha and Leopold in Los Angeles after the funeral was over, when her uncle had returned to the East Coast and her mother had gone back to Stockton to hold down a full-time job. In fact, Rhoda lived with her grandparents for two full years, from 1946 to about 1948, and this conversation with Bertha about the scars took place roughly in the middle of that time, in late 1946 or early 1947.

"I knew pretty much about it, but I never really had talked to her about it," Rhoda said of Lou's childhood accident. "I was curious about it and I asked her. We often had little talks. It was in her living room. It was just the two of us. Grandpa wasn't there."

Bertha told Rhoda the horrific details of the burning, though she told them calmly, without evident guilt or anxiety, as if it were just a story in which she had no great emotional investment. She did say, though, that she and Leopold had both been devastated by it. "And she told me that Grandpa, in particular, thought it would be better if he died, not only because of the scars but because of the psychological damage of being disfigured like that," said Rhoda. "But my grandmother said, 'No, he's going to be a great man.'"

Late in his life, Lou would recount this same story to an interviewer. By that time, in 1973, it had obviously become an oft-told family tale, gaining added luster from the fact that Kahn had turned out to be a great man, at least in certain circles. But when Bertha first told the story to her granddaughter in the mid-1940s, Lou was still a struggling architect, barely able to make a living from his profession. He had not yet turned into "the Louis Kahn that became famous," as Rhoda put it.

Lou himself, after Oscar's death, rarely if ever mentioned him. Many of the people who worked with him in the subsequent three decades never even knew he'd once had a brother. "He never talked about his siblings, or much about when he was young," Sue Ann recalled, and then she corrected herself: "He talked about Sarah, but not Oscar." Still, something of that old relationship—that close but distant, loving but embattled rivalry between brothers—persisted in a strange tale Lou wove into some of his writings in later life. Pondering the origins of human creativity, he remarked in one speech that man "is unable to make anything without nature, because nature is the material. But the desire of man is unique. I want to liken the sense of desire to the emergence of two brothers"—and then he went on to discuss "the luminous turning into flame and the flame subsiding into material." Elsewhere he repeated that he had "likened the emergence of light to a manifestation of two brothers, knowing quite well that there are no two brothers, nor even One. But I saw that one is the embodiment of the desire *to be, to express;* and one (not saying 'the other') is *to be, to be.* The latter is non-luminous, and 'One,' prevailing, is luminous, and this prevailing luminous source can be visualized as becoming a wild dance of flame which settles and spends itself into material. Material, I believe, is spent light." It seems odd, and yet somehow very important, that this imagined duality between light and darkness, spirit and matter—the kind of duality around which Kahn focused all his ideas about architecture, not to mention everything else—should take the form of a distinction between one brother and another, which is also in some way the separation of one self from another. Perhaps the fact that Oscar was never mentioned only indicated how deeply the dead sibling had burrowed into the living one.

■

Lou's grief at his only brother's sudden death may have been assuaged, in part, by the fact that a fascinating new person had recently entered his life. In September of 1945, Anne Griswold Tyng came to work for the firm of Stonorov & Kahn. A product of the Harvard Graduate School of Design, Tyng had come to the office to have lunch with one of her GSD classmates, Elizabeth Ware Carlihan, who was about to leave after working with the firm for a year. "By chance both Oscar Stonorov and Lou Kahn were in the office when I reached their ninth top floor unfinished loft space," Tyng recalled. "I had hardly been introduced before they asked if I would take my friend's place and work for them. Since I had heard they were a progressive firm known for low-cost housing, I promptly accepted."

At twenty-five, Anne Tyng was a very beautiful young woman who came from an unusual background. Descended from a long line of New Englanders of Northern European stock (the name Tyng was apparently Viking in origin), she had been born in a mountain village in China to a

Harvard-educated Episcopal clergyman and his Radcliffe-educated wife. Anne's mother had actually been invited to chair the Mills College economics department after her graduation in 1911, but she gave up that career to become a missionary's wife and the mother of five children. Anne, the second-youngest, was born in 1920 and spent most of her first twelve years in China, though with occasional visits back to America (including one hair-raising escape during the 1926 Communist uprising, after which the family eventually returned to a life in China in 1929). The product of Chinese and New England boarding schools, Anne was fluent in both Mandarin and English. By the time she got to Radcliffe, at age eighteen, she had lived in rural Kiangsi and urban Shanghai, had crossed the Pacific by ship several times, had driven across America by car with her parents, and had spent over a year traveling around the globe with her older sister.

She majored in fine arts at Radcliffe, after which she entered the Harvard Graduate School of Design in 1942, when women were just starting to be admitted. There she studied architecture with department chair Walter Gropius and his Bauhaus colleague Marcel Breuer; among her classmates and friends were Philip Johnson, William Wurster, and I. M. Pei. She did brilliantly in the program, but upon graduation she was only able to find a series of temporary jobs in New York ("The more established firms in New York where I had applied," she noted, "told me that they did not hire women architects"), so after a year she moved to Philadelphia to live with her parents and look for work there. In retrospect, it seems entirely unsurprising that Stonorov and Kahn would have hired her on sight.

Her own response to them—or at least to one of them—was equally instantaneous. "My first impression of Lou personally was his extraordinary intensity," she told an interviewer many years later. "He was not the kind of person I would consciously choose to be attracted to, though I do not know if one ever chooses whom one is attracted to. Yes, with my background he would have been a very unlikely person, but he had this intensity which I think must have been the strongest aspect of him."

Anne was the only woman in the firm, and both Oscar and Lou boyishly vied for her attentions, but it was Lou who won out. Anne was a bit naïve about worldly and sexual matters—"I found it difficult to believe that he was happily married and at the same time so intensely interested in another woman"—but she soon gave in to what she described as "a powerful physical attraction that I realized was mutual." She was not bothered by his scars, which she described as "part of a natural charisma," and she even suggested that the strength of his personality, combined with the shyness produced by the scars, was an especially appealing combination. Recalling the effect of his physical presence on her, she commented, "His wavy mop of reddish sandy hair was prematurely gray and his blue eyes, which tilted impishly upward at the sides, seemed to be on fire from within, compelling me to look beyond the scars. On sweltering hot summer weekend charrettes when Lou occasionally worked shirtless, it was hard not to notice how unusually broad his lightly freckled shoulders were in proportion to his slim hips. I had never met anyone remotely like him. He generated a profound energy—in his resilient walk, in the lively lines of his drawings, and in his ideas which seemed to take shape as he drew and talked."

Sexual attraction aside, Tyng was there to learn and work, and she immediately plunged into the life of the office, which had its difficulties as well as its rewards. "The space was not well insulated and was not air-conditioned," she pointed out. "Occasionally we were subjected to ammonia fumes when the *Bulletin* presses were being cleaned on the floor below. On the elevator at eight-thirty in the morning I was almost overpowered by the smell of Stonorov's cigar." But these minor complaints did not prevent her from taking pleasure in the firm's stimulating yet informal atmosphere. Everyone, including the principals, was on a first-name basis, and everyone was given a wide range of tasks to do. When Anne, in her first few months, managed to solve a particularly difficult architectural problem, one of her co-workers praised her for being able to "think like a man"—and though she was taken aback at the formulation, she couldn't help feeling pleased by the level of acceptance it indicated.

One of the first schemes she and Lou worked on together was a "solar house" for the Libby-Owens-Ford glass company. Anne also helped design a remodeled carriage house for a married pair of artists, a structure called Unity House for the International Ladies Garment Workers Union, a shoe store, a playground, and the Triangle Redevelopment Plan, on which she collaborated closely with David Wisdom, who had been with Stonorov & Kahn since 1943. She also had time to develop her own invention on the side—a geometrical toy for children which she called the Tyng Toy—and though it was not part of the firm's work, Lou generously helped her design the promotional material for that. All of this variety was satisfying, and she felt she was learning a great deal. But throughout her time at Stonorov & Kahn she was also vaguely aware of something unseemly in Oscar's dealings. "Stonorov was very much the entrepreneur," she said, "and we used to say that his left hand didn't know what his right hand was doing. He was always juggling things and was not necessarily straightforward about them. As a daughter of a clergyman, I was quite shocked by the fact that he was saying one thing and then saying something else later, never leaving things clarified."

The problems in the partnership came to a head with two memorable incidents. One was when Stonorov took some of Kahn's drawings to an architecture magazine to be printed, but allowed (or perhaps even instructed) the magazine to crop off Lou's name. This infuriated Lou. But he became even angrier when he learned that Oscar had gone behind his back to obtain a new design contract just for himself, going so far as to open up a secret office at Gimbels department store in which to carry it out. Lou found out about the deception when the clients, the Greater Philadelphia Movement, began calling Stonorov & Kahn about the project, thinking it was something the firm was doing jointly. This was the last straw, and Lou—having recently obtained a commission from the Philadelphia Psychiatric Hospital which he would be able to take with him—terminated the partnership and opened a new office of his own in March of 1947.

Kahn took both Tyng and Wisdom with him when he moved to 1728 Spruce Street, a charming Philadelphia row house whose first floor was occupied by the architectural office of Robert Montgomery Brown, the building's resident and owner. The new firm shared its secretary, Alma Farrow, with Brown—she too had been brought over from the Bulletin Building—and its second-floor office with the engineering partnership of Cronheim and Weger. Galen Schlosser, who came to work for Kahn at about this time and stayed with him until at least 1970, commented on the rather intense working conditions. "The office was originally all in one room at 1728 Spruce Street, the front of an old brownstone," he said. "Lou had his desk there, and there were just Anne Tyng, David Wisdom, another fellow and myself. That was the extent of the office, plus a secretary. There were also two engineers sharing our space. We were very intimate, because when you work for Lou you work every day and night, so you almost live together."

By now Anne Tyng had moved into the city from her parents' Main Line house, and she and Lou were spending more time together than ever. "We were both workaholics: in fact, work had become a kind of passionate play," she observed. "I think that for Lou and me loving each other and working together became integrated and took on a life of its own." Kahn did the visionary sketches, for the most part, while Tyng brought her geometrical sensibility to bear on turning their ideas into tangible models. Together they would hum snatches of Bach, Mozart, and Haydn to keep themselves awake through the long nighttime hours of hard work. Among the other things they designed jointly during their four years on Spruce Street (in addition to working on the major contract for the Radbill Building and Pincus Pavilion at the Philadelphia Psychiatric Hospital) were six private houses, of which three—the Roche house, the Weiss house, and the Genel house—were ultimately built. Tyng thought the Weiss house was the most fun to work on, largely because the clients, Morton and Lenore Weiss, were so delightful. It would also prove to be the building in which Lou first introduced several of his signature practices.

The Weiss house, which took from 1947 to 1950 to complete, was located about four miles outside Norristown in rural Pennsylvania. Constructed largely of stone obtained from a nearby quarry, along with exterior wood walls that aged to a silvery gray, it drew on the qualities of the surrounding landscape and regional building traditions in the way Kahn was later to do, for instance, with the locally made bricks he used in Exeter and Ahmedabad. At the Weiss house, he took care to choose and arrange the quarried stones carefully, so that their colors and patterns would make sense together (again, a habit he was to practice in his selection of the two very different kinds of travertine he used at Salk and Kimbell). He specifically asked the stonemasons to make a deep indentation in the mortar between the stones, so that each stone stood out clearly from the other—a procedure he had long admired in the studio built by an artist friend, Wharton Esherick—and this in turn led him to create similar recesses when two different materials, wood and stone, adjoined each other. That was the beginning of Kahn's idea of the "shadow joint," which he carried over to just about every major building he eventually designed. As Anne Tyng explained it, "The shadow joint is the idea of separation between materials so that if one has a door jamb in wood against rough stone-work, one actually lets it be separate, with its own straight edge away from the irregular edge of stone. The shadow joint is an indentation between them which would have a depth at least equal to the distance between wood and stone." This practice allowed each material to exist on its own, discrete and separate, even as it formed part of the coherent whole. It both emphasized the joint (for "the joint is the beginning of ornament," as Kahn was repeatedly to say) and at the same time made it disappear into nothingness.

Two other aspects of the Weiss house that stood out as characteristically Lou-like were the large, multipatterned mural on the living room wall—which Anne, who helped paint it, described as Lou's "concept of a 'giant pointillism'"—and the enormous stone fireplace that dominated the living room and divided it from the dining room. Such fireplaces, which Kahn referred to in his own notes as "inglenooks," were to appear in many of his designs from that point forward, not only in private houses but also, more surprisingly, in public buildings like the Rochester Unitarian Church and the Exeter Library. It was as if the fireplace represented, for him, something essential to the spirit of a place; its function was to provide physical coziness and at the same time to create a focus around which people could gather. Perhaps Lou was recalling the role of the open hearth in the wintry houses of his Estonian childhood. Or maybe his interest in domesticated fire had to do with its mythic qualities—most obviously in the Greek myth of Prometheus, less obviously in his own private myth about the "luminous turning into flame and the flame subsiding into material." Whatever the reasons, the inglenook was to remain for Kahn the actual and symbolic center of a house, and not only in *his* houses. Years later, for instance, when he came to visit his grown-up niece Rhoda and her husband, Marvin Kantor, at the Southern California home they had just bought, it was the massive stone fireplace that Lou singled out for praise.

Something else that lasted for the rest of his life started for Lou in

1947, and that was his teaching. In the fall of 1947, filling a sudden gap left by the Brazilian architect Oscar Niemeyer, whose visa had been denied because of his "Communist sympathies," Kahn was invited to be a visiting critic in Yale's architecture department. He had been offered a teaching post at Harvard the year before, but had turned it down because it would have required him to leave Philadelphia. The Yale position, though, took up only two days a week, a schedule that allowed him to commute to New Haven by train on his teaching days while retaining his Philadelphia practice.

Lou had come to Yale's attention partly as a result of his housing work with Stonorov and partly through the two Revere pamphlets (which had reached audiences of 100,000 and more within a few years of publication), but mainly because of his prominent role in the American Society of Planners and Architects, a forward-looking group he helped found in late 1943 and early 1944. The ASPA's members included noteworthy architects like George Howe, Philip Johnson, Richard Neutra, Eero Saarinen, and William Wurster as well as planners such as Edmund Bacon and Catherine Bauer, and though it fizzled out in 1948 without ever having accomplished anything tangible, its aims— to promote a new kind of socially responsible housing, as put forth in a program called American Village—struck many in the field as worth pursuing. By 1947, with the ASPA already nearing its death throes, Kahn had become the energetic leader of the group, and he kept it alive for an additional year largely through the force of his personality. Like the Architectural Research Group he had helped start in the 1930s, the ASPA showcased his abilities as a speaker, a theoretician, a man of ideas—abilities that must have persuaded the Yale dean, Charles Sawyer, and the department chair, Harold Hauf, that Kahn would be a good teacher.

At Yale, the architecture department was housed in the School of Fine Arts, and this gave the program a firmer link to painting and sculpture than it had at Harvard, where the study of architecture was more closely allied with urban planning. For Kahn, this meant a chance to forge alliances with colleagues like Josef Albers, the Bauhaus painter and designer who soon took over Yale's art department, and his wife, Anni Albers, the noted textile artist. At Yale he also met Vincent Scully, who started teaching there the same year Kahn did, and whose admiration for his architecture would be deep, lasting, and helpful. Writing about his first impressions, Scully later noted that Kahn "talked a good deal about structure . . . , sketched quickly and impressively with that black pencil, but as yet had no consistent approach to design." The man himself, as Scully recalled, was characterized by "deep warmth and force, compact physical strength, a printless, catlike walk, glistening Tartar's eyes—only bright blue—a disordered aureole of whitening hair, once red: black suit, loose tie, pencil-sized cigar. It was at this time that he began to unfold into the rather unearthly beauty and command of a Phoenix risen from the fire. Earlier he had looked as fey as Harpo Marx."

Perhaps some of the increasing gravitas came from being an official instructor of the young. The Yale post was significant, above all, in that it gave Kahn a chance to try out his architectural ideas, both practical and visionary, in the classroom. The habit of setting a "problem" for students and letting them solve it from scratch, either collaboratively or on their own, was congenial to Kahn's way of thinking, and he soon became a revered if somewhat eccentric teacher. Even in his earliest years at Yale he was known for getting his students to tear up their ideas and start afresh: he wanted them to get back to first principles and essential meanings, abandoning the well-worn solutions they had been taught by other architects. At the same time, he insisted on locating his students firmly in the here and now of a particular assignment. As Lou remarked to himself in one of the many notebooks he kept over the years, under the heading *On ways to teach structure in relation to architecture*: "The problems must come from real conditions." And indeed, by his second year at Yale he was getting his students to address an imaginary design problem set in a real, knowable space. He asked them to design a new UNESCO exhibition hall set in Philadelphia's Fairmount Park—not, that is, where the actual United Nations was to be located, in New York, but in the spot where Kahn had vocally argued the UN should be built. A second course he taught that year focused on a housing commission very much like his own Genel house, up to and including the client biography (again, an echo of that same notebook entry, where he observed, "If possible, the client should be known to the designer"). From that point onward, Kahn's architecture practice and his teaching methods would remain interwoven in this way, so that each enriched the other, bringing former students to his firm and practical examples to his classroom.

The teaching had another effect as well: it finally introduced a modicum of financial stability into the Kahn household. To supplement the constant ups and downs of his independent practice, Lou now had a steady income that was more than twice the size of Esther's. In the late 1940s she was earning about $2,300 a year from her full-time job at Jefferson Medical College; Lou's salary from Yale was $6,300, and even after subtracting nearly $1,300 in travel costs, he still had a healthy $5,000 or so to support his family. During this same period he was also continuing to receive income from projects associated with the dissolved Stonorov & Kahn partnership, sometimes amounting to $2,000 a year or more. On his tax returns this money would be set off against the annual losses from his sole proprietorship—a money-losing habit, ranging from hundreds of dollars a year to thousands, that lasted throughout most of the decades in which Louis I. Kahn Architect had its existence. But profit had never been Lou's chief concern, and he was far happier losing money on his own than making it with Stonorov. Among the reasons his teaching was to prove so valuable to him was that it allowed him the luxury of this preference.

With his new teaching duties added to his own busy architectural practice, Kahn was more consumed than ever by his work. But he did make time, in the summer of 1948, to take Esther and Sue Ann on a weeklong visit to his family in Los Angeles. Perhaps Leopold's guilt-inducing efforts had at long last succeeded, or maybe Lou was truly worried about his mother's declining health, which had included a recent diagnosis of diabetes. Among the other things Lou gleaned from the family letters of that period was a strong sense of Bertha's rapidly worsening vision. For example, after describing how much pleasure they received from a newspaper clipping about Lou's achievements, Leopold wrote, "When I finished it, Mother burst out crying, because she couldn't read it her self. Mother used to read her self all the time, now she can't, her eyes are bad and she worries a lot on account of that although the Dr. tolled her she shouldn't worry she will not get blind all together."

Other letters pathetically demonstrated the problem on the page itself, as the highly literate Bertha attempted to scrawl a few uneven, oversized words, first in wobbly paths across the page and eventually, after an operation, in ruled lines. "My dearest children, Thank you dears for your lovely Mother's Day gift. I can not write too much, but I am thankful to God for that," she wrote under Leopold's "Dear Lou, Esther & Sue Ann, I really didn't want Mother to strain her eyes for a while yet, but she promised not to write too much. We are very glad her eyes are a little improved." Faced with such heartrending appeals, Lou finally carved out some time for a visit and also undertook the substantial costs involved in getting a family of three across the country in those postwar years. (His solution was to send Esther and Sue ahead by train, while he flew out to Los Angeles to meet them; at the end of the trip, all three returned together on the train.)

This was the first time the eight-year-old Sue Ann had met either of her Kahn grandparents in person. "They were a devoted couple," she observed. "He used to carry her up the stairs. He did the cooking and she did the baking." Of Bertha, she noted mainly that "she was a roly-poly person." As for Leopold, "Pop was very tall. He spoke all these languages. He used to correct my pronunciation of Bach pieces or whatever I was playing."

Though Sue didn't realize it at the time, her musical talent was probably of more interest to Bertha Kahn than to anyone else. "She appreciated music," said Rhoda, who was still living with her grandparents when Lou's family came to visit. "She would sing songs in German." Her older brother Alan remembered Bertha "singing old Jewish melodies to me. I learned a lot about music from her: she loved music so much that she diffused it around her." But even Rhoda and Alan, who got to know their grandmother far better than Sue Ann ever did, never learned that she had played the harp as a young woman back in the old country. They knew her only as an extremely sweet, remarkably wise old woman with Coke-bottle glasses, a talent for cooking delicious apple tortes, and an uncanny ability to attract people to her.

"She had a warmth about her," noted Alan. "Neighbors from all over would come just to have tea with her." His sister's memories of Bertha were even more emphatic. "She was like a guru, in a simple way," Rhoda observed. "She was very intelligent, very refined. She was a quiet force.

She had a tremendous power to ameliorate problems. She would always say, 'Take care, take it easy. I foresee . . .' She would always say, 'I foresee'"—as if the future, in Bertha's view, always held some kind of helpful resolution in store.

When Lou brought Esther and Sue on this visit, the rest of the family congregated at Leopold and Bertha's house to welcome them. As they had since the 1930s, the elder Kahns were living at 1123½ 78th Street, in a relatively poor Los Angeles neighborhood where Jews, Germans, and other immigrant groups dwelt among small factories and commercial enterprises. The Kahns' own house looked something like a garage, and indeed a part of it—the guest room where Rhoda stayed for years—*was* a converted garage. Adjoining that was Bertha and Leopold's small apartment, and above them lived Sarah with her husband, Joe, and their daughter, Gerry.

Lou loved his sister and always praised her as an artist, both to others and to her face (though, never having received any formal training, Sarah only practiced her art on the side, while she continued to earn her living as a milliner). His brother-in-law, on the other hand, he described as "make-shift." The rest of the family was also a bit dubious about Joe Freedman. There was something coarse about him, they felt, and his relationship with the younger females in the family, including his own daughter, seemed slightly off. But none of this was ever discussed openly. It was not, on the whole, a family in which difficult subjects were confronted directly. There was always a great deal of warmth expressed, but there was also a lot that went unsaid or remained hidden.

One of the things that was not mentioned, at least in front of the children, was the fate of the relatives who had been left behind in Europe. By the time of Lou's 1948 visit, Bertha would almost certainly have learned that her brothers and sisters and nieces and nephews had not survived the war. After being forced out of the comfortable Riga apartments where Lou had visited them and sent to the city's old Jewish ghetto, they had been exterminated in 1941 or 1942. (The exception, her baby brother Isak Mendelowitsch, saved his family by fleeing to Russia, but he himself was drafted into the Red Army and killed at the front in 1944.) Yet none of this was spoken about during the Kahn family get-together, which was the first time they had all seen each other since the war ended.

"I knew," said Rhoda about the missing relatives, though what she had managed to gather was nothing specific, just snippets of overheard conversation. "I do remember my grandmother discussing it with someone. About family. They talked in general terms about that she did have some relatives . . . How much they knew, whether it was assumption or whether it was fact—I don't know." And if his parents knew, Rhoda guessed that Lou must have been told, too. "There must have been some discussion about it," she surmised.

But Alan Kahn was less sure of this. "They sort of protected him from any home or family problems," he said of Lou's relationship with Bertha and Leopold. "So it wouldn't surprise me if they didn't tell him something that was disturbing, and that didn't have anything directly to do with him." Alan himself never heard a word about the dead family members, at least not that he was aware of. If his grandparents ever spoke of such things to each other, "they would talk in a language we didn't know, whether it was German, Finnish, whatever: they knew a lot of languages."

They spoke accentless English, though, as far as he remembered ("Grandpop had a little accent," Rhoda amended, "Grandma none"). And English was certainly the language that prevailed during Lou's 1948 visit with his relatives. An outdoor photo taken at the time suggests the all-American family image they were aspiring to project, complete with white picket fence. Behind the fence and in front of a series of small houses, each with its own tiny front lawn, stand the five Kahns: Lou and his mother looking comfortable and relaxed, while Leopold, Esther, and Sue appear more tentative, though not unhappy or unwilling to be there.

Little Sue Ann struck her sixteen-year-old cousin as "closer to her father than her mother at that point. Esther as a person was more difficult, colder, more formal," said Rhoda. As for the relationship between the in-laws, well, that too was complicated. "I think there was a tolerance," Rhoda suggested. "Grandma was always—she always showed a loving side, but I think there was a distance. I think it may have been on Esther's part. You always had the feeling that she thought she was somewhat better, that they were peasantry. There was a general sense that she had married below her."

"She spoke very distinctly, like an aristocrat," mentioned Alan.

"Esther was not a very warm, demonstrative person. My uncle was," Rhoda stressed, and perhaps some of the special allegiance she detected in Sue Ann was also a projection of her own loyalty, her own fondness. But there never seemed enough of Lou to go around. At the end of the weeklong visit, "I remember telling him, 'I miss you, when will I see you?'" Rhoda recalled. "And he said, 'Well, you know, I have to work.'"

It was to be his constant refrain, and everyone around him learned to live with it, including his immediate family. Sometimes his absence could be a prolonged one, as when he flew to Israel in the spring of 1949 to work for a month on housing plans for the new nation. "Dearest Esther," he wrote three days after landing there, "Hy ye, my love!—We arrived Monday late and from the next morning on have been riding around in the government car inspecting questioning seeing etc etc the most amazing country and people." He excused himself in advance for his bad correspondence habits—"You mustn't mind if I don't write often to you. Our time is so solidly filled up working in committee that I can't pull away for long enough to make sense of a letter"—and then gave a detailed description of the remarkable things he had seen on the flight over. His handwritten note even included a bird's-eye drawing of the Mediterranean, with Naples and Vesuvius marked "N" and "V," as well as a sketch of the Acropolis viewed from its Aegean approach. For Lou, who had previously traveled to Europe only by ship, the trip offered a startling chance to observe from above how "the real flavor of ancient Europe unfolded itself," and his letter to Esther fully conveyed that sense of discovery and excitement.

This special trip was obviously justified by the employment it provided (though the housing scheme Kahn developed in Israel was, like so much else, never to be built). But there were other times when Esther took Lou's physical and emotional absence more personally, interpreting his habitually remiss behavior as outright neglect. In the summer of 1949, for instance, Sue Ann and Esther were vacationing with friends up at Lake Placid—the first of four summers that they were to spend there, leaving Annie Israeli to keep house for her son-in-law back in the sweltering city. The plan was for Lou to come up and join them on vacation for a week in August, and in most years he did manage to accomplish this. But when they were out of sight they were also completely out of mind, and in 1949 he was evidently so preoccupied that he forgot about Esther's August 9 birthday. ("She always made a very big deal of it," Sue Ann remarked about her mother's birthday. "We never made a big deal about Lou's.") Esther's reaction, on this occasion, was to write a complaining letter about Lou to her mother. Annie's reply, sent on August 14, 1949, gives a sense of the underlying family dynamic.

"Louis is in New Haven this week-end," his mother-in-law reported, "he really is very tired. I do feel sorry for him. He works like a slave and what does he have? It is of no use telling him anything, he only gets mad. Since I see how hard he works and how tired he is I would really advise you not to tell him about your birthday I would ignore it. I am sure he too would like to give you things, but he can't do it, he simply does not know how to make money."

Esther's irritation may have had other sources than Lou's chronic inability to earn a living or even his immediate crime of forgetfulness. By the late 1940s and certainly by the early 1950s, Anne Tyng had become something of a fixture in the Kahn household. She provided Lou's daughter with regular art lessons, gave the little girl one of the earliest copies of the Tyng Toy, and even involved her in putting together the architectural model of an elementary school. At one point she also surprised Sue Ann with the gift of a parakeet, a treasured pet to which the child later insisted on giving a first birthday party celebrated by the whole family at breakfast. This friendship between her daughter and the beautiful young woman from Lou's office could not have been entirely easy for Esther, especially if she had her suspicions—eventually to harden into certain knowledge—that something was going on between Lou and Anne.

But Anne too had to put up with Lou's absences, not only when he was with his family, but also when he was on his architectural travels. There were some compensations for this in terms of her role at the office: his 1949 trip to Israel, for instance, left her in sole charge of the Weiss house project for a month, and she was proud of the elegant roof-and-gutter solution she worked out during that time. But when Kahn was away, at least on the shorter trips, he tended to write to his office crew as a group, which left little room for intimate communication between him and Tyng. Nor did he seem to suffer at the idea of being

apart from either Anne or his family, as long as his travels were suffi-
ciently novel and interesting.

What was to prove the most significant trip of the new decade, and
possibly of his whole life, began in the late fall of 1950. Thanks to the
influence of his friend George Howe, who had recently vacated the post
himself, Kahn received an invitation to become the architect-in-
residence at the American Academy in Rome. He had earlier applied
for a fellowship there, but with no success. (Howe was apparently
enraged that he had been turned down.) Now, however, came an offer
of full-time accommodation in Rome for up to a year—though Lou felt
he could only afford to take three months away from his practice, and the
Rome Academy finally agreed to that term. All his expenses would be
paid once he was there, the Academy informed him, but getting to
Rome was up to him.

In the end, it was his sister-in-law Olivia and her husband, Mickey,
who paid for Lou's travel to Italy. He had remained close to Esther's two
sisters ever since they had all lived together at 5243 Chester Avenue in
the 1930s, and Regina, the youngest, had even moved back in with the
Kahns for a few years after her divorce in the early 1940s. Meanwhile,
Olivia and Milton Abelson, who were both trained as economists, had
gone to Washington to work on the Social Security Act under FDR. But
after Roosevelt's death and Mickey's subsequent blacklisting in the
early years of the McCarthy era, the Abelsons lost their federal jobs.
They had moved with their children (one of whom had Down syndrome)
from Arlington, Virginia, to New York City, where they were living when
Lou received the Academy's invitation.

"He got the prize but he didn't have the money to go over there,"
Sue Ann said of her father's Rome opportunity. "He and Esther approached various friends, people they were close to, and they all turned
them down. They said, 'You shouldn't go—you should stay with your
practice!'" These were relatively well-off friends, Sue pointed out: doctors, academics, people like that. But when the Abelsons, who had a
very modest income, heard of Lou's plight, they stepped in and offered
part of their savings. "They just gave him the money, no question," said
Sue. She didn't know exactly how much it came to, but "whatever it
was, it was a lot then."

By the beginning of December 1950, Kahn was settled in the

Beaux-Arts-style American Academy building on the hillside above Trastevere in Rome. There he was to spend a substantial part of the next few months in the company of the archaeologist Frank E. Brown, who took him around to all the local ancient sites, including Trajan's Market, the Pantheon, the Forum, and the ruins of Ostia Antica. Lou did a great deal of sketching in pastels and watercolors at this time: he produced some ninety pictures in the course of his three months abroad, documenting what he saw in Greece and Egypt (to which he took a three-week side trip) as well as in other parts of Italy, but mainly focusing on the massive old buildings he visited in Rome itself. He wrote to Tyng about the "overwhelmingly strong jolts that hit you when Rome appears again in all its power," though he also told her, from Egypt, "The Pyramids are the most wonderful things I have seen so far. No picture can show you their monumental impact."

Mass and weight became especially important to him during this period; so did the materials that possessed and embodied these qualities, like brick and concrete. Back in Philadelphia, he had designed his most recent building, the Psychiatric Hospital's Pincus Pavilion, in the lightweight steel so beloved of the modernists, but from this point onward he would abandon steel structures in favor of heavy masonry and reinforced concrete, materials that not only emphasized their relation to gravity, but also displayed on their surface the process of their own making. Inspired by Frank Brown, who spoke about anonymous Roman architects of the Hellenic and High Empire periods as if they were still alive, Kahn began to envision a way in which his deep-seated affection for the old and his admiration for the new could come together. As he said to Tyng about the city of Rome and his experience of being there: "as I see it again, I want to build all the more and better."

Part of what Kahn imbibed from Frank Brown was a respect for the weighty old materials and designs the Romans had discovered two thousand years earlier. "Roman architects were moved to seize on the arch as the formal substitute for post and lintel, and on the vault as a means of closing the shell of space in a continuous curve," Brown noted in his book *Roman Architecture*, published a few years after his conversations with Kahn. "In the heat of building, under the spur of their new incentives, they perfected old materials and invented new methods. From rubblework came concrete, laid between masonry forms, which yielded its permanent faces." In such passages, it almost seemed that Brown was recording the recipes from which Kahn would create his future monuments.

The influence Frank Brown had upon Lou went far beyond these technical descriptions, extending to the moments when he would talk, for instance, about "the choreography of space. In it the architect, like a ballet master, marked with inflexible symmetry the figures, the steps, and the tempo," Brown wrote. "His measures were the flow of vaults,—ramping, annular, coupled—the punctuation of arches, and the ripple of columns." That a building was something experienced in time, precisely through one's movement within and around it, was a great part of the lesson he gave Kahn. Or as Brown said in another passage: "The ample nave was to be grasped as a single whole, clearly scanned by the intervals of its framing. It placed men at its center or drew them to move lengthwise or crosswise of it. The ambulatory unfolded progressively with movement along it or subdivided itself in the stationary units of its bays. Within it special spaces of arrest might be signaled by tribunes, or alcoves or windows." Though he was speaking about the Roman basilica here, he was also uncannily foreshadowing such Kahn buildings as the Exeter library, the Rochester church, and the Dhaka parliament, each of which would similarly locate the human body, in movement and at rest, within a vast, inspiring space.

While he was still in Rome, in February of 1951, Kahn learned that he had been awarded the commission for the Yale University Art Gallery. Once again, this timely gift was at least partly due to George Howe, who had recently become the chair of Yale's architecture department. The project—to add a modern extension onto one of Yale's traditional Gothic-style buildings, thus creating room for both an art museum and classroom/studio space—would have been a major milestone in any career, and it represented a huge leap in Lou's. Yet he did not rush back immediately to America. Instead he made his way home in a comparatively leisurely fashion. Having flown to Rome on the way out, he chose to return via train through Venice to Paris, and from there by ship to New York. As he departed from Rome in late February, he sent a postcard to 5243 Chester Avenue addressed to "Dearest Esther Sue and Mother." In it he explained, "I might send a card from Venice but this might be my last note before leaving on the boat . . . I am really anxious to be back and see you all again and unravel the many tales & talk about far places and new impressions." He signed it "Lots of love to all, Lou."

■

Kahn returned to America on March 4, 1951, and by June he had moved his practice to new offices at 138 20th Street, at the intersection of 20th and Walnut. There he and his staff, which had increased to eight or ten by this time, occupied the second floor of a rather undistinguished two-story building. Adorned with an oddly fanciful arched ornament on the otherwise flat roof, this corner building was graced with large second-story windows on both of its outer sides, so the whole office was filled with light—though it could also get unpleasantly hot in warm weather (something that Lou, with his immense ability to focus on the project at hand, often failed to notice until long after everyone else was sweltering).

Besides housing the firm of Louis I. Kahn Architect, 138 20th Street was also the official address of a new entity called Architects Associated, a joint venture consisting of the partners Louis I. Kahn, Kenneth Day, Louis E. McAllister, Douglas G. Braik, and Anne G. Tyng. Braik left in 1952, but the other four continued to work together on various projects through the mid-1950s. Among the designs they did during this time were several neighborhood redevelopment plans and a set of row house studies for the Philadelphia City Planning Commission; a series of traffic studies for the Philadelphia AIA, never implemented but later published by Kahn and Tyng, along with beautifully colored illustrations, in an issue of the Yale magazine *Perspecta*; and the Mill Creek Project, another Planning Commission job that included closed-off streets yielding "greenways" around the housing. On most of these commissions, Kahn's group was collaborating in one way or another with Ed Bacon, the man who was to remain the dominant force in Philadelphia planning for more than two decades.

Kahn and Bacon had known each other since 1939, and they had joined together as housing activists in the early 1940s. Their families had also become friendly: Bacon, who had a daughter about Sue Ann's age, would invite the Kahns over for Sunday barbecues, and this friendship continued into the early 1950s. But the two men turned out to be very different types, with very different agendas and career paths. Bacon, a Quaker, fit neatly into the social conventions of old Philadelphia, whereas Kahn, an immigrant Jew, did not. Perhaps more importantly, Bacon was an extremely practical man with a clear-eyed, not to say self-serving, sense of politics. Kahn, on the other hand, focused his energies on questions of architecture and design—often involving highly visionary or inventive ideas and practices—and tended to imagine (or hope, or wish) that the politics of any given situation would just sort themselves out. Since they rarely did, this gave Bacon the upper hand, and he was able to take charge of the city's planning process and leave Kahn on the sidelines, eventually excluding him from most of the key decisions in Philadelphia's redesign.

Whether the falling-out between them stemmed more from Bacon's competitiveness and hunger for power, or from Kahn's woolly-headedness and impracticality, was a question that depended on whose side you took in their disagreement. At any rate, by the time Kahn left for the American Academy in late 1950, the two were no longer working directly together on specific plans, though Architects Associated continued to do projects for the Philadelphia Planning Commission and Ed Bacon continued to praise Louis Kahn as a "gifted designer" and the "greatest architect in the world." Kahn generously returned the compliment when he wrote to Bacon about Penn Center—a project from which Lou in the end was completely excluded—that "you have earned the distinction of being the Architect Planner. Few of us can really claim that title." But later the animosity between them became more pointed, as Bacon grew envious of Kahn's growing fame and was consequently less willing to give him even the planning credit he deserved—for instance, for the very practical ideas embodied in the traffic studies and the Mill Creek greenways.

Kahn may have resented Bacon's cavalier theft of these ideas (certainly Anne Tyng resented it on his behalf), but it was not his way to show overt antagonism. Nick Gianopulos, a Philadelphia engineer who met Lou in the early 1950s, remarked, "I never once heard Lou, ever, curse. I never heard him denigrate anybody. And he taught me something: he says, 'If you're angry, really angry, and you have grounds for your anger, when you write to them, kill them with kindness.'" Gianopulos

sensed that this principle applied directly to Kahn's dealings with Ed
Bacon; he also felt that Bacon deserved Lou's anger. "Bacon was an
autocrat," Gianopulos said. "I got to know him in his later years, and I
didn't like him."

Though Nick Gianopulos and Louis Kahn had met briefly at lunch
in 1951 or 1952, the project on which they really got to know each other
was the Yale Art Gallery, a technically demanding commission that
proved to be a turning point in Kahn's career. The art gallery was not an
Architects Associated project, but one carried out by Louis I. Kahn
Architect, involving close collaboration between Lou and Anne, and it
was probably Anne's relentless inventiveness which intensified the need
for engineering advice. According to Tyng, the unusual "triangulated
geometry" that ended up distinguishing the final design—in both the
tetrahedral indentations that made up the concrete ceiling and the triangular main staircase lodged within a concrete cylinder—emanated
from her influence. "Since the Yale Art Gallery was Kahn's first prestigious building, he was nervous," she noted, "and his first schemes indicated a conventional structure. I asked Lou, 'Why bother to build it if
you don't use an innovative structure?'" Yet those innovations were precisely what worried the New Haven planning department, which didn't
see how the tetrahedral ceiling could possibly be built to code.

The remarkable ceiling was certainly not a part of the initial design
approved by Yale in August of 1951. It didn't enter the plans until March
of the following year, when Kahn—in the kind of wholesale revision
that was to drive clients and co-workers crazy over the years—first introduced the idea of the tetrahedral space-frame. Working in steel in
one case and lumber in another, Tyng had already pioneered this kind
of structure in two prior commissions, an elementary school and a private house for her parents. For the massive Yale project, though, a wood
frame would never have been an option, and there wasn't enough steel
to do the job: the wartime economy that prevailed during the Korean
War meant that the Defense Department had to approve each domestic
use of steel, and Yale had already received its fixed allocation under the
earlier design. So the art gallery's three-dimensional space-frame had to
be composed of reinforced concrete rather than either of those lighter,
more flexible materials.

The structural viability of such a ceiling was a complete unknown, with the weight being the least of the potential problems. The real concern, according to the engineers, was the internal distribution of forces within the ceiling's elements. "It could fail in tension, it could fail in shear, which are the two primary forces a structure contends with," said Nick Gianopulos, whom Lou had called in for consultation. Gianopulos was representing the firm of Keast & Hood, formed after the recent death of Nick's old boss, Major Gravell, who had been widely known as the dean of Philadelphia engineering. What Lou told Nick was that "Anne Tyng and I had been to see the Major a week before he died, and he said the analytical tools to assess the structure did not exist yet. He said the only way to test it was to build a full-size model, load it with sandbags, and measure it with instruments."

In the event, that is exactly what Kahn and his contractor, George Macomber, did. But first Gianopulos made a slight adjustment to the design. He filled in the voids between the triangular tops of the tetrahedrons—the spaces on either side of the peaks, as it were—with additional concrete, turning them into "parallel canted joists" that would strengthen the structure's integrity. This change was invisible from below, so it didn't affect the look of the ceiling, though it did determine the way the ducts and pipes could be threaded through the space-frame. Nick's structural fix resolved at least one of the objections put forth by the City of New Haven, and the rest were met when the full-size test section, measuring about fourteen by fifty feet, was constructed and analyzed by Macomber. That test took place a mere two months before the ceiling's first pour, well into the building process itself, so it was only at the last possible minute that Kahn got the engineering reports allowing the pour to proceed.

One specific virtue of the ceiling, aside from its novel beauty, was the way it allowed ducts, cables, wiring, and even light fixtures to be embedded out of sight, deep within the shadowy recesses of the triangular openings. "I do not like ducts; I do not like pipes," Kahn once commented. "I hate them really thoroughly, but because I hate them so thoroughly, I feel they have to be given their place. If I just hated them and took no care, I think they would invade the building and completely destroy it." He was to come up with many different solutions to this problem, but at Yale he did it with the ceiling.

Yet even as he hid certain things, Kahn also wanted other things to show. "The Pyramids try to say to you, *Let me tell you how I was made*," Lou observed after seeing those powerful monuments, and now he invoked the same principle in his own first monumental building. He left the concrete walls, the steel staircase railings, the exterior and interior brickwork—everything, in short, except the wooden floors and the exhibition panels—bare and unfinished. "I believe in frank architecture," he explained to a student interviewer. "A building is a struggle, not a miracle, and the architect should acknowledge this."

The Yale University Art Gallery, completed in 1953, instantly met with an enthusiastic response. *Progressive Architecture* featured the building and in particular its tetrahedral ceiling in its May 1954 issue, along with illustrations of another Kahn/Tyng project, the City Tower. (The latter, which was even more indicative of Tyng's geometric influence, was to remain unbuilt, though it inspired several younger architects with its brash, zigzagging, intensely futurist design.) Vincent Scully praised Kahn's museum for its "honesty, reality, masculinity," observing that the rough concrete was "crystalline" rather than "muscular" in the manner of Le Corbusier, and that the "massive, repetitive, mathematically insistent canopy of the ceiling thus set off the specific works of art below it as, in my opinion, no white plane of plaster could have done." Yet despite the professional applause, Kahn himself was eventually to feel dissatisfied with the open-plan galleries, whose only interior walls consisted of flexible panels that could be added or removed, which lent them too heavily to redesign by others. In his later museums, as in all his later buildings, he would focus more on the careful differentiation of functional space: "Architecture is the thoughtful making of spaces," he would often say. Nor would he ever reuse the concrete tetrahedral ceiling in anything like that exact form.

The one thing from the Yale Art Gallery that seemed already to bear his mature signature was the staircase. Enclosed in a massive concrete cylinder vertically inscribed with the thin panels of its wooden formwork, the angular staircase mounted upward in a clean, enticing combination of open-work steel and solid concrete. "These stairs, now. They are designed so people will want to use them," Kahn said at the time. It was in this sense of pleasure combined with usefulness, of human motion in relation to architectural stillness, that he was starting to find his true vocabulary.

There's no guessing how much more powerful Tyng's effect on Kahn's work might have become, had an accident of history—or rather, biology—not gotten in the way. In the middle of 1953, shortly after the Yale project was finished, Anne discovered she was pregnant. She had planned to take a leave from the firm anyway, and had applied for a Fulbright to study with Pier Luigi Nervi in Italy. Now, however, she essentially had to go into hiding: the Fulbright Foundation would not have tolerated being represented by a pregnant unmarried woman, and even staying in Philadelphia would have proven socially difficult. So Anne resolved to go to Italy on her own, staying in Rome near her older brother Bill and his Italian wife. She didn't tell them in advance about the pregnancy, though, nor did she mention it to her parents when she visited them shortly before the trip. "Only Lou and the doctor knew I was pregnant," she recalled. "The collective projection onto unmarried mothers was that they were, at the very least, 'delinquent' and 'sinful.' I was not about to accept such archaic pronouncements. Having our baby in Rome might be positive, graceful, and even romantic for our love child."

What ensued during her trip was a series of letters between Lou and Anne that put into writing some of the thoughts and feelings previously audible only in their private conversations. Anne's letters to Lou have apparently been lost or destroyed, but she was able to save all of his, and when read in sequence they help to convey a sense of the couple's concerns, both mutual and separate, over the fifteen months they were apart.

Love, architecture, and money—not always in that order—were the primary subjects of the correspondence. "Dearest Anne, Your wonderful letters came I must have read them five times," Lou wrote early on, in November of 1953. He wasn't sure where she was, so he had forwarded their *Perspecta* publication of the traffic studies to Paris, sent a telegram to Bordeaux, and written to Rome. He filled her in on Howe's and Scully's enthusiastic response to their recent joint work, and then interrupted himself: "Darling Anne I do hope you are in good spirits and that you take heart in my love for you. I feel the same emptiness which I know I must counter with diligent work." Then back to some details about a possible new commission for a house, and finally: "Now Anne have a good time and let me know about money problems. I could send you a bill with each letter which would build up your dollar reserve which I know will do you the best financial good. By-By Honey, will write very soon again. With all my love, Lou."

His notion of sending her a "bill" in each letter (generally a ten, occasionally a twenty) was typical of Lou's hopeless approach to money problems—especially since, as the months wore on, his letters came less and less frequently. But though he was admittedly, even by his own reckoning, a terrible correspondent, he was doing his best for her, and his handwritten letters often ran to three pages or more. He tried to sympathize with her anxieties about telling her brother about the pregnancy, suffering the identity changes that would go with motherhood, and so on, though even his warmest words obviously couldn't take the place of his reassuring presence. Still, he made every attempt to convey to her his distinctive, passionate self: "My best regards to your people but if they treat you in some god damned Victorian manner I shall positively hate them."

Lou was eager for Anne to experience the architectural treasures of Italy, learning from them as he had done on his two earlier trips. "Don't fail to see Venice, Verona, Florence, Pisa, Siena. Even if you have to take a conducted tour," he urged. "Don't worry about the dough that is to be ever our least worry." Yet it clearly became a pronounced worry for her, one she must have reiterated in her letters, for he ended up telling her to fill out time sheets and send them to the office. That was evidently how he planned to provide at least *some* support for both Anne and their baby without directly draining the home coffers.

Alexandra Tyng was born on March 22, 1954. As if to assert her continuing independence, and perhaps also to avert scandal, Anne not only gave the little girl her own last name; she also put "Father Unknown" on the birth certificate. She sent Lou a coded telegram announcing the birth, and in return he sent her a cable on March 24: ALL MY LOVE TO BOTH OF YOU—LOU. A few days later he wrote, "Dearest Anny, Last night I dreamed about you. I was in our office telephoning you walked in and motioned to me that you could wait no longer. You had on a yellow dress and your golden hair was dressed in pony style. Your eyes some how were black and flashing looking at me reprehensibly. You were (and are of course) beautiful—Anny Anny I think of you always. I miss so much our meetings together. I hope nothing changes about our way of life—" A strange and rather naïve thing to say, per-haps, in the wake of a child's birth, but no doubt heartfelt. As if to reinforce that they were still intellectual partners as well as parents together, Lou launched immediately after that into a long paragraph about architectural projects past (a "lousy article . . . about the Yale Building") and future ("I might get a Synagogue to design").

And architecture did continue to be a subject of utmost interest between them. Most of the letters Kahn wrote to Tyng had at least one or two sketches incorporated within them—sometimes quite a compli-cated sketch, as when he detailed street patterns around Penn Center or drew alternative supports for a proposed roof. One letter contained a schematic arrangement of the words "Nature of Space," "Order," and "Design," with circles drawn around the first two terms and lines going between all three—the origins, it would seem, of Kahn's developing ideas about the relation between Order (which he saw as a given, some-thing inherent in nature) and Design (which was the human response to Order, at its best). Kahn also wrote to Tyng about his teaching, which by early 1954 was beginning to feel overwhelming. "Now that I am full of students from the rear and from the front I can truthfully say I would much rather have a big practice or a good practice with only some con-tact with the academic life," he reported. "When I see those faint scrib-bles after 3 weeks of seemingly stimulating directions I get a bit doubtful about the gain I give or take." This private confession contrasted inter-estingly with his oft-repeated assertion that he got an enormous amount out of teaching and would stop the minute he felt he was learning less than his students. Or perhaps it simply represented his bleak view on a rare bad teaching day.

Clearly Lou put a great deal of himself into these letters to Anne. Beyond the key insights he shared with her about their profession, there was the continuing and palpable feeling of warmth he expressed for both mother and child. "She is a perfect darling! I believe too she will be a beauty and will have much to offer this world—and You! You look so wonderful to me so beautiful—so loving," he wrote in response to the first mailed snapshots of mother and daughter. And when, in January of 1955, Anne finally arranged passage for herself and Alex on the S.S. *Constitution* to New York (having borrowed the $400 for the tickets from Robert Venturi, who was then at the American Academy in Rome),

Lou telegraphed excitedly to her, WILL MEET BOAT WHATEVER HOUR
IT DOCKS/LOVE LOU. He was not shirking his role as either father or
lover. He was doing his best to be warm, loving, and emotionally available. And yet, as usual, what he presented to Anne was not the whole
story.

During the fifteen months that Anne Tyng was away in Rome, a
young woman named Marie Kuo had started work at Kahn's practice,
and she and Lou had begun having an affair. Just as Anne had been,
Marie was in her mid-twenties when she came to work for Lou—it was
only her second job after architecture school—whereas he was by now
in his mid-fifties and beginning to be well known. Like Anne, Marie
was beautiful, though in a different way. And like Anne (or for that
matter, like Esther), she came from a distinctly higher social class than
Lou, though her family had suffered serious reverses and she had ended
up putting herself through college.

Marie Kuo was born in 1928 in Peking, China, the oldest child of
General Pehchuam Kuo, an important military and diplomatic figure in
Chiang Kai-shek's government. The Kuos, who came originally from
Manchuria, had been diplomats for generations. The general's wife,
Marie's mother, was the descendant of an extremely wealthy Manchu-
rian family, and Marie's first eight or nine years were spent in luxurious
surroundings. Then, in 1937, her father was sent to Washington, D.C.,
as military attaché to the Chinese embassy. Soon after, the rest of the
family—Marie, her mother, and her brother Joseph—hastily fled China
to escape the Japanese massacre that became known as the Rape of
Nanking. They joined General Kuo in Washington, but Marie was sent
off almost immediately to a Catholic boarding school, Villa Maria, on the
outskirts of Philadelphia, while her two younger brothers, Joe and the
American-born Jimmy, remained with their parents.

In 1941 General Kuo was posted to Moscow, at which point Marie's
mother and the two boys moved to a lower-middle-class neighborhood
in West Philadelphia. The family wealth had been greatly depleted by
this time, but Mrs. Kuo still had enough money to respond to her husband's requests that she send cash and silk stockings to Russia. In 1945
Marie's father paid them one last visit, during which he told Marie,
then only seventeen, that she needed to be responsible for the family and
so should not plan on getting married. Shortly after his return to Rus-

sia, Mrs. Kuo and her children learned that the general had a second family with a half-Russian, half-Chinese woman he had met at his Moscow posting. Marie's mother (who never divorced her husband but lived apart from him for the rest of her life) fell into an angry, moody state and began drinking a great deal. Marie herself left the house as soon as she could, going straight from Villa Maria to Penn. She had always wanted to be an artist, but the Chinese elders in Philadelphia advised Mrs. Kuo that this would not be a good way to earn a living, so Marie was steered into architecture instead.

Marie Kuo was neither as professionally ambitious nor as devoted to architecture as Anne Tyng had been. Though she graduated from Penn's five-year B.A. program in architecture, she never went for her license or became a member of the AIA. But she worked as a project architect, and by all accounts she drew beautifully. At Lou's office her artistic skills were considered quite useful: in one case, for instance, she traced over a quick drawing Lou had made and then spent a month perfecting it before it was eventually handed over to the Museum of Modern Art as a sample of Kahn's work. Her colleagues, in addition to commending her excellent draftsmanship, were charmed by her attractive appearance and delicate manners. Jack MacAllister, another Penn graduate who started working for Lou a year or two after Marie did, described her as "sweet," "intelligent," and "talented," and recalled that "she walked on her toes, like a ballerina." Lois Sherr Dubin, a landscape architect who met Marie at Kahn's office somewhat later, said she was "gentle, kind, bright, very pretty . . . My impression of her was a lovely, gentle woman."

But while Marie may have appeared soft and gentle to the outside world, her own family understood the degree of her strength and her forcefulness. Determined to rise above their poverty-stricken, recent-immigrant status—and, if possible, to drag her brothers up with her—she aspired to elegance in everything she did. She wore expensively tailored clothes, spoke in an accent that her brother Joe described as "almost British," and once advised him to "surround yourself with beauty in your life." Nor did she hesitate to criticize what she considered his boorish speech and bearing, telling him at one point that he should take ballet so that he would move more gracefully, less like a peasant. "Marie was classical," observed Joe, who also trained as an architect at

Penn. Then he added, "I never saw Marie that much. I guess I stayed away because she was so 'right.'" He admitted, though, that she could be extremely generous, as when she paid all the costs of their younger brother Jimmy's private schooling out of her earnings from Kahn's office.

No one could say exactly when or how the affair started, but by the time Anne Tyng returned to Philadelphia it was already in full swing, and Anne soon found out about it. Perhaps one of the men from the office told her; perhaps Marie herself gave it away. Certainly Marie felt possessive enough to pay Anne a visit, at a slightly later date, to ask her to give Lou up. Since Anne had the baby, Marie's argument ran, she should be willing to let Marie have Lou. Anne pointed out that this was not how things worked. Another time, at the office, Anne heard Marie speaking in Chinese on the phone, assuring the person at the other end (presumably her mother) that she would not get pregnant because she was using birth control. Of course, Marie could not have expected her conversation to be understood; she did not know about Anne's childhood in China. But what struck Anne most about the incident was that Marie felt able to use birth control despite Lou's dislike of it— something that she herself had not always managed to do, with the obvious consequences.

The intrusion of Marie Kuo into the equation, painful as it must have been to Anne on a personal level, became even more disturbing because of the way it affected her collaboration with Lou. This became apparent soon after her 1955 return to the office, when she was assigned to work on the Trenton Bath House, a building that was a key part (and, in the end, one of the few constructed elements) of a site plan for the Jewish Community Center in Ewing Township, New Jersey. According to Tyng, Kahn had been working with Tim Vreeland, one of their colleagues, on a roofless rectangular design, but it was she who came up with the final plan: four symmetrically arranged squares around a central courtyard, with each square roofed by an open pyramid that rested on four hollow columns. Some of these empty, partially walled-in corners could function as "servant spaces" that held things like water pipes, electrical equipment, and pool supplies. Others would form the matching entrances on either side of the boys' and girls' changing rooms. These "baffled entrances," as Anne thought of them, were something she remembered from her Chinese childhood, and at Trenton they lent both a simplicity and a mystery to the separation between public and private space.

"Lou and I were working together at a drawing board for the first time in over a year," Anne noted, and it pleased her that he went with her proposed scheme. But when it came time to paint the mural Lou had designed for the bath-house entrance, it was Marie that he took along on the weekend painting expedition. Only five years earlier, Anne had been his chosen assistant on the Weiss house mural. The change in her role could not have been starker.

Whether or not Kahn was consciously attempting to push Tyng to the margins of his work, he was effectively doing so. An entry in one of his notebooks—uncharacteristically dated, in this case with the notation "June 7, '55"—showed how this new alignment might have played out in the office. Kahn wrote:

> The last edition of the Sunday Times showed picture of Corbu's chapel at Ronchamp. Reactions differed wildly. I fell madly in love with it. Marie feels the same as I do. Dave thinks it arbitrary. Tim is not commital. Pen just repeats my words of praise, adding nothing. Beer, always superior, says it looks like hundreds of pictures in Switzerland. To me it is undenyably the work of an artist. An artist able to retranslate a dream into the concrete materials of architecture. A dream full of the known unrestrained forms symbolic of religion to the dreamer . . .

It is striking that Lou knew so immediately that this recently completed building of Le Corbusier's, seen only in a single photo, would be of such importance to his own work—not only in terms of its materials (poured concrete, local stone), but also with respect to its strangely affecting form, which was at once whimsical and serious, curved and straight, massively weighty and illuminatingly light. And one can almost hear the office conversation emerging from the page, as Dave Wisdom—the solid paterfamilias of the firm, the only voice routinely able to counter Lou's—chimes in with his opinion, while Tim Vreeland, the handsome former Yale student, resists committing himself at all.

Penrose Spohn comes through as the inevitable yes-man (though how do his comments really differ from Marie Kuo's wholehearted agreement?), and then Abraham Beer, the visiting Frenchman, takes on the role of the snooty foreigner.

But where is Anne Tyng in all this? Literally on the margins, it turns out, segregated off on the other side of the page—for to the left of this notation, across the vertical dividing line that separates each notebook page into a narrower left-hand column and a wider right-hand one, Kahn has written, "Anne is not satisfied with the power expressed only by form making not derived from an order of construction which is in all architecture inherent in form. Ann claims that if Corbusier had a growth concept of structure as I and she understands it he himself would not be satisfied with his work."

She was, it seems, the truer Kahnian of the two, always reminding him of the ideas he himself had espoused, the notions of order they had together explored in architecture and in form itself. Anne's special kind of intelligence—which included her passion for the purity of geometry—made her want everything to work out logically, neatly, so as to remain consistent with the underlying principles she saw at work in the universe. Lou had been immensely drawn to this quality in her and had responded to it, both in his words and in his work. Yet something in him also wanted to rebel against it, with an impulsive reaction of pure instinct: "I fell madly in love with it."

Despite their differences during this period, though, Kahn and Tyng remained a couple in many ways: as colleagues at work, as parents to little Alex, and even as lovers. Without permanently giving up Marie, as Anne must have repeatedly pressed him to do, Lou continued to be an important presence in the Tyng household. He would take Alex places or come visit her at Anne's, occasionally staying for dinner and sometimes spending the night. And Anne, too, was granted a flexibility at work that allowed her, despite everyone else's long hours, to have her "Alex time" at home with the child. As the little girl got older, she often asked her mother why her father didn't live with them, but Anne's answers, though intended to protect her, only succeeded in confusing her further. "She would say, 'We weren't married like other people were,' and I thought that meant they were married in a courthouse or something," the adult Alex remembered. So Alex grew up seeing her father no more than once or twice a month—about as often as a busy architect-father could manage it, she presumed.

One thing that made Lou slightly less busy, if not a great deal more available, was the change in his teaching location. George Howe had retired from his position as chair of the Yale architecture department in 1954, and in fact he was to die less than a year later, to Lou's great distress. ("He really adored him, and when George Howe died Lou disappeared; he just went to Atlantic City all by himself, and just walked down the beach all day and then came back home; but he did not want to talk to anybody," Esther Kahn later recalled.) Lou got along much less well with Paul Rudolph, the up-and-coming modernist architect who eventually took over the chairmanship of the department. The commute, too, was beginning to wear on him, and he wanted to be closer to his growing practice. So when G. Holmes Perkins, the new dean of Penn's architecture program, offered him a regular academic post starting in the fall of 1955, Kahn took him up on it. He had already taught occasional classes at Penn, starting earlier in the 1950s, and had become a familiar face to the architecture students. Now, however, he emerged full-blown as Professor Kahn. He was to take up visiting posts elsewhere—in 1956, for instance, he put in a term at MIT's School of Architecture and Planning, and he continued to do some teaching at Yale until 1957, as well as occasional stints at Princeton—but from the mid-1950s onward he remained permanently associated with Penn, as the figure around whom the influential "Philadelphia School of Architecture" cohered.

Richard Saul Wurman, who studied architecture at Penn from 1953 to 1958 and then went to work in Lou's firm, powerfully recalled Kahn's first appearance in one of his classrooms. It was one of the "crits"—those occasions when the master architect criticized (or, less frequently, praised) the drawings and designs of the students—and it probably took place around the time Kahn was abandoning Yale for Penn. In any case, Wurman already knew who he was, this teacher with the scarred face, the high-pitched "squeaky" voice, and the incredibly charismatic manner.

"I heard him give a crit in the beginning of my second year and I remember this distinctly," said Wurman. "It was an epiphany. I came home and said to my parents: I have just listened to a person who is going to be famous." Wurman didn't care to what extent his parents, a kosher butcher and a housewife, could understand what he was talking about. He just felt compelled to make the statement. "He's an astonishing person," he said to them about Kahn, "and the first person I've met who spoke the truth. He's different from we are—different from I am—and he's going to be famous."

■

Around the time Lou was beginning his professorship at Penn, or perhaps a few months later, the teenaged Sue Ann was riding the streetcar that took her from her home in West Philadelphia to her private high school, Friends Select, on the other side of town. As the familiar vehicle carried her along, she happened to glance out the right-hand window; then she turned her head and looked more steadily. There on the sidewalk stood Anne Tyng, whom she knew well, holding hands with a little girl she had never seen before. "And it came to me in this kind of otherworldly way: *This is my sister,*" recalled Sue Ann.

Her first impulse (though "impulse" made it sound conscious, and it never even reached that stage) was to ignore the realization entirely. "I thought, *I don't want to think about it,* and I just blocked it out," she said many years later. "Never talked to anyone about it. I don't know how I knew. Maybe I overheard something and wasn't aware of it. It was just like a flash of insight. Just information. I didn't feel distress. *That's my sister, that's my father's child:* I never articulated it to myself, but I'm sure it happened."

Up to that point, Sue Ann had no memory of hearing a single word about her father's infidelity. If her parents had ever argued about it, their discussion took place behind closed doors, well away from her presence. "They weren't display-type people," she pointed out. "Whatever they fought about was in private." But she must have heard something, or at any rate sensed something, that allowed her to recognize Alex Tyng the second she saw her. And if the recognition was instantaneous, so was the forgetting: the shock of the insight was evidently so great that her only alternative was to block it out until she was ready to retrieve and consider it.

What she did not discover until many years later was that her mother, too, was involved in a long-term love affair at the time. Lou's indiscretions were to become widely known, in part because of the children they produced, but Esther's remained completely hidden. In the end she told only her daughter and two other young relatives. The motive behind these eventual revelations was a kind of generosity, Sue felt. "It was 'This is how people manage their lives.' I think she was trying to sort of gently tell me that things are not black and white, that life takes paths that are not so, uh, 'normal.'"

Though Esther's straying from the marriage may have helped her cope with Lou's affairs, it did not seem to be a matter of *quid pro quo*. She had first met the man in question when they were both graduate students at Penn. Early on in their acquaintance, this colleague and his wife came to a party at Esther's house—a party at which, typically, Lou played the piano—and the wife was already conscious of feeling jealous about Esther. Her husband clearly thought this young psychology graduate student was exotic and brilliant and attractive. ("And I don't know that my father thought of her like that," Sue Ann pointed out. "She was his rock, but . . .") The man himself, who was tall and blond and not Jewish, was everything that Lou was not. He soon joined the Penn faculty as a full-fledged research scientist—something else that Esther, not to mention her parents, would have found admirably different from Lou's slow, often thwarted career path. By the 1950s at the latest, but probably starting much earlier, he and Esther were meeting for serious romantic trysts. They were discreet, but they were not always in hiding: in 1953 or 1954, for instance, he went so far as to drive Esther up to Sue Ann's summer camp. "I think Dad is seeing another woman," the man's daughter remembered hearing from one of her brothers, and they soon became aware that their mother, too, knew about the relationship. But the wife didn't, or couldn't, prevent it, and the affair persisted well into the late 1960s, when Esther's lover became too ill to continue with it. When he died she stayed home from the funeral, feeling it would not be appropriate for her to go, since his wife clearly knew about them by then.

Lou was actually acquainted with this man. As fellow Penn faculty members, they had lunch together occasionally, and Lou even attended the daughter's wedding. But the general consensus was that he knew nothing about the affair, was indeed "so engrossed in his own world that he probably never even thought about it," as Sue Ann put it. So Esther's affair was not revenge, it would seem, but self-assertion. "She had a very strong sense of herself," her daughter observed, "despite how she circumscribed her life. My mother treasured and supported Lou, but she had her own thing." And she was careful—unlike Lou—never to risk another pregnancy. Sue Ann's had been a difficult birth, a breech birth, and Esther also got the sense that Lou was not keen to have more children. The fact that she had a lover simply gave her an additional reason to take precautions.

All this, though, lay under the surface of family life, unspoken and in some cases unperceived. Lou apparently never knew about Esther's hidden love life, and while Esther knew about Anne Tyng—perhaps even knew about Marie Kuo—she did not discuss her knowledge or make it public in any way. So it was not out of character for their daughter, Sue Ann, to push away the sudden insight about her little sister. A certain willed obliviousness had become an ingrained habit in the Kahn family. It may even have been what allowed them to move forward.

Still, there were occasional moments when true suffering managed to pierce the emotional armor. In August of 1958, Lou got word from California that his mother was dying. Bertha Kahn was eighty-six at the time, and had been afflicted with type 2 diabetes for at least ten or fifteen years. Toward the end, she was confined to bed with a gangrenous toe. "I saw the toe," said Ona Russell, one of Bertha's great-granddaughters, recalling the too-vivid memory with a shudder, "because my dad and my uncle, who were doctors, had no awareness of how that would affect me. I remember her suffering, but still with a smile when she saw me."

Ona's uncle, Alan Kahn, had been watching over Bertha assiduously for the last few weeks of her life. When she finally died, in the middle of the night on August 20, he was sitting by her bedside. Leopold was downstairs in the living room, still awake, and Alan went down to tell him. "I came down and I looked at him, and he said in German, '*Mama ist gestörben*,'" Alan recalled. Leopold's English was completely fluent by then, but when he needed to acknowledge this terrible fact—*Mother is dead*—it was the old language he had spoken with Bertha throughout their lives together that came unbidden to his mouth.

The family had already notified Lou that the end was near, and he had caught the first available flight out of Philadelphia, but he arrived too late. He reached the house after Bertha died, but not long after. "He came in, and he came upstairs where she was lying," said Alan. "And I remember it because it was the only time I ever saw him cry."

Bertha Kahn was buried at the Home of Peace Cemetery in East Los Angeles, the same Jewish cemetery in which her son Oscar already lay. Lou attended the funeral and then he flew home, where he didn't say much about the death. But a few months later, in December of 1958, he remarked in response to an interviewer's question about his mother, "She was a compelling woman, a forgiving and adapting person but not gushy. She was idealistic, kind, understanding, humorous." Readily confessing that he identified more with his mother than with his father, he mentioned that his relationship with her had been "wonderful, inspiring, but not directly and/or continually close. It was warm but not with great personal intensity." During his childhood, if she had to correct him, she did it gently and reasonably: "Father whipped. Mother was understanding, with verbal teaching." And toward his father, too, she showed great forbearance and love. "He was volatile," Lou pointed out, and "felt the pressure of being a poor provider," but "he could be very jolly and happy, especially with mother." In reaction to one of the interviewer's rote questions—*Was your mother well satisfied with your father's earning power and position in life?*—Lou answered, "No, but she did not denigrate my father. She was noble." ("Subject looks back to her with awe and idealization," the interviewer noted parenthetically.)

Lou was answering these questions as part of a large-scale psychological investigation into creativity, conducted by the Institute of Personality Assessment and Research at the University of California at Berkeley. The man behind the study was a research psychologist named Donald W. MacKinnon, who had settled on architects (along with writers, mathematicians, and scientists) as a particularly fruitful creative species. To obtain his pool of respondents, he asked five architects associated with UC Berkeley—William Wurster, Vernon DeMars, Joe Esherick, Don Olson, and Philip Thiel—to nominate forty-five or fifty architects each. Though Louis Kahn had thus far built little of note beyond the Yale Art Gallery, the Trenton Bath House, and a few private houses, he was nominated by all five architects on the panel. Others in this prestigious category included Marcel Breuer, Walter Gropius, Ludwig Mies van der Rohe, Frank Lloyd Wright—all of whom declined to participate in the study—and Philip Johnson, Richard Neutra, and Eero Saarinen, who, like Lou, accepted.

MacKinnon worked his way down the list, starting with the fives and then progressing in order to the fours (Paul Rudolph was in this category), the threes (who included I. M. Pei, José Luis Sert, and Charles Eames), the twos (Buckminster Fuller), and finally the ones (Oscar Stonorov, G. Holmes Perkins). In the end the psychologist arrived at forty participants—all, by the way, men—who were subdivided into four groups for purposes of testing and conversation. Kahn's group, which also included Pietro Belluschi, I. M. Pei, and Richard Neutra, was brought to Berkeley on December 12–14, 1958.

By the time Donald MacKinnon got around to publishing his results, the whole process had become so diffuse, not to mention so unscientific by modern research standards, that there was little he could really say about creativity. Some interest, however, still attaches to his composite biography of the creative individual, which has striking affinities with Lou's own life story. This generic creative person was apparently an introvert who, early in life, had developed a sensitive awareness of his own thoughts, symbolic processes, and imaginative experiences. This inward-turning development would have been caused by childhood unhappiness or loneliness, possibly due to sickness or else to natural shyness; and this child would also have had special skills of a creative nature, which were encouraged by at least one parent or some other adult. MacKinnon also posited a child who would have been free to make his own decisions and thrive independently, largely because of a healthy absence of smothering closeness to his parents. Finally, and perhaps most remarkably, the researcher deduced that this person would have moved frequently as a child, "often from abroad to this country," and that he was, moreover, someone who felt unusually able to postpone the steps in his professional development until *he* was ready, without regard to outside pressures. One might almost call this a textbook version of Louis Kahn.

But whereas textbooks, like creativity studies, aim to iron out the differences between individuals, the raw material often tells another story, and it is here, in the interviews and exercises, that Lou's personality actually emerges. He dealt for the most part with an interviewer named Joseph Speisman, a man who went on to have a substantial career in research psychology himself, though he was only in his early thirties when he interviewed Kahn. From the "character sketch" he was obliged to compile, it would seem that Speisman was well-disposed toward his subject. "He was warm, serious and quite intense and absorbed in the task—he was not at all dependent on the examiner but was quite alert to subtleties and nuances of questioning procedure," Speisman noted. The interviewer also expressed a certain degree of admiration for Kahn's "great clarity and fluency," as well as his ability to order his memories chronologically while at the same time making connective leaps across time. In a checklist he filled out after the interview, Speisman reported that Kahn "seemed to enjoy being interviewed," "made considerable use of his hands in talking," and had both a "quick tempo of movement" and "an alert, 'open' face."

Overall, the character sketch seemed accurate in its main conclusion: that Louis Kahn's outstanding quality was "an intense dedication to his work," such that "sense of tradition and antecedents, historical perspective and even intellectual drive and curiosity are sublimated through and filtered through what he refers to as his 'artistic creativity.' This does not mean that he is in any sense withdrawn; on the contrary it appears to be an extreme in focussing and in utilizing his work as an integrating frame of reference—albeit a broad frame." Speisman was also insightful in regard to how that work was accomplished. "He is extremely active; nonetheless, he likes to broadcast his ideas even when not fully thought through in order to get feedback," the psychologist correctly observed. But he was taken in, or at least misled to a degree, by Lou's self-effacing manner, for Speisman decided "he is not really personally secure enough to repudiate anything with directness or completely . . . despite his abilities and talents he is not a man of great confidence nor certainty about himself." (Perhaps it is in the nature of such studies to contradict themselves, but this conclusion sits oddly with the one expressed in a separate "rating sheet," where Speisman ranked Kahn average-to-high for most of the listed cognitive and intellectual traits, but practically off the charts—with a 9, the highest score—on "*Sense of destiny*: Has clear notion of life goals, and unquestioned confidence in his eventual attainment of them.") Finally, Speisman theorized,

"He leaves the impression that he does not live and experience directly enough but rather everything is filtered through his 'art,' his work, and even this is further covered by a 'mysticism.'"

The so-called mysticism is perhaps traceable to Kahn's answers in response to a series of routine questions about his practice of architecture. *When did you feel you had arrived as an architect?* "8 years ago," Lou responded (which would make it December of 1950, when he was at the Rome Academy). "I felt secure," he continued. "I realized a sense of order and design." And then, three questions later: *Do you feel that you have any exceptional or unusual talents in architecture?* "Yes," said Lou. "A sense of order from which design flows. I am unique in this!" Later still: *How would you define creative achievement in architecture?* "A sense of order and position, a relationship to existing life," he repeats. And again: *Do you consider yourself to be a creative architect?* "Yes." *If yes, in what ways?* "Order! out of which stems true design and structure." One can sense a certain impatience in that exclamation point, a concern that he is not really being understood. The interviewer seems not to realize that Kahn means something quite specific by "order," not just as a guiding principle in his own work but as a critique of how architecture is generally practiced by others. Kahn explicitly set out to capture the essential spirit (of a place, or a function, or a need, or a desire) and allowed *that* to dictate the design. Perhaps this was mystical, as Speisman insisted, but if so, it was also very practical.

And if Speisman inaccurately characterized Lou as insecure, or felt he was unable to live and experience things directly, Lou himself was partly to blame, for he omitted as much as he conveyed. He readily confessed to his own shyness, tracing it back to his childhood accident: "I suffered severe burning. My scarred face and hands contributed to my shyness." He also presented himself as a dreamy, imaginative boy, full of daydreams about knights and other fairy-tale characters. He was forthcoming, when asked, about his early sexual experiences, saying that he had learned about sex at "13 or 14. I experienced an emission while alone," and confessing to the interviewer that he didn't have actual sex until after college, when that unnamed woman who owned the hotel in England seduced him during his 1928 tour. But he did not mention—perhaps because Speisman did not ask—anything about the role of sex in his later life.

In regard to Lou's current family life, the record is apparently incomplete, because Speisman took only fragmentary notes when they were talking about the subject, so that he had to reconstruct Lou's answers from memory much later. "As far as the questions about his family," the interviewer wrote in an apologetic cover letter to the researcher, "I simply did not place enough confidence in my memory to write in what did occur to me, but if it is any help to you this is what I remember: One wife, two children (boy and girl). Wife devoted to his career, supportive—warmth, etc. Wife a musician? Relationship with all three excellent—contributes to his sense of security and provides him with a feeling for the 'continuity' of human existence." This imaginary musician wife may have stemmed from a mix-up between Esther, who enjoyed concerts but was not a musician, and Lou's mother, daughter, or brother, all of whom were. ("My brother was musical, had extreme talent, but no interest in school," Lou had mentioned during the interview, in one of his rare allusions to Oscar.) As for the boy and the girl: if Kahn told the interviewer he had two children, one named Alex and the other named Sue Ann, Speisman might well have deduced that the former was male, the latter female. But because the interview results are so haphazardly reported, one cannot conclude that Lou said anything at all about his second family—especially given the fact that, on the Personal Data Blank he filled in himself, he indicated that he had only one child.

The official test results are, for the most part, even more inconclusive. The Rorschachs were done in a nonstandard way and are therefore uninterpretable; the Minnesota Multiphasic Personality Inventory and the Architect Q-Sort Deck are unreadable without a key; the Strong Vocational Interest Test is just plain useless; the Metaphors tests and the Study of Values test, while intriguingly titled, yield only numerical responses; and so on. Still, there are a few moments in this three-day battery where something important seems to emerge from the overall static.

In a test called Semantic Differential, for instance, Kahn was asked to rank various subjects—Architecture, Science, Art, Creativity, Success, and Myself—on a spectrum of descriptive words that ranged from one extreme to another. For the most part the evaluations came out pretty much as expected. Architecture, for instance, was absolutely "permanent," "strong," "deep," "stable," "safe," "pleasant," and "good." Lou defined Success as utterly practical, masculine, and active, but also characterized it as completely difficult, unstable, and complex. Yet there were some surprises too, especially on the page that referred to Myself. Whereas every other category—including Architecture, even including Creativity—got the most "public" rating possible, Lou located himself far over on the other side of the spectrum, toward "private." He also put himself one step away from fully masculine (though this was not necessarily a negative in his eyes: Creativity, Art, and Science were all centered midway between masculine and feminine). On the beautiful to ugly spectrum, he placed himself exactly in the middle.

This is all mildly illuminating. But by far the most interesting results, from a personal point of view, came in the Thematic Apperception Test, where Kahn was asked to make up verbal descriptions for five rather complicated visual images. The first of these pictures shows an older woman in profile, looking out a window, while a younger man stands behind her; both are unsmiling. "The son has just told his mother about his plan to leave the household," Lou responds. "Constant disagreements with his father are the cause of his decision. The Mother's looking out in space as though reflecting times gone by when care-free happiness was all every one knew. He remembers these days too, but is bitter though unhappy determined."

In reaction to an image of a young woman with dark hair next to a wrinkled old woman in a cowl or hood, he says, "It was so obvious, the same face years ago. To think that so fresh and inviting a figure would one day be but just interesting, no longer desired. I knew her mother when she was the image of her."

A semi-abstract, semi–Social Realist stairway, with a doll-like figure climbing upward near its base, yields the description, "The massive structure brutally made with the least sensitivity was before her every day as she climbed the stair of endless treads to her work. She was so young. Some day she thought I will own this dump and install an elevator. But how can anyone penetrate this mass. Not even dynamite is able."

Another picture shows a masculine figure in coat and hat standing alone in noirishly lit obscurity. Lou's response is: "Waiting in hopes she would pass again. Though he knew it would not happen still he counted off seconds, minutes playing the game of love and circumstance—a fairy tale of existance, unreal though still real because he was alive and capable of such a turn of mind." Unlike the other descriptions, this account abruptly changes its viewpoint in the last sentence: "There I was watching him suggestively shaped by the light in a drooped pose of resignation."

And then there is an image composed merely of shapes and voids, so abstract that it reads equally well vertically and horizontally. About this indeterminate chaos Kahn says: "This is the best way I can express my dream. All the movement made by the wind and the waves seemed to form themselves into clanging spirits undulating and inter mingling. Nothing was I knew things to be, still, I knew that they are part of existence. A dream, a manifestation of order is real though only to the single being. The wind became the flame the flame became water."

In the face of such material, interpretation seems utterly beside the point. These little stories are the thing itself: the Avernus leading directly down into the cauldron of personality. In contrast to the cool placidity of the rest of the test results, these TAT descriptions are white-hot with a man's living presence. You are there with him, at least for the moment, inside his wishes and dreams and fears and regrets; and you are also standing outside him, just as he occasionally stands outside himself: "There I was watching him . . ."

■

This romantic fellow—the Louis Kahn who presumed that a man waiting alone on a street must be waiting for a beloved woman to pass by—was evidently the one who showed up for a Christmas party at Wharton Esherick's house later that month. For it was there, in December of 1958, that Kahn first met an attractive young woman named Harriet Pattison.

Harriet, who came from Chicago, was the seventh and last child born to William and Bonnie Pattison. Her ancestors on her mother's side, the Abbotts, had arrived on the shores of New England in the seventeenth or eighteenth century, and Bonnie Abbott Pattison, who graduated from Wellesley in 1906, was a member of the Daughters of the American Revolution. After settling in Illinois, the Pattisons produced five daughters and two sons, one of whom—Abbott Lawrence Pattison—was already an established artist by the time his little sister Harriet reached high school. Abbott's massive, WPA-style *Kneeling Woman* won the Art Institute's prestigious Logan Medal for the Arts in 1942, and in the subsequent decades his semi-abstract, semi-figurative sculptures in bronze, steel, and marble could be found all over Chicago.

Harriet herself, after attending a progressive school called Francis Parker, went briefly to Wellesley and then to the University of Chicago, from which she graduated in 1951. After that she enrolled at the Yale Drama School to study set design, though she ended up transferring to the acting program. Along the way, she also took a course in color theory with Josef Albers. Leaving Yale without an advanced degree, she traveled to Europe and lived for a while in Scotland, where she spent a semester in the graduate philosophy department at the University of Edinburgh. By the late 1950s she had decided to concentrate on the piano, which she played extremely well, and she had come to Philadelphia in order to study with a teacher named Edith Braun.

When they met in December of 1958, Pattison had just turned thirty and Kahn was nearly fifty-eight. Harriet had come to the Christmas party with Robert Venturi, a young architect who, like Kahn, taught at Penn. Lou had great respect for Venturi ("Bob Venturi knows more about architecture than all of us combined," he told a colleague many years later), and Venturi's personal life had already overlapped with Kahn's in curious ways. For instance, during Venturi's Rome Academy fellowship—which coincided with Anne Tyng's stay in Rome—he had driven Anne and Alex to the American Episcopal Church in Florence for the baby's baptism, had stood up as her godfather, and had then loaned Anne the money to pay for their passage back to America. Now he had brought Harriet Pattison as his date to Esherick's party, and though she left with Venturi that night and continued to see him for a while, she and Lou had instantly become smitten with each other. Lou soon began visiting her in secret, and though he referred to her in public as "Bob Venturi's girlfriend," he thought of her as very much his own.

This was made abundantly clear in a letter he wrote to Harriet from Europe in September of 1959, less than nine months after they first met. "Dearest·Best My Wonderful Sweetheart," the letter began. "How your image and all that I feel gives radiance that is ever with me. Once it appeared unbelievably real. The wife of Aldo Van Eyck, a Holland architect of unusual ability, reminded me right away of you—with cut of her beautiful face and graceful body. But above all I felt you in me by the loving closeness to her husband and her artful way of sharing her faith in him."

Kahn had been invited to the Netherlands to give a talk at the Congrès International d'Architecture Moderne meeting in Otterlo, and as he said in the letter to Harriet, "After my talk at the conference it was expressed as the presence of a new beginning. Harriet it was a good moment." But the trip was even more important for other reasons, because during his two-week stay in Europe Lou also went south to France to see two key works of Le Corbusier's: the Ronchamp Chapel he had so loved when he first saw its photo five years earlier, and the monastery at La Tourette. He found Ronchamp to be "a great great work"—the letter to Harriet included a quick sketch of it—but perhaps even more telling in terms of his own career was his exposure to La Tourette. "The building is a coming together of spaces boldly and even violently meeting each other with its own light quality," he said in another letter to Pattison. "I felt all humility before this masterpiece of Corbusier's. I kept telling the monk who guided me thru of my reactions—the meaning profound in the nakedness of every form. The joyous courage that comes from realization in art and that only a religious man could act with such fearless invention for the sheer need rather than the desire for creation."

Le Corbusier's varied and striking use of light in this monastery was to have a profound influence on the work Kahn designed from that point onward—not just in explicitly religious buildings like the Rochester church and the mosque at Dhaka, but also in the other light-filled structures he proceeded to create, including the Exeter Library, the Kimbell Museum, the Yale Center for British Art, and the Indian Institute of Management, among others. What's more, Kahn seemed to comprehend almost instantaneously the impact Corbu's work would ultimately have on his own. "All the time I talked to him," he said of his conversation with the monk, "I was thinking of course if my own realizations are testing against what I saw. I felt nothing but humility and strength and a powerful will to continue more than ever . . . an artist never sets out to solve a problem for which there is a known solution and a known appearance (or feeling). He draws from the circumstances and need the essence of new clusters of affinities, which he models into a new image."

When Kahn returned to Philadelphia from this European trip, it was not only his architectural life that had changed its direction. Personally, too, things were realigning themselves. He was still committed to maintaining his domestic life with Esther (for even as he was writing extensively to Harriet from France, he was also sending postcards to 5243 Chester Avenue, including one in which he entertained his wife with a small bout of conspiratorially tongue-in-cheek French pretentiousness: "Tout le monde, Tout La France est beaux et sympathique. Carcassone—c'est l'architecture tres importante"). And he was still working closely with Marie Kuo at the office, sharing his most important projects with her. But the relationship with Anne Tyng had taken on a new form. After nearly fifteen years of being his lover, Tyng had announced to him that though their work together would of course continue, their sexual life was over. "I suggested to Lou that our relationship should become platonic because I realized he was involved with someone else" was how she discreetly put it—though in fact, by 1959, she had been forced to confront not just one but two rivals. The affair with Marie was painful for her, but it seems to have been the passionate connection Lou felt with Harriet that finally persuaded Anne to end things between them.

"When I was about five, my parents separated, but I wasn't told of the separation," Alex Tyng recalled as an adult. "I suppose that, since they weren't married, they (even my mother) didn't think it was necessary." But still, Alex noticed that something had changed, because her father didn't come around as much. The little girl went through what she later remembered as "a period of not seeing Lou as often—probably between the ages of five and seven. By the time I was eight I saw him regularly again."

Up to that point, Alex would have called hers a happy childhood. Her mother was reliable and supportive, and her father was a steady if intermittent presence. "I remember him drawing with me, bringing me blank books to draw in and colored pencils," she said. "When he visited, which seemed often, he would be there when I went to sleep and be gone when I woke up. A couple of times I woke up and saw him leaving my mother's room in the middle of the night." The drawings she did at that time reflected her confidence in this setup. There was one she called "Family," for instance, executed at age three, which showed three enthusiastic stick figures—a mother and daughter in triangular skirts, a foregrounded father in pants—all smiling widely, their arms raised in joyful triumph. The colors were as bright and cheerful as the people being depicted.

But when her parents separated, her drawings began to alter. She became obsessed with scary things—witches, ghosts, pirates, and especially haunted houses, which she drew frequently from the age of six onward. "Sometimes I drew houses in perspective and sometimes I drew what I called 'cut-throughs,' showing the rooms inside," Alex noted. In one such cut-through, the Victorian-style structure's irregular rooms and multiple stories were peopled with ghosts and skeletons, all drawn in a blood-red line of paint. Another drawing, entirely in pencil, showed two identical houses from the outside. A few lines of childish printing at the top of the page explained that "once upon a time there was a haunted house and a unhaunted house they looked alike only [one] was haunted and the other wasn't." Alex also composed an illustrated story called "House of Secrets" at around this time. "I think I became aware that there were things I didn't know and couldn't find out," she observed many years later, and one result was that, from the age of seven or eight, she found herself seeking out and reading books "in which kids solved puzzles created by adults to cover up the truth."

"If you could go into the Land of Oz every day or a reality show, I'd go into the Land of Oz," said Richard Saul Wurman, attempting to explain why the men who worked with Kahn couldn't have cared less about the complications in his personal life. "The reality show is not of interest. This was a place, for most of us, that never was before and never would be again." They knew—or most of them knew—that Lou's private life was "odd," but what they really cared about was "When is he going to get back to the office? We all wanted a piece of Lou's time."

According to Wurman, the atmosphere surrounding Kahn's work and ideas was electric. "The passion to be an architect then was palpable. It was a special time to be alive. You knew that then. It was like being in Paris and knowing Picasso. So you're in the midst of a historical moment and you know it disappears. So yeah, you felt special. It was a special moment."

In his first experiences at the office, Richard Wurman, as Kahn's student, had been set to work on occasional charrettes—those brief, intense, all-hands-on-deck periods when a model or a plan was being prepared. (The word itself came from the nineteenth-century French term for the kind of cart—a "chariot," as it were—that was sent around in the École de Beaux-Arts to pick up the just-completed models from the hardworking architecture students when their projects were due.) Later, a couple of years after he graduated, Wurman was invited to come work for the office full-time.

"My working for him started when he called on a Christmas Day— he didn't even know it was Christmas—and said, 'Ricky, can you come into the office?' And I said, 'Lou, it's Christmas,' and he said, 'Well, can you come in tomorrow?'"

(Lou's Christmases were in fact something of a mystery. Wurman placed him at the office, as did other employees over the years. But his family, including nieces and nephews as well as his daughter Sue Ann, remembered him dominating the celebrations held at 5243 Chester. "I remember Lou mostly from those Christmases," said his nephew-by-marriage Edward Abelson. "Lou seemed to do most of the talking at the Christmas dinners: I remember him telling stories about the people he had met and the places he had been." Sandra Abelson, Lou and Esther's niece, fondly recalled that "when he brought Christmas gifts for Esther and Sue, he always had one for me too." But she also noted that "sometimes on Christmas Day he'd leave the house for a while, saying he was going to the office. Once I must have shown how sad I was, because he assured me he'd be back as quickly as I could say, 'Jack Robinson.' I said it repeatedly that afternoon and thought it worked eventually, because he was back in time for dinner." Yet even as his family consistently mentioned his presence at Christmas dinner, other people remembered his being with them instead. "He spent more than one Christmas with us, and not with his family," insisted his colleague Jack MacAllister. It al-

most seemed that there were two or three Louis Kahns, enough to satisfy everybody—or, as Wurman was later to put it, "Everyone had a
different Lou.")

Soon after Richard Wurman showed up for work in January of 1961,
Kahn sent him off to England to discuss the development of a Thames
barge for the American Wind Symphony Orchestra. What the twenty-
four-year-old architect didn't realize until he got to London was that
the working drawings (which did not yet exist) were supposed to arrive
there with him. Having packed for a week, Wurman stayed for six
months, finishing the job himself. "I had no funding, I had no money to
live from day to day, and Lou wouldn't take my calls. It was trial by
fire," he commented. Swearing to himself that he would never work
for Kahn again, Wurman stopped off at the Philadelphia office briefly
on his return to pick up his final paycheck. Lou, who had been out,
came in and said, "Oh, Ricky, what are you working on?" and immediately put him to work on another project. "His innocence was disarming," Wurman observed. "It was the 'emperor has no clothes' innocence.
That's seductive. He was incredibly seductive because he meant so much
to us."

And they, as a group of needed colleagues and associates, apparently
meant a great deal to him, too. "He wanted to do good work. Doing
good work and finding realizations of patterns had to do with hearing
himself talk. So we were all sounding boards," Wurman pointed out.
Or, as Sue Ann put it, "He ran the office like an atelier. He had this idea
of competing ideas, letting other people come up with various things, and
then he would choose."

Among the odder sounding boards Kahn attracted into his atelier
was a fellow named Gabor, variously described as a philosopher-genius,
a crazy Hungarian, a crackpot, and a young architecture student
(though completely without drawing skills) who had walked all the way
from Ohio to learn at Kahn's feet. Gabor did have a last name—it was
Szalontay—but nobody ever used it; he was simply Gabor. He showed
up sometime in 1960 or early 1961, at the age of about twenty-two, and
he stayed forever.

His function, it seemed, was to listen to Lou talk and occasionally
to make enigmatic responses. Sue Ann, who by this time was an undergraduate at Penn, would sometimes drop by her father's office at nine or

ten at night and would find just the two of them, Lou and Gabor, having a conversation. "Everyone remarked on this strange relationship. He would talk to Gabor for hours," said Sue. "It was very fruitful to keep explaining himself." At the end of each session Lou would hand Gabor a twenty-dollar bill; sometimes he even put in a time sheet for him. "Gabor earned his twenty bucks by listening raptly. I don't think he debated him, but maybe he did," Sue Ann added.

Even years later, when Lou had become much busier and much more famous, Gabor remained a notable presence. Gary Moye, who studied with Kahn in the late 1960s and then went to work in his firm, recalled first noticing Gabor in Lou's master's class studio. "Early in my first semester he appeared nattily dressed in a dark suit and bow tie and sat among the students as Lou addressed the class," said Moye. "Lou was talking about light and when he paused Gabor asked, 'What if the light were blue?' Lou took the question in stride and began a new stream of speculation. I remember thinking at the time—Wait! What the hell?"

Gabor, despite the absence of any obvious means of support, never seemed down and out. On the contrary, he was always neatly attired in a variety of outfits. Many people assumed he had a series of women willing to take care of him. "My classmates and I would sometimes observe him in the cafeteria picking up girls," noted Moye. "He seemed to be quite successful at it." Later, when Gary was employed by Lou, he happened to be at the office working one weekend when the telephone rang and he answered it. "A young woman asked for Gabor," Gary recalled. "When I explained that I knew him but he actually didn't work there, she responded by saying, 'You must be mistaken, as he is Mr. Kahn's personal assistant.'"

Moye also remembered one other tale that exemplified, for him, the weird philosopher's role in Lou's life. "One of the stories that became legend in the office," he observed, "was about Gabor being assigned to work on a project charrette." The project coordinator set Gabor up at a board and gave him a drawing to work on, but when he returned some hours later, hopeful that the task might have been completed, he found Gabor contemplatively staring at a still-blank piece of paper. The angry coordinator, faced with a looming deadline and burdened with this unhelpful assistant, "stormed off to confront Lou with the problem," said Moye. "As the story goes, Lou responded by saying, 'I pay the rent, I pay the electricity, I pay the water, I pay the gas, and I pay Gabor.'"

Lou himself explicitly acknowledged Gabor's importance to him in a talk he gave before a group of Rice University students in 1964. "About a month ago, I was working late in my office, as is my custom," Kahn began, "and a man working with me said, 'I would like to ask you a question which has been on my mind for a long while: How would you describe this epoch?' This man is a Hungarian, who came to this country when the Russians entered Hungary"—in other words, in 1956, about four years before Gabor first showed up in Lou's office.

Kahn told the students that in response to this question he sat absolutely still thinking for at least ten minutes, "and finally I said to Gabor, 'What is the shadow of white light?'" (The non sequitur was apparently a conversational strategy they shared equally.) "Gabor," Lou continued, "has a habit of repeating what you say. 'White light . . . white light . . . I don't know.' And I said, 'Black. Don't be afraid, because white light does not exist, nor does black shadow exist!'" Lou went on to bring up the possible colors of light, and from there he moved to the writing of fairy tales, and thence to the various qualities of words—all of which set him thinking about three untitled talks he was about to give at Princeton. "After that night of discussion with Gabor, I knew the titles," Kahn announced triumphantly, adding, "How rewarding it is to have a person who is concerned about everything, not just little things." From Lou's account of this largely one-sided "discussion," one might conclude that the titles emerged from Kahn's comments alone rather than from any words of Gabor's, but that, for Lou, seemed to be the point: the membrane between his thoughts and Gabor's was so permeable as to make attribution impossible.

"Gabor was bizarre," Richard Wurman acknowledged, "but Lou would get something out of talking to him." And however much he may have irritated the younger architects who came to work in Kahn's practice—one of Lou's final group of employees, a woman named Reyhan Larimer, became so exasperated with Gabor that she once took off her shoe and threw it at him—he was clearly there to stay.

The period of Gabor's first appearance at the office, when the late 1950s were shifting into the early 1960s, was a particularly important time for Lou. On the basis of his rising reputation, a number of new architectural commissions were coming into the firm, and among the most significant of these were two Philadelphia assignments, the Richards Medical Building and the Mikveh Israel synagogue. One was to elevate Kahn's reputation, promoting him to the acknowledged first rank of modernist architects; the other was to prove one of the most frustrating disappointments of his career.

The Alfred Newton Richards Medical Research Building at the University of Pennsylvania came to Kahn's firm largely through the good offices of G. Holmes Perkins, the dean of Penn's design school. The commission was awarded in early 1957, and construction on the laboratory towers had already begun by the very next year, at which point the project was extended to include a set of similar towers for a biology building next door. Though Kahn had worked on other hospital and medical buildings in the Philadelphia area, this was the tallest, as well as the first to use precast concrete. As a design project, the Richards Building practically trumpeted Modernism, with its large glass windows blending uninterruptedly into flush concrete and brick walls on the multistory structures housing the scientists' labs and studies. Yet there was also something faintly archaic and monumental-feeling in the looming, windowless brick towers that held the exhaust stacks, the stairwells, and other "servant" functions. It was the first Kahn project to articulate so clearly what he had listed, in response to the 1958 Berkeley questionnaires, as one of his primary architectural innovations: "The distinction in the planning of spaces between the 'spaces which serve' and 'the spaces served.'"

In that same series of interviews, Kahn had been asked, "Do you feel that you are lacking any particular skill or subject competence for the practice of architecture?" and had answered, "Engineering and mechanical skills, although this is a minor lack."

Nick Gianopulos, who was one of the many engineers Lou employed in the course of his career, pretty much agreed with this self-assessment. "Yes," he said, when asked if Kahn indeed lacked these skills. "But he recognized competency and talent in others, because he had a very strong intuitive nature. Lou had this knack of being able to intuitively grasp an idea and translate it into something structural. And he was so well grounded in the classics and classic architecture. He knew how huge stones came together. Well, in a sense precast concrete is huge stones coming together."

Perhaps it was Lou's intuition that allowed him to understand, from the moment he first worked with August Komendant on the Richards Building, how useful this brilliant engineer would be to him. Komendant and Kahn had originally met in the mid-1950s, when Gus, as he was called, appeared in Lou's office to make a case for his company as a subcontractor on the Trenton Jewish Community Center. That project never reached completion. But in 1957 Lou briefly consulted Gus about a design he was entering (unsuccessfully, as it turned out) in the Enrico Fermi Memorial competition. Later that year Kahn brought his students to the concrete factory in Lakewood, New Jersey, where Komendant worked as a consulting engineer, and the two men had an even better chance to take each other's measure. Like Kahn, Komendant had been born in Estonia; unlike Kahn, he had spent his youth and early manhood in Germany, where he trained and began working as an engineer. After the war he was hired by General Patton to redesign bridges and develop other concrete work in Europe. Now, in the 1950s, he ran his own American consulting practice that specialized in pre-stressed and post-tensioned concrete.

Kahn had already formed close connections with a number of engineers before Komendant, and at least one of these men, the Paris-born Robert Le Ricolais, became a lifelong friend and Penn colleague, someone with whom Kahn frequently taught seminars. Le Ricolais was something of a visionary himself; among other things, he had helped develop the whole idea of space-frames (though since he and Kahn didn't meet until 1953, the ceiling for the Yale Art Gallery probably came to Tyng and Kahn indirectly rather than directly from Le Ricolais). He was a poet as well as an artist, and in the semesters when they were both teaching, Lou enjoyed meeting Le Ricolais outside of school time, often for weekly drinks at Le Ricolais's Philadelphia apartment. But partly because they shared what others might have viewed as a certain degree of high-flown idealism, Robert Le Ricolais could not fill the down-to-earth function in Lou's work life that came to be occupied by the scientifically knowledgeable August Komendant.

When Kahn decided to include Komendant as the consulting engineer on the Richards Building, he had already hired Keast & Hood as the official structural engineers. So Nick Gianopulos and Gus Komendant inevitably found themselves working together, on this and later projects. "We had this love-hate affair for years," Nick said of Gus. "He always got the best of the deal. He's a born winner." But irritated as he may have been by the man's character, Gianopulos had to acknowledge Komendant's remarkable level of engineering skill. "I had no doubts about his talents," he affirmed. "His motivations were something else. But he was a superb mathematician, and he could use mathematics creatively in a structural sense." He was, Nick felt, "an excellent engineer." And if Komendant was difficult, Kahn seemed able to handle those difficulties. "A lot of people never used him a second time," Gianopulos observed. "Lou did, because Lou could cope with him."

With Gus Komendant at his side, and with Fred Dubin, a mechanical engineer, assisting with the actual ducts and wires and pipes, Kahn was able to build in a new way at Richards, using massive pieces of precast concrete that could be lifted into place by cranes and assembled with unusual speed. The structure's strong yet flexible Vierendeel trusses, which allowed Kahn to eliminate diagonal supports, also gave him greater freedom in the design of the tower floors, and this in turn meant that the architect could indulge in uses of space—making each lab floor essentially continuous, for instance, with eight precast columns dividing the space into cantilevered squares, and no corner columns interrupting the windows—that might otherwise have been impossible. Kahn had used Vierendeels before, in his short-lived AFL Medical Services building (built in Philadelphia in the mid-1950s, it was to be demolished in 1973), but it took Komendant's expertise to show him how these beams could be deployed most effectively in the creation of large open spaces.

Ultimately, there proved to be some practical problems with the Richards design: the wide-open labs made privacy difficult, and the glassed-in corner offices had a tendency to grow too hot in the direct sun. But this did not interfere with the passionate adoration that the Richards Medical Research Building inspired in the architectural community at large. In the summer of 1961, just a year after its completion, the building was honored with a solo show at the Museum of Modern Art in New York—the first time MoMA had ever allocated a whole architectural exhibit to a single structure.

Yet even as he was embarking on this notorious success, Kahn was already setting the pattern for the kinds of failures (perhaps they are better labeled "incompletions") that would also define his career. Of the seven other projects that his firm undertook in 1957, the year of the Richards commission, only two were ever built: a small private house for Fred and Elaine Clever, most of which was actually designed by Anne Tyng, and some limited alteration and remodeling on the Biology Services Building at Penn. All five other projects—including houses for two different families (one in Pennsylvania, the other in Oklahoma), a private school campus in Chestnut Hill, a Thermofax sales office on North Broad Street in Philadelphia, and a remodel of the American Federation of Labor Medical Center on the same street—came to nothing in the end. All architects suffer through unbuilt projects, but Lou appeared to be coping with more than the average number, and their proportion was not to diminish as his career progressed.

One of the saddest examples of the hauntingly unbuilt, at least in his own eyes, was the Mikveh Israel synagogue, which he worked on for eleven years before finally being told the congregation didn't want his plans. That disappointment still lay far in the future, though. In 1961, when Kahn was awarded the synagogue commission, it seemed yet another sign of his growing success, a hometown victory to match the national honor of the MoMA show.

"Awarded," however, was perhaps not the right word to describe the decision-making that led to Kahn's selection. Mikveh Israel, the oldest Jewish congregation in Philadelphia (and, by their own reckoning, the oldest continuously operating synagogue in the United States), had not conducted any kind of competition or formal selection process in choosing the architect for their new building. Instead, a couple of powerful board members—namely, Dr. Bernard Alpers, Esther's longtime employer and Lou's friend, and Dr. Lillian Alpers, his wife—had put forth Kahn's name, and Kahn's name alone. The Alperses were attempting to make up for what they perceived as the slight to Louis Kahn perpetrated by the City of Philadelphia, which had built so little of his work; they were also trying to secure for their synagogue the services of an architect whose accomplishments they knew and admired. Yet even though they were able to get a majority of the board to vote for Kahn in May of 1961—at which point he began feverishly working on the design—resentments continued to simmer under the surface. The vote was not unanimous, with two trustees voting against giving out the contract: one because he felt it was too early in the process, the other because he objected to the absence of choice. There was also some concern that an architect who belonged to the Mikveh Israel congregation, Alfred Bendiner, would feel offended at not getting the commission himself (as indeed he did).

Part of the problem, both then and later, may have had to do with Lou's insufficient Jewishness. He did his best to learn about the guiding principles of Orthodox Judaism and the specific Sephardic tradition that this congregation derived from. But he could not conceal from the Mikveh Israel members his own lack of religious education. "Kaddish/kiddush," he noted at the side of one of his architectural drawings, as if to help himself remember the difference between the prayer in memory of the dead and the traditional blessing over the weekly ceremonial meal. He kept referring to the sanctuary as a church and the sukkah as a chapel—blatantly Christian terms which, though they fed into Kahn's ecumenical idea that all religions were essentially one, would have offended the ears of his clients. Kahn also had his own firm convictions about the nature of a religious building, and they included a distinct separation between secular and sacred spaces. This was something the congregation, on its limited budget, felt it couldn't afford, and one of the final battles took place over the architect's refusal to put the gift shop under the same roof as the sanctuary. At least in conversations with his own staff, Kahn cited as part of his reasoning Christ's insistence on keeping the money changers out of the temple. For the Mikveh Israel worshippers, this New Testament quotation (if they ever learned about it) would have been the last straw.

All these conflicts still lay in the future, though, and in May and June of 1961 Kahn threw himself fervently into the newly won commission. His initial design, with light filtering delicately into an enclosed chamber through pierced outer walls, was clearly inspired by Ronchamp and La Tourette, the Corbusier religious buildings he had seen two years earlier. Had these plans for Mikveh Israel reached completion, the building would have been far more memorable in every way than the rigorously vertical Richards Building, with its unmodulated, relatively unsubtle lighting effects. And yet, even as he began work on the synagogue, it was the Richards Building for which he was being celebrated.

The MoMA exhibit honoring the Alfred Newton Richards Building opened on June 6, 1961, and the private viewing and celebratory cocktail party were held the night before. It was a grand occasion: the show's curator, Wilder Green, had praised the structure as "probably the single most consequential building constructed in the United States since the war," and the mood on the part of Kahn's colleagues, friends, and family was correspondingly high. The party itself was held in the Sculpture Garden, at the end of a warm, sunny day, with the daylight blending gradually into twilight as the cocktail hour wore on. More than a hundred people had been invited, and most of them came.

Leopold Kahn had traveled all the way from California for the event, and at the opening festivities he could be seen talking to Anne Tyng, whom he was meeting for the first time. "Why is a beautiful young woman like you not married?" he asked her. She teasingly responded, "I was waiting for you," and Leopold roared with laughter. Harriet Pattison, standing at some distance from the two of them, wondered what Anne had said to make him laugh so. Closer to the central cluster of dignitaries, Esther Kahn performed her role as official consort and also hovered protectively over Sue Ann, who had just graduated that morning from Penn, with both her parents present at the ceremony. (The University of Pennsylvania's president, Dr. Gaylord Harnwell, had also been invited to the MoMA opening, but he politely sent his regrets on the grounds that it fell on the same day as his university's Commencement, even as he also chimed in with praise for the honoree.)

The architectural celebrities in attendance included Philip Johnson, chair of MoMA's architecture committee, and Vincent Scully, who came down from Yale, accompanied by a number of Kahn's other former colleagues. Several practicing Philadelphia architects and Penn architecture professors also showed up. A few of Lou's newer, younger staff were present, including Dave Rothstein, who had done most of the work on the architectural model displayed in the show. But it was mainly the older guard from Kahn's office that was represented here, proudly gathered together on this noteworthy occasion to celebrate their late-blooming and now widely revered employer.

Yet even at the time, Louis Kahn knew that the Richards Building was not his definitive achievement, nor even a true indicator of the direction he was to take. "If the world discovered me after I designed the Richards tower building," he told an interviewer many years later, "I discovered myself after designing that little concrete-block bath house in Trenton." In this judgment he was to prove singularly correct. It was the Trenton Bath House, begun three years before the Richards Building, that more accurately forecast the remarkable buildings of his later years. Something about that modest yet precise structure, it turned out, was capable of giving its users the same kinds of pleasures that would be generated by his masterpieces: a sense of being safely enclosed while at the same time gaining access to the world outside; a delight in the various forms of natural illumination, which changed according to the time of day; a tactile appreciation of sturdy materials like unpainted wood and rough concrete; and a feeling of grandeur even in the most quotidian of circumstances.

Picture a girl from nearby Trenton—an adolescent, say, just a year or two younger than Kahn's oldest daughter—who might have come to the Bath House for a swim shortly after it opened to the public. After passing by the front wall's mural and reaching the central courtyard, she goes left to get into the women's changing room. Slipping through one of the twisty, doorless concrete entrances that lead in from either side, she finds herself released into the surprisingly grand space of the room itself, all the larger in comparison to the tunnel-like approach. Above her, the high arch of the pyramidal wooden roof guides her eye upward to the square hole from which light pours down, making everything, even her own body, seem to bask in the ceiling's glory. At one side of the room, a five-foot space between the roof and the wall—one of Kahn's earliest and largest "light joints"—allows the sun to shine directly on her shoulders as she sits on the changing-room bench. Looking around, she notices how lightly the massive pyramid rests on its four corner supports, so that the ceiling almost seems to float above her head. Even the construction materials, the coarse wood and the undisguised concrete blocks, take on a kind of rough sublimity from their placement in this setting, as if to suggest that humble things could have their own form of elegance. As the girl sits in the light and watches it alter over time, with clouds passing over the sun and the sun itself slowly shifting position, she might well take this message about transcendence to apply directly to herself.

The Trenton Bath House was a building that Louis Kahn could not have designed without Anne Tyng—not only because specific aspects of the final plan were her idea, but also because the structure's rigorous, symmetrical geometries borrowed something of her essential sensibility. And yet it was also, ironically, his first step away from her. In its use of complementary heaviness and lightness, on the one hand, and contrasting darkness and light, on the other, the little Trenton building crucially signaled the path he was destined to take. It was a path influenced not just by his close collaborator Tyng, and not just by the more distant figure of Le Corbusier, but also by his Brutalist and Bauhaus colleagues at Yale and his Beaux-Arts instructors at Penn. Perhaps, above all, it was a path marked out for him by the ancient Roman architects to whom he had been introduced by the archaeologist Frank Brown. If the Trenton Bath House was not exactly the Pantheon, it was nonetheless Kahn's first real step in that direction.

IN SITU:
PHILLIPS EXETER LIBRARY

Interior of Phillips Exeter Library with circular cutout
(Photograph by Bradford Herzog © Phillips Exeter Academy)

It doesn't look like anything else on the campus. A squarish structure about eighty feet high, it is noticeably taller than any of the three-story, brick-and-marble neocolonial buildings that populate the rest of this New England prep school. It sits alone on its own patch of grassy ground, set well back from Front Street, the main city road that divides the campus in half. At night, its lit-up windows beam invitingly from every floor, guiding you toward it along the paths that cut diagonally across the grass. In the daytime, especially when viewed from a distance, it manages to look somewhat forbidding, and also to seem both modern and ancient at once. Its cube-like bulk, consisting mainly of framing brick around rows and columns of rectangular windowpanes, signals its twentieth-century origins, but the glassless openings in the arcades at the top and bottom levels suggest something much older. Standing on the other side of Front Street and viewing the roofline from afar, with patches of sky peeking through the gaps between the narrow brick columns, you might almost imagine you were looking at a Roman ruin.

And that sense of an older architecture is reinforced as you approach, for around all four sides at the ground level runs a gallery of the sort one might find in a medieval monastery. This arcade is protected from the elements by a heavy brick overhang, but it opens to the air on the outer sides, its rows of shadowy doorways recessed between the brick supports. A fierce symmetry guides the design: each opening in the arcade is at the base of a column of windows that rises directly above it, and only the tiniest differences distinguish the four sides of the building from each other. One of these differences involves point of access, for although you can circumnavigate the entire building from within the covered brick gallery, you can only enter the library through two of its four chamfered edges—that is, the two corners that are closest to Front Street.

Anyone can just walk in. There are no guards checking bags at the door, no librarians manning desks on the ground-floor level. You find yourself wondering how secure this is. "Will my coat be okay if I leave it here for three hours?" you ask the small group of Exeter students standing near the coatracks just inside the door. "You could leave your iPhone here for three hours and it would be okay," one of them answers. They have no doubts at all. They feel utterly safe and protected in this place.

The ground floor is apparently meant for pleasure reading. Peering through the glass doors that lead from the entrance hall to a carpeted area further in, you can see freestanding magazine racks, comfortable chairs, wooden tables meant for small-group gatherings, and natural light flooding in through large windows. But you have no desire to explore this lower region now, because an immense, alluring, semicircular staircase is drawing you up to the next level. On both sides of its curving, symmetrical arms, the wide travertine steps and handsome, solid balustrades beckon you upward toward the castle-like notches that mark either side of the landing; and as you approach this landing, you sense that something colossal and surprising awaits you there. It is the classic Kahn seduction: the somewhat opaque exterior, the elusive front door, the low-ceilinged entryway, and then the sudden arousal and fulfillment of one's previously unknown desire. Desire, not necessity, is the motivating force. "Need is so many bananas. Need is a ham sandwich," Kahn once remarked. "But desire is insatiable and you can never know what it is."

Elsewhere in Kahn's buildings, at the Rochester Unitarian Church, say, or the Yale Center for British Art, you need only move forward through an opening or a doorway to receive your gratification. But here, at this place for youthful learning, you must actively take control of the discovery by climbing up one side or the other of this inviting staircase (and even that—the choice of which of the two curved arms you ascend—is a decision you must make on your own). The staircase itself becomes part of your education, part of your experience. "Because it is not just a matter of being wide enough to go *up*, you see," Kahn said about stairs in another context, "but to be *assertive* enough to realize that to go up is *one of the events of the building*. It's an event of the building, and you know how much of one. It plays on your mind as being important and welcomes you as you rise on the stairway."

What greets you when you reach the top of the Exeter staircase is one of the grandest and most appealing spaces Kahn ever built. Grandeur here is not just a function of size (though the library's atrium, which reaches to the very top of the building, does feel satisfyingly huge); it is more a matter of proportions, materials, and above all natural light. As you stand in the center of the atrium, you are aware of the vast space above you, extending up the light-filled, concrete-and-wood room to a ceiling that is high above your head. Coffered in a tic-tac-toe pattern of nine large squares, the concrete ceiling rests atop a series of glassed-in clerestory windows that fill all four sides. Directly beneath them a cross, also made of concrete, extends diagonally over your head, meeting the wall at a wide strip of elegantly incised wood paneling. You can tell by looking at this joint that the concrete X is massive—at least one full story in height, if not more—but from down on the floor of the atrium it appears to float delicately overhead, letting through the sunlight from above as if it were a two-dimensional tracery.

Below the cross, on each of the four walls, is a gigantic circular cutout through which you can see at least three floors of stacks and reading rooms, each level marked by a beautifully paneled half-height wooden wall that is actually the back of a waist-high bookshelf. These edge-defining bookshelves come more fully into view as you mount to each level of the library and look across at them, or down on them from above. The perspective alters constantly as you move up or down through the four-story space; it alters even when you stand still and raise or lower your glance. But that is a discovery you only make as you climb higher and begin to perceive the library's full complexity—its structural variations on each level, its discrete sections and rooms and corridors hidden on every floor, its mysterious and sometimes vertiginous views. From the floor of the central atrium, the overall shape of the place seems graspable, finite. And this sense of security, this realization that everything joins up at the center, allowing you to locate yourself visually, persists through all the surprising, sometimes unnerving discoveries that the building yields up as you explore it.

The design is often described by architects and architecture critics as if it were a simple series of concentric rings, with a central area containing the full-height atrium, a middle section (largely protected from the direct sun) which houses the stacks, and an outer ring in which the carrels and reading rooms are bathed in natural light from the exterior windows. This is true enough as far as it goes, but it doesn't begin to convey the complicated feel of the space. For someone actually moving through the library, it is not easy to distinguish among the three rings. The division is blurred, for instance, by the narrower mezzanine levels that hang, balcony-like, above each full floor, containing their own rows of carrels set well back from the library's exterior wall. Sunlight reaches both sets of carrels, inner and outer, through the big rectangular windows that pierce the library's brick skin on all sides; it reaches the center of the building not only through the high clerestory windows, but also through two large side windows on the atrium level; it even reaches the ground-floor reading room through floor-to-ceiling windows that face out toward the arcade on multiple sides.

The effect of this pervasive natural light, in combination with each floor's orientation toward the inner atrium, is to create a sense of unity throughout the building, without any kind of artificial divisions among functional rings or bands. At the same time, the local design on every floor is different. The fourth and highest floor has seminar rooms off corridors on two adjoining sides of the square, and sumptuous reading rooms with sharply slanted ceilings on the other two. The third floor has a sitting area with a triple-sided fireplace on one side only, with the usual stacks-and-carrels arrangement on the other three sides. There is a staff room on one side of the lowest mezzanine level and a row of offices on the adjoining side, but there is no third or fourth side on that level: on those "empty" sides, the staircase simply offers a view of the atrium through an interior window, rather than access to any space.

Confusion is the least of the terrors this building is capable of producing. If you go up to the highest floor, you will find four small windows opening mysteriously out of an internal corridor, with each pair overlooking a corner at which the massive concrete X joins the wall. These windows have no glass—they are open to the atrium—and if you stick your head through them, you will see a vertigo-inducing slice of the atrium floor, cut off at a severe angle by the heavy block of concrete, which seems to hang in the air in front of you. You are only four stories up, but they are tall stories, and something about the abbreviated view combined with the open window frame makes the ground feel slippery beneath your feet. Even more likely to send a chill through you is the unimpeded Escher-like view from the top of the "back" staircase all the way down to the bottom. And for those hardy souls with no fear of heights, there is the top-floor arcade, which runs all around the building. Here the square, open window spaces sit above head-high brick walls pierced by five-inch-wide vertical slits—slits of the sort that medieval knights might have shot arrows through—and these wide cracks run all the way down to the brick paving of the terrace floor. If you were so inclined, you could easily stick a limb through one of the slits; alternatively, you could, with some effort, climb to the top of the relatively low brick wall. Perhaps it was some such inclination on the part of past Exeter students that resulted in the decision to keep the doors leading out to the arcade permanently locked.

A strong feeling of security combined with the thrill of fear: how many modern structures manage to engender them both? And these are not the only contradictions embodied in the Exeter Library. The sense of symmetry is overwhelming, but the use of asymmetry is equally important in the design. You can easily lose yourself in this building, and yet you can always find out where you are by orienting yourself toward the atrium. The materials—Kahn's usual concrete and wood—may be mundane, but the finish on them is beautiful, and the way they fit together supremely elegant. Opposition plays with complementarity, as the enormous circular cutout nestles within its square, the triangles of oak paneling set themselves off next to the polyhedrons of concrete, and the grand curve of the highly visible travertine staircase contrasts with the sharper-edged, more functional design of the enclosed, steel-railed, slate-paved corner stairs. The whole building is like a puzzle that asks you to fit its odd pieces together, whether these are the angular shapes of wood and concrete meeting at a shadow joint, or the over-arching and mysterious mismatch between interior and exterior views.

There is always something new to be discovered here: that is the main thing this library appears to be saying.

Some of the discoveries, though important, may remain at the unconscious level. For instance, a great deal of the pleasure one gains from that central atrium has to do with the perfect proportions of the space. The relation of the length of each side of the square floor to the room's overall height turns out to be exactly 1:1.618, the ratio known as the "golden section" or the "golden mean" in Greek mathematics. The same pleasing ratio governs the relationship between the diameter of the massive circular cutouts and the height of the rectangular planes in which they are embedded. Outside, the building manifests a similar obsession with precise measurement, for as the stories rise, the brick columns framing the windows narrow by exactly one brick's width at each successive level, and the windows widen accordingly. None of this is instantly visible to the casual or even the serious glance, and yet it all has an effect: one feels the grace of the design intuitively even if one can't measure it. At Exeter, geometry has truly triumphed in Kahn's work, as Anne Tyng always hoped it would, but it has done so in part by effacing itself—or rather, by merging its hard, abstract shapes into the softer lineaments of human wishes, desires, and fears.

That Louis Kahn could so beautifully fulfill this particular commission was never a given. Even at its last and most highly developed stage, his architectural career had its failures, and one of them sits immediately behind and beside the library building. If the Exeter Library is one of Kahn's finest constructions, the Exeter Dining Hall—designed and built at exactly the same time—is surely one of his worst.

The students call it the Crematorium, after the towering brick chimneys that surround it on all sides. Like the library, the dining hall has an exterior composed mainly of brick and glass, and it too is a distinctly modern building, but all similarity ends there. Though substantial windows light either side of the bifurcated dining room, the overall atmosphere is one of gloom and oppression. A noticeably slanted ceiling rises to a high peak in the center, but the space nonetheless seems squashed and horizontal, as if something heavy were bearing down overhead. The acoustics are so noisy that one can barely hear oneself, much less one's dining companions, and the traffic patterns from entrance to food lines to tables to tray returns are so nonsensical and confused that people are always banging into each other. It is a deeply unpleasant environment, and no one chooses to spend more time there than necessary.

Various theories have been offered as to why the dining hall is so inferior to the library. One line is that Louis Kahn left the design and construction almost entirely in the hands of his novice project architect, a recent addition to his firm. Another is that during this period he was extremely busy with the "Second Capital" in Dacca, East Pakistan, a massive project begun in 1963, and so had little time left over to focus on anything else. But neither of these explains why the library, which was supervised by the same project architect during the same busy period, turned out splendidly. The responsibilities for the dining hall's insufficiencies cannot be sloughed off so easily, for although Kahn routinely delegated many tasks to his employees, he prided himself on being a one-man firm, and no plans left his office without his approval.

The fact is, Lou did not care much about food. Cooking was a necessity in his eyes, not a source of intense delight or serious pleasure, and as a result he never gave a great deal of thought to it. He may have enjoyed his meals as much as the next man, but he was singularly incurious about how they were produced. You can see this in the kitchens he designed for his private houses, which for the most part are cramped quarters tucked away from the primary social activity. (Even the notable exceptions prove the rule: the charming kitchen at Esherick House was designed by the client's artist uncle, Wharton Esherick, and *not* by Kahn; and the lovely, glass-walled, brick-floored kitchen-dining area at Korman House was the result of emphatic instructions on the part of the clients.)

Louis Kahn did, however, love books, and he viscerally enjoyed being among them, whether in bookstores, libraries, grand palaces, ancient monasteries, or his own office. "He loved used bookstores," said Jack MacAllister, recalling Lou's trips to La Jolla when they were working on the Salk Institute together. "He insisted on being taken to a used bookstore in San Diego, sometimes even missing meetings to go there. He'd buy a book and tell you he'd read it. Actually, he'd open it in the middle and read one page and say, 'This is what the book's about.'"

Lou's own take on his reading habits confirmed this story. "I like English history, I have volumes of it," he said, "but I never read anything but the first volume, and even at that, only the first three or four chapters. And of course my only real purpose is to read Volume Zero." Treasuring the origins of things meant that he necessarily had a somewhat ambivalent relationship to books, for in some ways he was always trying to get back to the point before anything was written down. When, as part of the Berkeley creativity study, he took a test called Consequences that asked him (among other things) to come up with multiple responses to the question "What would happen if all books were suddenly destroyed?" his answers were surprisingly upbeat: "We would look for fundamentals." "We would see things in wonder." "We would hear things for the first time." "The mind would improve." But he also acknowledged, mischievously: "We would start writing them all over again." Books, despite his ambivalences, were an essential part of his idea of human existence.

This meant that when he was asked to design a library, as opposed to a dining hall, he was able to dig down into his own character, his own way of occupying the world. "You plan a library as though no library ever existed," he said, and this search for beginnings is what ultimately allowed him to come up with something remarkable. First principles came before any specific design. "A man with a book goes to the light. A library begins that way," he remarked. After seeing the carrels in medieval monasteries, he also formulated such notions as "the carrel is the room within a room" and "the carrel is the niche which could be the beginning." Out of such observations grew the design for Exeter Library's glorious wooden carrels, those light-filled, comfortably private, semi-enclosed desks that ring the building on all four sides and on several levels. But the carrels were not the only parts of the library that needed natural light. "I see a library as a place where the librarian can lay out the books, open especially to selected pages to seduce the readers," he said. "There should be a place with great tables on which the librarian can put the books, and the readers should be able to take the books and go to the light." Hence the profuse and welcome sunlight flooding into the atrium, pouring into the top-floor reading rooms, and even shining into the ground-floor periodicals room. The whole of Exeter Library is meant to be a place where one can take a book and go to the light—where one can be seduced into reading for pleasure.

A great deal has altered, in the school itself and in the world beyond, since Louis Kahn finished the Exeter Library in 1972. Once a school for boys, Exeter has become coeducational. This has no doubt had many consequences, but on a practical level it has meant that half the library restrooms, the ones on alternating floors, had to be allocated to girls. Laptop computers and the Internet became a commonplace element in education, so the library needed to be wired for wireless, leaving a small visible extrusion—an odd gray disk attached to one of the atrium's pillars—in a place Kahn would have left bare. Card catalogues are, as everywhere, a thing of the past. Exeter has kept its lovely wooden catalogue cases (which, like virtually all the woodwork in the library, were designed by Kahn himself), but they are now merely a decorative element, a visual shield between the main part of the atrium and the new computer room. The library will never run out of stack space, not so much because of wise planning, but because fewer and fewer bound books are acquired for the stacks as more and more texts become electronic. And with the advent of recent technology, one no longer has to carry a book to the light to read it, for the screen itself is backlit.

None of this could have been foreseen by the architect, and yet the building he designed is as useful and important as it ever was. It is still a central feature of the Exeter campus, not just for the librarians who work there, but for the faculty and students and even townspeople who come there regularly. Concerts and public events are held in the atrium, and at such moments the library feels like one big room, with the sound reaching up to the highest levels. At various times of the day or evening, individual students can be found occupying whole tables in luxurious solitude in one of the special-collections rooms on the fourth floor, while other students lounge on sofas, quietly conferring, or study at their assigned carrels. Occasional oddities occur, such as a spontaneous performance amid the stacks by students in the dance program. A small-group sleepover once took place, supervised by the current head librarian, Gail Scanlon. "It was eerie," she said. "You heard different sounds at night. But it wasn't scary. It was comforting, because there's that middle ring where all the books are—it was kind of like arms around you."

Scanlon has her complaints about the physical plant. The heating and air-conditioning system is inadequate, so it is often too cold or too hot. Cracked pipes located deep within the walls sometimes leak a sewage smell. The windows don't open. Lightbulbs and vents on or near the high ceilings are almost impossible to reach. The fireplace in her office, though enticing, can't be lit without releasing smoke into other rooms. But the library, she feels, is nonetheless a remarkable place. "The space is beautiful. The light is gorgeous," she comments. She's also pleasantly surprised by the different *kinds* of spaces one finds here. "There's almost a sense of formality or seriousness as the floors increase," Scanlon remarks. "The ground level is the most vibrant floor: newspapers, plasma screen, events with food, exhibits." On the atrium floor—the floor containing her office—are the service desk, the card catalogues and computers, several comfortable chairs, a couple of marble benches with views out the front windows, a grand piano, and a large oval table perched on a Persian carpet. Then, "as you go up higher in the stacks, it's quieter, more about the work: individuals rather than groups. At the top floor, with the special collections, it's more a hushed space." And at every point one is not only aware of the specific nature of the interior space; there is also a constant sense of the outdoors. "The light changes. The fall is just gorgeous," Scanlon says. And in the winter, "when it starts to snow, you can hear people run to the windows. When there's a bad storm, it echoes upstairs. You are always aware of what's outside."

Gail Scanlon has been at Exeter for only a few years, but one of her fellow librarians, Drew Gatto, has been working there for over a decade, and his connection to the building and its architect feels unusually intimate. "I really think he had the students in mind, spiritually, when he designed the carrels," Gatto says. "Louis Kahn understood light like no other architect." He goes on to tell a little anecdote from his own experience: "I remember one time, late May or June, I was up on the third floor shelving books. The light was coming through the windows by the carrels. And all of a sudden I got this impression that I was being bathed in light; it seemed like there was a beam of light coming in and hitting me and nothing else. It was very"—he pauses for a long time, as if the feeling he recalls is impossible to describe properly—"pleasant."

Gatto has clearly thought a lot about the space in which he works. He talks about "finding beauty and symmetry in something utilitarian rather than artistic"—a notion that would have pleased the architect, who often disparaged "so-called beauty" and insisted that "No space is a space which does not show how it was made." Gatto comments on the heaviness of the building materials, and the way the light itself offsets them. He also points out how "those open circles soften the building, because predominantly it's a square building." In this too he seems in tune with the architect, who was fond of remarking that "the wall does not want an opening, it resents an opening. When you make an opening, it cries. When you make it really well, it feels all right."

The panopticon structure of the library, with all those well-made openings, is bound to emphasize the process of seeing and being seen, and Gatto imagines that new students might feel a bit intimidated as they ascend the grand travertine staircase. "It's impossible not to feel you're being watched when you come up those stairs," he points out. "All the knowledge looking back at you, the people watching you: it's imposing in the same way the school is imposing." Asked how he feels about those vertiginous open windows looking down into the atrium from the fourth floor, he says he finds the view exhilarating rather than scary. "I feel like I'm getting away with something," he comments, "because hardly anyone in the library can see me, but I can see them. I don't find it frightening, because there's so much concrete to protect my body."

In focusing on this, the placement of his own body in relation to all that concrete, Gatto has arrived at something central to Kahn's design. Logically, one should feel threatened by these massive structures— potentially crushed, or at any rate crushable. Instead, one feels elevated. It is almost as if the weight of the heavy materials exists not to bear down on you, but to lift you up. Drew Gatto describes it as an "overall feeling that the building is floating, on air or on a body of water, like a large cruise ship: like I'm suspended above the ground." And this, for him, goes hand in hand with another feeling, equally important in making the library such a satisfying place to work, or read, or simply sit and think: the sense one has "that the center of gravity is not below us, but above us. The building is flip-flopped, with the huge X, the foundation, above us, and the lightness below us." Is the lightness that is below us the opposite of weight, or is it the opposite of dark? In a building that somehow manages to blur the boundaries between sight and the other senses, there can be no firm answer to such a question.

ACHIEVING

"Dr. Salk to office, 1501 Walnut," said the sole entry in the office calendar for March 1, 1962. The address was underlined because it signaled a departure: this was the first appointment in the new office, to which the firm of Louis I. Kahn Architect was finally moving from its cramped quarters five blocks away. In the new location, at the corner of 15th and Walnut, Kahn and his employees were to occupy two floors instead of one; and because this solidly undemonstrative, pale-stone-clad building jutted a full story above its adjoining neighbor to the west, the top floor in particular was filled with natural light. That fifth floor was where Lou's own office would be, next to the long, high drafting room that was lit by tall windows on both sides.

His daughter Alex was just turning eight at the time of the move, but she distinctly remembered both offices. "He lived—slip of the tongue—he worked at 20th and Walnut when I was a little girl, on the second floor of a two-story building," she recalled. "He moved to 1501 Walnut from there." The new location, as it happened, was on one of the classiest blocks in downtown Philadelphia, with a fashionable men's clothing store located diagonally across the intersection and the brokerage house of Butcher & Singer directly opposite, its ticker tapes visible through large glass windows in front. But these trappings of affluence were not the kinds of things a child would notice.

"I remember the smell, which smelled like plasticine and pencils and paper," Alex said of her father's final premises. "A good smell, kind of sweet, like people were working. It wasn't elegant—just a big space.

His personal office was kind of small but it had nice big windows. It was a corner office. It was kind of spare. There was a table in light-colored wood and some bentwood chairs. He had a colored pencil sketch by an architect, Doshi—just a colored, lively sketch, maybe 24 by 30—taped up on the wall. And then he had books everywhere. He had a little mat in the corner where he would take naps. There were things sitting on windowsills and tops of shelves. They changed; probably if he traveled somewhere and people gave him things, he would put them on the windowsill."

But that process of accumulation was still to come. In March of 1962 Kahn had only just moved in, and he was using the new space mainly as a formal setting in which to greet his most important client. In fact, it was the steady income provided by the Salk project (along with contributing amounts from other jobs like the First Unitarian Church in Rochester, the Carborundum factory in Niagara Falls, the private houses built for Margaret Esherick and the Shapiros in the greater Philadelphia area, and the beginnings of the Fort Wayne and Bryn Mawr commissions) that had allowed Lou to acquire the larger office.

The recent improvement in his financial condition was clear from the tax return that Louis and Esther Kahn filed jointly that spring. The income from Kahn's architecture practice was listed as an astonishing $366,309—an enormous jump from the $66,757 he had reported four years earlier. More to the point, Lou's substantial 1961 income enabled him to show a profit for almost the first time in his career. Of the $28,445 the Kahns declared as their taxable income that year, a full $13,713, or nearly half, came from Lou's architecture firm. Considering that his practice had generated a loss throughout most of the previous two decades—a loss that was always offset against Esther's steady earnings as a medical technician and, more recently, Lou's as a professor of architecture, which together rarely totaled more than $13,000—this year marked a serious change in his ability to earn an income.

That the Salk Institute commission was profitable (and indeed would remain the only profitable project that Kahn ever undertook in his career) was hardly its major virtue in his eyes. Lou was notoriously careless about money matters. "There's a picture of a bad businessman," he once said about a photograph of himself that was hanging in the office, and though his employees felt he intended the comment as rueful self-mockery, it could also have contained an element of pride. What Jonas Salk was offering him was worth much more than dollars and cents. It was a chance to try out innovative ideas with a sympathetic and intelligent collaborator. It was an opportunity to build something that could be strangely, unexpectedly beautiful, and at the same time enduringly useful.

When the two men first met in 1959, Louis Kahn was just beginning to be recognized as an architect, while Jonas Salk was already a world-famous epidemiologist whose successful vaccine against polio had put him on the cover of *Time* magazine. Salk had recently decided he wanted to build his own biological research institute, and the City of San Diego had given him, free of charge, a stunning twenty-seven-acre site overlooking the Pacific Ocean. The buildings themselves would be paid for by the March of Dimes, Salk's supporters and allies in the fight against polio. With the site and the funding both assured, all that remained was for Salk to find the right architect for the job. Scientific colleagues who had heard Kahn speak about the Richards Building at a bicentennial event at Carnegie Mellon told Dr. Salk that perhaps this man could give him some useful advice about the architectural selection process. So in December of 1959 Jonas Salk came to Philadelphia to meet with this potential advisor and visit the Richards site.

He was not greatly impressed by the towering brick-clad building (which proved, when completed, to be the bane of those who had to work inside it), but Salk and Kahn hit it off personally. Both men came from Eastern European Jewish immigrant families, and Salk, like Kahn, had grown up in one of the poorer sections of a large East Coast city—in his case, New York. Yet this common background was not enough to explain the instant sympathy that arose between them. It may have had more to do with the fact that the two of them were at once intense realists and intense idealists. "I found being with him a very warm, stimulating experience," Salk said. "The kind of person he is— the poetic, mystical type—always warms my heart." From the very beginning, they found themselves able to treat each other as equals, despite the obvious gaps in age (Kahn was thirteen years older) and status (Salk was infinitely more famous and successful). "I have to say he exhibited as much respect for me as I have for him," Salk commented toward the end of their project together, "and because of this, the two of us were able to struggle through many difficulties."

Kahn's take on the relationship was, if anything, even warmer. "When you ask who has been my favorite client," he said toward the end of his life, "one name comes sharply to mind, and that is Dr. Jonas Salk. Dr. Salk listened closely to my speculations and was serious about how I would approach the building. He listened more carefully to me than I did to myself, and then he recorded these things in his mind. During the time for our study, he constantly reminded me of premises which were not being carried out. These premises, which he thought were important, were also the basis of his questioning in his own way of thinking. In that way he was just as much the designer of the project as myself."

Shortly after their initial meeting, the two men went to La Jolla together to visit the empty site—a second visit for Salk, the first for Kahn. That was in January of 1960. Somehow the status of "advisor" got converted, without any formal discussion, into the position of architect for the project, and by March of that year Kahn's office had produced a model that Dr. Salk could take around in his efforts to publicize the project. By November the City of San Diego had signed off on the plan, and Kahn's firm moved rapidly ahead with its work.

Sixteen months later, in March of 1962, the design had already gone through one major revision, shifting from a Richards-like complex of eight high-rise towers to a more site-suitable, lower-height scheme involving two-story laboratory blocks grouped around two garden courts. In addition to the labs, this scheme included the Village (a set of residential apartments for visiting scientists, located to the south of the main complex) and, to the north, a grand communal structure called the Meeting House. When Salk had first discussed his proposed institute with Kahn, he had mentioned that he wanted it to be a place to which Picasso could be invited: a place, in other words, where the best in art and science would mingle freely. The Meeting House was Kahn's response to that idea.

Working with the engineers August Komendant and Fred Dubin, his collaborators on the Richards Building, Kahn put together the "folded plate scheme" that replaced the initial towers. The name derived from the V-shaped hollow beams that were designed to carry ductwork and other services along the full length of each lab block— the point being that the fold, as in a creased piece of paper, would enable the beams to carry greater weight. It was a clever feat of engineering, and all of Kahn's associates on the project, whether architects or engineers, were extremely fond of the design. They proudly presented the scheme to Salk when he visited Philadelphia in January of 1962, and when he voiced certain criticisms, they made revisions that were shown to him in March. Things seemed all set to proceed toward construction.

And then the project shifted direction once again. On March 27, out in Southern California, Salk and Kahn met with potential contractors to select a construction team. Later that day, after the meetings were over, Dr. Salk strolled through the site on his own. "It was twilight," he recalled. "I tried to imagine how the buildings would look, and I must say, I suddenly became terribly unhappy." The following day, March 28, Kahn and Salk had an appointment scheduled in San Francisco to present the status of the project to its funders. "Well, I told Lou on the plane the next morning that I thought we had to start over again," Dr. Salk said, "because I really was not happy about the plans. And I sketched for him what I thought I didn't like, and also what I thought was needed." Salk's objections centered on the extreme narrowness of the two gardens—"not gardens at all, but two alleys," as he described them—and on the excessive width of the lab buildings.

Kahn, though he had invested more than a year of his firm's time in the folded plate scheme, felt the truth in Salk's criticism. As an architect he was always willing to change course, even on a nearly completed project, if he saw that something better could be done. It was one of the most characteristic aspects of his method, and it often proved frustrating for both employees and clients, though in this instance it served him well. "He was always very gracious in saying that this gave him an opportunity to build an even greater building," Jonas Salk would later remark. Lou worked quickly to come up with a new design, and it was the revised plan—with its mirroring rows of six-story labs standing behind rows of study towers, which in turn faced each other across the sole open space—that finally got approved for construction a few months later.

■

"When the folded plate went out, a lot of the kids lost interest," said Fred Langford, who at the time had only recently started working at Kahn's office. "But I was new and young and still interested. Then we got the Vierendeel truss."

Langford was referring to the new scheme's key engineering element, the long, flexible beams that August Komendant had adapted so as to make possible both the open-plan labs and the innovative full-height service floors between them. When Dr. Salk saw the plans for these Vierendeel-supported interstitial floors, he reportedly said he liked them because they reminded him of something he knew about from biology—that is, the mesodermal layer that separated the external skin from the tissues beneath it. Vierendeels had already served a significant function in the Richards project, but now Komendant lengthened and strengthened them for the Salk. "That was good for earthquakes," Langford pointed out, "because as Komendant said" (and here he adopted the engineer's distinctive German-Estonian accent), "*It vill r-r-roll back and fort' like a drunken sailor.*"

With construction ready to commence, Kahn sent two of his young employees out to La Jolla to keep a close eye on the project. Fred Langford was thirty-four at the time; Jack MacAllister was only twenty-eight. Jack had been with Lou part-time since 1955, full-time since 1956, and he was known as a problem-solver. "Jack is quick on his feet. He'll get us out of it," Lou would say when a crisis arose, particularly one involving money. Fred had just joined the firm in 1961, but something about him inspired Lou's confidence. Perhaps it was that he got along easily with people. Maybe it was because he was one of the few architects in the office who seemed fully on board with the new Salk design. It may also have had something to do with his commendable drafting skills, which definitely impressed Lou ("He would look at something I was drawing and say to the others, 'This man can draw!'" Langford grinned). In any case, Kahn decided to send him out to California before he had even worked a year in the Philadelphia office. "Fred, you get to go out there and be tough," Lou told him.

Knowing that Langford had worked in construction before becoming an architect, Kahn asked him, "Fred, what do you know about concrete?"

"Nothing," Fred answered.

"That makes two of us," said Lou.

Of course, as trained architects they already knew a great deal about this material, not least the distinction that always eludes laypeople: the difference between concrete and cement. Concrete, as Langford would later put it, "is everything: sand and stone and cement. Cement is the matrix, your powder. It starts with limestone. You grind it up, you heat it up in furnaces, until it becomes powder."

That cement powder, as he and Kahn soon came to realize, could vary considerably in color, which in turn would affect the color of the finished concrete. "Lou didn't like the first samples he was seeing from California—they were too blue, too green, not warm enough," said Langford. "One of our first assignments was to call up the cement plants and get them to ship us samples. We got them from, oh, ten or twelve places. And finally the one with the warmest tone—pinkish-like—it came from Santa Cruz. They were adding something, the pozzolanic ash, to get the color Lou loved." It would not have escaped Kahn's notice that a similar ingredient, a volcanic sand called *pozzuolana*, was what the Romans had used in constructing the Pantheon and the Colosseum.

Those who worked closely with Lou on this project were well aware of the connection between his love of ancient monuments and his feeling for concrete. "The permanence—he liked the idea of the old castles, the old Roman buildings, the Colosseum," commented Langford. In fact, Kahn seemed to be attracted to anything old and ruined. Once, when he was talking to Fred about the remnants of the old Spanish monasteries in California, he said, "There's a beauty in the fact that they're now in repose." It was an effect he actively sought out in his own work, and according to Jack MacAllister, concrete helped him to achieve it. "Lou loved ruins," said MacAllister, "and with concrete, the building *before* it's built is already a ruin, in a way." But Jack also felt that Lou's affection for concrete had a rational basis in his ideas about form and materials. "Lou loved concrete because it had substance," he observed. "Steel buildings have no substance because the structure disappears. With concrete, you can see the structure. And it's already architecture when it's unbuilt—without the finishing, without what comes on top—because you can see what it will look like."

For the concrete to end up looking the way Louis Kahn and Jonas Salk wanted it to look, many obstacles had to be overcome, and it was probably both men's perfectionism that resulted in the Salk Institute's special variety of architectural concrete. To begin with, they agreed that the concrete should be poured in place, since that would make it structurally more solid as well as visually more distinctive than anything precast could be.

"Precast is much easier—you can reject something before it goes in place. Pour in place requires much more skill," noted Langford. "Precast is like a Lego set as opposed to a monolith: the monolith is more difficult to construct, but stronger in the end. Lou favored poured in place." And part of his reason, Fred felt, was that the precast look was "more machine-like," whereas Lou always wanted his buildings to look constructed by human hands—even, or especially, when the material was as industrial-seeming as modern concrete.

The key to good poured-in-place concrete lies in the formwork, that containing plywood structure into which the fresh concrete is poured, and which must then be stripped off as the concrete begins to dry and cure. Fred Langford became obsessed with how to design the formwork so as to produce the effects Lou wanted. The decision to coat the plywood in polyurethane resin rather than oil had already been made before Fred arrived at the La Jolla site, and the resin coating was what gave the smooth, almost marble-like feel to the concrete. But precisely because of its delicacy, the concrete from resin-coated forms was more likely than the normal variety to show the "bleeds," those places where the cement granules had oozed out of the forms at the corners.

"Lou wanted a perfect corner. Most builders would put in a chamfer," said Fred, referring to the sliced-off diagonal corner often used to soften the edge of a building. "A chamfer could accept a little more bleeding. But that wasn't what Lou wanted. He liked the idea of the light and the shade being definite." Yet even as he insisted on the sharp ninety-degree edge, Kahn also made it clear that he didn't want any bleeding, because of its effect on the visual quality of the finished concrete: "It becomes a scar," Langford pointed out. So all through the sample panel work, Fred struggled to eliminate the bleeds, even going so far as to invent a new formwork design that made the wooden frame much more solid and airtight at the corners. He was also anxious to save money by conserving the plywood forms, which tended to break up as they were stripped off. "My goal was to satisfy Lou with the articulation of the surface, but get more reuse out of it," he said. In this, too, Fred ultimately proved successful—so successful, in fact, that he was able to patent the system of rubber blocks used to protect the forms.

Fred Langford's significant contribution to the Salk project did not go unnoticed. "He was very interested in doing perfect concrete," Jack MacAllister recalled. "So he worked on it and figured all that out: how to do the forms and the tie-holes so that they were rational, how to allow the reuse of forms, how to make the forms not leak. And the end result was the most perfect concrete the world has ever seen. When Lou saw that success, he got even more deeply into concrete, because he saw how perfect it could be. In his own way, Fred elevated Lou's vision of concrete."

Fred, on the other hand, always attributed the guiding vision to Lou: "The main thing on all his formwork was 'I want to show the hands that built the formwork.'" So even the tie-holes—those circular punctures marking the spots where the plywood forms had been tied together before the concrete was poured—were left visible and filled only with rust-preventing lead, not patched over with acrylic or concrete as they would have been in standard construction. And they were arranged symmetrically because, as Fred put it, "there was a logic to it." It was a logic that MacAllister, at least, saw as Langford's handiwork. Certainly the symmetrical tie-holes were already visible in the detailed working drawings Fred made for the site, which showed every little circle lined up in its proper place. (Even the holes on the sharply angled walls were exactly rendered—they were elliptical in shape, to account for the diagonal perspective.) It was a case of Fred's precise draftsmanship and Lou's relentless search for "articulation" lining up as perfectly as the tie-holes did.

"The fact that they are organized in a way that the pattern is rational, not random," said Jack MacAllister, was "an opportunity for design rather than just construction. Lou was leaving behind evidence of how things were made, including the flaws. He never wanted the concrete patched. I think that was directly related to his face."

No one who met Lou could fail to notice his scars, but for some they played a more important role than for others. "When I first saw him, at first I was shocked," confessed Fred Langford, "but in minutes you forgot about it because of his personality." That was how most of the people who worked with him felt, or said they felt.

But for Jack MacAllister, the flaws that marked Lou's face were an ever-present factor. "I think it was 'all about the scars," he said, referring to Lou's energy—sexual and otherwise—as well as his approach to architecture. "If you're that ugly, you try to look for beauty in some other way." MacAllister could never get over the ease with which this "ugly man," as he thought of him, attracted women. There were parties at Jack's Del Mar house, for instance, where "he would glom onto some younger woman or other and just press them to the wall—very attractive women, too. And some of them fell for it," marveled Jack. "He mesmerized people, especially in California, where there were a limited number of people with three-digit IQs."

Kahn's love life was not necessarily a subject of office chatter, but those who worked regularly for him in 1962 could hardly have remained ignorant of his serious, long-term affairs. Anne Tyng was still working at Louis Kahn's practice in the early 1960s, and so was Marie Kuo. There were evident tensions between the two women, just as there were tensions between Lou and Anne over Marie. And by the time of the move to 1501 Walnut, Kahn had already become deeply involved with Harriet Pattison. Some of the architects at Kahn's office may have been aware of the fact that these three major affairs had overlapped in time, but most probably were not. "I think he was serially monogamous," said David Slovic, who worked for Lou in the mid-1960s. "He wasn't, like, juggling mistresses that I know about. It wasn't discussed; it was just accommodated. It's not like people thought it was normal. They wouldn't have expected to have such a life themselves."

His colleagues may not always have known about each stage in his relationships, but people around him nonetheless became aware, sooner or later, of his latest love interest. Sue Ann Kahn, for one, began to suspect that her father and Harriet were having an affair when Pattison made special efforts to befriend her in about 1961. Harriet had taken a job in the antiques department at Parke Bernet auction house in New

York, and Sue Ann was a recent Penn graduate who had just moved to the East Village. When Harriet relocated to Philadelphia a short time later, Sue felt her suspicions had been confirmed.

But now, in the spring of 1962, Lou and Harriet's relationship reached a kind of crisis point when Harriet found out she was pregnant. She told Lou, and the first thing he said was "Not again!" This was hardly encouraging. If he viewed her pregnancy as simply a rerun of the Anne Tyng situation, he would not necessarily feel obliged to get a divorce this time either. But Harriet was not ready to give up, and when she conveyed the news that she was going to have a baby to her rather patrician WASP family, her underlying implication was that she hoped soon to be married to the father. She did not, however, feel it was her obligation to inform anyone in Lou's circle. That would be up to Lou.

Late in the spring, Sue Ann got a call from her father saying he was going to be in New York consulting with Noguchi and would like to drop by and visit her afterward. (Kahn was collaborating with Isamu Noguchi on a very engaging playground design for the Upper West Side, which—like so many of his projects over the years—was doomed never to be built, in this case because it was *too* engaging: the neighbors feared it would bring in "outsiders," presumably of a darker, poorer kind.) Sue Ann had been trying to get Lou to visit her ever since she had moved into her first grown-up apartment the year before, and now he was coming at last. He told her he planned to be there at two o'clock, which would allow her to serve him tea, so when she got off the phone she rushed out to buy special tea things.

Lou didn't show up at two, but Sue knew he was often late, so she waited. Three o'clock came and went and still he wasn't there. As it got closer to four, Sue Ann called Louise, Lou's secretary, to find out what had happened. Had the meeting with Noguchi run over?

"There is no meeting with Noguchi," Louise told her. "He's coming to New York just to see you. He's on the train now."

When Lou finally arrived at about five, Sue Ann said, "How did the meeting with Noguchi go?" But if she thought Lou would confess his strange lie, she was disappointed; he just said, "Fine, fine." They barely had time for him to sit down for a few minutes and make a few critical comments about the apartment ("Why don't you get some antiques?" was the one that stuck in her mind) when he announced he had to go.

"I suggested we take a cab together uptown, since I had to go to my rehearsal," recalled Sue Ann, who at the time was just beginning her career as a professional musician. She would drop him at the train station, she said, and then go on from there. "We get to Penn Station, he opens the door, hands me a twenty-dollar bill—twenty dollars was a lot of money in those days—and he's standing outside the door and he says, 'Harriet's pregnant.' And I say, 'Oh, that's great, Daddy,' and the door closed and he was gone. I'm not even sure if he heard me."

Sue Ann never did figure out why Lou felt obliged to tell her this. Perhaps Harriet had pressured him to do so, or possibly he himself just wanted her to know about it. Maybe he expected her to transmit the information to her mother. Sue Ann certainly had no intention of doing *that*. But the subject came up anyway, when she was staying at her parents' house over the summer.

Esther and Lou were still living at 5243 Chester Avenue, though now the West Philadelphia neighborhood, once solidly middle-class, was starting to decline. The household continued to function much as it had during Sue's childhood, with Esther's mother, Annie, occupying a bedroom on the second floor, Lou and Esther on the top floor with their own sitting room and bedroom, and Sue Ann's bedroom sharing the rest of the third floor with the empty room that until recently had belonged to their longtime lodger, Aunt Katie, who had moved to an old-age home. Though Esther had at long last retired from her career as a medical technician and was home more often now, her elderly mother still did much of the cleaning, cooking, and laundering. (It was said that when Annie Israeli reached her eighties, the family had tried sending Lou's shirts out to a Chinese laundry for a while, but he didn't like the way they were done, so his indomitable mother-in-law went back to ironing them.)

On that summer day in 1962, Sue was downstairs in the kitchen drying silverware when she heard a knock on the door. She opened it to find a stranger standing on the porch. He said he wanted to speak with Esther Kahn.

"Who shall I say is calling?" asked Sue Ann.

"My name is Pattison," he said, and Sue thought: Uh-oh. She ran upstairs, told her mother that someone was at the door to see her, and then shut herself in her bedroom, wishing she could lock the door.

A short time later Esther came upstairs, flung open the bedroom door, and said, "And what do *you* know about this?" Without waiting for a reply, she went on, "It's not like the other one—" and then clapped her hand melodramatically over her mouth, because Sue Ann was not supposed to know about Lou and Anne's daughter, who had never been mentioned in her presence.

"It's okay, Mom, I know all about Alex," said Sue. ("It was kind of a relief to say I knew about it," she reflected later.) Her mother then told her that the man downstairs was Harriet's brother. He had come to ask Esther to give her husband a divorce so he could marry Harriet, who was pregnant with Lou's child. Esther firmly showed him the door.

One wonders how this played out in the privacy of the marital relationship. Did Esther ever discuss the encounter with Lou? Did she even mention that she knew about the other children—first Alex, and now this new one? "I'm sure they talked about it," Sue Ann remarked many years later. "In those days people didn't get divorced. They worked it out. They slept in the same double bed for forty-four years." She paused, reflecting on her mother's character. "She was a very capable person," she observed. "She supported him all her life."

■

That summer Kahn was more reliant on his wife's support than ever, for at the beginning of July he underwent eye surgery. Over the years his eyesight had been getting progressively worse. He remembered the blue-tinted spectacles his mother used to wear, and the way her handwriting had gone from sharp and clear in the early 1930s to loopily oversized in the letters she wrote him in the 1940s. For a while he must have worried that he too might slowly be going blind. But the doctors told him his problem was just cataracts, which they assured him were completely operable.

The surgery took place at the Wills Eye Hospital in Philadelphia, and in anticipation of it, Lou cleared his office schedule for several weeks. "Mrs. Kahn will be at home July 2–9," said the note scribbled at the top of the July calendar, the assumption being that she would field any questions and concerns from the office. "No calls" was written under July 3 and 4. Otherwise the calendar remained practically blank until late in the month, though there was a reminder on July 13 of a 9:30 a.m. meeting at Bryn Mawr, perhaps to be attended by someone other than Kahn. On Tuesday, July 24, things finally began to pick up again, with a 9:00 appointment at Esherick House and a lunch with a Korean visitor. By the following weekend Lou was back at work full tilt, meeting up with Jonas Salk in Maryland and Pittsburgh. But it would be months before his eyesight fully returned, and then only with the help of thick, heavy-framed glasses that made his eyes look enormous.

The two projects mentioned by name on the July calendar, Esherick House and Bryn Mawr, were among the more significant commissions taking place in the background while Kahn was working on the Salk Institute. They were significant, in part, because they actually resulted in finished buildings, unlike many of the other commissions his firm undertook in those years; and they were also both in the Philadelphia area, where remarkably little of his built work could be seen. That July, the Bryn Mawr dormitory design was still in its early phases, while the Esherick project was just winding down.

Of the nine private dwellings that Louis Kahn was to complete in the course of his working life, Esherick House may well have been the most appealing. He designed and built it for Margaret Esherick, a single woman in her early forties who ran a bookstore in Philadelphia and who had, until recently, been living with her aged parents. Margaret was the niece of the artist Wharton Esherick and the sister of the architect Joe Esherick, both of whom were friendly with Kahn. When Lou agreed in 1959 to design Margaret's new house, he also agreed to collaborate with Wharton on it—an arrangement that caused some tensions and delays, though the project ultimately survived them. In the end Kahn did most of the work himself, but Wharton Esherick retained sole responsibility for the singularly pleasant kitchen, where Gaudi-esque curving counters, a copper sink, and quirky knots in the wooden cabinetry prevailed over Lou's sterner aesthetic. Wharton also found and installed the huge, rough-hewn, slightly warped piece of wood that ran along the divide between the living room and the stairway—not a choice Kahn would have made, but one he was able to integrate and even enhance with his own surroundings.

Esherick House was designed as a small, two-story, one-bedroom residence set on a large, lushly wooded lot adjoining a park in Chestnut

Hill, one of Philadelphia's most fashionable suburbs. From the street, the building did not look particularly inviting. Flat-roofed, stucco-clad, and oddly fenestrated, with a narrow bronze-railed balcony sited directly over the half-hidden doorway, it radiated a sense of resistant modernism. Only when you stepped inside did the delicate beauty of the place begin to reveal itself.

To the right of a small entrance room and past the elegantly simple oak staircase lay a double-height living room that ran the full width of the house. In the daytime, light poured into this room from three sides, subtly altering with each hour that passed. The narrow, vertical front window that could be glimpsed from the sidewalk turned out to be a slit between built-in bookcases, topped by a larger horizontal window with which it formed a T shape. On the long side wall, a wider vertical window extended above the fireplace to the roofline, offering slivers of woodland view on either side of the concrete chimney—and because the chimney tower itself was located at least a foot away from the external wall, the changing daylight also fell entrancingly on that smooth concrete face, creating the sense of a living gray panel between the two living green ones. At the back of the room, which faced onto a private garden and the parkland beyond, the wall was almost entirely windows, cunningly placed within various-sized wooden coffers. The way these shuttered windows were set within their wood frames emphasized the comforting fifteen-inch depth of the embrasures, and the fact that you could open and close the windows, both front and back, meant that the long, high room could be cooled by breezes in the summer.

The upstairs possessed many virtues of its own, including an airy bedroom that was as deep and wide as the living room, with a low wall of charming built-in cabinets designed by Kahn; a luxurious master bathroom whose tub faced a nearby fireplace (this had been the client's special request); and a gallery from which the hostess and her guests could overlook the beautiful living room. But it was that ground-floor room, with its light-filled windows and soaring height, which marked this house as one of Kahn's first great successes. He had managed to express his unique vision in small parts of a building before—in the cylindrical concrete column containing the triangularly ascending staircase at the Yale Art Gallery, for instance, or in the open pyramids of the Trenton Bath House's wooden roofs, which seemed to rest with miraculous lightness on their corner supports. But Esherick House was perhaps the first complete building that exhibited his keen understanding of the pleasure a person could take from an enclosed space. Like the larger, grander masterpieces of his later years, this small house was capable of giving its inhabitant both a feeling of exuberant expansion and a sense of intimate protection. So Margaret Esherick must have thought, at any rate, for she insisted on moving into the house in October of 1961, before it was even done. As it happened, she spent only six months there: she died suddenly the next April. Work continued on the house, though, and Lou's meeting in July of 1962 was probably with the landscape designer, who had not yet finished the garden.

If Esherick House was one of his stellar achievements, Erdman Hall at Bryn Mawr—a much larger, more expensive project that allowed him to bulk up his employee rolls for years—was at best a partial failure. It was the last project he attempted to design in tandem with Anne Tyng, and perhaps the fraying of their personal relationship lay behind some of the problems. Tyng, with her usual penchant for precise geometry, wanted the bedrooms to be octagonal in shape, nestled together in a kind of molecular design around the circumference of the building. Kahn preferred a pattern of interlocking Ts and rectangles, with some rooms having a wide outside window and some only a narrow one. In Anne's design, the college girls' rooms would all have been equal; in Lou's, some were obviously more desirable than others. At each meeting with the Bryn Mawr administration from 1960 onward, Lou and Anne would come equipped with their competing schemes, which they would then present, argue for, and revise before the next meeting. The conflict was overt, and it didn't just affect the client. "There were two teams, the Anne Tyng team and the Lou Kahn team," Richard Wurman said about office life during that period. "It was horrible to be in the office then." Finally, sensing everyone's impatience and discomfort, Lou told Anne that the era of competing schemes was over: only one design would be presented at each Bryn Mawr meeting, and it would be his. From that day forth, she ceased to participate in the project at all.

To be honest, the finished structure had more wrong with it than just unequal bedrooms. Though the lobby included a gracious, naturally lit atrium punctuated with intriguing cutout shapes, the rest of the build-

Bertha Kahn as a young woman
(Anonymous photograph from the collection of
Sue Ann Kahn)

Leopold Kahn as a young man
(Anonymous photograph from the collection of
Sue Ann Kahn)

Louis and Sarah Kahn as small children in Estonia
(Anonymous photograph from the collection of Alexandra Tyng)

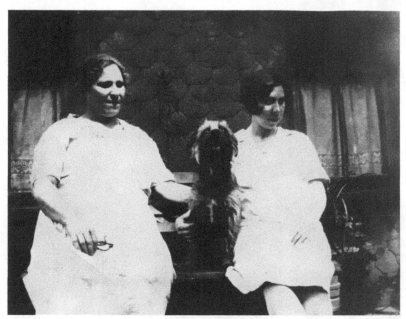

Bertha and Sarah Kahn in Philadelphia
(Anonymous photograph from the collection of Alexandra Tyng)

Oscar Kahn in his late twenties or early thirties
(Anonymous photograph from the collection of Rhoda Kantor)

Louis Kahn in his early thirties
(Anonymous photograph from the Esther Kahn Collection, The Architectural Archives, University of Pennsylvania)

Esther and Lou Kahn in Atlantic City,
1933
(Anonymous photograph from the collection of
Sue Ann Kahn)

Lou at Brookwood Labor College, 1936
(Anonymous photograph from the collection of
Sue Ann Kahn)

Self-Portrait with Pipe, 1928–29
(Drawing by Louis Kahn, from the collection of
Sue Ann Kahn)

Lou's portrait of Esther, 1931
(Drawing by Louis Kahn, from the collection of
Sue Ann Kahn)

Lou's portrait of Regina, 1930–34
(Drawing by Louis Kahn, from the Regina
Soopper Collection, The Architectural Ar-
chives, University of Pennsylvania)

Olivia with a Grape, 1939
(Painting by Louis Kahn, from the collection of
Olivia and Milton Abelson)

Lou, Esther, and Sue Ann Kahn
in Atlantic City, 1947
(Anonymous photograph from the
collection of Sue Ann Kahn)

Bertha, Lou,
Leopold, Esther, and
Sue Ann Kahn in
Los Angeles, 1948
(Anonymous photograph
from the collection of
Lauren Kahn)

Anne Tyng in 1944, age
twenty-four
(Photograph by Bachrach, from
the collection of Alexandra Tyng)

Alex and Anne Tyng, 1965
(Anonymous photograph from the
collection of Alexandra Tyng)

Louis Kahn in the Yale University Art Gallery
(Photograph by Lionel Freedman, from the Louis I. Kahn Collection, University of Pennsylvania and the Pennsylvania Historical and Museum Commission)

Marie Kuo in the 1950s
(Anonymous photograph from the collection of Morton Paterson)

Marie Kuo Paterson with Jamie Paterson in the late 1960s
(Photograph by Morton Paterson, from his own collection)

Trenton Bath House exterior with mural
(Photograph by John Ebstel © Keith De Lellis Gallery)

Trenton Bath House interior courtyard
(Photograph by John Ebstel © Keith De Lellis Gallery)

Salk Institute study towers
(Anonymous photograph from the author's collection)

Phillips Exeter Library exterior
(Anonymous photograph, courtesy of the Phillips Exeter Academy Archives)

Louis Kahn teaching at Penn with (left to right) Norman Rice, Robert Le Ricolais, and August Komendant
(Photograph by John Nicolais, from the Richard Saul Wurman Collection, The Architectural Archives, University of Pennsylvania)

Kahn drawing ambidextrously
(Photographs by Martin Rich, from The Architectural Archives, University of Pennsylvania)

Kimbell Art Museum exterior
(Anonymous photograph from the author's collection)

Central Market in Riga
(Anonymous photograph from the author's collection)

Lou and Nathaniel Kahn, late 1960s
(Photograph by Harriet Pattison, from the Harriet Pattison Collection, The Architectural Archives, University of Pennsylvania)

Lou, Alex, and Nathaniel at Alex's high school graduation, 1971
(Anonymous photograph from the collection of Alexandra Tyng)

Harriet Pattison at George Patton's landscape architecture firm
(Anonymous photograph from the George E. Patton Collection, The Architectural Archives, University of Pennsylvania)

Louis Kahn in the
auditorium of the
Kimbell Art Museum
(Photograph by Bob Wharton,
from the Louis I. Kahn
Collection, University
of Pennsylvania and the
Pennsylvania Historical and
Museum Collection)

Louis Kahn at the Indian Institute of Management with Samuel Paul,
the Institute's director
(Anonymous photograph from the Louis I. Kahn Collection, University of Pennsylvania
and the Pennsylvania Historical and Museum Collection)

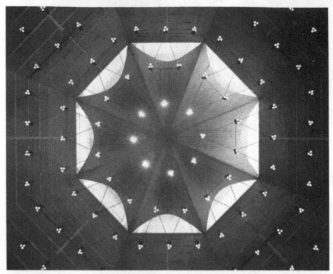

The roof of the Dhaka Assembly Building
(Photograph by Raymond Meier, courtesy of the photographer)

The mosque in the Dhaka Assembly Building
(Photograph by Raymond Meier, courtesy of the photographer)

ing's interior felt somewhat cramped and dark. The angularity of the diagonals combined with the harshness of the concrete walls to produce a feeling of coldness and impersonality; even the ground-floor inglenook, with its brick chimney-face and wooden floor, could not warm up the institutional space. In addition, the slate Lou had chosen for the exterior panels turned out to be too porous, and when it eventually had to be sealed with a shiny finish to prevent leaks and weathering, the building looked as if it had been covered in dark gray acrylic. But the really serious problem was that the Bryn Mawr students hated the dorm. No one moving away from her parents for the first time could find anything homelike in this modernist experiment, and for many decades after its 1965 completion, Erdman Hall remained the last-choice dormitory among incoming freshmen.

In July of 1962, though, most of these problems still lay in the future, and much of Lou's staff was working at least part of the time toward the Bryn Mawr bid date, which was set for the spring of 1963. When Lou returned from his cataract surgery, there were probably a dozen architects and draftsmen employed at his office; by the end of the year the number would increase to twenty or so, and that would be the range within which the staff would continue to expand and contract. "They had these huge projects and very few people in the office," commented David Slovic, who came to work there in the mid-1960s: "Lou had his own pace." Fred Langford confirmed the small ratio of workers to work, noting that "we did work a lot of hours. In the six years I worked for him, I know I averaged sixty to seventy hours a week."

Ed Richards, who joined the firm in late 1962 to work on Erdman Hall, had his own take on the idiosyncrasies of Kahn's process. Like other staff members, he understood that it was essentially a one-man office, with design directives issuing from Kahn alone. But he was disturbed by the inefficiencies in the system. "He could really only work on one project, because he was so involved in it," Ed remarked. "Our Bryn Mawr was a stepsister to Salk." And then, once he'd got things rolling, Kahn would adopt a new project without regard to scale or cost. "Lou would work on a house," pointed out Richards. "The time you spend, any big firm would lose money on a house or a church. You make money when you have a repetitive thing like an apartment building. My understanding is, with Kahn, he really only made money on Salk"—and that was probably because, unlike any of his other commissions, the Salk project paid him an hourly rate and not a fixed percentage of the final costs. "He was a terrible businessman," Richards said. "The thing is, he didn't care."

Neither, for the most part, did the people around him, because he made the task at hand seem so compelling. "Lou brought emotional depth and poetic discussion to architecture," said Lois Sherr Dubin, who studied at Penn's School of Architecture in the late 1950s and had some contact with Kahn's office in the early 1960s. "He was very, very moving when he talked about things." And for those who worked with him, this approach could be tremendously inspiring. "The biggest lesson from Lou on the positive side was to be relentless in seeking the right answer," said Jack MacAllister. That was why, toward the end of any design process, his employees would urge each other to keep the finished drawings out of Lou's sight— otherwise he was likely to think of a new approach just before construction began. For Lou, the excitement was all in the search for the building's essential nature. And if that search was sometimes difficult, it could also be terrifically enjoyable.

"Lou was very much alive. Fun to be with. Uplifting," Fred Langford pointed out. "He could complain about something, but he was never down. Great sense of humor. He would sit down and we would all gather round and listen to him. He was not an efficient businessman—there we all were, supposed to be working for him, and in his own mind there was no difference between us and his Penn class."

■

The class at the University of Pennsylvania was something Lou had continued to teach even as his workload at the office increased, and in 1962, despite his recent cataract surgery, he began the fall semester promptly on September 10. Every Monday and Wednesday at 2:00 he would show up at his studio at the top of the Furness Building and talk about architecture with his students.

"It's very hard to tell, but he could have been the best teacher in the world," said Ed Richards, who was one of Kahn's students in the 1950s. "The reason is he had fabulous ideas. For almost three weeks you don't understand what he's saying, because he has his own language and he's kind of a staccato sort of person. But once you get it, it's fabulous."

The Philadelphia architect Charles Dagit gave an example from his own studies with Lou, which took place about a decade later. According to Dagit, the class would begin with Kahn sitting in complete silence, just stroking his chin until the tension became unbearable. Then he would start talking about the "universal elements" of architecture: the stair, the column, the wall, the window, and so on. "Who invented these things?" he would ask. "Who now owns them? How did the vault begin? These are the things of our expression. They exist because they must. When did they become?" And then Lou would tell the students his parable of the wall, in which the wall has a window ripped in its side and feels weak and sad until it is strengthened with lintels above and below, and with piers on either side. "And Lou's parable continued and continued," said Dagit, "drawing ever closer to its ultimate and inevitable end. And so, he said, 'the walls parted and the column became.'" This was one of his trademark ideas, always expressed in this phrase, and he loved passing it along to younger listeners.

Kahn was deeply committed to his students, allowing them not only a full measure of his time ("If he owed you three hours, he gave you three hours," Ed Richards observed), but also offering them both wide latitude and close attention. "He gave fabulous crits," Richards said. "He would do things like—one of the fellows in my class was designing a church. He said, 'The way you approach this design is excellent. I would never design a church like that, but it's a process.'" Lois Dubin remembered something similar, remarking: "He didn't want you to copy. He wanted you to use what was within you. He wanted to introduce an order to your thinking that freed up spaces that were wonderful spaces."

But Lou could also be a bear if he was in a bad mood. Charles Dagit recalled the risks of pinning up one's work for the regular crits. "Lou would walk around the room in the beginning of class surveying the drawings," noted Dagit. "He often would stop at those that intrigued him and start to speak. On the other hand, he sometimes would approach a student's work that he did not care for . . . He would pause and, with his hand to his thick glasses, he would examine the drawing ever so carefully, with his nose nearly touching the paper. He would maintain that pose for thirty or forty seconds—a veritable eternity—then he would pull his head back slightly and talk to the drawing. He would say in his high-pitched voice, 'The building is a crab' or 'This building is a turd on the landscape. Whose is it?'"

Ed Richards remembered a similarly unpleasant occasion from a decade earlier. "He came in one night—he was in a terrible mood—he just went around the class and tore everyone apart," said Richards of that evening session. "It was late at night, he was tired—I don't know, maybe something bad had happened that day. He could be that way. But on the other hand he could be so wonderful." When he came to work at Kahn's office, Ed noticed the same vacillation between extremes. "It was heaven and hell," he said. "The hell part of it was when you worked all evening and Lou would go home to sleep and he would come in in the morning and say it was crap."

To be fair, it wasn't as if the boss was always sleeping while the staff was working: most of his other employees described Lou as working at night as well. If he went off to a movie house for a few hours in the course of the evening, as he occasionally did, it would be to catch up on his sleep. "The time that Lou was there was at night," David Slovic pointed out, because he had so many client meetings and other things to do in the day. So Slovic tried to work nights, too, in order to be part of Kahn's world. "It was always exciting to work there," he said. "Nobody was cynical. Everyone was there to help it happen, and everyone felt it was important, that he was onto something that would change what architecture was about."

But even this young enthusiast saw that Lou could be highly critical at times. Once, for instance, they had all been working on a model so that Kahn could bring it to a client, and "towards the end a bunch of us were working on it probably two or three days straight, without any sleep, trying to get it ready for the presentation. Basically, we butchered the model," admitted Slovic. "Lou comes in five, six in the morning, and he starts looking at the model and he says, 'I can't take it. This is no good.' He wasn't angry; he was just very clear. 'I'll take the drawings. I'm not going to take the model.' It wasn't *you idiots*, it wasn't insulting to us; it was just the work. We'd not been able to pull it off."

For Ed Richards, who arrived at the firm just as Lou was starting to recover from his cataract operation, Kahn's critical nature and his actual vision somehow coincided. "He went from someone that was a little blurry to someone with these thick glasses," said Ed. "He would see the grain on the vellum; he saw too much." But for Fred Langford— who, practically alone among Kahn's employees, always found him "easy to work with"—the blurry vision was just another side of Lou's charm. "When people came into the office," Fred remembered about the regular morning routine, "Lou would shake their hands. He would just stand there and shake everyone's hand. Finally, the window washer came in, and Lou shook *his* hand. And he said, 'I'm just the window washer.' And Lou says, 'I'm Mr. Magoo.'"

The Mr. Magoo personality came to the fore when Lou made a trip out to California in October of 1962. "He would say, 'Where am I here? Tell me where I am on the site,'" Fred Langford recalled. Jack Mac-Allister said that he, too, had to act as Lou's eyes during Kahn's visits to the Salk site. "He was just totally blind, I mean when he first got his glasses," said Jack. "And I'd have to walk him to the job and hold him by the hand. And he'd whisper in my ear, 'Tell me when something's bad so I can scream about it.'"

It was during this period, too, that Lou began to draw almost exclusively with charcoal on yellow tracing paper. He no longer did the detailed pencil drawings he had done earlier in his career, or even lively crayon sketches like the ones he had made in the initial stages of Esherick House. Now his medium was a stick of charcoal, sometimes clasped directly in his hand, sometimes lodged in a "broker's pencil" that had been designed to hold a very thick lead. "We all had Lou's kind of pencil," said David Slovic. "He had a fabulous one—silver, with a big fat lead. I had one or two; everyone had one. You had to find them in antique shops." Slovic described how Kahn would draw over someone else's drawing, "put a trace over it and correct it as he drew." And Lou would also make his own original drawings in charcoal. "It was when his eyes went bad that he started drawing in charcoal, so that resulted in some very beautiful drawings," Slovic said. The younger architect remembered how Kahn would constantly erase and redraw, so that "it had all the traces of his thoughts—what we don't have with computers— embedded in the drawings."

To Ed Richards, though, it seemed as if Kahn's avowed affection for charcoal went back much further. "When I was a student, he'd try to get everyone to start with charcoal," Ed pointed out. "Charcoal is easy, and if you found something wrong you'd just . . ."—and here he mimicked the gesture of erasing a line with a brush of his hand. "If you had drawn all that and found something wrong, you'd be much more hesitant to change it. You're much freer with charcoal." And Fred Langford seconded this notion, commenting about Lou's approach: "I think he would say he liked the charcoal because he could erase it quick. 'Give me a hard line and then I don't want to change it!'"

■

All throughout his initial months of recovering from his cataract operation, Lou was planning another great adventure: a voyage to India, with an exciting new project to work on. Earlier in 1962, his friend Doshi had telegraphed him asking if he would like to design the new Indian Institute of Management in Ahmedabad, and Lou, after some hesitation, had accepted. "I will help you realize your dream," Doshi assured him.

The two men had known each other since the late 1950s, when Balkrishna Doshi—then a young Indian architect who had already worked with Le Corbusier in Paris and Ahmedabad—was visiting the United States on a Graham Fellowship. Brought to Kahn's Philadelphia office by a friend from New York, Doshi showed Kahn photographs of some of his work, and the older man seemed impressed by the affinity between their ideas. After looking at the design of Doshi's own house, which separated off the kitchen, bath, and staircase from the living and sleeping rooms, "he started talking about the master and servant spaces, a concept of which I was quite ignorant," Doshi reported. "He then pulled out his embassy project in Luanda and mentioned about the similarity of approaches between my house and the embassy plan."

The 1959 design for an American consulate in Luanda, though it was never built, became the seed behind many of Kahn's ideas for the buildings he later did in hot climates, including Salk and Ahmedabad. "I came back with multiple impressions of how clever was the man who solved the problems of sun, rain, and wind," Lou was to say upon his return from Angola. In particular, the Africa project had caused him to come up with two new design possibilities. One involved having windows face a sunlight-reflecting wall across a space that was open to the sky; this would cut down on glare while still allowing an abundance of natural light into the room. The other entailed placing a "sun roof" at a six-foot distance from a sturdier "rain roof," so that breezes could waft in and cool the space between. Perhaps most tellingly, Kahn's consulate design gave rise to a phrase that would not only define that particular project, with its inner walls protected by outer walls, but would also echo down the years of his future work: "I thought of wrapping ruins around buildings."

But on the occasion of Doshi's visit to Philadelphia, it was the Richards Building—first the drawings and models, then the site itself—that most impressed the thirty-one-year-old Indian. It was here that Kahn had produced what Doshi considered "the new idiom of a modern skyscraper . . . manifest in the service tower made of bricks, juxtaposed with the glass windows without any mullions at the corners. The stark contrast between the stoic brick towers and the transparency, reflections and details of glass windows even today haunt me," Doshi wrote in one of his commentaries on Kahn's work.

The other thing that stuck in his mind from this first encounter was that when Kahn offered to take his young visitor out to dinner, he had to borrow cash from his secretary to do so. That Louis Kahn was someone who didn't think much about money was evident from the beginning, and it was to remain central to Doshi's view of him. "Till the last day he remained a generous person. He only gave," Doshi noted, "and all he wanted in return was to know more about others and their pursuits."

(Others did not necessarily share Doshi's take on Lou, at least in this regard. "He was very worried about not having any money," commented Richard Saul Wurman. "He was not a giving person. He was not particularly nice in a lot of ways. He was bitter about other people getting jobs he didn't get." And yet even he acknowledged that doing things the right way was far more important to Kahn than earning money. "He almost purposely would shoot himself in the foot, he so much didn't want to compromise," Wurman said. "He would give up a building rather than compromise." So Wurman's Kahn turned out in some ways to be as much of a self-denying saint as Doshi's, despite the rather unsaintly selfish streak.)

After his initial visit to Philadelphia, Doshi returned to Penn in 1961 to teach for a few weeks in the architecture school, and it was then that he and Lou solidified their friendship. When he got back to India from that trip, he met with two important clients, Kasturbhai Lalbhai and Vikram Sarabhai, about their plans to develop an Indian Institute of Management along the lines of Harvard's famous business school. Lalbhai, a textile-mill owner whom Doshi described as "the grand old man of Indian industry and a great patron of architects," had already hired Le Corbusier to design two major buildings in Ahmedabad. Dr. Sarabhai, a prominent scientist and industrialist, was to be the director of the new management institute; he was also a member of an important local family for whom Corbusier had designed a private house. Both men, though they wanted Doshi to take responsibility for the IIM project, also wanted him to collaborate with an international architect comparable in stature to Le Corbusier. (Corbu himself was unavailable for this job, since he was by now busy with Chandigarh and other new projects.) They proposed the names of a couple of American architects they thought would fit the bill. "I said no, I will get you someone as good as Corbusier," Doshi recalled, and that's when he contacted Kahn. According to their informal arrangement—Lou being Lou, there was never a formal contract—Kahn would be the official architect and Doshi his local consultant. The project was to be run out of the National Institute of Design offices in Ahmedabad and subsidized, in part, by the Ford Foundation, which gave a grant to cover Lou's travel and accommodation costs.

On November 4, 1962, Kahn flew to India. Though this was his first trip to the subcontinent, it had been preceded by at least one other encounter with Indian culture. In 1959 Lou had joined the recently formed Tagore Society of Philadelphia, an organization whose aims were "to promote a knowledge of Tagore's artistic contributions in literature, dance, music and painting" and "to promote Tagore's ideas of peace and universalism." Perhaps Kahn's growing friendship with Doshi had led to his interest in the multitalented Rabindranath Tagore, the first non-European to win the Nobel Prize in Literature; more likely, he was urged to join by Adelaide Giurgola, his friend Aldo's wife, who had been active in the Tagore Society since its beginning. Whatever his motive, Lou remained a full-fledged, dues-paying member of the group for at least a year.

But learning about the country through one of its great writers was one thing; India in person, with its vast range of intense, sometimes disturbing, often astounding experiences, was something else. And this first trip represented a complete immersion for Lou. In between pilgrimages to the Taj Mahal, Chandigarh, and other architectural wonders, he spent a sustained period in Ahmedabad with Doshi and the two clients. His "consultant" took him around to various local places of interest—not only the four modern buildings designed by Le Corbusier, but also the most notable ancient monuments in the area. Together Lou and Doshi visited the nearby fifteenth-century Islamic complex called Sarkej Roza, where shaded, colonnaded walkways surrounded a central open square facing the mosque, while a large pond of shallow water, accumulated during the rainy season, crept up on the outermost steps. They also saw the primary mosques in Ahmedabad itself, including Sidi Saiyyed, whose extraordinarily delicate stone tracery in the shape of a tree was to inspire the IIM logo. And they journeyed northward to the Adalaj Stepwell, a lovely Hindu ruin where visitors descended from the unobtrusive ground-level entrance through five stories of intricately carved sandstone to reach the well-water at the bottom. Here, at midday, the sunlight shone directly on the water through an octagonal opening at the top (not unlike the oculus at the center of the Pantheon's ceiling—or, for that matter, the square holes Lou had created in the peaked roofs of the Trenton Bath House). But a diffused, watery light also filtered down to every level through the oblique openings that surrounded the central staircase. It was this powerful impression of filtered light, mingled with the direct heat and the deep shadows elsewhere in the landscape, that would remain with Kahn long after his journey was over.

He returned to the United States in late November, just in time to attend the dedication ceremony for the First Unitarian Church in Rochester on Sunday, December 2. In the three years Lou had spent working on the Rochester church project, he had become increasingly interested in Unitarianism, and he and Esther had even made a $1,000 tax-deductible donation to First Unitarian in 1961. (By comparison, the

American Friends of Hebrew University got only $80 that year, and the Allied Jewish Appeal a mere $50.) This is not to say that Kahn ever considered converting. Adopting *any* religion would have been extremely out of character for this man who, despite his apparently mystical tendencies, described himself in the 1958 Berkeley creativity study as a complete rationalist who "dislikes irrationality thoroughly." When asked, during one of the psychological interviews, "Have you ever had an intense experience of mystical communion with the universe, life, God, etc.?" Lou responded with an abrupt "No." And though the interviewer observed that in his work as an architect Kahn "places great emphasis on a spiritual-value approach," he also noted that he "consciously rejects any formal religion." Perhaps because the Unitarians seemed inclined in the same direction, Kahn found their, approach congenial.

His Unitarian clients, for their part, were delighted with their chosen architect. Among other things, they derived great pleasure from seeing how much his public stature had increased since they had hired him. In the spring of 1959, when they selected this relatively unknown Philadelphian over Walter Gropius, Paul Rudolph, Eero Saarinen, Frank Lloyd Wright, and other high-profile names, their preference might have seemed a trifle idiosyncratic. By the end of 1962, though, Kahn was widely seen as belonging in that august company. There was even a new book about him, for Vincent Scully's *Louis I. Kahn*—part of Braziller's series on "Makers of Modern Architecture"—had come out just a month prior to the Rochester dedication. "He is the one architect whom all others admire, and his reputation is international," Scully's little book announced, contrasting this with Kahn's obscurity a decade earlier. His buildings, Scully went on, "are hard and normally without finishes; they are exactly what they seem: not for the fainthearted, which is as it should be. Kahn therefore requires wise and courageous clients who are willing to forgo the gloss of superficial perfection in order to take part in a sustained and demanding process of which they may one day be proud." The Rochester Unitarians were pleased and honored to count themselves in this select category.

The formal dedication, with its unveiling of the building to the congregants, only confirmed their sense of having made the right choice. Forbidding as the nearly windowless brick exterior might have seemed on that December Sunday, there were ample rewards for the people who found their way through the church's well-concealed front door and past the low-ceilinged entrance lobby. As they walked through a low, wide, open doorway to the right, they were greeted by their first sight of the astonishing Sanctuary.

High above their heads was a concrete cruciform ceiling that reached its lowest point at the center, where the eight smooth panels that together formed the cross shape met in eight triangular points. The fact that the roof of this large and beautiful room sloped downward toward the congregants did not feel at all oppressive. On the contrary, the sensation was rather like being sheltered under a colossal set of wings. Suspended a good six feet off the high concrete walls and seemingly held in place only by thin beams and brackets, this remarkable ceiling seemed to float rather than loom, and the whole glorious effect was enhanced by the natural light pouring in from the four corners of the room, where the high-set clerestory windows, located in four tall light-towers, let in the sunlight in a way that was mysterious because not fully visible.

The worshippers on the ground could sense the vast empty space over their heads as something luxurious and exalting, and at the same time they could sense themselves as individually significant bodies inhabiting that grand space. Seated in one of the movable chairs on the Sanctuary floor, a congregant could almost feel the oppositional pull between the downward curve of the ceiling and the upward lift of the light-wells—as if the former enabled the latter, like a dancer bending his knees before taking off in a leap. There was an atmosphere of great repose, but it was a thoughtful, sometimes unnerving repose, filled with the knowledge that light requires darkness to set it off. There was something, too, about having the light delicately entering from the corners as the roof descended slightly in the middle that conveyed an entirely different spiritual quality from that of a domed or arched building. In those more traditional churches, one was meant to sense an all-powerful God drawing everything upward toward himself. Here, in contrast, the sense of power was more diffused and less focused, as if what was being worshipped was more like sunlight, say, or humanity in the aggregate, or simply the possibility of peaceful contemplation.

Kahn returned from his Sunday in Rochester to the usual plethora of tasks in Philadelphia, including more appointments at Bryn Mawr and Esherick House, a dinner with his old friend and opponent Ed Bacon, a lunchtime meeting with his young Penn colleague Denise Scott Brown, and a nine-hour architecture jury held in Penn's Fine Arts Building. But he made sure to schedule a substantial amount of free time—five evenings and one full day, as marked on his office calendar from December 15 to 19—for a special purpose of his own.

He was using this time to pay his first visits to his son, Nathaniel Kahn, who had been born on November 9, while Lou was away in India. Shortly after the birth Harriet had gone with the baby to a cottage called The Twig in Longridge, Connecticut, and it was to Longridge that Lou came on those December evenings. Snapshots taken at the time show the gently smiling gray-haired father, a bit formal-looking in his suit and tie, holding his tiny son in his arms. Soon after, in the early months of 1963, Harriet moved with Nathaniel to Charlotte, Vermont, where they were to remain for the next eighteen months. Lou and Harriet kept in frequent touch by phone and letter, but except for a flying two-day visit Lou made to Vermont when his son was one and a half years old, they did not see each other again until Harriet and Nathaniel moved back to Philadelphia in the fall of 1964.

A great deal had happened in Lou's professional life by then, and much of it involved the Indian subcontinent. To begin with, there was the IIM project, which brought Kahn to Ahmedabad at least two or three times a year. Whenever he was there, he and Doshi would spend every waking minute together. "First of all he would come, he would go to the hotel and rest," Doshi said. "Next morning he would come to the campus." Early on in the process Lou had unfurled his plans for the buildings, which were to be constructed almost entirely of brick. "He wanted as much brick, as little concrete, as possible. In order to eliminate the beams, you had to make an arch," Doshi explained. So the material itself dictated the most frequently repeated motif in the design, a rectangular open span surmounted by a wide arch, with only a thin concrete lintel in between.

Brick was an obvious choice in one way: it was local and it was cheap. Everywhere in northern India, the landscape was dotted with small to medium-sized brick factories, each with a chimney rising above its kilns. According to Doshi, most of the brick for the entire IIM complex ended up coming from a single kiln, so that the color would match. For Lou, the fact that these bricks were handmade, and looked it, would have had a special appeal, despite the opposition of certain younger modernists, who felt that the Indians should have concrete and steel just like everyone else. "Why don't you take them out of the Stone Age?" objected the twenty-five-year-old Moshe Safdie, who was working on the Ahmedabad drawings in Kahn's office. ("I was the only nonstudent of his in the office; I was perhaps the most critical," Safdie confessed later, while also admitting that he had been wrong about the brick: "You have to work with what people have.")

When Kahn and Doshi were not at the site itself, they were sometimes visiting Kasturbhai Lalbhai at his house in the Old City. This was a house the mill owner used as an office, not the place where he slept, and it was located in the most mazelike section of the city, off one of the narrow streets and partially enclosed courtyards that made up the *pols*, as the people of Old Ahmedabad called their tiny local enclaves. Lalbhai usually spent afternoons at this office. "From 2:30 to 4:00 every day he would be at his office, in the mornings at the textile mill— Kasturbhai was very organized," noted Doshi. When Lou and Doshi came to visit him there, they would sit on the floor in the traditional manner.

Sometimes Lou would try to explain to Lalbhai the philosophy behind his designs, and at such moments the old industrialist would turn to Doshi and say in Gujarati, "Tell him just to come to the point. Whatever he says is fine."

"What's he saying?" Lou would ask, and Doshi would answer, "Nothing, nothing."

But sometimes Lalbhai would have very specific critiques of the plan, and Kahn would always pay attention to them. "It was Kasturbhai's idea to have the classrooms in a line, not in a turning corridor," Doshi pointed out. In typical fashion, Lou responded to the client's request for a change by producing his best work. That long, straight classroom building eventually became the alluring centerpiece of the whole complex, and Kahn was always eager to give Kasturbhai full credit for it. "He is a man of thorough magnificence," with a remarkable "sense of art," Lou said of his venerable Indian patron, "and he suggested why don't I line them all up as one. And it was infinitely stronger. It's very unusual that a client will give you an aesthetic argument, and that he is dead right. In his case, he is made of good stuff."

As work progressed on the construction of the IIM, Kahn found it necessary at a certain point to pay a more prolonged visit to Ahmedabad. It was the only time he stayed for a full week, and his purpose was to teach the brickworkers how to do the brickwork in the proper way. When he saw their first attempts, he was upset with the way the walls looked. Doshi had apparently instructed them to lay the bricks as Le Corbusier had wanted it done, but Kahn wanted something different—a much thinner joint, with as little mortar between the bricks as possible. He also wanted the corners of the bricks to be rubbed off so they would fit more cleanly into the arches (and perhaps, also, so they would look even more handmade). "This is like old times," Doshi remarked, describing the scene after Lou gave his instructions. "People sitting on the floor, squatting and rubbing: you would think you were in another century."

Later, Lou would convey his teaching approach in his own words when he talked about that training session in Ahmedabad. His aim, he commented, had been to get the brickworkers to "duplicate the work that I did, but in their own way." He started by building a sample arch to show them how the brick and mortar should be combined; then he watched as they did it themselves. "I learned a few words in the language, and I would say to a worker, 'This is good,'" Kahn said. "It all comes because you give a little praise to the guy, make him feel he has something worth living for."

Ahmedabad was not the only place where Lou would find himself dealing with non-English-speaking workers in a foreign country. By the beginning of 1963 he had also embarked on a major project in Pakistan. To begin with it was actually *two* major projects: a presidential palace for the new capital city of Islamabad, in West Pakistan, and an entire government complex in Dacca, the country's secondary capital, located far to the east in the poorer and less developed East Pakistan. Ever since 1947, when the primarily Muslim regions that made up Pakistan had been partitioned off from India, the smaller country had consisted of these two unequal segments gripping the gigantic mass of India from either side. To the west, in the Urdu-speaking area, lay most of the power and wealth. To the east, in what had once been part of India's Bengal province, lay a Bengali-speaking region that was always treated as the poor stepsister.

When Field Marshal Ayub Khan—who in 1958 had become president of Pakistan during a period of martial law—resolved in the early 1960s to move the capital from Karachi to Islamabad, he also promised to do something for East Pakistan. The contract for the new government buildings was initially assigned to Mazharul Islam, a well-respected East Pakistani architect who had studied in the West and had already done significant work in his home country. Islam, however, did not think much of the two international firms, one English and one French, that had been awarded the subcontracts for the job, so he rather selflessly renounced the commission for himself and told President Khan they should seek out a world-renowned master architect for the job. He suggested three names: Le Corbusier, Alvar Aalto, and Louis Kahn. Corbu was too busy. Aalto was suffering from "ill health" (code for a severe drinking problem). So the commission went by default to Kahn. Mazharul Islam, who had known of Kahn from his Yale days, offered to remain peripherally involved with the East Pakistan project throughout its development. Much as Doshi had done in Ahmedabad, he took Lou around to see the local ruins, including a 1,400-year-old monastery called Shalban Bihari that was a short helicopter ride away. He loaned the American architect useful books and gave him various leads and instructions. He also showed him some of the modernist buildings that he himself had designed and built in Dacca, including the clean-lined university library and a very appealing fine arts institute. All this caused one local architect to say, many years later: "When you look at the Parliament Building in Bangladesh, you can hear Mazharul Islam whispering in Kahn's ear."

Lou's first journey to Dacca took place in January and February of 1963. He returned in March and again in July, and then made separate trips in November and December. Some of this time was also spent in Karachi and Islamabad, where Kahn was working on the presidential palace at the same time. But that commission soon came to nought, for when the committee overseeing the West Pakistan project saw Kahn's model, they rejected his plans and hired Edward Durrell Stone instead. The reason given was that Kahn's design was too austere, with no minarets, no gold leaf, none of the decorative frou-frou desired by the client. Apparently in this case Lou did not want to accede to the client's wishes, or perhaps he was not given the chance to do so. At any rate, he still had the Parliament contract in East Pakistan, and the discouragement of losing the West Pakistan assignment only made him more determined to accomplish something special in Dacca.

On that first trip to Dacca, Kahn was joined by a young American architect, previously unknown to him, who was based in Pakistan. Henry Wilcots had done his training at the University of Colorado and, after working briefly in Denver, had gone to work for an architect named Bill Perry at his overseas office in Karachi. That's where Wilcots and his wife were living in early 1963, when he was summoned to Dacca to meet Kahn. "I was asked to tag along by the office of the public works department," Wilcots said. "I didn't know anything about him—maybe read something in a couple of the professional journals." Perhaps because they were both Americans, or perhaps because Wilcots was a known quantity to the locals and Kahn was not, "whenever he would come out and I was around, I was invited to be there. Someone would call me and say, 'Professor Kahn will be here,'" and Henry Wilcots would go.

At first Wilcots felt uncomfortable in his anomalous role. People in Karachi would ask him to look over Kahn's drawings as they were sent in, and because he didn't work for Kahn, he felt awkward about it. "This is not right," Wilcots said when he reported one such incident to Kahn, confessing that he didn't like being asked to be a supervising intermediary. "And he just smiled and said, *It's okay.* He always just smiled and said, *It's okay, it's okay.*"

The real breakthrough, though, came when the two men were sitting together at a meeting in Dacca. "Lou and I were being very formal with each other," Henry recalled, "and one day we just broke the ice. We were sitting in a meeting somewhere, and everyone always referred to him as Professor. And I, being a country guy, might have chuckled a little bit. And he turned to me and said, 'In the office, everyone calls me Lou.' And I said, "Well, I'm Henry.' And that was it."

As Henry saw it, these new jobs on the Indian subcontinent were not just a potential source of fame and fortune for Lou; they also gave him a deeper kind of satisfaction. "He liked going out to India and Pakistan. It's a chore, and it's long, and it gets hot out there, but he enjoyed engaging with the folks there. It's a different culture, and the demands are different. And he received so much respect there. He was a complicated guy," Wilcots mused. But that realization still lay in the future. "At our initial meetings," said Henry, "he was just sort of a nice person to be around. He and I got along quite well, really."

Part of the reason for that, Wilcots felt, was the palpable sense of respect between them, and part of it was their mutual willingness to leave a great deal unsaid. Each man was able to be private, almost secretive, in the presence of the other. "We only talked about architecture," said Henry, "the process of it, the spirituality of it. We had nice drinking sessions too: in a bar, a hotel, a plane . . . Malt whiskey," he recalled. "We always drank that together"—although there was also Lou's notable fondness for acquavit, not to mention the ubiquitous gin: "In Dacca, before I knew him, he came to my door and asked if I had gin, and he filled his flask with it. He said Esther packs his bag and she always includes his flask, but he had run out."

Still, the drinking and talking, however pleasant, were always secondary to the work. For Kahn, the problem was essentially how to make something out of nothing—how to take a flat, featureless site, "a no man's land completely without distinction," as he called it in a letter to Harriet Pattison, and turn it into a place "worthy of the thoughts I had before I saw it." When he first arrived in Dacca, he had been taken for a boat ride on the Buriganga River, and this inspired him to do a lovely little sketch of a man poling a boat along in the water. It may have been this image, as well as his recent memory of Le Corbusier's Chandigarh, that caused him to think of setting the Assembly Building in the midst of a shallow lake. Other aspects of the final design might have derived in part from his recent work on the Rochester church: the ambulatory, for instance, that wound round and round the core of the building, creating a twisty, mysterious route that divided the outermost offices from the more central functions; or the light-wells that brought sunlight down to the shadowy lowest levels from high above. But there was at least one crucial element in his Dacca plan that could only have arisen in response to the local culture.

"Then at lunch it dawned on me to include in the assembly group a mosque," he wrote in his detailed letter to Harriet. "This somehow twisted me from the hopelessness of the location. I was sure then that I could design something that could be its own force and even if an inspiring location would have other spaces suggest themselves it would not have been valuable if I had not thought of the mosque. Religion," he pointed out, "is the basis of separation from India."

Apparently this radical idea—to include religion prominently within the legislative building—appealed to the clients as much as the architect. "When I presented that afternoon the idea of an axial relation of the Assembly complex and a mosque," his letter continued, "it was as though heaven descended on the authorities. They thought it was IT! I am stunned by the completeness of their approval, because they said, 'You have put religion in this capital. Just what it needed to give the meaning it lacked.'"

Elsewhere, Kahn gave a slightly different version of the same story. "In Dacca, where I am building a Second Capital of Pakistan," he declared in one public speech, "I was given a long and wordy program . . . On the third night I thought of the devil of an idea. A house of legislation is a religious place. No matter how much of a rogue you are as a legislator, when you enter the assembly, there is something transcendent about your view . . . The mosque was an absolute necessity for the assembly, because the way of life involved the mosque five times a day."

Whether the idea came at lunch or on the third night, in response to the religious history of East Pakistan or the transcendence of democracy, one thing proved consistently true: the mosque (sometimes referred to as the "prayer hall") turned out to be an essential piece of the finished structure. A grandly proportioned, cube-shaped room with huge, symmetrically curved windows embracing all four corners, it became the heart of the Assembly Building, exuding an indescribable power that could be felt by daily occupants and occasional visitors alike. As with Kahn's other similarly stirring spaces—not just explicitly religious ones like the Unitarian Church, but the more secular ones too, the "churches" he designed for art and books and research and education— the question arises as to how he managed it. How did a man who practiced no particular religion, who believed in rationality and disdained irrationality, have such remarkable access to the spiritual element in architecture?

"Spirituality has nothing to do with religion," observed Shamsul Wares, a Bangladeshi architect who met Kahn when he was working in Dacca. "Religion is a set pattern of rituals; religion is caught between rituals. Kahn was a man of the mind: he explored mind. Mind wants to know the truth. Religion never provides the truth—it's a belief. Kahn was a spiritual man. He was trying to understand the truth in terms of how things happen. If atheists say, 'We have come from nothing, go to nothing,' what is that nothing?"

In Wares's view, this was an investigation that Kahn pursued through light. "He found something in the light," Wares went on. "You feel that you are washed clean. The light has some existence. It is not totally abstract. It is also visible, it is also feelable. Light is sensoriality. This sensoriality is somehow connected to spirituality: that is how light works on us. We get the idea of spirituality through the senses. His architecture," Wares stressed, "is sensorial, not just formal."

And this in turn, Wares felt, was linked to Kahn's pursuit of the truth. "That we come from nothing, go back to nothing, was also at the core of his being. So he was interested in space—big spaces, giving you the sense of awe. He also knew that truth can never be known. Truth is ever hallucinatory, obscure. So he made the ambulatory, a labyrinthine process: you lose your way. And this disorientation within the building is another way of saying that truth is obscure."

■

On February 7, 1963, just as he was returning from his first long trip to Pakistan, Lou got word that his father had died that day in Los Angeles. Leopold Kahn, who had belonged to his local synagogue and regularly attended services on the High Holidays, would have counted on having a traditional Jewish funeral as soon as possible after his death. So the day after Lou landed in Philadelphia, he took off again for California, arriving in time to see Leopold buried at the Home of Peace Cemetery in East Los Angeles, next to his wife, Bertha, and their son Oscar.

According to Richard Wurman, Lou "didn't have a good relationship with his father; he mentioned that once." But at least on the surface they were not at all estranged. Colleagues of Lou's remembered a visit Leopold paid to the 20th Street office, where Lou set his father up with a drawing board. The man was a skillful artist, and people knew he had worked for a while in stained glass during his younger days, though that employment had been short-lived. In fact, none of the younger members of the family could remember Leopold consistently holding down a job. "Leopold was never the most ambitious man," observed Leonard Traines, whose father had been Leopold's first cousin. Traines also pointed out that the elder Kahn had depended for years on the younger one's financial assistance and had learned to husband his resources: for example, when "Lou sent him the money to come to the East Coast by plane, he didn't want to spend the money, so he came by bus."

Despite his weaknesses as a provider, or perhaps because of them, Leopold was always the stricter parent, the family disciplinarian. "He demanded respect, and he was very authoritarian, and the only person who could handle him was my grandmother," said Lou's niece Rhoda Kantor. Her brother, Alan Kahn, concurred. "He was the noise, she was the sounds of nature," he said about his paternal grandparents.

"I think that in terms of influence on Lou, his mother had the greatest influence," Alan commented. "Her aura, her approach to life— she had a magical quality to her that attracted everyone. His intelligence came from her. But much of his personality came from Leopold. I think he had a very strong ego, like his father. I don't think he had an arrogance, but I think he was pretty assured; he would stand his ground. He got that from his father."

Leopold was not only a proud man; he was also, according to his grandson, a bit of a dandy. "He was very meticulous—very clean too. He starched and pressed his own shirts. I never remember seeing him in casual clothes. He always looked like a bandbox," said Alan.

Ona Russell, Rhoda's daughter, also recalled her great-grandfather's formal clothing. "I remember Leopold with his suit on, carrying Hershey's Kisses in his pocket," she said. "He always had Hershey's Kisses and he would give me one. I don't have warm feelings about him—I was afraid of him on some level—but the Hershey's Kisses ameliorated that."

Fifty years later, Ona could still conjure up the sight of Leopold on his deathbed in the hospital. "I remember his face looking strained," she said. "He looked like he was in pain. I remember him speaking with difficulty, but not incoherent or anything."

Yet the dying man did have his moments of delirium, according to Alan Kahn, who as a trained doctor was monitoring his grandfather's care. "He was seeing bugs all over," said Alan, "even though he knew they were phony." Medically speaking, there was no specific cause of death, no definitive final illness. Although Leopold had for decades been encouraging if not inventing rumors about his own ill health (it was for the sake of his health, for instance, that he and Bertha had originally moved out to California), Alan ascribed his grandfather's death simply to old age, or "system breakdown," as he put it.

Lou's entire West Coast family—not just his sister Sarah, his sister-in-law Rosella, his nephew, and his nieces, but also grandnieces, grandnephews, and assorted varieties of second cousins and cousins once removed—continued to be an important part of his life even after Leopold's death. Yet few of Lou's colleagues, even among those who worked with him on the Salk Institute, knew anything about his Los Angeles relatives. It was as if they occupied two completely separate spheres in his life. When he came to La Jolla, he would stay with Jack MacAllister in Del Mar, and either Jack or Fred Langford (depending on whose turn it was to "babysit") would drive him around, go out drinking with him in the evenings, and swap stories about baseball. When he visited Los Angeles, he would stay with his sister, Sarah, in her tiny house on 78th Street—the same house she had occupied with their parents since the 1930s—and get driven around by Alan or Alan's ex-wife, Eleanor. And in either place, Lou would seem fully to belong to the people he was with.

"I remember him playing the piano at Sarah's house," said his grandniece Ona. "On family gatherings I would see him in his rumpled suit. There was a twinkle in his eye. You would never imagine his greatness, in that setting." One of his grandnephews, Alan's son Jeff, also remembered the suits ("Brooks Brothers suits, always dark gray, all the same—that was his uniform, always the same suit, always the white shirt, and the bowtie, askew"), but more than that, he remembered Lou's conversation. "His metaphors were far-reaching," said Jeff Kahn. "It was all pretty abstract. And we got it! I remember Dad would debrief us: What was Lou saying?" Jeff's sister, Lauren Kahn, particularly recalled the quality of her great-uncle's attention. "When he talked to you, you were the only person in the room," said Lauren. "This was true even as kids. He would not dumb down what he was saying."

For Rhoda, the memories were mostly of Lou having fun. "It was hysterical. He loved to play the piano, but he played by ear. He thought he could play really well. My brother, who *could* play really well, would laugh." But Lou was never offended; on the contrary, he was obviously doing it in part to produce that laugh. "He was a fun-loving person," Rhoda added. "He never said anything negative about anyone. He had this charm about him; he had a great smile and laugh. He had a sense of humor." And what Rhoda especially remembered was how comfortable Lou was with everyone in the family. "They'd have big parties to get together—it was a big family, cousins and everything. And he was very egalitarian. He made everyone feel his equal."

Yet there was also something special about having him in their midst. "There was a mystique about him," Ona observed. "If there was a family event and Lou was coming, it was like 'Lou is coming!'"

It wasn't just the West Coast relatives who felt this way about Lou's invigorating presence. "Your father is coming to dinner!" was how Anne Tyng would announce to Alex that Lou would be dropping by their odd little vertical house on Waverly Street in Philadelphia—as if something thrilling were about to happen. Even when there was no longer any romantic connection between her parents, Alex could hear the breathlessness in her mother's voice as she ran downstairs with the news of Lou's imminent arrival.

The dinners themselves were, in Alex's view, rather boring. "Basically, my parents would talk about theories at dinner—their latest architectural theories, their ideas," recalled Alex. "My mother would talk about new geometrical ideas; he would talk about silence and light. Most kids don't want to be asked *How was your day?* I was dying to be asked *How was your day?*"

Yet however close the intellectual bond was between Louis Kahn and Anne Tyng, it did not prevent Tyng from leaving the firm. "In 1964, though Lou had plenty of work in the office, he 'let me go' by simply not giving me work," Anne wrote in a memoir she published long after Lou's death. Other people offered somewhat different accounts of their pro-fessional parting. "Anne would go off and do her own scheme when we were working on a project. It was crazy-making," said Jack MacAllister, who was never Tyng's greatest fan. Even Ed Richards, who was fond of Anne and friendly with her outside the office, insisted that "Lou would never have fired her. When she dropped out of Bryn Mawr, she worked on other stuff. Some of the time she worked on her own geometry. She would come into the office and say, 'Oh, I'm so excited, I crossed a do-decahedron with a whatever'—no one could understand what she was talking about."

To Moshe Safdie, it seemed that Tyng's departure stemmed directly from the personal tensions between her and Kahn. Safdie, who had not been in the office long, assumed that this had something to do with Marie Kuo, even though the affair with Marie was long over by then. (Marie was still working at Kahn's office in 1964, but by that time she had met and married Morton Paterson, an executive with the drug company Smith Kline & French; as if to signal how thoroughly that episode in his life was closed, Lou even attended their wedding.) Safdie thought he could recall the exact moment when all the simmering re-sentment between Lou and Anne came to a head. "One day the three of us are working—Lou, she, and me," Safdie recounted. "To start with, the atmosphere seemed charged." Then, according to Safdie's memory of events, something set Anne off, though he couldn't say exactly what it was. "There was a big fight," he said. "She stormed out and never came back."

Yet it was Anne and not Lou with whom Safdie developed an endur-ing friendship. "Anne was a brilliant thinker, even beyond architecture. She was a mentor. She kind of invested in me, more than Lou," Safdie observed. He and his wife and young daughter made up an informal extended family with Anne and *her* daughter during the sixteen months he spent in Philadelphia, before he moved to Montreal for the World Expo and the creation of Habitat 67. Alex Tyng was about nine or ten at the time.

"She was cranky," Safdie said of the little girl. "I've seen it since with several single mothers who cannot somehow deal with the disciplinary issues. The kid just grows up without any sense of limits. At the same time," he admitted, "she had something in her."

Ed Richards, who had once visited Anne and Alex at their Waverly Street house, put the case even more strongly. "Anne made the decision that Alex was not going to be disciplined because it would affect her creativity," he said, adding: "She was a little terror."

From the point of view of the grown-up Alex, a highly accomplished painter, there was never any question of Anne's *deciding* not to discipline her; she was simply too willful, even as a small child, to do what anyone else told her to do. And the adults around her—even and perhaps especially her father—seemed to reinforce her own sense of herself as a fully formed person. "I think he just assumed I was an artist, or would become an artist," she said of Lou's attitude toward her. "He was very encouraging. He'd buy me art supplies. Sometimes he was too early: he bought me an oil painting set when I was ten."

Lou also made her feel that she was very much his offspring. "He always scrutinized me," Alex recalled, "and since he thought that there was a strong resemblance between us, he was always trying to find more things about me that were like him." She remembered, in particular, their playing a game of pickup sticks together. "All of a sudden he grabbed my hands and said that my hands were just like his, a feminine version of his hands. He couldn't get over it," said Alex. But it was more than that. "He also sensed that my mind worked a lot like his . . . This likeness between us did not make our relationship any easier," she pointed out, "because sometimes it is hard to communicate on a day-to-day basis when one is a lot like somebody else. We shared the same self-motivation, the same stubbornness, the same intensity."

■

Even after Alex's mother stopped working with him, Lou continued to see his daughter regularly. But now another child, Nathaniel, entered the picture as well, for shortly after Anne Tyng left Kahn's firm, Harriet Pattison returned to town. After spending a year and a half apprenticing with Dan Kiley's office in Vermont, Pattison had decided to earn a formal degree in landscaping. She enrolled in the University of Pennsylvania's master's program in landscape architecture, and in the fall of 1964 she and Nathaniel moved back to Philadelphia.

Around the time she began her first semester at Penn, Lou set up a tiny office for Harriet on the fourth floor of his building. "He was on the fifth floor in the corner," said David Slovic, who worked at Lou's firm throughout the three years Pattison was studying at Penn. "Harriet was downstairs. They had made a little place for her in a storage room—a place for her drafting table and her things. She would work on her schoolwork, and Lou would give her crits."

David didn't know whether or not she was involved in any of the firm's projects, but "we all knew who she was, and that she was Nathaniel's mother. In the office it was known about Lou's various adventures, and we all protected him." One of the ways his employees did that was to make sure Harriet and Esther never encountered each other during Esther's unannounced visits to the office. "I can remember times when they would say, 'Esther is in the lobby; she's coming up.' I don't know how they knew—maybe the elevator operator," said Slovic. "They would make sure that Harriet's door was closed. Esther would just stop by and leave. It happened maybe every couple of weeks, not in any overbearing way, just because she needed to connect with Lou about something."

For Harriet, being shut away in an eight-by-ten-foot windowless storage room, sometimes with the door locked from the outside, could not have been a pleasant experience. Years later, when her son suggested that her position must have been very uncomfortable, she acknowledged, "It was humiliating in some ways." But when Nathaniel asked why she always protected Lou, why she didn't express anger at the situation he had put her into, she denied feeling any anger. In the end, she said, the deal was worth it: what she got in exchange for whatever she had to give up was more than enough.

As for Esther, she endured her own form of humiliation, though the people at the office tended to underestimate her awareness, regarding her instead as some kind of oblivious battle-ax figure in a rollicking marital comedy. "We always used to say that Lou's wife was one mistress behind," chuckled Ed Richards. Neither he nor anyone else at the office seemed to know that Esther had learned about Harriet's pregnancy before Nathaniel was born. And if the shutting of the storage-room door had its farce-like aspects, the theater piece was one that Lou helped to perpetuate by performing his expected role. Ed recalled one day, for instance, when he and a friend were returning to the office after lunch, and "Lou comes down the steps with a big smile on his face. Usually he would have taken the elevator, but he was coming down the steps. We get up to his office, and there was Esther; somehow he had got around her, and that's why he was smiling."

For the most part, the men who worked with Lou had no problem with his various lovers and his children out of wedlock. On the contrary, they seemed to get a kick out of it, as if it proved something about how special he was, or maybe how *un*special he was. "We just thought, here's this very famous person, but on the side he's just a guy that had mistresses," said Ed Richards. Jack MacAllister took it as a symptom of the times. "It was the age of Henry Miller," Jack pointed out. "We were all reading Henry Miller." Jack recalled hearing from David Zoob, Lou's lawyer, about a client of his, or maybe it was a client of someone else's, whose invention was going to revolutionize the world; that turned out to be the Pill, which was finally approved for general use in 1960. "In the Fifties and early Sixties, everyone was screwing everybody," MacAllister remarked. "It was a giant free-for-all." In this atmosphere, to be critical of Lou's behavior was seen as a sign of prudishness, or perhaps excessive religious zeal.

One of the few men in the office who openly disapproved was Carles Enrique Vallhonrat. Vallhonrat was a Spanish-speaking, Argentine-trained architect who worked with Kahn for most of the 1960s, starting with the Salk project. An intelligent and capable man much respected by Lou, he struck some people as austere or arrogant; others characterized him as honesty and rectitude personified. Observing that most of his colleagues didn't comment one way or the other on Lou's extramarital love life, Fred Langford recalled, "The only one definitely had an opinion against it was Vallhonrat. He was very much against it."

As for Harriet's presence in the office, Fred himself simply took it in stride, the way most others did. "They were certainly not lovey-dovey, kept it pretty businesslike," he said about Harriet and Lou. "Everyone knew that she was Lou's paramour, and everyone knew there was a boy involved."

Not everyone learned it at the same time, though. Balkrishna Doshi recalled how, on one of his fall stints at Penn, where he came annually to give a short course of lectures in the architecture department, Lou took him over to Harriet's place without telling him where they were going. Once they were there, Kahn introduced the little boy to Doshi as his son. Doshi had not heard a word beforehand about the relationship with Harriet or the birth of Nathaniel; now the child was simply being presented to him. He felt he had been allowed this sudden peek into Lou's private life because "I was an outsider, and yet family to Lou." Nor did he wish to make anything of the revelation. "A sage may have other affairs, but you don't want to know about that," Doshi pointed out. "You wanted to know what he was talking about."

When Henry Wilcots first mentioned to Louis Kahn, around the middle of 1964, that he was planning to move back to the United States from Pakistan, Lou suggested that he stop by for a visit in Philadelphia on his way home. As it turned out, however, Wilcots wasn't staying on the East Coast long enough. "I called him and said I won't be able to get to Philadelphia because there's a family event in Des Moines, and then I'm going on to Denver," Henry recalled. He and his wife had missed Colorado, and they wanted to return there even though Henry had no firm offer of employment. But Lou had other plans. "He asked for an address where he could reach me in Des Moines," said Henry, "and then I received a cablegram at my parents' address in Des Moines: *Welcome when ready. Lou.* So I changed my ticket and went to Philadelphia." Henry started working at Kahn's office in September of 1964, and meanwhile he began looking for a place to house his family, which ultimately included two sons as well as his wife, Eileen.

One day, soon after his arrival, he got a phone call from Esther Kahn. "We met on the telephone," he said. "When I first came to the office, she called and wanted to speak with me. Lou must have told her about me. We just chatted on the phone."

Then Esther asked him a pointed question: Where was he looking for housing? And Henry understood right away why she was asking. As an African-American, he was well aware that although landlords and realtors might pretend to show him their available places, only a limited number would actually be willing to rent to him. There were relatively few black professionals in Philadelphia at the time, and even fewer black architects. "I think there might have been a couple," Wilcots guessed. "I never got a chance to talk to them, we were so separate."

So Esther's phone call really made a difference to him. "The good thing about her, she was very straight," Henry said. "She told me about the neighborhoods where I would be welcome and where I would not be welcome." After their conversation he just stopped looking in the hopeless places, and his family ended up settling permanently in Germantown. Someone of a different temperament might well have been taken aback by Esther's direct, not to say brash, approach, but Henry found it enchanting. "Wonderful woman," he emphasized, and it was an opinion from which he never deviated.

The other person who made Henry feel welcome was Dave Wisdom, the architect who ran Lou's office. "When I came here, other than Esther, he was the one who—he and his wife invited me to dinner at their house," Henry explained. In fact, the Wisdoms invited both Henry and Eileen to come have dinner with them. "So we got out there, to Swarthmore, and had Sunday dinner with he and his wife, and he introduced me to his daughters," said Henry. In other words, the evening had all the earmarks of a casual social event between work colleagues, which is precisely what made it so unusual in the genteelly segregated Philadelphia of 1964.

"His house was filled with magazines and books and *New Yorker*s and artworks," Wilcots recalled. "He had the Smithsonian collection of jazz work on vinyl—maybe some of it on shellac records." Dave was a big reader, Henry discovered, and so was his wife, Helen, who volunteered at a local library. And they were both Quakers. "Helen attended services, but Dave as far as I know didn't," Henry observed. "He practiced it in his own way. He never flaunted it, never pronounced it. He was an old Pennsylvanian. He was a terrific guy, and he and I got along."

Actually, there was no one in Kahn's office who did *not* get along with Dave Wisdom. That was one of his essential qualities, part of the means by which he had been holding the place together for more than twenty years. First at Stonorov & Kahn, then at Lou's solo offices at 1728 Spruce and 138 20th Street, and finally at 1501 Walnut, Dave supervised all the employees and coordinated an ever-growing number of projects. It was Wisdom—"the well-named Quaker," as Jack

MacAllister called him—who had the calmness, the intelligence, and the steady practicality needed to keep the firm going. "Dave was different. Dave was benign. Dave was agnostic," said Richard Wurman. "Nobody disliked Dave. Dave was glue. You needed glue to keep the packing case together."

"Dave *was* the office," said Henry Wilcots. "Of course everyone knew that there was only one architect in the office, and that was Lou. Yet Lou was in and out. Dave held things together. He was the day-to-day person." According to Henry, "he was involved in every project that came through that office. Often times when a new job came in, the first person that Lou talked to was Dave." And as the project progressed, Wisdom's role became even more important. "During the working drawing stage, he was consulted by everyone who was in charge of a job," Wilcots said. "They would go to Dave about things: 'How should this work?' He would sit down and work out the detail. When you had a problem, you went to Dave. Sometimes Lou would come in and say to Dave, 'What do you want me to do? You tell me.' And Dave would say, 'Do such and such.'"

This is not to say that the relationship between Kahn and Wisdom was uniformly placid. Dave, unlike many others, was always willing to raise objections to Lou's ideas. ("Dave was not a rah-rah man," Wilcots pointed out, and in Kahn's firm "there were a lot of those.") Although Lou had once told Henry that Dave was his best critic, he would still resist the criticism if he didn't like it. Gary Moye, who came to work at the firm a few years after Henry Wilcots, remembered a time when he and Henry had felt that the project they were working on, Temple Beth-El, needed to be redesigned if it were to work. "We brought this matter to Dave's attention," said Moye, "and he arranged for us all to meet with Lou. I remember that at a crucial point in the meeting, David, knowing the status of the work and the amount of fee left, suggested that we 'couldn't afford to back up.' Lou got very angry and said, 'We can't afford not to!' That was where it was left, and Henry and I revisited and reconfigured the structural elements so they were buildable." But Moye, despite the fact that he himself had advocated the reworking, took away from the occasion "great respect for David's point of view (as Lou's financial straits affected all of us) and for his willingness to speak up to Lou."

"Dave's details were all very practical," said Wilcots. "He would say, 'I don't know, Lou. What's this for? What's it going to do? It's meaningless!' Sometimes Lou would get angry with Dave and would go storming out." But he would always come back sooner or later, and generally sooner. To Henry, it just seemed as if their relationship was that of "old-time friends. You know how you can live with your friends, you can get angry at your friends. Sometimes Lou would get angry at Dave, and then he'd turn around the next day and appreciate him." Henry felt that an underlying feeling of mutual respect bound them together. It also helped that Dave's own strong sense of self allowed him to remain calm in the face of Lou's outbursts. "Nothing bothered Dave," said Wilcots. "He didn't appear to get upset, and others would get upset that Dave didn't get upset."

Some of the others took this composure as a sign of weakness on Dave's part. "Dave Wisdom was a wonderful, sweet man, very smart, but not aggressive, not individually strong," commented David Slovic. "Dave Wisdom was a kind of saint," said Ed Richards. "He loved Lou, but Lou treated him badly like everyone else." Fred Langford called Dave "a real nice person, a very cooperative guy," but felt that Lou didn't really rely on him for design input. "He did rely on Dave for construction details— the flashing, the way the building was put together," Langford observed. "He'd say to some young guy, 'Go ask Dave, he'll know.'" And as Langford and others pointed out, Dave was never too busy to answer questions: he was always available, and he used his availability to guard Lou's time. "He'd say, 'Don't bother him, he's busy.' He was like Lou's protector," Fred recalled. "Dave was always respectful of Lou. And we knew that there was respect from Lou toward Dave, but it didn't show. They'd been together so long, there was no warmth there. It was sort of like antagonistic brothers," Fred concluded.

Wisdom's privileged position at the office did show in one way, though, and that was in the hours he worked. Everyone else put in the same crazy hours Lou did. "Day or night made little difference to Lou," Gary Moye pointed out. "If the work needed to be done it had to be done, even if it couldn't be achieved within conventional working hours. Keep in mind that the office was operated more as an artist's studio than as a professional business." But Dave Wisdom kept strictly businessman's hours. "He was there in the morning, 8:30 or whatever, and would quit about 5:30 or 6:00," said Fred Langford. "Sometimes, if things were really busy, he would come in on a Saturday or Sunday. But for the most part he did not work the long hours everyone else did." Henry Wilcots agreed: "Right. That's true. He'd go home." One time, Henry remembered, they were all working around the clock, "weekends and everything. And Dave told Lou he wouldn't be in that Saturday or Sunday. And Lou said to him, 'Oh, you mean because of your religion?'" Henry never knew for sure if that was supposed to be a joke or not. (Neither, apparently, did Dave. Years after Lou's death, Wisdom was to say to an interviewer, "To the end of his life, Kahn led himself to believe that certain Quakers had religious scruples against working on Sunday.")

During regular hours, at any rate, Dave Wisdom presided over an office that, despite its elements of chaos, had definite patterns and routines. Dave himself sat at a desk that was just to the left of the fifth-floor entrance, the first desk you came to in the main drafting room. If instead of going left you turned to the right, you would come to Louise's desk, which was parked just outside Lou's enclosed office and immediately next to the bathroom. Louise kept the office calendar open on her desk and facing outward, so that anyone who wanted to know where Lou was—or had been, or was shortly going to be—could come by and consult it, and Lou often added his own handwritten additions and corrections to the schedule.

On the days when Lou was there and planned to stay a while, he would go into his own office, take off his jacket, and put on one of the cardigan sweaters he kept there. Then he would walk around the drafting room looking at the projects, speaking to the architect who had lead responsibility for each, and finally ending up at Dave's desk, where they'd talk over various issues. Sometimes, especially later in the day, Kahn would spend time in his office with the door closed, either on the phone or napping. Occasionally he would be in there sketching, and then he would come out with his roll of yellow tracing paper and show the new design to the person working on that project, explaining what he wanted changed. "He would come to your table and say, 'Could you move this . . .' He always had the yellow paper handy, the cheap tracing paper," said Langford. Kahn also had a little sketchbook that he always carried with him, so that if he got an idea on a train or a plane, he could capture it in a quick drawing and then bring it back to the office. But mostly he seemed to come up with his ideas on the spot. "The beauty of watching him work out a sketch," Wilcots recalled. "He would come and push you off your stool and start sketching: putting it down, rubbing it out. And he would be talking about the second floor, wipe it out, do the third floor—and you had to follow that."

Of course, there were many days when Kahn didn't come into the office at all, usually because he was away on a work-related trip. Louise made all his travel plans, and over the years she learned to avoid the kinds of calamities that had plagued her job at the beginning. One of her first travel mistakes occurred soon after she began working for Lou, when he had to go up to Rochester for the Unitarian Church project. "Never having traveled by train, I knew nothing about the accommodations," Louise recalled. "I reserved a roomette for him, which proved a disaster. His comment to me: 'I may be only 5'6", but even a midget couldn't dangle his feet in one of those.' I got the message."

After her second travel mistake—sending him off on an overseas trip with an expired passport—Louise had offered to resign, but Lou insisted she stay on. "Even baseball players get three strikes," he told her. "I can't let you go yet because I want to see if you can top this one." She never did, and by the mid-1960s she was handling more travel for him than ever.

One of the most interesting foreign trips she sent him on was not, in fact, connected to any specific project. In the summer of 1965, Kahn was invited to travel to the Soviet Union as part of the State Department's cultural exchange program. Vincent Scully, who went along on the same trip, later reported on the experience of looking at Russian architecture with Lou. "Once during one of those summer nights in Moscow we walked around the Kremlin," Scully said. "The Kremlin towers are wonderful, romantic—they were built by Italian architects—and I said to him, 'Lou, look how they point.' And they do, if you read it that way. But Lou said, 'Look, instead, at the way they bring the weight down.' It is true, they are all masonry, and one can really see the compression coming down the wall. It is beautiful. I always thought that was the key to Kahn's architecture."

An equally telling moment occurred when they were in Leningrad, at the opening of an American-sponsored show about American architecture. Scully called it "a disgracefully unprofessional exhibition, chosen to astound the Russians with the glitter and glamour of our material culture." When Kahn was asked to speak about the exhibit to the mayor of Leningrad and his entourage, he refused. "He said it was a disgrace and he wouldn't do such a thing," Scully recounted. "But he agreed to walk along and be there in case there was a question." And in the event a question did indeed arise—regarding Kahn's own Rochester church, about which the Russian mayor commented that it didn't look like a church at all. "That's why it was chosen for exhibition to the Soviet Union," Lou instantly responded, smiling. The interpreter ("a terrible square," according to Scully) didn't translate Kahn's remark, but that didn't prevent the Russians from laughing heartily.

■

As the 1960s progressed, life back at the Philadelphia office got more and more frenzied. "It was busy," remarked Wilcots, waving his hands in all directions to indicate the apparent confusion. "There was a lot of shuffling going on. No one was gotten rid of. There was a lot of coming and going. People would arrive to work on a charrette, work a short time, and then they would move on. I don't think anyone was ever fired." Perhaps not, but some people were certainly laid off, particularly when the project they were engaged on was finished. "At the end of Bryn Mawr he let everyone go who had worked on it," said Ed Richards. "They were laid off. He had run out of money."

From about 1965 onward, the shortage of money became an increasingly desperate theme in Kahn's office. Louise—whom Henry described as "the mother hen, a very jolly kind of person"—had to hold down a second job with a catering firm to support her family, as the income from her secretarial job became more and more erratic. Henry himself, despite the fact that his wife worked as a nurse, had problems paying his bills because his paychecks often didn't come on time. Gary Moye once found himself getting so far behind financially, even with moonlighting jobs added to his regular work, that he told Lou he had to quit. "He turned on the charm and asked me to stay," Moye remembered. "He said that he would be receiving payment soon for one of the projects and that he would pay me up. I told him I couldn't accept that since everyone else was in the same situation." Then Lou told Gary to take the weekend off and come back on Monday, by which time he would have something worked out. "On Monday he called me into his office and gave me a personal check from Esther to cover some of my back pay," said Moye. "I have always wondered how many other times she may have helped Lou in this way."

David Slovic, who was paid at an hourly rate while he was still in architecture school, would find himself negotiating with Louise or Dave Wisdom about the arrival of his checks. "They were very open about it. 'We'll have a problem paying you until two weeks from Wednesday— how much do you need to survive until then?' And then two weeks from Wednesday the check would come through," Slovic recalled. "This didn't happen every time: maybe half or a third of the times. I think that Dacca was a very irregularly paying proposition," he added.

It was so irregular, in fact, that at one point Lou sent Jack Mac-Allister over to Pakistan to collect the half a million dollars the firm was owed by the government. "President Khan was a great, big man," Jack remembered. "He spoke perfect English because he had been at Sandhurst. He called me Mr. MacAllister. After a few preliminaries, he said, 'What can I do for you?' I said, 'Pay us.' 'Do I owe you a lot?' he said. 'Enough to shut us down,' I said." MacAllister told him that if they weren't paid, the Dacca project would be left unfinished. According to Jack, the money was in Lou's bank account by the following Monday morning.

MacAllister also figured in a financial negotiation involving the Salk project. As it turned out, even this stellar client did not have bottomless pockets, and at a certain point Basil O'Connor, the head of the March of Dimes, decided to intervene. He made a conference call to Lou that also included Jonas Salk, and the two of them asked Lou to put Jack on the line as well. "O'Connor said, 'Lou, we're going to fire you. The project's not on schedule, you're not paying your bills, it's a mess,'" Jack recounted. "Lou says, 'Is there anything I can do?' They said, 'Yes. You can put Jack as the head of the project, in charge of everything.' And Lou said, 'Why didn't I think of that?'"

By 1965 the budgeting problems at Salk had become so severe that the Meeting House had to be eliminated from the plans. For most of the people working with Kahn then, and probably for Kahn himself, this represented a terrible loss. The Meeting House was not only the conceptual heart of the project, the place where artists, humanists, and scientists would encounter each other's ideas; it was also one of Lou's most entrancing designs, with large windows surrounded by tall, pale concrete walls that allowed reflected light to enter the interior from all angles. This was a notion that he would eventually revive to stunning effect in the mosque of the Dacca Assembly Building, but that consolation still lay in the future.

What preoccupied Lou at the moment was what to do with the Salk's central garden. He had hired landscape architect Lawrence Halprin to come up with an initial design, but Halprin's suggestion that they plant shrubs and trees right up against the concrete pleased no one. Then Lou came across some designs by the Mexican architect Luis Barragán, published in a Museum of Modern Art book that also contained the plans for Kahn and Noguchi's playground. Early in 1965 Kahn decided to contact Barragán by phone, but since he spoke no Spanish, he had one of his employees, a Puerto Rican architect named Rafael Villamil, make the initial call.

"I introduced myself and said, 'I am calling from the office of Louis Kahn,'" Villamil remembered. "Barragán said, 'Who is Louis Kahn?' I was sitting next to him, and I said, 'He says, who are you?'"

Lou, undaunted, answered, "Tell him to ask some of his architect friends." A friendly conversation apparently ensued, because a week after the phone call, on January 20, 1965, Kahn wrote to Barragán in Mexico City and thanked him for the time spent on the telephone. He emphasized how much he looked forward to getting Barragán's guidance on the Salk project, adding (in his typically peculiar Lou-language, which always sounded like a translation from some unknown tongue), "I also feel from the work of yours I have seen, you are in touch with the virility of approach to man's will of shaping the ground and the planting of shrubs, compared to the ways of nature." A few months later, in Mexico, the two architects met in person for the first time. It would seem that they already felt comfortable enough to joke with each other, for Kahn, on seeing Barragán's brightly painted walls, admitted that they were beautiful but nonetheless argued that concrete should always remain unpainted, to which Barragán reportedly responded, "Okay, you win the argument but I'm going to keep painting the walls."

Then, in a later encounter that was to become the stuff of legend, Luis Barragán, Louis Kahn, and Jonas Salk all met together at the nearly completed Salk Institute on February 24, 1966. The two rows of study towers were already in place, with their respective labs standing behind them, but they faced each other across an undeveloped mud expanse, and the question was what to do with it. According to Lou's version of the story, he had brought Barragán in because of the wonderful things he had done with gardens, but when the Mexican architect actually saw the space itself, he said, "There should be no garden. It should be a plaza."

"I looked at Salk," Kahn recalled, "he looked at me, and we both agreed that a garden was not what we wanted; it should be a plaza. Barragán said, *If you make it a plaza, it will give you a façade to the sky,* and it killed me, because it was a wonderful idea. I could only counter it by saying, *That's right, then I would get all those blue mosaics for nothing,* meaning, of course, the Pacific."

So the marvelous plaza—possibly the most powerful, intriguing part of the Salk Institute's final design—was practically an accident, or at any rate the unpredictable result of a confluence of visions. Nor did the matter end neatly there. Kahn's first impulse was to pave the plaza in *recinto*, a dark volcanic stone that Barragán had used in Mexico. "Lou liked it because it was like an elephant's hide," observed Jack MacAllister. "Then for some reason he decided against that and wanted a pinkish stone, the one used for the cathedral in San Miguel de Allende." But that would have required reopening the Mexican quarry which had produced the stone, so it was prohibitively expensive. "It was about then that Lou suggested Roman travertine. It turned out that it cost less than vinyl tile. And that," said Jack, "was the largest single shipment of travertine ever to come into the United States." With its pale, finely textured surface and its subtle relationship to the color of the concrete, the travertine turned out to be crucial to the character of the Salk plaza. The whole space would have been unimaginably different if chance (in the form of cost and availability) had allowed Lou to pave it in dark gray or even pink, for it was the ivory-colored travertine that in the end gave the Pacific-facing complex its resplendent luminosity.

Now that the Salk project was starting to wind down, Kahn sent Fred Langford out to Dacca to deal with a new and different challenge in concrete. The National Assembly project—or, as it was still called in 1966, the Second Capital project—was the biggest job of Kahn's career, and it was in many ways the most difficult. Not only did he have to deal with the Pakistan Public Works Department and all their requests and requirements; he also had to face the fact that East Pakistan was an extremely poor region with relatively primitive building techniques. In India he had got round a similar problem by building almost entirely in brick, with structures that were never more than three or four stories high. In Dacca, by contrast, he was going to be putting up an immense nine-story building reaching 140 feet at its peak. For the nearby two-story residential structures, designed to house visiting Members of Parliament, Kahn could use the traditional brick—and indeed, with their elegant cutouts and graceful arches, those residences ended up looking a great deal like the Ahmedabad buildings. But the central structure, the massive Assembly Building itself, had to be done in concrete, and that called for Fred's expertise.

When Fred Langford arrived in Dacca in February of 1966, he was met at the airport by his brother Gus, who also worked for Louis Kahn (and indeed was to continue working for Kahn until the very end, long after Fred had left to found his own concrete consulting firm). The two brothers went straight from the airport to a local golf course, where they played a couple of rounds together and were amazed to discover that the caddies applauded after every shot. Then they settled down to work. Gus Langford's duties in regard to the Dacca site were various, and were to remain so during the many years he spent working on the project, but Fred's, for that relatively brief period in 1966, were exclusively focused on concrete construction techniques.

By the time Fred arrived, certain crucial decisions had already been made. The Parliament Building would be set on a patch of built-up land in the middle of an artificial lake, which would separate the Assembly from the surrounding brick residences. In addition to adding substantial visual interest to the site, the shallow lake would suggest an affinity with the surrounding countryside, where monsoon-level rains and converging rivers often inundated the lowlands. The building itself would be octagonal at its core and roughly diamond-shaped on the outside, though from the viewpoint of an external observer, that central structure would be so disguised by curving outer walls on one side, and gigantic triangular, circular, and square cutouts on the others, as to be nearly indecipherable in shape. And as if to complicate the essential symmetry even further, the mosque, which was to occupy one of the four points of the diamond, would be shifted ever so slightly off its axis, emphasizing the fact that it faced directly toward Mecca. Yet despite all these potentially confusing elements, Kahn managed to unify the whole building through its consistent materials: a medium-gray concrete textured by narrow wooden form-boards and striated at regular intervals with thin bands of white marble.

Those distinctive marble stripes, one of the most noticeable features of the finished design, actually arose in response to a local construction problem. In the Dacca of that time, the only way to pour this amount of concrete was to have many individual workers, each carrying a panful of wet concrete on his head, march single-file from the cement mixer across hundreds of feet of rough terrain and up long ramps of bamboo scaffolding, where they would then dump their pans into the prearranged forms. What this meant was that the walls could only rise by about five feet a day. Looking at the results of the early pours, Lou was disturbed by the evident join, the place where one day's work met the next. So he resolved to recess the concrete every five feet, leaving a six-inch gap that would later be filled with a horizontal strip of white marble. He then introduced intermittent vertical bands of marble into the design as well, creating a wall that would look from a distance as if it were composed of rectangular gray blocks edged in white.

Fred Langford's job was to make this laborious construction process succeed. He had nothing to do with choosing the color of the cement (which was imported in bulk from Russia and China, the only places where sufficient quantity was available at an affordable price), and though he checked to make sure the stone and sand brought in from the Sylhet region of East Pakistan were good enough to use in the mix, that decision too had been made before he arrived. Plywood was simply not available in East Pakistan, so the forms had to be built out of a mahogany-like wood instead; the work was done by a furniture manufacturer in Chittagong, a city more than a hundred miles southeast of Dacca. The workmanship on the form construction was much poorer than what Fred was used to—the unseasoned boards warped easily, among other problems—so Fred compensated by making the panels stronger than he had in La Jolla. On Lou's instructions, he also made them with an indentation at each juncture point, which produced an attractive V-shaped extrusion as a regular pattern in the concrete.

Another local problem Fred encountered in Dacca was the nature of the steel rebar. "Standard Western reinforcing rods have deformations all along the length, protruding ridges that grab the concrete," Langford explained. But the bars in Dacca were smooth, something he had never seen before. Luckily, "Komendant and Nick Gianopulos figured out how to make these smooth rods work, by putting hooks at the ends to make up for it."

Actually, Komendant and Gianopulos worked sequentially on Dacca, not simultaneously—and they were not the only engineers Kahn employed on this lengthy commission. Keast & Hood, Nick's firm, had agreed to be part of the Second Capital team when it was put together in 1963, but in 1965 they withdrew from the project. They were forced to bow out, Nick said, "because Lou owed us so much money that we were going bankrupt, and the banks wouldn't loan us money. He owed us $90,000." (They continued, though, to do other jobs for him over the years, and eventually they were even paid back the full $90,000, albeit in piecemeal payments. Kahn may have been bad with money, "but the obligation was always honored," Gianopulos pointed out; "Lou always paid us what we agreed on. He never came back and said, 'I lost money on this so you have to reduce your fee.' The man had honor, but it may not have been the conventional honor.")

At some point after Keast & Hood left the Dacca project, Gus Komendant was brought in, mainly to work on the very difficult problem of the roof. But he too quit before it could be solved. It was left to a third engineer, Harry Palmbaum, to come up with a satisfactory way to cover over the Assembly Hall. In its final incarnation, this ceiling was an eight-sided concrete parasol that hovered over the parliamentary meeting space, resting with apparent lightness on its eight points of contact with the wall and allowing light to seep in under its edges. Such an engineering miracle would have been astonishing in any location, but in Dacca it seemed like something that had flown in from outer space—as, indeed, did the entire Assembly Building. Yet in this version of the science-fiction visitation, the aliens from the future did not obliterate the past, but somehow managed to preserve a sense of the ancient and the traditional even as they brought in the new.

That, in a practical sense, was Langford's task in the four months he spent on the site. Even as he worked closely with the laborers and their supervisors to train them to produce high-quality, modern concrete, he also paid attention, whenever possible, to their preferred way of doing things. For example, when he suggested that vibrators needed to be used to settle the concrete after it was poured, the laborers insisted that they could instead stir it with bamboo poles, as they had always done. Fred let them do this, and at first the concrete looked smooth from the outside; only when it was stripped did he discover that it was filled with rock pockets. "A disaster," Fred termed it. "They had to take it down by hand: two men with hammers, taking down a wall five feet high and eighteen inches thick and about thirty to forty feet long." He ended up importing at least one electrical vibrator (the mechanical ones available locally were pretty much useless) and he got the workers to use it during the rest of the construction.

The days got hotter and hotter from February to May, eventually requiring a two-hour rest period in the middle of the day. The workday should have started at nine and ended about seven, but Langford's entire crew always worked until at least nine or ten, and often they stayed until midnight. "A pour which here would take twenty-five minutes would take two or three hours there, because you're only using a dishpanful at a time," Fred observed. He decided to speed up the process and also make the laborers' work easier by doubling the size of the concrete pans and putting handles on either side, so that they could be carried by two workers instead of one. Yet even when the pan sizes were doubled, the laborers still continued to carry them individually on their heads. When Fred protested, they would say, "Oh, it's not so heavy."

To help him create the metal accessories required for the pouring process—all the loops and bolts and brackets and clamps and plates that were needed to put the wooden forms together and take them apart—Langford employed a group of students from a nearby vocational school. These young men, he noticed, would often address him by a name he didn't understand. "What does it mean?" Fred asked his driver one day, and the man answered, "Favorite uncle." That May, shortly before Langford left Dacca for good, a photograph was taken of the entire group, including two supervisors, about forty students, and the Favorite Uncle, all standing together in a semicircle, their construction tools laid out neatly in the space in front of them. Although the tall, thin American, hands clasped behind his back, was captured at a distance and was wearing sunglasses, it was still possible to read from both his facial expression and his body language how proud he was of what they had accomplished together.

. Fred Langford must have been pleased with the photo, too, because he included it in a 98-page "Report on Concrete and Formwork" that he submitted to the Pakistan Public Works Department in June of 1966. Like most reports of its kind, this one was filled with abstruse technical information and repetitive details, but it ended on an uncharacteristically personal note. "I would also like to thank the men in the field who participated in the formwork and casting operations. Their wonderful spirit and willingness to cooperate in spite of the limited facilities and trying conditions," Fred wrote, "was an inspiring lesson in life that I will always treasure." And he did. All through his long career of working in concrete, the memory of that Dacca period remained etched in his mind, though he never returned there in the subsequent half-century, and hence never saw the Parliament Building in its finished state.

IN SITU:
NATIONAL ASSEMBLY
BUILDING OF BANGLADESH

Interior of National Assembly Building
(Photograph by Raymond Meier, courtesy of the photographer)

Just seeing it in photographs fairly takes one's breath away. In Raymond Meier's color pictures and, especially, in Nathaniel Kahn's film *My Architect*, the National Assembly Building comes across as Louis Kahn's most supremely beautiful accomplishment. Particularly in the shots taken at dawn or twilight, the structure glimmers across its surrounding pool of water like a fairy-tale castle or a visionary dream brought to life.

The building is indeed remarkable, and it may well be Kahn's masterpiece, but the experience of encountering it in person is much more complicated than those lovely images would suggest. At first glance, when seen at some distance, it is downright strange—so strange that its oddity rather than its beauty is the dominant impression. Hulking alone against the skyline, looming above an otherwise flat plain, this weirdly striped cluster of variously shaped walls, some curving, some flat, some punctured by giant cutouts, defines itself first of all as unique. It is not just the only building of its kind in Dhaka or Bangladesh. It is the only one in the world.

This is not to say that there are not discernible influences, as there always are when something is this powerful. No one can build such a masterpiece alone: a good architect needs to stand on the shoulders of others. In this case, you can see traces of Le Corbusier's Chandigarh (another government complex set on an artificial lake) as well as older and more anonymously designed structures like Sarkej Roza in India or Castel del Monte in Italy. The former is a geometrically patterned

Islamic structure lapped at its edges by water, its sunlit squares alternating with deep shade; the latter is an octagonal castle with full-height corner towers, carved out of pale limestone and visible for miles around. One cannot swear that Kahn was thinking of any of these buildings when he designed the Dhaka Parliament, just as one cannot be sure how clearly he remembered the medieval castle surrounded by a moat that he saw on his childhood island of Ösel. But some or all of these buildings were almost certain to have gone into the making of his Dhaka Assembly. (This is, after all, the man who simultaneously denied and admitted being influenced by any architectural antecedents, dryly noting, for instance, "I have a book of castles and I try to pretend that I did not look at this book but everybody reminds me of it and I have to admit that I looked very thoroughly at this book.") Even so, none of these possible predecessors is quite as startling, in its context, as the National Assembly of Bangladesh. Part of what Kahn's building seems to declare, in fact, is the very impossibility of its presence in that place—as if the surprise of its having been constructed at all were to be preserved in perpetuity.

As you approach, this initial strangeness does not wear off. Depending on the angle of your approach, the building takes on different shapes, with one side emphasizing its cylindrical towers, another its obliquely angled walls. There is no way to grasp the pattern of the whole from down on the ground. All you can be sure of, as you get closer and closer, is that something important takes place here. The high walls have an imposing quality that is strengthened rather than softened by the alternating textures of concrete and marble, the wood-patterned gray marked off vertically and horizontally by the smoother white. It is as if a giant had been playing with these blocks and had shaped them into this whimsical pattern in order to tempt you closer. The temptation works. You are ready to risk all to get inside.

There is a grand entrance at the front, but these days it is used only for ceremonial occasions. These days, too, the plazas and steps and lawns surrounding the structure are empty and desolate at all hours. Heightened security has banished the general population from this place that was meant for them, this public spot where they once exercised or strolled or simply stood and admired the massive hall built in their name. "They've destroyed it. I do not visit—only in photographs," says the architect Shamsul Wares, who cannot bear to see the effects of the twenty-first century's security measures on a place he so much loved.

Once the guards have checked your pass and your identification, and confiscated your cell phone and your shoulder bag, and ushered you through the metal detector at the end of the entrance tunnel, you will find yourself on the building's lowest level. Practically the first thing that greets you, on the facing wall, is a sort of shrine to Louis Kahn, with two photographs of him, one young, one old, along with a display of architectural plans and a scale model of the building. The setup suggests a degree of reverence that Kahn rarely if ever met with elsewhere, and this sense of a personal debt to the architect is reinforced by the fact that many ordinary Bangladeshis actually know his name. The building itself is pictured on a standard piece of currency, the thousand-thaka note—another honor Kahn never received from any other country, including his own. When pressed, citizens ranging from taxi drivers to prominent politicians will say that they are grateful to him because "he brought us democracy," as if the building and its function were one and the same.

Looking at the plans and the model that are located beneath Kahn's photos, you can see that the building is structured in the shape of a diamond, one of whose four points lies at the entrance you have just come through. The octagonal assembly hall is at the center of the diamond, the mosque is somewhere directly over your head, and a series of offices and chambers line the four outer walls, set off from the interior functions by an ambulatory that runs around the entire building. It all looks simple and understandable in the plan. In actuality, it is just the opposite. The building is so changeable, so complicated, and so different at every level that you will repeatedly find yourself lost. "This is the process of learning truth: through disorientation," notes Wares.

It is an appropriate methodology for a building that houses the apparatus of democracy, and it applies even to those at the pinnacle of the political structure. "Yes, yes, I'm like Alice in Wonderland," says the Speaker of the Assembly, Dr. Shirin Sharmin Chaudhury, when you ask her if she has ever gotten lost in this vast space. "You can't go everywhere by lift," she points out. "You need to know the access. Otherwise you will lose your way."

In fact, it is only with the assistance of a clever guide that you've managed to wend your way up the ramps and stairs and balconies to Dr. Chaudhury's elegant double-height office, located near the top of the nine-story building. Barely even aware that there *were* lifts, you would have hesitated to use an elevator even if you could find one. At least from the ambulatory you have a continuing sense of the space above you and the space below you: you know where you are vertically, even if you have no idea about anything else.

Still, the sense of disorientation that you experience in the Dhaka Parliament is countered by something much rarer, and that is a feeling of profound wonder. No photo or even film image of the interior can begin to convey what it feels like to occupy these spaces. Visual enticement enters into it—the shimmer of light on the marble-banded walls, the brief glimpses of the exterior landscape through the slits of windows, the Piranesian views from the higher balconies, the pale diagonal ramps slicing across gránd circular cutouts, and the other pleasing geometrical patterns formed by the structures and materials. All this is spellbindingly beautiful. But that is the least of it. There is something dreamlike about your passage through the building (and occasionally something nightmarish, in those terrifyingly vertiginous views from the upper balconies—but even the fear is an aspect of the wonder). As you go higher and higher, observing the minute, delightful idiosyncrasies that Kahn wrought at every level of the complex design, you cannot help but feel that the building itself is changing you. The person who emerges from it will not be quite the same as the person who went in.

From inside this building, it is possible to gain an understanding of Kahn's genius that none of his other marvelous structures is quite prepared to give you. For here is where he most clearly demonstrates what is implicit everywhere else: that the inside and the outside do not match up. Being outside a Kahn building (or any building, for that matter) is primarily a visual experience, something that can tend toward static appreciation. But what a Kahn building offers you on the inside is a drama, a journey, a narrative with a plot. The drama may be set off by visual elements, but even that is more complicated than it seems. Light and shadow, for example, are not purely visible. They are also tangible, or "sensorial," as Shamsul Wares puts it. You can feel the sun on your body, or the gratifying coolness as you move into the shade; even without actually feeling these things, you can imagine them as sense impressions rather than just visual stimuli.

Which is not to discount the tremendous visual effects created by Kahn's Assembly Building. For instance, there is one "room," for lack of a better term, that exists entirely for the purpose of letting you stand in the light and look up to the very top of the building. It is an oddly shaped little space, enclosed within a semicircular wall that meets a flat one, like a crescent moon laid on its side. You have reached it after climbing two flights of zigzagging marble steps from the lowest level of the building, and up to now the concrete ceiling of the staircase has hovered closely above you. Now, however, you are released into this smile of a space, looking up at the ceiling many stories overhead, with light pouring down on you through slim glass openings in the roofline and also through a huge, round, glass-paned window. You have emerged from shadow into light, and when you leave this room you will go back into shadow, but now you know that this alternation will be a central and continuing part of your experience of the building. Had you not already done so, you would, from this time forth, view light itself as one of Kahn's primary building materials.

The variety of lighting effects in the Parliament Building is remarkable. At one point you are out on an exterior terrace overlooking the lake, with bright sunlight glinting on the water; a man poling along in a skiff looks exactly like the picture Kahn sketched when he first came to Dhaka. You re-enter the building in near-blinding darkness, and it takes you a moment to discern that you are already back on the lamplit main "street" of this structure's interior, where shadow is your constant protection against the harsh exterior heat. Elsewhere, as you stand on one of the upper balconies that look out over that internal street, you can see two distinct varieties of light playing against the marble-banded concrete walls: a golden light coming directly down through the series of Japanese-made glass blocks that form the roofline windows, and a silvery, reflected light that bounces off one of the outermost façades and shines onto an interior wall. Both kinds of light are entrancing, especially in combination, and yet neither overwhelms the cool shade.

The assembly hall itself offers still another kind of visual and dramatic experience. Having progressed up several levels of the ambulatory, you are at long last ushered into this central space—the whole building's reason for being, the heart of the democratic process. Unlike anything else you've seen thus far, this grand space is instantly grasp-able. You can clearly discern the eight sides of the octagonal plenary hall; you can count the ranked tiers of strongly raked seating assigned to delegates, visitors, and press; you can spot the podium at which the Speaker presides, the doors by which she and the delegates enter. The room is tall but not excessively tall for its width. People are not dwarfed by it. Rather, their presence defines it, so that its height seems to be a function of human dignity. And capping it all is a ceiling that appears to float overhead with unbelievable lightness. The roof is a tent, but a tent made of concrete, delicately tethered to the wall at just eight points, so that natural light shines in under each of the tent flaps. This covering shields the roof from the outdoors and at the same time lets the out-doors in.

"In the plenary hall you can hear the rain, if it's raining," comments Dr. Chaudhury. "In the daylight you can see the light, and at night you see the night." She thinks of Kahn as "a person who felt that it was important to be close to nature. He had an idea for the environment. And also the broadness and spaciousness—that has an impact. I think there's a calmness. It is a building where there's so much hustle and bustle and argument, but within a serene context."

In saying this, the Speaker is describing not only the assembly hall itself, but also the whole building. "It's very spacious—the corridors, when you move from one end to another, it's not cramped," she points out. "This is important for a people's place, with many people moving together."

It is true that overall the Dhaka Assembly Building is designed for multitudes rather than solitude. Most of the time, in order to take in the sensations aroused by a Louis Kahn building, you need to have time by yourself. You need to sit quietly in the space—whether it's the plaza of the Salk Institute or a gallery of the Kimbell Art Museum or the grand atrium of the Exeter Library—and take in what it has to say. Kahn's buildings, for the most part, speak to you as an individual: they give rise to the kind of private communion that he felt could only take place between two people in a room together, when what is said is so particu-lar that it "may never have been said before." With most of Kahn's great buildings, that companion is the structure itself, and you need to be

But the Parliament Building in Dhaka, in this as in so many ways, is different. You are never alone here. It's not just that you are not allowed to go unescorted into the building; it's also the fact that the business of the building is public communion, public encounter, public argument and agreement. It is a place meant for many people, and whatever serenity it produces (which is considerable) is a serenity snatched from the crowds.

"*What is assembly?* is the conceptual question behind the Parliament Building," observes Wares. "Why do people assemble in a single place to talk about one thing?" He then proceeds to elaborate on the idea of community that underlies such a structure. "A shopping center is not a community," he points out. "In an Assembly Building, people come together to talk about one thing; then it becomes a community. When the souls unite, then it becomes a spiritual place. He was concerned with soul," he remarks about Kahn, "or mind. Mind can be analyzed. Soul cannot. It is more mysterious."

That Kahn was indeed concerned with soul, in whatever way he may have defined it, seems clear from the breathtaking, mysterious space he designed for worship here. The mosque is located at the front of the Parliament Building, but because it is on the third floor, you cannot get to it directly from the outside. Its external walls are hidden behind cylindrical sections of concrete, so you cannot see into it, either. In this sense it is a kind of Holy of Holies, a relatively inaccessible core. The only way into it is up a branching flight of steps from the brightly illuminated crescent-moon space where you first viewed the building's full height.

The plenary hall may be the Assembly Building's *raison d'être*, but the mosque is its heart in a different way. That Kahn viewed it in those terms is suggested by the heart-shaped corner windows, each composed of two semi-ovals with a slight downward dip at their ninety-degree joint. Thus each pair together, linked across adjoining walls, forms a multipaned heart through which light pours into the space below. Concrete buttresses at the roof level follow and extend the curves of the windows, so that each ovoid shape seems three-dimensional on its own, and thus doubly three-dimensional when it joins its mirror image at the corner.

Constructed of glass, concrete, and the omnipresent marble band-
ing with walls that are partially paneled in wood to lend the room a

traditional warmth, the mosque is a precise cube, measuring just under seventy feet in each direction. While Kahn no doubt intended this as a reference to Mecca's sacred cube, the Kaaba, the shape also has a visceral effect even on those who don't recognize the allusion. To be held inside a cube is to be contained with an exactitude that is both pleasing and stirring. One is aware of one's placement in relation to all six equal surfaces, just as one is aware of their congruence to and distance from each other. Things seem in balance from within a cube—and if the cube is as beautifully lit as Kahn's is, from above and also from the side, the feeling of serenity is magnified.

That all the light within the mosque is reflected light accounts in part for its special feeling of repose. You cannot see the outdoors, because the high, curved, outer walls block your view, but the light nonetheless reaches you. The room has affinities with church architecture (those flying buttresses at the roof level, for instance), but it is clearly not a church. It honors the principles of a mosque, yet without any appearance of exclusiveness or specificity. One can partake of its contemplative nature without belonging to its religion, or indeed to any religion at all. Whoever you are, it will speak to you. And unlike the rest of this avowedly public building, it speaks to you in your capacity as an individual—a soul, if you like, or a mind. When you leave it, the desire to be back inside will stay with you, lastingly.

ARRIVING

By the end of 1966, Kahn's firm had acquired two of the most important commissions of his career. One was a library building for the Phillips Exeter Academy, an elite private school in Exeter, New Hampshire. The other was an entirely new museum in Fort Worth, Texas, designed to house the small but excellent art collection initiated by the late Kay Kimbell.

These were not the only big jobs the practice was undertaking during that time. Among other projects, Kahn was simultaneously working on the Maryland Institute College of Art in Baltimore, the Broadway United Church of Christ in New York, the Dominican Motherhouse in Media, Pennsylvania, the Mikveh Israel synagogue in Philadelphia, the Memorial to the Six Million Jewish Martyrs in Battery Park, a large office building in Kansas City, Missouri, and two private houses, one in Philadelphia and one in Washington, D.C. None of these projects was ever built. Kahn also devoted twelve years to a massive fine arts center in Fort Wayne, of which the Performing Arts Theater, finished in 1973, was the only part to be constructed. Then there were projects like the Olivetti-Underwood typewriter factory in Harrisburg and the Beth-El synagogue in Chappaqua, both of which got built but then underwent substantial alteration over the years, so that Lou's contribution ultimately became undetectable.

One of the few lasting emblems of his work on American soil from this period—aside from Exeter and Kimbell, that is—was the Fisher House in Hatboro, Pennsylvania, which Kahn finally completed in

1967. Norman Fisher, a doctor, and his wife, Doris, a landscape designer, had waited patiently for seven years, and in the end they were delighted with the woodsy, two-story, three-bedroom home, in which deeply recessed windows, a massive stone fireplace, and a double-height living room created a cozy, inviting place for the whole family to gather. But it was a quirky house, with its acutely angled walls, its dark bedrooms, and its minuscule kitchen, and it would be hard to argue that it stood up against the major public buildings Lou was designing at the same time.

The Exeter Library and the Kimbell Art Museum, on the other hand, extended the level of achievement that had begun with Salk and confirmed Louis Kahn's reputation as one of America's greatest architects. The Exeter building, which came first chronologically, was in many ways the easier of the two projects. When the enlightened principal of Phillips Exeter Academy, Richard Day, and the thoughtful and farsighted head librarian, Rodney Armstrong, approached Kahn in late 1965 with the offer of the commission, he had already been thinking about libraries for quite a while. As far back as 1956 he had entered a competition for the Washington University Library with a design that focused on the importance of individual carrels. By the time he was awarded the Exeter job, he was actively working on another library— the Vikram Sarabhai Library at the Indian Institute of Management— and though the Ahmedabad and Exeter buildings ended up being quite different, both designs had a similar airy-yet-sturdy feeling, with solid, brick-clad exteriors and high-ceilinged reading rooms lit by oversized cutouts in the walls.

In contrast to many of Lou's building plans, which tended to go through several extreme revisions, the Exeter Library design reached its ultimate form fairly quickly. From the start Kahn was focused on the notion of three concentric spheres of activity: a central open area in which people could gather, a middle section containing the stacks, and an outer layer where study carrels would be lit by natural light. That he had always meant to house these concentric "rings" in a square structure was part of the beauty and the complexity of the design. Brick, too, had been part of the plan from the beginning, and when Lou learned that the local brickyard from which he intended to obtain the perfect-colored material was on the verge of bankruptcy, he had Exeter buy up

its inventory and store the bricks on campus for the duration of the design and construction process.

By late 1966 or early 1967, Kahn had essentially worked out the
plan for a four-story cube of brick and glass with an open arcade running
around the bottom and a parapet around the top. At just about that
time, the town of Exeter passed an ordinance forbidding buildings of
more than three stories on that site. The Academy exerted its local pull
and managed to get a variance for the library. But a year later, when
faced with the kinds of budgetary overruns that had become typical in
Kahn's projects, the building committee itself asked Lou to reduce his
structure by one story. At first, under pressure, he agreed to do so. He
found, though, that he couldn't bring himself to make this compromise in the geometrically perfect design, and he ended up explaining
his position in an eloquent letter to Rodney Armstrong written in April
of 1968.

Lou pointed out that when he sat down to make the revision, "without surrendering the simple beauty of the building and with the least
loss of function," he found that the more he worked on it, "the more I
realized that I could not accomplish a fully worthy solution. You must
understand that my intentions were to adjust to new conditions without
losing any aesthetic values nor any functional values. But judgement in
this work is not mathematical in nature nor is a full validity reached
solely by deductive reasoning . . ." He was willing to do anything necessary to persuade the Buildings & Grounds committee that "the only
right way to build is to the height and proportions we so painstakingly
worked out over so many months . . . You are perhaps better acquainted
than we are as to the disadvantage of the loss of the Seminar Rooms
and the mixed function of rare books, staff lounge and conference
rooms, faculty offices, visitor's office that would have resulted from
eliminating a story. A very great additional loss would have been the
value of the high ceiling in the public areas of the first, the main
floor. This loss alone, I am convinced now, would have been a drastic
mistake."

Kahn went on in the letter to say that his close scrutiny of the plans
had resulted in numerous cost-saving possibilities that he was now able
to propose to the building committee, savings which would nearly pay
for the expense of preserving the extra story. But Lou finally rested his

argument on aesthetic rather than financial grounds. "The building from the exterior is intended to present a rhythmic development . . . The regularly spaced brick piers diminish in size as they rise in a slow rhythm of double-story units. The loss of one story broke this rhythm and the grace and simplicity was lost," he wrote. Then he came down firmly on his *own* bottom line, which was significantly different from that of an accountant or a zoning official. "My fullest consideration has convinced me that my hopeful proposal of saving a story would have presented an intolerable condition that I must now firmly say I cannot accept," he concluded. "I must say that I have come to a stronger confirmation of my aesthetic judgement and I was misled by my willingness to make adjustments."

Armstrong was persuaded. The Buildings & Grounds committee was persuaded. And Exeter Library was built to its full four stories, exactly as Lou had wanted it.

Complicated as it was, this was a simple process compared to the one Kahn went through to produce the Kimbell Museum. Yet by almost everyone's account, the difficulties were well worth it. "It's my favorite building," Kahn's daughter Sue Ann said of the Kimbell. "There's something about the space it creates and the way it makes you feel—I would love it no matter whose building it was. It's just a space that works, with the human spirit." A somewhat more objective source, the architect and design professor Robert McCarter, came to much the same conclusion in his monumental study of Kahn's buildings. "The Kimbell Art Museum is rightly considered Kahn's greatest built work," McCarter noted, "in that it fully integrates and brings to the highest level of resolution all the elements composing Kahn's conception of architecture." Even Lou himself seemed to have a special attitude toward the Kimbell. Privately, he told Richard Wurman that he thought it was his best building ("If you liked Exeter, you're going to *love* Kimbell" was how he put it), in large part because it did not call undue attention to itself. And publicly, at the museum's official opening, he expressed a similar preference when he said, "This building feels—and it's a good feeling—that I had nothing to do with it, that some other hand did it."

Many other hands certainly had something to do with it, and they ranged from reliable old allies, such as Komendant on the engineering and Langford on the concrete, to local collaborators and contractors forced on him by the Kimbell's board, who feared the kinds of construction delays and cost overruns that had become endemic in Kahn's work. But Lou's comment was referring instead to an apparent perfection of form, almost a feeling of inevitability, that the finished building radiated. It was as if Kahn, as an individual maker, had disappeared silently and completely into this thing he had made.

Like Rodney Armstrong at Exeter, Richard Brown, the Kimbell's first director, was a strong personality who knew what he wanted in his building. Among the competitors he rounded up for the Kimbell commission were Mies van der Rohe, recently finished with the Neue Nationalgalerie in Berlin, and Marcel Breuer, who was just completing the Whitney in New York. Compared to them, Louis Kahn—who had built only one small museum, the Yale Art Gallery, thirteen years earlier— might have seemed underqualified. But Brown felt that Kahn, unlike the others, would approach the new building with an open mind and an "all-embracing" attitude. "He's willing to let the specific situation posed by the creation of a building guide him and tell him what the structure, engineering, and aesthetics ought to be," Brown concluded. So in October of 1966 Kahn's firm was awarded the commission, though with the proviso that they work with a Texas architect, Preston Geren, and his local engineers.

From the first drawings submitted in March of 1967 to the building's completion in the fall of 1972, some things remained constant. It was clear from the beginning that Kahn envisioned the Kimbell as a series of long, thin galleries or vaults, joined at their sides and featuring identical arched roofs through which natural light could flow downward. Everything else changed radically, though, in the course of the design process. The initial plan covered a square block six hundred feet on a side; it was eventually scaled down to less than half that size. For the arched roofs, Kahn had originally proposed a folded plate scheme involving trapezoidally shaped arches. He then revised this into semicircular vaults. But as Brown pointed out, the height of these proposed galleries was totally out of proportion to the paintings that would hang within them. "The average size picture on the walls of the KAM will be about 2 1/2 feet in one direction and 3 or 4 feet in the other," Brown reminded Kahn in an emphatic memo. "I'm worried about how a little old lady from Abilene is going to *feel* looking at our 15 inch Giovanni di

Paolo on a wall 15 feet vertical, with a vault above which goes up to 30 feet."

Kahn was not the kind of architect who viewed it as beneath his dignity to consider the gallery's visitors. On the contrary, it was a way of thinking that came naturally to him. In many of his sketches for the Kimbell Museum—including some of the earliest drawings, when the rooflines had not yet reached their final shape—he included fleeting, stylized human figures. At times they were just a scribble, with a pair of compass legs attached to a roundish head. But sometimes they were much more individualized: a parent holding a child by the hand, a woman in a cloak, a person in the museum's library putting something on a shelf, a cluster of people outside sitting on benches in the portico. Occasionally there was even more detail, as when a sketchy violinist appeared in one drawing of the auditorium, or a figure behind the counter in the kitchen wore a chef's hat. These were not like the generic cutouts most architects use only in their finished presentations. Instead, they embodied future inhabitants of these as-yet-imaginary rooms, people who had already colonized the spaces that were just taking shape in Lou's mind. For it was in these sketches—loose, free, drawn in black charcoal on yellow tracing paper, with an occasional touch of turquoise or red—that Kahn did his thinking. It was as if he were musing to himself about the bits and pieces of the developing plan: what if it were like this? or like this? or with that tiny alteration? And what he was thinking about, as he held his charcoal in his hand, clearly included people.

But even if Lou understood what Richard Brown wanted, obtaining it was not easy. The question was how to preserve the grandeur he sought in the arched top-lit galleries while reducing the height of the rooms. He needed a curve—did it even exist?—that would accomplish both aims at once.

The person who found it was a staff architect, Marshall Meyers, who had just come back to Kahn's office after two years with another firm. According to Henry Wilcots, Meyers was one of Lou's best architects, but he wasn't consistently part of the Kahn practice. "Marshall would leave, then come back, then leave," Henry commented, and this seemed to have something to do with the fact that Lou was "still a one-man show, even when Marshall was lead person." Lou made him the lead architect on the Kimbell project when Meyers returned to the office in the summer of 1967, and shortly after that they jointly arrived at the solution to the roof problem.

Describing the kind of "gentle collaboration" that took place in Kahn's office, where nobody took credit for his individual role in a design, Marshall would later say about Lou: "He never worked alone. He couldn't. He needed to talk to someone, he needed a dialogue." Meyers recalled how Kahn would "sketch something and then go away and then about three days later he would come back to see what had developed . . . He was always testing his ideas, looking for a consensus, and you weren't helping him at all if you just thought that every scratch on paper he did was something handed down from on high." Marshall also noted that, especially in the early stages of a project, Lou "worked best with one person. He said that if I talk to many people it is a performance, while if I talk to one person it may perhaps be an event. So he tended to work with one person, because then there would be a discourse."

Prior to Marshall's involvement on the Kimbell, Lou had already tried designing the vaults with a semicircular arch (too high) and a flattened arch (not very graceful), but what Meyers suggested—apparently after reading the section on barrel shells in Fred Angerer's 1961 book, *Surface Structures in Building*—was the cycloid arch. The cycloid had been around at least since the days of Galileo, and it was based on the pattern described by a moving circle: that is, if you attached a pencil to the outer edge of a wheel and rolled it along next to a strip of paper, the repeated shape traced by the pencil would be a cycloid arc. It was a long, low curve, but it was also a pleasingly natural one, a continuous arch shaped by a continuous process, so that the eye did not feel cheated even as the roof height was lowered.

When Meyers and Kahn discovered this solution, they also came up with two other crucial ideas: a way of dividing the arch down the middle, by creating the curved roof out of two unmeeting shells that each formed a pair of "wings" with the adjoining shells on other roofs; and a way of transmitting but also diffusing the bright sunlight that came through the gap, by placing a silvery reflector or "beam splitter" directly underneath the opening. All three elements were included in the November 1967 plans that were submitted to the Kimbell board, and they were again part of the final reduced design that was approved in late 1968. This final plan included three parallel sets of cycloid vaults, with a middle set housing the public functions and two side sets for the galleries, placed on top of an understory that contained offices, the conservation space, and the loading docks. The front approach to the museum would be through the middle set of vaults, which would be diminished in number to allow for an entrance court; on either side, the flanking vaults would be extended out to include a shaded portico.

This design had not been arrived at by the architects alone. As always in Lou's most adventurous work, the engineers had to be called upon to make it work. Nick Gianopulos was consulted first, but he frankly admitted that the calculations of stress, weight, and balance were beyond him, and he recommended they ask Gus Komendant. Komendant quickly approved the cycloid design with the light-slot on top, but he insisted on certain modifications, among them the inclusion of post-tensioning cables throughout the roof, so that the concrete shells would be cast around steel. He also persuaded Kahn, though not without some difficulty, to reshape the concrete frame surrounding the arched windows at the end of each vault, so that the concrete thickened at the vault's peak, the point of greatest stress. This in turn meant that each curving glass window had to narrow correspondingly as it rose from its base on the vault's wall toward its pinnacle in the roof—an important revision that ended up giving the Kimbell's clerestories their subtle but distinctive affinity with church architecture.

August Komendant proved essential to this building in other ways as well. After the local engineers had declared the job impossible and insisted on having a flat roof instead, Komendant got himself put in charge of the whole project and pushed through Kahn's designs. If he later tried to take credit for the designs themselves, perhaps that was forgivable. Lou, at any rate, seemed to forgive him for all his grandiosity when he said in response to a direct question about his engineer: "Komendant is very sensitive to the nature of structures. The fact that he's an actor and a great performer is of no importance . . . I don't live in concrete, I don't live in steel, I just sense their potentialities. But he lives in them. He feels the strain of every member. He knows when a thing is pulling away, or when it's staying at rest. He knows repose very

well. He's not worried about symmetry, he's just a great balancer. He feels that the thing is out of balance without analyzing it."

Perhaps the most surprising thing about the design of the Kimbell, in the end, was that it triumphed so powerfully over all the conflicting stresses—not just the physical stresses imposed by concrete and glass and steel, but also the personal rivalries among various strong-minded designers, the built-in conflicts between the museum's needs and the architect's wishes, the financial and professional imperatives of all the collaborating, competing parties. That it got built at all was remarkable. That it became Lou's most highly praised building, his and yet transcendently *not* his, came to seem almost a matter of fate.

Despite his nomadic existence during these years—which might entail rushing from Dacca to Exeter in any given month, or from Media to Fort Worth to New York in the course of a single week—Lou managed to maintain some semblance of a personal life. On June 27, 1965, he gave away Sue Ann at her wedding to Harry Saltzman, celebrated at the Curtis Arboretum in Wyncote, Pennsylvania. Friends of Sue's and Harry's who met her father at the marriage festivities described him as affable and charming, though even these musical types were a bit intimidated by his famous name, which had by now begun to spread beyond the realm of professional architects.

Fame brought with it certain expectations about an improved quality of life, and shortly before their daughter's wedding, the Kahns decided to give up Esther's old family home in declining West Philadelphia and move with her mother to a nicer place. What they ended up buying—largely with an inheritance of Esther's, so that she became the legally designated owner of the new house—was a traditional Philadelphia row house, four stories high and clad in brick, at 921 Clinton Street. This South Philadelphia neighborhood, with its brick-paved sidewalks and quiet, narrow streets, was coming up in the world rather than going down, and their block of Clinton, near the corner of 10th, was only a brisk ten-minute walk from Lou's downtown office. Still, the house itself needed a lot of work, both structural and cosmetic. Various people from the Kahn firm were assigned to supervise the renovation project, but it was mainly the province of Luis Vincent Rivera, a young man who had started out as the "office boy" and, with Lou's encouragement, had soon progressed to draftsman and beyond. Lou being Lou, the work on his own house always came last in priority, so the remodeling process dragged on for years. The improvements were initially intended to include an elevator for Annie Israeli, who had become too frail to climb stairs, but before she could be moved out of her beloved old house on Chester Avenue, she fell and fatally broke her hip. Annie died on December 23, 1966. Esther and Lou moved into their new house (now without an elevator) during the following year.

Around the same time, Harriet and Nathaniel also changed their address, moving into the place they would occupy for the rest of Nathaniel's childhood. When Harriet had first returned to Philadelphia to attend Penn, she had rented a flat at the Cherokee Apartments on Walcott Drive—coincidentally, a building designed by Oscar Stonorov, Lou's former partner. A few years later, after taking her master's degree, she moved with her son to a little white house at 8870 Tawonda Avenue in Chestnut Hill. Their benevolent landlord was Francis Adler, one of Kahn's old clients, who occupied the large house at the front of the property. Harriet and Nathaniel's three-story, two-bedroom house, which included an attic that Harriet could use as a studio, sat behind the bigger house at the end of a long driveway. About once a week, when he was in town, Lou would come out there to see them—though often not until the middle of the night, when his long hours at the office were over.

"Lou didn't drive," said David Slovic, who frequently shared the night shift with his boss. "As a student I had this old jalopy, and late at night, when we were done working, I'd take Lou home, out to Chester Avenue. But after a while sometimes he wouldn't go home. He would say, 'Take me out to Chestnut Hill.' And there would be this little boy, standing in the driveway, who had been woken up—at 3:00, 3:30, 4:00 a.m.—because his dad was coming. So that's how I met Nathaniel: he was the kid at the end of the driveway."

Not all of Lou's visits were so late. Sometimes he would arrive in time for dinner, and Harriet would cook him an elaborate meal, with a specially prepared martini beforehand. Less frequently, there would be a visit during the day, perhaps on a weekend, when Lou and his son would play or read or draw together. Nathaniel's memories of his father from this period were like the well-preserved fragments of an ancient mosaic, bits and pieces of clarity that remained uncannily intact.

"He had very warm hands, physically warm to the touch," Nathaniel recalled. "He could make coins disappear, for sure." Those hands were delicate and expressive, but they were also very strong. "I remember he used to be able to split an apple with his hands," Nathaniel said. "And he wouldn't use a nutcracker when he came to our house: he would crush a walnut in his hands." The little boy somehow associated his father with knights and their brave deeds, perhaps because Lou loved King Arthur. "He gave me four beautiful books about the Arthurian legend. He loved fairy tales—the idea of chivalry, of having to stand up and fight for what was right, what was good." Mostly, though, Nathaniel remembered the glowing intensity of Lou's attention. "He was the kind of person that made you feel you were the only one in the universe, when he was talking with you. When he turned his light on you, it was intense, it was warm, and it made you grow."

He was also a kind man, Nathaniel felt. Once, for instance, "he was at our house and he couldn't get a taxi, and there were no taxis available—or there was just one taxi on the road." But instead of getting irritated with the dispatcher, Lou started joking with her. "Suddenly Lou is having a hilarious conversation with the dispatcher, a woman, and he's saying to her, 'It's like the Depression, when there was only one meatball to go around.'"

Usually, though, Lou didn't need a taxi after one of his late-night visits, because Harriet would drive him home. She would bundle Nathaniel into the back seat of the car and take Lou to 921 Clinton, where he would arrive in time to have breakfast with Esther. "Since we moved here we generally talked at breakfast because it was the only time we had together," Esther told an interviewer some years after Lou's death, implying that what took up all the rest of his time was his work: "architecture was the most important thing in his life and everything else came second." Though a bit evasive as an explanation of his schedule, this statement also happened to be true, and the other two women in his life perceived it as well. Later, as a grown-up, Nathaniel came to understand that both Harriet and Anne valued Lou's work—"his mission," Nathaniel called it—and knew that architecture was always what came first with him. The social discomfort they endured in having children out of wedlock (not to mention the financial hardship and emotional distress entailed in sharing Lou with others) was "the price they had to pay, but it was worth it because of the work that was being done," Nathaniel said.

By 1968 that work was being done with his mother's collaboration, for Harriet Pattison had become the *de facto* landscape architect on a number of Lou's jobs. After graduating from Penn in 1967, she went to work for George Patton, whose office space was located just below Kahn's at 1501 Walnut. Patton was the designated landscape architect on the Kimbell project, but it was Harriet who actually did much of the work. For those who visited the Kimbell after it opened, the luxurious grounds that led up to the museum door, with their groves of yaupon trees, their lawns of resilient Texas grass, their soothing, splashing fountains and crunching gravel walks, were an integral part of the experience. And yet Harriet herself wasn't allowed to attend the opening ceremonies. Instead, Patton represented the whole firm. Was the reason for her exclusion "that you were a woman, or that you were involved with him?" Nathaniel asked his mother many years later. "Yes, all of those things," Harriet answered.

One further memory from his childhood stuck with Nathaniel very strongly. He was in first grade, he remembered, and Lou was walking him to class. Even the little boy could see that something was wrong with his father on that early March day in 1970. "He was devastated. It was a very traumatic event, a very sad day for him," Nathaniel recalled. "I remember because he took me to school that day and he was clearly in distress." When Nathaniel got home, he asked his mother why Lou was so upset, and she told him it was because Marie Kuo had died in a car accident.

Marie had left Kahn's practice in 1966, when her son, James, was born. "She said Jamie was going to be her creation," said her husband, Mort, explaining why she decided to give up her architecture work completely. She seemed happy in her new life, and she took her son with her everywhere, even on the all-day trip to the nearby snow country she was making that last Sunday. When her little VW bug swerved off the Germantown Pike late in the afternoon of March 8, 1970, Marie was killed by the impact of the steering wheel, which crushed her pancreas; three-year-old Jamie, who was in the back seat, survived with only minor bruises. Her husband, who had been rehearsing in a community theater play, was driven by a neighbor to the hospital where she and Jamie had been taken, and that was when Mort learned she had died in the crash.

Marie had not worked at Lou's office for nearly four years by that time, but the bond must have run very deep, for Sue Ann, too, was struck by her father's response to her sudden death. "Lou cried," she said. "I had never seen him cry, and I asked my mother what happened. And she said, 'Marie Kuo died.'"

But Lou didn't have much time to mourn, for by now his professional life had grown more chaotic and distracting than ever. The office was full of young new employees and employee-hopefuls, all drawn by Kahn's fame. The firm had recently lost its longtime secretary, Louise Badgley, who had married an oil engineer and moved with him to Saudi Arabia. Her replacement was a younger woman named Kathy Condé, quite competent but less playful and humorous than Louise had been. Meanwhile, on the business front, the practice was continuing to lose money at a rapid rate, despite Dave Wisdom's best efforts. Lou himself seemed to be traveling constantly, whether to faraway Kathmandu (where he was asked to design a family planning clinic) or nearby New Haven.

A few months earlier, in October of 1969, Kahn had been awarded a lavish and inviting new commission: to design a new art museum at Yale that would house Paul Mellon's collection of British art. This came on top of two other prestigious jobs he had recently undertaken, the Hurva Synagogue in Jerusalem and the Palazzo dei Congressi in Venice. Any one of these would have been a career-capping assignment, and now Lou was faced with all three at once.

The Hurva Synagogue project, which began in 1967, was in many ways an ideal Kahn assignment. *Hurva* means "ruin" in Hebrew, and this particular building had been ruined more than once: built and demolished in the eighteenth century, it was rebuilt in the nineteenth and finally toppled in the 1948 war that immediately followed Israel's founding. Lou, with his oft-stated passion for ruins, planned to preserve the remnants of the older synagogue, located in the heart of Jerusalem's Old City, next to his newer construction.

Kahn was not a newcomer to Israel—he had been a consultant on housing policy as far back as 1949, and in the 1960s he had joined the seventy-member Jerusalem Committee, an advisory group which included his friends Buckminster Fuller and Isamu Noguchi—but this was by far his most important commission in the Jewish state. It came, too, just as his work on Philadelphia's Mikveh Israel synagogue was beginning to founder, and it must have soothed his feelings to realize that even if the local Jewish community didn't appreciate his architecture, the international one did. (The Mikveh Israel commission, after limping along for a few more years, finally came to an end in 1972, when another architect was brought in to replace Kahn. "If something fell through, he just stopped talking about it," said Sue Ann, but "the Mikveh Israel—the fact that it didn't get built—was one of the greatest disappointments of his life, I think.")

As he so often did, Kahn went through three designs on the Hurva project. The first entailed an outer wall made of the traditional golden Jerusalem stone and an inner room constructed of silvery concrete; the two were separated by an ambulatory, and the whole thing was lit from above as well as through vertical slits between the pyramidal columns of the outer structure. The second plan, completed in 1969, was both darker and more monumental than the first. For the third plan, sketched out in 1973, Kahn added a square oculus to the top of the central room, much as he had in the changing rooms at the Trenton Bath House. It was somehow typical of him to link in this way the ordinary recreational activities of New Jersey's lower-middle-class Jews and the high pomp of Jerusalem's magnificent synagogue—and to do so by connecting them both with his favorite building, the Pantheon. Mayor Teddy Kollek, who functioned as Kahn's chief client on the Hurva Synagogue (and who was, incidentally, one of the most peace-loving politicians ever elected to office in Israel), told Lou he felt ready to build after receiving those third plans. He urged Kahn to deliver the working drawings so that construction could begin.

Meanwhile, the Venice project was proceeding at the same time. Awarded in early 1968, the commission was to design a large conference center that could hold up to two thousand people for major public meetings. For Lou, both the site itself—in beautiful, ancient Venice—and the project for a public assembly space had tremendous allure. Because he had been working for years on the Dacca Assembly Building, his mind was filled with ideas about how to gather people together for purposes of public discussion. But here Kahn took a completely different approach from the concrete, marble-banded Dacca building. To accommodate Venice's cramped space, he planned to take a bowl-shaped amphitheater structure, slice it in half to produce a longer, thinner meeting hall, and raise the whole thing up on end-supports and a suspended bridge.

Originally the project was to be located in Venice's Giardini Pubblici, but by 1972 it had been moved to the Arsenale, where Kahn planned to suspend it over the Canale delle Galleazze, on the west side of the Arsenale lagoon. Hanging above the water, its exterior composed largely of glass and stainless-steel panels, the Palazzo dei Congressi would have been a striking if unusual addition to Venice's architecture. With its reflective surfaces and its encircling arms, the building would have made its occupants feel they were floating between sky and water, just as Venice itself does. Kahn was so aware of the watery, dreamlike, historic city, and so proud of being asked to design something there, that he volunteered to do his part of the job without charging a fee. When Dave Wisdom protested at this idea ("Who's going to pay the engineers?"), Lou simply answered, "How could you charge for having your work in Venice?"

The new Yale art museum—another structure that used glass and steel on its exterior, though to very different effect—obviously required no international travel, but Kahn still put in a great deal of time on it. First he met with the project patron, Paul Mellon, not only to get the wealthy donor's personal approval of his selection as architect, but also to understand the art collection as the collector himself saw it. Then, over the course of several years, he worked closely with Jules Prown, the first director of what came to be called the Yale Center for British Art. Prown was one of those intelligent, forceful, yet sympathetic clients who, like Jonas Salk or Richard Brown, helped shape Kahn's design in ways that even the architect admitted were useful. This was to be Lou's third art gallery, and his second in New Haven; the somewhat mangled Yale University Art Gallery, on which he had collaborated with Anne Tyng in 1951, sat across from the new site. The Center thus represented both a chance to address past misfortunes and an opportunity to try something completely new.

As it emerged from its final design (which, typically, was the third complete plan submitted by Kahn, after earlier plans had foundered on issues of scale and expense), the Yale Center looked unlike anything Lou had ever built before. From the street it could almost have been an expensive office complex, with its alternating panels of matte gray steel and shiny glass. One entered at the corner, through an external foyer whose heavy concrete-coffered ceiling recalled the unwelcoming entrance to the Richards Building. But once inside, the museum's visitors were rewarded with a tall, light-filled atrium that nearly rivaled in grandeur the central spaces at Exeter and Dacca.

The materials that made up this atrium and the rest of the museum had a smoother, sleeker look than anything Kahn had used before. It wasn't just the presence of the dark-hued steel. Even the oak and concrete panels, though similar to what Lou had employed at Exeter, Kimbell, and elsewhere, seemed more elegantly finished here at Yale. The form-holes were still visible in the concrete, but they were even more discreet than at Salk; the shadow joints were there to separate concrete from wood or wood from metal, but they too were somehow less evident, becoming mere lines of demarcation. The galleries, as they rose floor upon floor, were perfectly tailored to their different purposes: a light-filled space for special exhibits, a darkened level suitable for drawings and prints, and finally a top-lit, side-lit, grandly roofed upper gallery, where glorious natural light poured in on gloriously light-filled Turner paintings. The whole thing had something of the feel of an elegant gentleman's club that had been hijacked for artistic purposes.

Nowhere did this feeling come through more clearly than in the long, high, second-floor Library Court that occupied the center of the museum. This was a room designed to soothe the weary museum-goer, the overstressed Yale student, or the casual visitor escaping from the frenzied urban street. With its high paneled walls, its gently muffled skylights, its comfortable dark brown leather sofas, and its large Persian rug spread across an oak floor, the room invited one to sit and rest. On the walls hung Paul Mellon's largest and in some cases most treasured

British paintings. (That Lou had envisioned precisely this arrangement from the very beginning was demonstrated in an early sketch of his, which showed Stubbs's gigantic *Lion Attacking a Horse* on exactly the wall where it eventually ended up.) The room was the acme of gentleman's-club perfection.

And yet Kahn had allowed a primeval intruder to venture into this inner sanctuary, subtly altering the feeling of the whole space. At one end of the long room, and visible from every point within and around it, stood a massive concrete cylinder that seemed to have flown in from another universe entirely. This freestanding gray tower, which in fact housed a staircase leading up to the higher galleries, was like a giant piece of the ancient world plunked down in an upscale London interior. The curved windowless façade that it presented to the room, textured as only Lou's concrete could be textured, was implacable, indomitable, unforgiving of the niceties of club behavior. *It* was the important thing, the memorable thing about the room. Its gesture toward the harshly archaic, toward the seeming ugliness that always precedes a new idea of beauty, gave it a strength that the merely beautiful lacked. ("Picasso said something very wonderfully, that everything that is created must be ugly," Lou observed at about this time. "I, not having read Picasso until just recently in a booklet by Gertrude Stein, tried to say it by saying that a thing must be archaic. But it has historical connotations which are not as good as Mr. Picasso's harsh word, *ugly*.") Yet despite its insistence on its own centrality, the concrete cylinder also offered something to the room at large, transmitting its power and its strangeness to the more sedate elements, so that even the Stubbs animals gained a demonic side in its presence. Kahn had used a similar effect in smaller settings before—in the tall, curved, stone fireplace, for instance, that dominated the living room at Fisher House—but here at the Yale Center it finally made complete sense.

■

Even as he was starting work on his plan for Yale, the forthright and the implacable were, in their own ways, getting ready to intrude on Lou's extended family life. As her older sister would later point out, Alex Tyng had never been one to take any guff. For years Alex, like her mother, had accepted the fact that Lou's schedule meant he wasn't often available for family dinners and so forth. Ever since elementary school she had thought of herself not as a fatherless child but as a child whose father was extremely busy elsewhere. Now that she was in her mid-teens, though, her perceptions began to change.

It started late in 1969, when Alex was fifteen. She was supposed to go to a Christmastime concert of the Vienna Boys' Choir with two friends. Afterward Lou promised to take them for tea at the Hunt Room, an elegant Philadelphia gathering place in the grand old Bellevue Hotel. He duly met up with the three girls, and they were all sitting together in the Hunt Room, having a good time, when someone came up to the table and said, "Hi, Mr. Kahn." Alex never really focused on who this person was—it wasn't anybody she recognized—but when Lou made the introductions, "he introduced me as Alex Tyng, and he didn't say I was his daughter," she recalled. "I mean, we went to a lot of places together and people knew I was his daughter. He used to take me to the art store, and we used to go to rare book stores together. I never thought he was trying to hide it. I think he was just caught in an awkward moment and didn't know how to introduce me. But it just struck a raw chord. Things were not quite right."

The following year, when she was sixteen, she was talking to a good friend of hers, a very direct, matter-of-fact boy, and he asked her how often she saw her father. "And I said, 'Oh, once a month or so,' and he said, 'Is that all?' And I'd thought, well, a busy guy with three families . . ." But this exchange got Alex thinking in a new way.

She had always known about Nathaniel, ever since the day he was born. "I remember being told by my mother as we were crossing the street. She said, 'By the way, you have a baby brother.'" That happened when Alex was eight and a half. Nearly eight years later, shortly after that signal conversation with her friend, she decided to call Nathaniel and Harriet on the phone. "I told my mother what I was going to do—I didn't ask her, but I told her—and she was okay with it," said Alex. So she just looked up the phone number and called their house. "Nathaniel answered, and I said, 'Is your mother there? This is Alex Tyng.' But I didn't want to say this is your sister. He said she would be in later. So I called back later when she was there, and she was delighted and said, 'Why don't you come over?' and I did."

From the first moment they met, Alex and Nathaniel got along really well, despite the significant age gap. They had plenty to talk about together. It was as if each had been waiting for someone exactly like that to come along—someone with whom to compare notes about their mysterious father. "Like: why didn't he ever show his teeth when he smiled?" Alex remembered. "My mother told me he didn't have good dental work as a child, so he was self-conscious about them." Neither Alex nor Nathaniel could recall seeing or hearing Lou brush his teeth; perhaps, Alex suggested, he didn't have any. (Nathaniel had in fact seen his father laugh and knew for sure that Lou had teeth, but he kept silent, not wanting to ruin his older sister's fun.) Together, they worked out a complicated plot that would allow them to take a picture of him caught in a sudden smile, using a Rube Goldberg–like camera device that they invented on the spot. Of course the plot was never executed— it was undoubtedly not executable—but Alex, at any rate, found the whole game highly entertaining.

Anne and Harriet, too, became friendly through their children, to the point where they would occasionally rely on each other for child-minding. "I have great memories of going to their house," said Alex, who found Harriet to be "a people person, very understanding and warm— great to talk to. She was like an alternate mother. And also she always had great food, and my mother wasn't much of a cook. Harriet was a really good cook." Nathaniel, meanwhile, had fond memories of eating at Anne Tyng's house. "The meals she served were so different from my mother's," he recalled. "There were a lot of seeds involved—I never had a sunflower seed before I went to their house. And she made a wonderful big salad with lots of radishes." The physical environment, too, struck him with its novelty when he went to visit Alex and Anne at 2511 Waverly. Anne had recently remodeled the house to create an architectural aerie for herself at the top of the narrow building, but the downstairs remained much as it had been for years, with a single long room containing kitchen, dining space, and living area. "They had these stained-glass lamps that cast a beautiful colored light," Nathaniel remembered. "No candles. My mother was big on candles, Anne on stained glass—a very different kind of light."

Most of all, though, what Nathaniel recalled about Anne Tyng was her personality. "Anne was a lovely person, an interested person," he said. "She was interested in me. I remember long discussions with her about geometry, particularly the spiral: about how things came back to the same thing again, but they were better. Her vision of life—I don't mean an individual's life, but life itself—was very orderly. It was positive. Things were getting better in the universe, according to Anne." Nathaniel paused to bring to mind this unusual woman, his sister's mother. "I still remember the sound of Anne's voice," he said. "She did not make small talk. She thoroughly engaged you, whether you were eight years old or an old person."

Alex's experiment in-seeking out her younger brother had gone so well that she decided to try the same thing with her older sister, someone she had known about all her life but had never met. "I just decided I would call her up. It was ridiculous that we didn't know each other," said Alex. "She was about thirty, living in New York with her husband, and she said fine, come see me." So Alex and a friend went into New York on a shopping trip and stopped at Sue Ann's for lunch. "And it was fun," observed Alex. "She said she was just waiting for me to call her— waiting until I was old enough to want a relationship."

Now that Alex had gotten things out in the open, she wasn't about to let her father lapse back into silence. On behalf of herself and Nathaniel, each previously so isolated, she would probe him about the existence of other relatives. Did they have any cousins? Where did they live? What did they look like? (Alex was very aware of not looking anything like the members of her mother's family; she looked, in fact, like Lou.) Did he have any photographs? Could he bring some back the next time he went to Los Angeles?

Alex also, as part of her effort "to inject some normality" into their lives, took Nathaniel with her on her visits to Lou's office. She wanted them both to be as involved in his regular world as possible. When she happened to find out, in the spring of 1971, that Lou was about to get some kind of big award, she insisted that all four of them, the two mothers and their two children, be invited to the ceremony. She succeeded in procuring the invitations, but Harriet and Anne declined to go, so Alex and Nathaniel, aged seventeen and eight, went on their own.

The occasion was the Bok Award, formally known as the Philadelphia Award, one of the most prestigious honors that could be conferred on eminent native sons. (The previous year's winner had been Eugene

Ormandy, internationally renowned as the conductor of the Philadelphia Orchestra.) Louis Kahn was the 1970 recipient, and the ceremony was held at the elegant Pennsylvania Academy of Fine Arts on April 21, 1971. The event marked such a significant milestone in Lou's life that his sister, Sarah, flew in from Los Angeles to attend. So did Jonas Salk and his wife.

For the presentation itself, the audience was asked to sit down. Alex had "started to notice that people would try to shove us to the back of the room—this would happen at every event. This time someone said, 'The seats in the front are for important people,' and told us to go to the back, but then I saw just regular people, not important people, sitting in them." After the presentation, there was a receiving line that included the Salks, some local political figures, and Esther and Louis Kahn. Alex persuaded Nathaniel that they should go through the receiving line. When they reached Esther, Alex put her hand out. Esther looked straight at her, clasped her own hands behind her back, and said, "Hello, Miss Tyng," in what Alex thought was a very cold voice. "And when Nathaniel put his hand out—he was a very polite little boy—she ignored him," reported Alex. "She just looked over his head."

Lou was standing next to Esther in the receiving line, and this encounter did not go unnoticed. He reacted by hugging his two children warmly. Then he took them with him and introduced them to various people in the room. Alex remembered meeting her aunt Sarah; Nathaniel remembered meeting Jonas Salk. Both were convinced that the people to whom Lou introduced them as "Alex and Nathaniel" knew that they were his children—though if Sarah understood this, she never mentioned the fact back in California, where the relatives remained completely ignorant of their existence.

"To be fair to Esther, it was not an easy thing, to have your husband's other children show up," the grown-up Nathaniel Kahn pointed out many years later. "You have to say to Lou: What did you have in mind here? How did you think this was going to go?"

For Esther, the ceremony was meant to be one of the crowning moments of their married life, an occasion when her decades-long support of Lou and his work at last yielded public acknowledgment for both of them. "I think she recognized his genius. She admired his talent and wanted to have a part in it," said the Philadelphia architect Peter Arfaa, attempting to explain why Esther had stayed with her wayward husband in spite of everything. And Lou, too, must have been aware of the stakes for her, because he knew how much he owed her. Part of the debt was emotional, and it was linked to guilt; as Arfaa put it, "He appreciated her loyalty—he appreciated the fact that she had accepted his disloyalty, and he was obligated to that acceptance." But part of it was solidly financial, though in ways that added up to other and more important kinds of debt. If not for Esther's steady support, her years of being essentially the sole breadwinner, Lou's dream of setting up his own practice and making a go of it might never have become a reality. "Without Esther he could not have made it," Arfaa asserted. "I mean that literally."

And Lou knew this. Once, a few years earlier, he and David Slovic had been driving home from an important presentation that followed an all-night work session, and David, groggy and relieved, had felt relaxed enough to bring up the subject of Lou's marriage. He had asked—"in a kind of innocently young person's way"—why Lou stayed with Esther rather than getting divorced, given that he'd obviously fallen in love with other people and even had children with them. "He said, basically, she'd been supporting him for many years, all through the Depression," Slovic remembered. "So he felt it was appropriate that he stay with her. He felt an obligation—that it was the right thing to do, to be with her." Alex Tyng sensed that, more than just an obligation, it was an actual feeling, a warm feeling of loyalty. "I think his loyalty to Esther was admirable," said the adult Alex, recalling the difficulties brought about by Lou's multiple lives. "She did support him all those years. But then there should have been loyalty to other people too. I don't think the way he dealt with the situation was good." Later, she recalled, when she would try to talk to her father about why he had created these strange family circumstances for them all, he would never answer. "He would be silent," Alex said. "But he would think about it. In the few years before he died, I think he was starting to think about us as people."

■

"He was a man of agony," said Shamsul Wares, the Bangladeshi architect. "He had disturbances inside. On the exterior, he was a very nice person. Probably women were attracted to him because of this: his greater understanding of humanity. He was a sensitive person." And this, Wares felt, was at least partly because "he had a difficult life in his childhood. People who have a difficult life always become more perceptive. Sometimes they also become more reckless—they want to grab things."

Among the other difficulties, clearly, had been his scarred appearance. "He never talked about it," said Fred Langford, referring to the childhood accident that caused the scars. "But I certainly thought about it many times, and how it shaped him. I imagine as a child his classmates would call him ugly, so it made him reclusive, left him alone a lot, and that's how he developed his drawing, his art. A lot of artists develop that way."

But if Lou had initially lacked self-confidence, it would seem that he eventually came to possess it, or something like it. "Probably growing up he was very self-conscious and unconfident. In my time with him he acted very confident," Fred remarked. "I saw him give a speech in La Jolla. He never made notes. He'd walk out on the stage, start rambling, and then he'd tee off like a jazz trumpeter. That takes confidence."

Increasingly as he grew more famous, Kahn was asked to give these oddly intimate, entrancing, free-form lectures of his, not only in the classroom, as he had always done, but also at all sorts of formal occasions. The audiences ranged from the general public to music and art students to architecture professionals. The venues could be as local as Philadelphia and as far-flung as Zurich. One of his most passionate and comprehensive lectures, titled "The Room, the Street, and Human Agreement," was delivered in Detroit in June of 1971 on the occasion of his receiving the American Institute of Architects' Gold Medal for lifetime achievement, an award given to only one architect annually. Lou was singularly, almost childishly proud of such recognition, as Richard Saul Wurman realized when Kahn came to give a talk in Aspen in June of the following year. At that point Kahn had only just returned to Philadelphia from the British Isles, where on June 13, 1972, he had been given the English equivalent of the AIA prize, the Gold Medal of the Royal Institute of British Architects. When Wurman met him at the airport in Colorado a few days after the London ceremony, Lou arrived cupping within his hands the British gold medal, which he had carried through multiple flight changes from Philadelphia and beyond. "Ricky, look at this!" he exclaimed, holding out his hands like a boy with a new treasure.

But that was in private. In public, at the 1971 event where he received his first gold medal and delivered his lecture, Kahn was appropriately mature and serious. A version of the talk he gave to the AIA was captured on film by Duncan White elsewhere during that same year, and in the movie you can actually see what could only be sensed in the printed transcript from Detroit: the way Lou directly addressed his audience, without notes and without any evident nervousness or embarrassment, his trademark bow tie askew, his white hair and thick eyeglasses gleaming in the light.

The room, Lou argued in his talk, was "the beginning of architecture," and he went on to call attention to its special attributes: "Enter your room and know how personal it is, how much you feel its life. In a small room with just another person, what you say may never have been said before. It is different when there is more than one person. Then, in this little room, the singularity of each is so sensitive that the vectors do not resolve. The meeting becomes a performance instead of an event, with everyone saying his lines, saying what has been said many times before." In delivering these lines, Lou appeared to be referring to his own "performance" at that very moment, even as he also raised the possibility of a more intimate, personal, fresh encounter that could only take place between two people in private. Yet because of the way he spoke, the public and private conversations seemed to intermingle. "This room we are in now is big, without distinction," he said. "Yet I know that if I were to address myself to a chosen person, the walls of the room would come together and the room would become intimate."

A feeling of close connection with one other person at a time: that was Lou's whole way of being in the world, whether he was engaging in a love affair or designing a building. By beginning with the room and working outward from it to the street and thence to the whole of "human agreement," he attempted to bring some of that private intensity into the public realm.

"The street is a room of agreement," he said in that Detroit talk.

"The street is dedicated by each house owner to the city in exchange for common services . . . The street is a community room."

He could have been thinking, as he spoke, of his own design for the Dacca Parliament Building, where the ambulatory that carried people from one level to the next actually had the physical characteristics of a city street, up to and including street lamps. These hallways of the National Assembly, which were supposed to foster random encounters and fortuitous meetings, were intended to produce the kind of human agreement known as political collaboration. That Kahn did indeed have Dacca at the back of his mind as he spoke these words was suggested by a section later in the talk, when he actually brought up his work on the subcontinent. "I realized in India and Pakistan," he said, "that a great majority of the people are without ambition because there is no way in which they are able to elevate themselves beyond living from hand to mouth, and what is worse, talents have no outlets. To express is the reason for living." Yet self-expression on its own wasn't worth much, in Lou's eyes, if it didn't lead to something larger. "I believe that the greatest work of man is that part which does not belong to him alone," he said.

Kahn seemed convinced that the culture at large had reached a moment of crisis. "A city is measured by the character of its institutions. The street is one of its first institutions. Today, these institutions are on trial," he remarked in Detroit in 1971. This was certainly true of American cities and institutions at that time (and not just at that time). But it was also true, in a different way, of the faraway place that was always at the back of his mind. For even as Lou was speaking these lines, he was aware that Dacca had become enmeshed in a bloody war.

The Bangladesh Liberation War, as the conflict over the new country's independence came to be known, officially began in March of 1971, when East Pakistan's leading political party, which had won a majority of National Assembly seats in that year's election, demanded the right to form a government. This would have made Sheikh Mujibar Rahman, who was head of the separatist Awami League, the prime minister of East Pakistan. When West Pakistan's leader, Zulfikar Ali Bhutto, refused to recognize the sheikh and instead sent one of his generals out to take over as governor of East Bengal, Rahman issued a formal declaration of independence. That declaration was made on March 26, the same day the sheikh was arrested by Pakistani forces.

The resulting war was notoriously violent. After the Pakistani army had invaded and taken over Dacca, there were numerous reported incidents of genocide, both in the capital and in the outer provinces. The surviving rebels fled westward to India, and a Bangladeshi government-in-exile was set up in the city of Calcutta, just over the border in West Bengal. Finally, on December 3, India entered the war on Bangladesh's side and mounted a three-pronged attack on the Pakistanis in Dacca. The city fell to the Indian forces on December 16, a date that became known as Victory Day in the new country of Bangladesh.

Throughout the nine months of the war, during which the people who had been paying Kahn—the West Pakistanis—were trying to wipe out the people he was directly working for, Lou had virtually no contact with his clients in Dacca. The half-poured concrete walls of the Assembly Building stood roofless and incomplete, looking less like a building under construction than an ancient pile of stones that had long been abandoned. (In fact, one theory held that the Kahn building made it through the bombings and strafings relatively unscathed because it *already* looked like a ruin, especially when seen from the sky.) Most of the Western contractors who had been hired to do projects in East Pakistan pulled out and quit during the war, but Kahn just kept working on his commission. Sometimes Henry Wilcots was the only architect assigned to the job, while the rest of the office occupied itself with more current projects. But all through 1971 the design process for Dacca slowly continued in Philadelphia, and it was during this period that Lou, with the aid of the engineer Harry Palmbaum, worked out his final plans for the National Assembly Hall's roof.

When the war was over, Kahn signed a new contract with the fledgling Bangladeshi government and went back to completing the job. Before it was done there would be the usual alterations and reductions that always took place in a Louis Kahn project. Dacca's Supreme Court, initially scheduled to be included on the Assembly site, was given its own building elsewhere in the city, designed by a different architect in a more traditional style. A major hospital on which Kahn's firm worked for years was ultimately reduced to its single outpatient wing. And there were smaller changes as well: among other things, the V-shaped extrusions that Fred Langford had so lovingly taught the concrete workers to make were eliminated from the higher stories of the building because they kept breaking off during stripping. But such design alterations were relatively minor, and the building as a whole slowly took shape in much the way Kahn had envisioned it all along.

Lou went out to Dacca in August of 1972 and again in January of 1973, in both cases joined by Henry Wilcots, who generally arrived first to prepare the ground for their work. On the early 1973 trip, for instance, Lou and Henry both left for London on January 20; from there, Wilcots proceeded immediately to Bangladesh while Kahn flew to Tel Aviv, remaining in Israel for the next few days. Lou then joined Henry in Dacca on Friday, January 26, for five intensive days and nights of meetings.

On the agenda were discussions about various design and construction issues at the capital site, including plans for a proposed Secretariat building. Among those Lou met with on this visit were the newly appointed and very capable Minister & Secretary of Works, Moinul Islam, as well as the new prime minister himself, Sheikh Mujibar Rahman. Professor Kahn, as they called him, was also invited to help develop a master plan for the whole of Dacca, whereby the existing city would be joined with new developments to the north of the Parliament area, including an air terminal, a diplomatic enclave, commercial space, and some housing. In conversations with Dacca's chief planning commissioner, a man named Mr. Zaman whom he much admired, Lou discussed bridges, waterways, and dwellings built on mounds or over water, while he and Henry were shown maps and diagrams illustrating the flood levels during monsoons.

And finally there were the evening events to attend—in particular, a dinner held at the home of Larry Heilman, a USAID planner in Dacca. The guests included not only Lou and Henry, but also a number of USAID staffers, along with the orthopedist who was going to head up the new hospital, Dr. Goss, and his wife. During the dinner-table discussion that evening, several people expressed their concern that so much money was being spent on the government buildings when housing needs in Dacca were so acute. Wilcots found their arguments specious, but Kahn listened carefully.

That night, back in his hotel room, Lou had a dream that was so intense it woke him up. He searched for a piece of paper on which to jot it down, and ended up grabbing his BOAC receipt from the London to Tel Aviv flight. On the back of this index-card-sized sheet, in minute and at times nearly indecipherable handwriting, he scribbled down what he could remember of the dream:

> The burnt wood figure, recognizable as one I met. Clean up man to destroy chared wood – 3 inches long. The beauty in blue seemed to constantly appear lately detected at a distance. The outfit tried on trousers placed them back where gotten try to conceal having taken them. As leaving a figure meant to hid this from inquired whom they belonged to. The bottoms marred though platd.
>
> Some artist friends leaving in a certain car – had other plans – left them with an idea to go my own way. Crossed again found them not having left and had to join them after all.

To those unfamiliar with Lou-speak, and even to those who know it well, these sentences might seem obscure to the point of impenetrability. He is talking to himself here, after all, and he is recounting something that does not obey any laws of logic or narrative sequencing. Still, precisely because Lou *is* speaking only to himself—both unconsciously (in the dream) and consciously (in his attempt to unravel it)—this account brings to light some of his deepest preoccupations. There are the references to something having been burnt: a charred wooden thing three inches long (or at least somehow connected to the number three) which is also a "figure . . . recognizable as one I met." There is the anxiety of having been caught in an illicit or forbidden action and trying to "conceal" it (especially with regard to the person from whom it is "meant" to be "hid"), though that shameful act appears only to involve trying on some trousers that don't belong to him. And there is the desire to "go my own way" when confronted with some "artist friends," accompanied by the later discovery that he "had to join them after all."

Having captured what he could of the fleeting, strangely disturbing dream, Lou attempts to ground it in the preceding day's events. "*Last night,*" he writes directly under his summary of the dream, and then notes down brief phrases from the dinner-party discussion about "the impropriety of building the capital in light of desperate housing needs" and other planning issues. Eventually he turns to the guests he had met at dinner: "Young people there at the Larry Heilman's also the Doctor and his wife seem nice giving people." He realizes he had "Said many things related to my relation with the authorities . . . I wonder now since I cannot sleep (it is early morning) how wise I was stating to these people which if reported I am afraid would not rest well with me." And then, on a new line all by itself, he writes, "I wish I did not so much the determination to finish the capital"—characteristically but also suggestively omitting a crucial word (have? feel?), as if the congruence between himself and his determination was so complete as not to require a connecting verb.

In this half-waking, self-communing language, Lou now returns to the dream and its meaning. "The dream above was like a warning," he muses. "This strange unrelated dream somehow is recognizably connected One would not be without the other. The old thing bothers and one afraid of ones own folly which could lead to treachery." Though he had "intended to do good for the nation," he worries that instead he may have been "feeding another point of view for my destructive position." Then hope surges back, and he wistfully concludes, "Yet heightening them to constructive criticism."

The Dacca Assembly Building was important to Lou, in part, because of his intense if somewhat amorphous feelings about democracy. This project, above all others, had given him a chance to put into built form the various emotions and ideas he had about the nature of assembly and the mechanisms of human agreement. And now, at long last, it seemed he was finally to be granted a commission in America that dealt with similar public issues, though admittedly on a much smaller scale.

In early 1973, Kahn was hired to design a memorial to Franklin Delano Roosevelt on the newly renamed Roosevelt Island in New York. The project made a nice bookend to the period that began with the Salk Institute commission, for FDR, himself a victim of polio, had been the founder of the March of Dimes, and the dime itself—or at any rate the profile of Roosevelt that graced the dime—ended up making an appearance in both the La Jolla and New York structures. But Roosevelt's significance in Kahn's life went back much farther than that. The years of FDR's presidency, 1932 to 1945, coincided with the era of Lou's youthful idealism, and during this period he was actively political in a variety of ways. Roosevelt's socially minded federal programs inspired much of Kahn's early architectural and urban planning work, and Roosevelt himself remained Lou's favorite president of all time.

Yet in his later years Kahn explicitly denied having any politics at all. In the early 1960s, for instance, he refused to sign a petition against nuclear weapons that some Philadelphia artists were circulating—and this despite the fact that his much-loved sister-in-law Olivia Abelson was one of the founders of the Sane Freeze movement. "He said no. He just didn't want to be associated with politics," said Sue Ann Kahn, who was embarrassed at her father's refusal.

"I would say Lou was completely apolitical," Esther Kahn told the architectural historian David Brownlee about fifteen years after her husband's death. When pushed, she suggested that any apparent radicalism in Lou's past could be attributed to Oscar Stonorov and other outside influences. She had clearly managed to obliterate Kahn's activist years of the 1930s and 1940s from her memory, just as Lou himself had attempted to do.

There could be many reasons for someone to move away from political activism as the twentieth century progressed, including shame about Stalinism and the other depredations of Soviet Communism, distaste for American presidential elections and their increasing reliance on television, fear and concern about America's military engagements abroad—not to mention the natural retreat toward the personal that comes with aging and financial stability. But in Kahn's case, the McCarthy era probably had something to do with it. Joseph McCarthy's widespread, ruthless, and damaging investigations into anybody and everybody's left-wing past would have been particularly frightening to an immigrant who had pulled himself out of poverty and was just beginning to get a foothold in the upper middle class. Many people, and not just Lou, tried to efface their activist histories in order to preserve their jobs. For an architect like Louis Kahn, the need to qualify himself anew every time a public commission offered itself would have underlined the desirability of a squeaky-clean record. And though one cannot be certain the red-baiting scare determined Kahn's choices about politics, one *can* be sure that Lou was aware of the problem, for in a 1973 speech at the Pratt Institute he warned against a way of thinking that would be "as ruinous as McCarthy, who spoiled our true consciousness, our sense of democracy."

In that same talk, delivered before a group of Brooklyn art students, Lou brought up "the Roosevelt Memorial in New York, which I am now engaged in doing. I had this thought that a memorial should be a room and a garden. That's all I had." He then went on to suggest his reasons for the choice: "The garden is somehow a personal nature, a personal kind of control of nature, a gathering of nature. And the room was the beginning of architecture. I had this sense, you see, and the room wasn't just architecture, but was an extension of self. I'll explain this because I think it has qualities that don't belong to me at all. It has qualities which bring architecture to you . . . there is something about the emergence of architecture as an expression of man which is tremendously important because we actually live to express. It is the reason for living."

And this, for Lou, came back to politics of a different and perhaps deeper kind: his long-held conviction that everyone in the world, including the poor of India and Bangladesh, deserved the right of self-expression. That his memorial to FDR came to be called Four Freedoms Park was thus singularly appropriate, for it was in his 1941 speech about the "four essential human freedoms" that Roosevelt championed "freedom of speech and expression—everywhere in the world," along with freedom of worship, freedom from want, and freedom from fear. In the monument's final incarnation, these words from FDR's speech were engraved on a stone wall that marked one edge of the roofless, three-sided Room from which one could look out onto Queens, Brooklyn, Manhattan, and the wide expanse of the East River.

Kahn's plans for the FDR memorial went through the usual series of extreme changes, but now in compacted form. From February 20, 1973, when he first brought the proposal for the memorial into Harriet Pattison's office, and the autumn of that same year, when he came up with the final design, there were essentially three different versions of the Room: a large brushed-steel monument, a smaller but still substantial concrete edifice, and the final granite structure. The Garden, too, went through several transformations, as Harriet and Lou argued about whether there should be a long approach through allées of trees (Harriet's idea) or something more limited and enclosed (Lou's idea). In the end the clients—who included the city of New York, the state of New York, and Ed Logue's Urban Development Corporation, which was in charge of new construction on Roosevelt Island—favored Harriet's landscaping plan, just as they insisted that the concrete be replaced by granite; and Lou complied.

While he was working on the FDR plan, his nephew Alan's children, Lauren and Jeff Kahn, came on a trip to Philadelphia and visited Lou at his office. Decades later, Lauren vividly remembered her great-uncle explaining to her a particular segment of his design. "He was trying to make a ha-ha," Lauren recalled, and when she asked him what a ha-ha was, "he said it's something a farmer has in his field when he wants to keep the cattle in but doesn't want to build a fence, so he makes an indentation in the ground, and the cows know instinctively not to go beyond it, and it's more beautiful than a fence. And he wanted to do something like this at FDR, so people could look out without an obstructed view, but so they would also know where the edge is, and feel safe."

That same summer, Lou wrote a letter to Harriet and Nathaniel containing a sketch of his current ideas for the FDR monument. The August 1973 letter, handwritten and undated, was sent to Harriet's summer place, a lighthouse on Indian Island off the coast of Maine. This was where Nathaniel and Harriet retreated to every summer, hoping that Lou would visit them there as promised, though he never did. The single-page note was filled with affection (it was addressed to "My dearest ones" and referred to Nathaniel as "our little hero"), but it also hinted at a slight, perhaps momentary sense of despair. "The little little little looms so full of joy in the depressing state of big trying to be bigger bigger all bigger emptiness and unhappyness—bladderesque," Lou wrote. Then he seemed to recover his spirits, adding, "I know you are having fun and above all feeling that a part of the world is your domain . . . Have made a scheme of the monument all in stone." He marked up his sketch with a few tiny handwritten phrases about his plans for the granite structure, including several "gaps" that were indicated with arrows.

Nathaniel was to have his own direct encounter with those gaps a few months later. It was during the design's final phase, in the fall of 1973, and the eleven-year-old boy had been brought to the office at night because both of his parents were hard at work on the FDR project. Lou was fiddling with a model of the Room, in which the different sections of the wall came apart to leave a space in between—an almost literal rendering of his oft-repeated idea that "the walls parted and the columns became." As he pulled the wall apart and brought it back together, over and over but with a slightly different gap each time, he said to Nathaniel, "How far apart do you think it should be?" Nathaniel the child was delighted to be asked; Nathaniel the adult, reflecting back on the occasion, thought it offered a crucial insight into how his father worked. "He liked to talk as he worked," said Nathaniel. "And it didn't matter whether you were young or old or an architect or not. He wasn't necessarily interested in your solution, but he was interested in what a conversation with you might bring out for him."

The FDR memorial wasn't the only project on which Kahn was working with Pattison in 1973. He also enlisted her to do the landscaping on Korman House, the final private residence he designed. Lou's clients in this case, Steven and Toby Korman, had money to spend, and they were both very particular. They wanted a modern family house composed of glass and wood (Steve's lumber business made him an expert on various kinds of wood), and they insisted on having Kahn design it, despite his repeated insistence that he was too busy with larger projects. "He turned me down seven, eight times," said Steve Korman. "I just showed up and kept asking."

Weekend after weekend, once he had agreed, Lou would go out to the piece of land the Kormans had selected in rural Whitemarsh Township, a few miles northwest of Philadelphia, and talk with them about their specific needs. Toby wanted a window she could look through when she was doing her laundry, and she wanted a private dressing area all to herself, away from her husband and their three boys. Steve wanted a lot of light, even in the basement ("I'm a scared person," he said, "I don't want dark places that will scare me"), and because of his allergies, he also wanted to be able to see the outdoors from behind walls of protective glass. All of this Lou ended up giving them, in a beautifully scaled, lovingly constructed house that looked more like an *Architectural Digest* ideal than anything he had built before.

When it came time to landscape the extensive grounds—to shape the view that one saw from the glassed-in breakfast area and the glass-walled living room and the upstairs window over Toby's dressing table and the downstairs one in her laundry room—Lou brought in Harriet. "You would have thought they were a typical married couple," commented Steve, who got to know them both well. "They'd be out there arguing, and then they'd say let's go have lunch. He was very comfortable in his relationships."

He must have been, because he also suggested Harriet as a landscape architect to the Shapiros, for whom Anne Tyng was in the midst of building a major addition. Lou and Anne had worked together on Shapiro House from 1958 to 1962, when the first phase of construction was completed. Even before it was finished, Norma Shapiro—a lawyer, later a judge—and her husband, Bernard, a doctor, suspected that their house would eventually need to be larger to accommodate their growing family. By 1972 they had three children, and they asked Lou to do the addition. He instead recommended Anne, who at that point was teaching in the architecture department at Penn (also on Lou's recommendation) as well as pursuing her own practice. Lou knew that Anne would take as much care as he would have in making the new rooms of the house fit with the old, and he also knew that she and the Shapiros would get along, since they had worked together in the earlier phase. "When Lou brought her into it, he showed her great respect," Norma Shapiro said. "I would never have known about their relationship if she hadn't talked about it. And he never did mention it."

But Anne talked about it quite freely to Norma, and it was through Anne that Norma learned about Lou's involvement with Harriet. "She told me about Alex, about Sue, about Nathaniel. She told me how often Lou visited," said Judge Shapiro. Anne also told Norma how much she wanted the three children to get to know each other. Norma, who had only ever been with Bernie, couldn't really identify with Anne over the love affair itself—"it was out of my realm," she commented—but she liked and respected Anne very much. "I was tremendously impressed and admired Anne because she was so accepting of the illegitimacy of her child and Harriet's," Shapiro said. "She may have felt sad that he had left her, but she didn't resent it—and she liked Harriet. She would say, 'When someone is an extraordinary man, you don't hold him to ordinary standards.' To the last day I saw her she was sure she was the preferred mistress, and part of it was how much she contributed to his work. In my view she was still in love with him, and I think she felt she was the love of his life."

When Lou recommended Harriet Pattison for the Shapiro House landscaping, Norma asked Anne if she minded, "and she said no, she just wanted what was best for the house." Norma confessed to enjoying the complexity of the situation ("It was kind of fun to have two women associated with him involved in my house"), but in the end she couldn't use the plan Harriet came up with. "The design she gave us was very formal, Victorian—concentric circles, a maze—very beautiful but totally inappropriate for our house," Judge Shapiro explained. "This is a tree house in the woods. And it cost as much as the house! We told her we were not interested. We offered to pay for her time; she refused. I think it's fair to say she did not enjoy working for us."

Norma Shapiro's outspoken sympathy with Anne Tyng sometimes put her at odds with those colleagues who openly sided with Esther Kahn. For instance, Eddie Becker, one of Philadelphia's leading lawyers, was "very prejudiced" in favor of Esther "and resented this whole situation," Norma recalled. It would appear that Lou's secret life was not very secret, if even people in the legal community, totally outside his sphere, were discussing it with each other. And the lawyers were not the only ones. "Philadelphia was a very small town," Sue Ann Kahn observed, "and everyone knew about the affairs."

Steve Korman agreed, acknowledging that the broad facts about Lou's private life were widely known in Philadelphia. But Steve also felt that he himself had a special kind of access, having gotten unusually close to Lou during their months and years of working together on Korman House. "I spent a lot of time talking to Lou about his personal life, Esther and all that," Korman said. "Marriage to him was something you were supposed to do. He really cared about all the people he was involved with. He wasn't conventional. He didn't want to hurt people. He did, but he didn't want to."

■

Shortly after Korman House was finished, Steve and Toby invited Lou and Esther to come have dinner with them in their beautiful new residence. The couples spent most of the evening in the long, double-height room that served as both living room and dining room. On that cold February night, a fireplace warmed the seating area at the far end, a grand piano stood next to the elegant dining table, and the floor-to-ceiling windows brought together the reflected light from indoors and the darkness outside. Everyone had a great deal to drink. Lou played the piano. There was a lot of laughter and a sense of joyous occasion. "It was one of the most wonderful dinner parties," said Toby. "I remember Esther writing me a note telling me it was one of the great evenings of her life."

On this everyone agreed. But Toby and Steve Korman (who subsequently got an amicable divorce, remained close during their respective remarriages, and eventually handed on their beloved house to their oldest son) had very different memories of the events of that evening. Toby, for one, recalled that another couple had been present as well—Suzanne Binswanger, who designed the furnishings in the house, and her husband, Frank. None of the conversation from that evening stuck with her, and she might have missed part of it when she was out in the kitchen, but she didn't think there had been any prolonged or emotionally charged discussion.

Steve, though, remembered an intense conversation between Esther and Lou that lasted for a long time, possibly even an hour. ("Steven tends to exaggerate a little bit. He does get a little carried away," advised Toby. "It doesn't mean there wasn't a line or two said, but an *hour*?") As far as Steve was concerned, the bystanders just faded away during it— "blacked out," he said, "as if we weren't there." He didn't mention the Binswanger couple: from his perspective it was just Toby and himself, watching and listening as if they were the audience to a play. And what they heard was an extremely intimate, warmly affectionate conversation about the relationship between Lou's marriage and his other loves. "He says to Esther, I care about you because I care about others," Steve recounted. "You're my rock. But I care about each person differently. The other people I care about, I care about." From Steve's perspective, "the whole conversation was: I care about you." That was the context in which Esther was hearing what she was hearing. And that, according to Steve, was what made her write to the Kormans several weeks later about how significant the evening had been for her.

In any case, it remained a major event in her life—in her and Lou's shared life—because of the timing. The dinner party at the Kormans took place on the last weekend in February, 1974. Two weeks later, Lou set off on his final trip to India.

IN SITU:
INDIAN INSTITUTE OF
MANAGEMENT AHMEDABAD

Main plaza of Indian Institute of Management
(Anonymous photograph from the author's collection)

It would be possible, if you were so inclined, to view this entire campus in terms of the influences upon it. Looking at the broad expanses of the Institute's softly faded brick walls, intermittently broken up with arches and other cutout shapes, you could imagine you were seeing the ruins of Trajan's Market in Rome. The vast open-ended rectangle defining the central space between the classroom wing, the faculty wing, and the library wing might make you recall the mysterious grandeur of the desolate, abandoned piazzas at Ostia Antica. On the other hand, this same central plaza could remind you of something much nearer: Sarkej Roza, a fifteenth-century Islamic structure located just south of Ahmedabad, whose series of mosques, tombs, and covered walkways were built around open squares of heat-filled light. Yet another local ruin, the beautiful Adalaj Stepwell, built in 1499, could have influenced Kahn's design by suggesting the ways in which rays of filtered light could penetrate deep into the cooling darkness. And then there are the *pols* of Old Ahmedabad itself, those closely clustered neighborhoods in the oldest part of the city, whose gated courtyards and narrow alleys lead continuously from one into another. These mysteriously interlinking compounds seem to be echoed in the winding pathways, unexpected courtyards, and abruptly terminated views of the Institute's campus, where everything finally connects up, though in ways that cannot be predicted from a distance.

Then again, perhaps the whole complicated design, with its brick-paved walkways and irregular cut-throughs and medium-height brick buildings, makes reference not to Rome or Ahmedabad, but to another city entirely—that is, the early-twentieth-century Philadelphia of Louis Kahn's youth. Or maybe the influence is even closer in time. Maybe Kahn was borrowing from Le Corbusier, the only other foreign modernist to design a significant amount of work in this part of India. Kahn certainly saw the four buildings Corbusier built in Ahmedabad in the decade before his own arrival, including two private houses, the City Museum, and the headquarters of the Mill Owners' Association. Though one cannot trace exact echoes, one could point to the brick cladding of the City Museum, the long approach by ramp to the Mill Owners' center, the use of concrete as both a structural and a decorative material in all four buildings, the fiercely geometric shapes that define their outer surfaces, and the continuous play of light and shadow from within the internal courtyards, all of which Kahn could have been reusing or reinventing when he came to design the Indian Institute of Management.

"I don't think there is any influence from anybody," says Balkrishna Doshi. "It is all what the brick wants to say." At eighty-six, Doshi is still vital and active; he is also generally acknowledged to be Ahmedabad's pre-eminent living architect. Yet he retains a youthful sense of admiration for the friend who has been dead for forty years, that master architect whom he still views as a kind of yogi. "There are higher sensibilities by which people discover the traditions of the past," he insists, and in his view Kahn possessed those intuitions. "Deep inside, he must have connected himself to the classics period. If one is able to connect with things far beyond, either in time or space, you connect with your soul—no, not soul, with your inner self. So the relationship is not physical. A building is no more a building, it's a sacred space."

There is perhaps some irony in the fact that the inner self of a man as notoriously unbusinesslike as Louis Kahn should have manifested itself in an Institute of Management. And yet if the irony is there, it is not a damning one, but a gentle joke of the sort Kahn himself enjoyed. The gods of management may be money and efficiency, but this campus's sacred space seems dedicated to something else besides: to a sense of community founded on like-minded aims, to the possibility of tranquil contemplation amidst a chaotic world, and to a notion of education that goes back to the original idea of a school as Kahn always formulated it, something which "began with a man under a tree, who did not know he was a teacher, discussing his realization with a few who did not know they were students." Even the specific goals of an economic institute would not necessarily have been alien to Kahn's nature, for as he said in one public lecture, "Economy has nothing to do with money. Economy is doing the right thing, and money is just what money can buy."

The IIM campus encourages exactly the kind of meandering that the classical students under a tree—Socrates' pupils, say—would have associated with their peripatetic education. Kahn's plan creates room for serendipitous encounters, frequent small discoveries, and approaches to light-filled endpoints through shadow-filled corridors. The heuristic method is invitation, not coercion, and until a few years ago anyone could have just walked in off the streets of this well-heeled collegiate neighborhood to enjoy the lushly landscaped grounds. Now the heightened security that prevails all over India requires you to stop by the guard station and leave your ID in exchange for a pass. But after that you are free to wander the campus on your own, passing from the parking lot at the front to the pedestrian precincts beyond.

Immediately to the right of the parking lot sits a Kahnish-looking auditorium building—complete with perfectly round cutouts and mottled brick—conceived and executed by another architect, Anant Raje, who helped finish the campus after Kahn's death. Ignoring this for the moment, you will find yourself drawn instead to the strangely angled staircase that sits at a diagonal to the building it leads up to. At the top of the broad granite stairs, and visible from some distance away, is a square opening in the brick façade, surmounted by a semicircular arch; the two openings are separated by a quirky cement lintel, whose outer edges lift in a kind of angular smile. This, you will soon discover, is the most frequently repeated pattern on the campus: the square, the arch, and the concrete strip between them. You will see it everywhere. And yet you will never tire of it, because it appears in so many variations: small or large, with an open arch or an arch filled by glass or brick, the lintel usually present but sometimes absent or with brick replacing the

concrete, and the arch occasionally appearing on its own, mirrored by a
reflecting arch below, or even turned into a circle crossed by a cement
band. The square openings, too, will wander away from their arches,
becoming doors at the corners of a brick room, or ground-level windows,
or stacked rectangular shapes in differing or matching sizes. But wherever you turn you will eventually come back to that pattern of the arch
and the rectangle and the smiling concrete lintel. And it will please you
each time you see it, not only because it is rather lovely in itself, but
because it will give you a sense of familiarity and firm location in this
otherwise slightly confusing place.

The confusion is not severe. You can cover the whole campus in a
few hours of casual strolling, and you can pretty quickly get a sense of
how the various parts—the classroom building, the library wing, the
student dormitories for men and women, the faculty offices and the
faculty housing, not to mention various functions strewn over the regions beyond—relate to each other in a kind of mental map. It is not
possible to get seriously lost. And yet there are always local surprises.
Before you round a corner, you will not know whether the path ahead of
you is to be a set of steps or a bridging walkway. Until you descend into
a tunnel and follow its shadowy route, you cannot be positive where it
will take you, though you can be sure it will take you *somewhere*. Courtyards appear suddenly before you and have multiple exits, some of them
sliver-thin, as if inviting you to squeeze between buildings. Concentric
ground-level arches lead your eye into a distance that is light-filled but
otherwise indecipherable until you get there. Buildings turn out to
have whole extra stories that are only visible from one side. But none of
this is permanently disconcerting or in any way frightening. On the
contrary, it gives you a sense of pleasure to be mildly tricked in this way,
to be sent on a picaresque journey that is somehow guaranteed to end
happily.

It is not a campus that stands on its own dignity. There is humor in
the design as well as grandeur, and sometimes the grand scale itself
gives rise to a witticism. Consider, for instance, the gigantic concrete
lintels that rest above the walls of the men's dorms, each lintel span-
ning a huge brick cylinder that holds an interior staircase as well as the
two concave brick walls on either side of it. This smiling lintel, set beneath a pair of elongated arches, takes the same form as its smaller

cousins elsewhere on the campus, but here it is so long, so oversized, that it almost seems a kind of Claes Oldenberg joke. Yet even with its evident sense of humor, it remains elegant and serene, at once a joke and not a joke.

An even bigger grin can be found farther down those same walls, in the paired arches set within the slightly concave brick faces. Here the open arches are designed to mirror each other—one arching upward, the other downward, with an hourglass-shaped span of brick between them, so that there is a curve at the bottom of each arch as well as the top. But because the walls in which these arches appear are *themselves* bent inward, there is a further ripple to the design, a further dimension to the curve. In the harsh glare of the sunlit exterior, the convolution is barely visible to the eye: while you can sense that each arch is concave, you can't fully see the effect. But if you enter the stairwell and look at the design from within the dark interior, so that the inward-flooding light highlights rather than flattens the contours of the arch, you can see that this three-dimensionally curving shape resembles nothing so much as a widely grinning mouth, of the sort a skilled child might carve into a jack-o'-lantern. It is a delightful joke—a pun, almost, since it causes you to smile at a smile—but it is also a serious and beautiful piece of construction.

The men's dorms, located off to the left as you enter the campus, are the only ones with these grinning arches, just as they are the only ones possessing the tall, windowless, cylindrical stairwells. In the women's dorms, which lie just behind the main classroom building, the design is wider, lower, and rounder. Curved surrounding walls with dry gullies below them segregate the buildings from the adjoining walkways, and arched doorways manned by guards at desks mark the entrances. The ladies appear to have been given the role of damsels in a moated castle, whereas the men are more like frat-boy knights, with their phallic stairwells and jack-o'-lantern cutouts. Whether this says anything about how Kahn viewed the sexes, or whether it was just another kind of allusive game he was playing with design, is not something a casual observer could ever hope to answer. Both sets of dorms appear spartan and attractive in equal measure; both feature ground-level buttresses that emphasize the medieval fort look, and that seem to call out for water to lap at the foot of the brick. They are probably not all that different, as living places. But the women's dorms, especially as glimpsed from the big side windows of the central classroom wing, possess an added level of mysterious allure, a whiff of inaccessibility, that makes them seem like something out of an old fairy tale.

The classroom wing is the heart of the campus, and you are likely to find yourself repeatedly drawn back to it. A long, straight, thin wedge of brick, punctured at regular intervals by large open rectangles and their crowning arches, the building is both a welcome refuge from the sun and a privileged recipient of its filtered light. If you approach it from the direction of the adjoining Vikram Sarabhai Library (which, with its obliquely angled entrance and radiant brick-lined reading room, offers yet another evocation of Trajan's Market), you will probably find yourself at the main classroom level, one floor up from the ground. Here the corridor soars to a double height, and the cutouts stretch all the way from floor to ceiling, with only a concrete bench set within them to keep you from falling out the open window. Though long and high, the hallway feels perfectly proportioned, with the brick walls set close enough so that you feel embraced but not smothered, and with the concrete ceiling high enough above your head to give you a sense of grandeur and ease. You can see light coming in from the end of the tunnel and also from the cutouts along the way, but you find yourself enjoying the relative darkness, for in this climate deep shadow is more often friend than foe. As you pass by the large side openings, you notice not only the entrancing views they provide (of the nearby women's dormitories on one side and the faculty offices across the plaza on the other), but also the cooling cross-breezes they bring in.

Moving further down the hallway, you are drawn forward by the light at the end, and as you approach you can see that this light comes mainly from an immense circular window set high in the far wall, as well as from smaller square windows bunched into the lower corners of the end-room. Far behind you, at the other terminus of the central corridor, there is a similar room that serves as an exit lobby, its square windows converted into doors; but at this end the small room has no exit except the door you came in by, and no visible function except to serve as a place of rest and contemplation. Benches are set into each of the floor-level corner windows that abut each other at right angles, so you can sit with your back to one window and glance out another;

meanwhile, in front of you, an inner brick wall pierced at three levels with differently shaped windows runs up to the very top of the building. As the sunlight passes through the high circular opening on the outer wall, it plays on the brick walls and the stone floor in constantly changing shapes, calling to mind Kahn's oft-repeated misquotation from Wallace Stevens, "What slice of the sun does your building have?" (to which he famously added the gloss "as if to say that the sun never knew how great it is until it struck the side of a building").

· If you ever tire of this remarkable internal view, you can always look out through the lower windows at the tall, stately, square-cut water tower that stands at some distance from the rest of the campus. Closer to hand, you can glimpse small clusters of students seated beneath you on the grass. A slight murmur of their conversation may reach you in your secluded chamber, but mainly there is silence, and tranquility, and room to think.

Toward the very back of the Institute, past the dormitories and a playing field and a small road and some luxuriant gardens, lies a corner of the campus where Louis Kahn has left his personal mark. These are the "sample arches," the hand-fashioned structures he created and left behind to show the workers how to lay the bricks and mortar, and how to rub the corners of the bricks so they would fit more closely together. "He wanted a thin joint," Doshi says, contrasting this to the way Le Corbusier had the workers lay a thick mortar between his bricks. And indeed, if you look at the brickwork in the City Museum, you will see how much rougher and messier it looks than the walls of the IIM. But then, Le Corbusier was going for a rougher appearance in general: his concrete often looks like something from an industrial process— almost as if it were still in its wet state, still emerging from the cement mixer—whereas Kahn's concrete is singularly smooth and fine, a finished product.

Both the concrete lintel with its upturned tips and the patterns of brick forming the arch itself are clearly visible in the sample Kahn created. They are like a tangible signature, reminiscent of the quick sketches of forms and joints preserved on the basement wall of the Salk

Institute: a lingering sign of his presence, testimony to his actual hand in the work. Here, at the very back of the Institute campus, you can look at these remnants in peace, surrounded only by the sound of birdsong, the rustle of wind in the trees, and the occasional splash of a spray hose as a gardener hand-waters the plants.

It is a much more moving memorial than the explicit one, which consists of a sign affixed to one of the columns of the central piazza announcing in Hindi and English that this space has been officially named "Louis Kahn Plaza." In fact, this central courtyard, grand as it is, may strike you at times as one of the less functional parts of Kahn's design. On sunny days, its enormous length and width make it too hot to traverse comfortably. Even the eternal Indian dogs choose to lie only in its shaded patches, cooling themselves against the paving stones. Humans hug the buildings as they navigate around the plaza, or else choose to go inside the tunnels that line it. They will generally walk the extra distance it takes to adhere to the right angles rather than cut across in the direct sun. In rainy weather it must be even worse, with the monsoon pelting down and the grassy part of the rectangle turned to mud; then everybody, including the dogs, must stick to the inside corridors.

Admittedly, there is a magnificence to the views this great space creates as one looks across it or down its length. Without them, you would not be inclined to think of the Roman Forum or Ostia Antica. And yet the design falls short on a practical level, because if people are not drawn to walk across it, then the plaza serves no communal function; it just feels vast and empty. However grand the visual effect is, there is something missing, and one intuitively feels the lack. Kahn himself evidently recognized the problem, for up to his very last day in Ahmedabad he was still tinkering with plans for this area. His final sketch of the plaza—a rough, thought-filled drawing, done in charcoal on yellow tracing paper—was dated March 15, 1974. Perhaps, if he had lived, he would eventually have come up with something to fill the gap.

Time has, to a certain extent, ravaged the buildings of the Indian Institute of Management. Moisture has seeped into the softly rubbed bricks and corroded the steel rebar that lies within the walls. Cracks have appeared in the concrete lintels and ceilings, some of them large and jagged. An earthquake in 2001, so severe it knocked the concrete caps off the cylindrical stairwells, caused widespread damage that took years to repair. The bricks that pave the central plaza are half torn up, awaiting new bricks to take their place. And everywhere the walls have been faintly or in some cases grossly stained by the constant tug between intense rainfall and severe heat.

Yet the essential feel of the place remains unharmed. It is not just that the structure was built to look like a ruin, so that even time's damage can't make it look bad. That may be partly true, but it is not the whole story. The campus itself remains a congenial place, its buildings and arches and shadows and light a never-ending source of pleasure that you hesitate to leave for the last time because there still seems so much to explore. What you feel when you walk·through the Institute is that Kahn at long last got to build the kind of city he was envisioning when he helped make plans in the 1950s for Philadelphia's center. It is a pedestrian city, quiet and peaceful but still interesting, where you are surrounded by old brick buildings that are high enough but not too high, and where winding paths and secret courtyards and hidden exits through alleys and tunnels bring people together in unexpected ways. Kahn never got to construct his pedestrian Philadelphia: those who opposed him argued that he was being egotistical, utopian, and willfully unable to accept things as they are. But what you sense in the Indian Institute of Management is precisely the opposite of egotism. It is a kind of letting go.

"It's like an offering," says Doshi of the shapes between the buildings, the way the massive structures create a sense of organic, human space. "See, one has to be modest, and Kahn was extremely modest. He was very shy. When you respect something, you want to give it some distance." Yet it seems he was also proud of what he had done. "He said, 'This is perhaps my best campus,'" Doshi recalls.

That affection may have had something to do with the role the project played in Kahn's life. He had reached a certain age when he started it, a certain stage in his career, and the project itself—its large size, its slow pace—gave him time to think. "Twelve years: time to reflect," says Doshi. "So when you look at Lou at the age of sixty-two or sixty-one, when he came here, and then twelve years on, you can almost imagine his mental state—searching for what he does in life. In India, the sixties start the last phase. You know you have to now serve, and not covet." In Kahn's case, the constant need to go away and come back may have reinforced the lesson. "Here you come, and the work has happened a little bit more, little bit more. You think about time, and why it takes so much time, and why you want to be here. If you don't think about time," Doshi concludes, "you don't think of memory."

BEGINNING

I like English history. I like the bloodiness of it somehow—you know it's
horribly bloody—but out of it came something . . . I have one of eight
volumes, and I only read the first volume and only the first chapter,
because every time I read it I also read something else into it. And the
reason is that I'm really interested in reading Volume Zero. And maybe,
when I get through with that, Volume Minus-One.

—Louis Kahn

Naturally, he couldn't remember everything about the beginning—
not only because a small child's memory is vague to nonexistent, but
because much of it happened before he was born. And there were other
things, too, that hid the past from him.

Many of the names changed. The Russian province of Livonia,
whose capital was Riga, got parceled out between two separate countries, Latvia and the southern part of Estonia. The island known as
Ösel turned into Saaremaa, and the town of Arensburg came to be
called Kuressaare. Leib and Beila-Rebeckah Schmulowsky renamed
themselves Leopold and Bertha Kahn, and their son Leiser-Itze became Louis Isadore. So the historical record—already fuzzy, especially
in the case of Jews in that time and place—became even more confusing, more difficult to penetrate, harder to read. People covered their
tracks, and what they didn't intentionally cover up, history disguised
for them.

The man who came to be known as Louis Kahn always said, and
believed, that he had been born in the town of Arensburg on the island

of Ösel. But in the official record that was kept at that time, Leiser-Itze's birth—like that of his younger sister, Schorre, and his even younger brother, Oscher—was registered in the mainland town of Pernau (now Pärnu, on the Estonian coast). This does not necessarily mean he had his facts wrong. In 1901, when Leiser was born, all Jewish births in the province of Livonia, to which both the island of Ösel and the city of Pernau belonged, had to be recorded by a rabbi; under Tsarist rule, it was the responsibility of the rabbis to keep track of the Jewish population and report to the authorities. Ösel was one of the largest islands in the Baltic Sea, second in size only to Gotland, and the town of Arensburg, with a population of 5,000, was its biggest settlement. Yet the Jewish community of Arensburg, which numbered fewer than a hundred people in 1901, was not large enough to sustain a full congregation. So any Jewish child born on the island in the early years of the twentieth century would have had to be registered in Pernau, where there were enough resident Jews to support a rabbi.

Of course, it's possible that Beila-Rebeckah and Leib actually traveled to Pernau for the birth, or even lived there for a time. After all, their first child was born on February 20, in the dead of winter, when there was no regular ferry service linking the island to the mainland. Perhaps the young parents, nervous about being isolated, temporarily moved to the mainland for their child's winter delivery—though this would not explain why their second and third children, born in June of 1902 and June of 1904, were also listed as Pernau births. Or perhaps they moved to Pernau in advance of each birth to make sure that there would be a professional *mohel* who could perform the ritual circumci-. sion, if necessary, since they could not know beforehand whether the child would be a girl or a boy. Certainly there *was* a circumcision, in the case of Leiser-Itze; it is recorded as having taken place on February 27, a week after the birth.

But it's also possible that the rabbi just recorded the birthplace inaccurately, putting down the place of registration instead of the actual place of birth. (Such errors invariably crept into the records: Leiser-Itze, for instance, was listed in some documents as Itze-Leib, though an Ashkenazic Jewish family would not have named a son after a living father.) Or possibly the confusion arose because the Schmulowsky family was trying to finesse the issue of their address. Jews in Tsarist

Livonia were not really supposed to live for any length of time outside the legally approved locations, such as Riga, and while the town of Pernau was already outside the official settlement areas, Arensburg was even farther out.

Yet Arensburg was certainly where Beila-Rebeckah's family was based. Of her six living siblings, five had been born in Arensburg between 1881 and 1890, and the town was listed in a census report as the "constant residence" of her parents, Mendel and Rocha-Lea Mendelowitsch. Beila herself, the oldest of the Mendelowitsch children, had been born in Riga in 1872. Two younger sisters, including one who died at the age of seven months, were also born there between 1874 and 1878. Then the family moved to Arensburg, a popular Baltic resort town which, as of 1875, had a direct ferry connection to Riga. The trip took only nine hours; steamships between the two ports ran twice a week in summer, then somewhat more irregularly through the end of November, when winter finally closed in. So it was easy for Arensburg's Jews to go back and forth between the Livonian capital, where most of them had come from, and the Ösel resort. By the time the Mendelowitsches arrived, Jews constituted the fourth-largest ethnic group in Arensburg, after Estonians, Germans, and Russians.

Mendel Mendelowitsch, who was variously described as an artisan, a shoemaker, and a tinsmith, apparently adapted to the resort environment by opening a rooming house: at least, his grandson remembered that he owned a "hotel," which in the case of a Jew was more likely to be a small boardinghouse. Relations between Jews and non-Jews on Ösel were comfortable if not close. The island had been ruled by so many different nations over the years—including Estonians, Swedes, Danes, two varieties of Germans, and Russians—that it was much more mixed and cosmopolitan than most of the mainland. Catholics, Lutherans, Russian Orthodox, and Jews were all buried in a single cemetery in Arensburg (though in different sections). Tourists, especially German tourists, came through all the time to take the waters and luxuriate in the health-giving mud baths. An elegant Kursaal, in appearance a bit like Bath's Pump Room, provided a social focus for these visitors, with its grand dining room, its sunny terrace, and its bandstand set within a large city park. The town itself had a number of charming old buildings clustered around the market square, including not only the venerable Town Hall, but also an ancient weigh house which had been built in 1633 and was later transformed into the local post office. Older even than the weigh house was the Bishop's Castle, a massive fourteenth-century structure on the outskirts of town that was set within a sixteenth-century fortress and surrounded by a moat. A well-preserved ruin in 1901, the castle was one of the defining features of Arensburg, with its two square towers visible from any point in the town.

Life for the Mendelowitsch family continued to move back and forth between Riga—the place where they remained officially registered, in case deportation became necessary—and Arensburg, where they actually lived. In 1900, for instance, Mendel and Rocha-Lea were recorded as living with their son Abram at 108 Maskavas Street, in the heart of the Riga ghetto; yet by 1901 the family had a tinsmith shop at 16 Tolli Street in Arensburg. By that time, too, they had acquired a new family member, for on May 28, 1900, Beila-Rebeckah married Leib Schmulowsky, a twenty-five-year-old Lithuanian Jew who had recently served as a paymaster in the Russian army. The marriage took place in Riga, but when Leib and Beila's first child was born nine months later (by which time Leib's status was vaguely described as "tradesman"), they were already in either Pernau or Arensburg.

No residential or employment records from the turn of the century hint at where Leib Schmulowsky might have lived or worked before or after coming to Riga. Nor did he seem to have any relatives of his own nearby (the marriage register simply lists his father's name, Mendel Schmulowsky, and his place of origin, the Lithuanian city of Rossieni). Later in life Leib apparently told his oldest son that on Ösel he had worked for a while as a clerk at the Arensburg fortress, though nothing but his word supports this. Employment, in any case, was never his strong point. But he was a good-looking man, he wrote a fine hand, he spoke five languages, and he and his wife doted on each other. Beila-Rebeckah was twenty-eight at the time of the marriage, and her family must have been immensely relieved that she had been saved from spinsterhood, as well as grateful to the suitor who claimed her.

And if the new husband proved restless—he was already planning to decamp for America as soon as his wife delivered their third child—that was to be expected of an ambitious young man in his circumstances. Certainly things did not look promising for the Jews in Tsarist Livonia. Rumors of Russian pogroms had penetrated even Arensburg, setting off a migration that caused the local Jewish population to decline from 111 in 1881 to 35 or fewer at the start of the First World War. To this general motive for flight Leib added a more specific one: he wanted to avoid being drafted again into the Russian army, which in February of 1904 had just embarked on a war with the Japanese. Spurred into action by this latest development, Leib Schmulowsky began plotting his move to Philadelphia, where he had a half-brother who he hoped might help him find work.

A building that is being built is not yet in servitude. It is so anxious to be that no grass can grow under its feet, so high is the spirit of wanting to be. When it is in service and finished, the building wants to say: "Look, I want to tell you about the way I was made." Nobody listens. Everybody is busy going from room to room. But when the building is a ruin and free of servitude, the spirit emerges telling of the marvel that a building was made.

—Louis Kahn

They told him the Arensburg Castle was a ruin, and he loved the word *ruin* almost as much as he loved the word *castle*. It was his favorite place in the whole town. He wasn't allowed to go there by himself—even the short fifteen-minute walk was too far for a small boy alone, and the long-uninhabited structure was too dangerous to play in—but sometimes his mother or father would take him there, down the cobbled length of Lossi Street, past the park surrounding the Kursaal, across the wooden bridge that spanned the moat, and into the dark tunnel that led through the fortress's thick wall. One of his favorite moments of the walk was the point at which the tunnel curved and you could see for the first time the sunlight shining at the far end, with the castle's tall corner tower framed in the arch of the tunnel exit. It was always exciting to come around that turn. And then to emerge into the vast forecourt, now occupied by the Russian garrison, with the fortress walls far away on either side and the immense stone front of the castle itself looming above you—that was even more thrilling. Not everyone was allowed inside this part of the fort, but because of his father's job with the garrison, he was sometimes permitted to wander around there. He liked the way, when you stood in front of it, the left side of the castle was not quite the same as the right: the two corner towers, though both were square and capped with pointy pyramids, were of different heights and widths. They matched and at the same time they didn't match.

The castle felt enormous, and the closer you got to it, the more impossibly tall it seemed. Yet though it was impressive, it was not at all frightening. He loved to go right up to the front wall and stroke the rough texture of the closely fitted beige stones. He also liked walking to either side and feeling the curve of the stone as it rounded the corner. And when he got back to the front, if his parents allowed it, he especially liked to go inside the castle itself, through that tiny off-center door, only a bit larger than the doors in their house—a door that seemed too small for such a grand place. But he liked that too, because it made him feel as if something in this gigantic structure had been shaped to his own small size. He had the same feeling when he got all the way to the interior courtyard of the castle (which was as far as you were allowed to go, because the rooms themselves were in a ruined state) and looked around at the four inner walls that surrounded him. They were not far away, as the fortress walls out front had been, but comfortably close, and somehow shorter than they had seemed from the outside, so that he could sense the presence of the sky above him as he stood in this little space which was at once a room and an outdoors. And as he stood there he thought: *The inside is different from the outside.*

Or perhaps not. Maybe he didn't think any of this. No reliable records survived from this early period of his life, just hazy family memories and hearsay. What was certain, though, was that he loved the Arensburg Castle—he was to remember it and speak about it as an adult—just as he loved ruins of all kinds for their qualities of stillness and repose. Yet even ruins, he would discover, did not always stay the same. In 1904, when he was three years old, renovation work began on the castle in an effort to make it a place that tourists and townspeople could visit. All the building activity was no doubt fascinating to a small boy, who would have enjoyed watching men and equipment at work. But it was the castle as he first saw it, as a ruin, that was to stimulate his imagination for the rest of his life.

The fact that you could see the castle from anywhere in town was just one of the things that made Arensburg a good place for this little boy. Everything important to him was within walking distance. If he and his mother set out from his grandparents' house at 4 Kohtu Street to walk to the market square, they could get there in about three minutes—maybe five minutes if his sister was with them, because she was a year younger and slowed them down a bit. The market square (which was actually shaped like a rough trapezoid rather than a formal square) was not only the center of town, the gathering spot where beautiful buildings like the town hall and the old weigh house lined the wide-open space. It was also the recognizable landmark which told him he had almost reached his uncles' shop.

From the point at which Kohtu Street entered the square, you could see across to the long, symmetrical two-story building, just to the right of the town hall, that was 1 Lossi Street. This fine address, with its multiple arched entrances on the ground floor and its wrought-iron balcony on the second, was where Abram and Benjamin Mendelowitsch had their butcher shop. If, after visiting his uncles, he and his mother walked down Lossi in the direction that led away from the market square, they would pass the intriguing-looking Russian Orthodox church called St. Nicholas and eventually (if he was lucky) end up at the castle. If instead they turned off the main cobbled street to the left or the right, they would find themselves on one of the town's many unpaved roads, their surface made up of dirt that turned to mud when it rained. These streets led to his relatives' houses, or to the little school where his aunt taught, or to the address at 16 Tolli Street where the family tinsmith business was located.

Sometimes he was taken down by the harbor, where the fishermen's boats and small pleasure craft came in. (The big ferries from Riga, he knew, docked at the larger port at nearby Roomessaare, from which you had to take a little train to travel the few kilometers to Arensburg.) On the rare occasions when he was driven in a cart out beyond the city limits, he found himself in a flat, seemingly endless countryside filled with trees. But even here there were pleasant surprises—sudden clearings in the forest, for instance, where there might be an old stone church or a newer wooden farmhouse. The houses out there had much more land around them than the tightly packed city houses. But whether in the town or the country, most of the buildings on the island had the same kind of steeply pitched roof, often made of square metal tiles, though sometimes thatched or shingled. In winter the snow would pile up on all these steep roofs, getting thicker and thicker as it froze in layers, until the warm days of spring finally melted it off.

The little boy did not mind winter. One of his very earliest memories—he must have been about two—was of drawing designs on a frosted window from inside a snowbound house. Still, he loved the moment in the year when the snow began to slide off the sloping roofs, because it meant that the light of summer was coming soon. He did not fear the dark, but he loved the light.

On most summer nights he was asleep long before the sun set, so all his waking hours were in the light. But sometimes, when he was allowed to stay up later than usual (after a dinner at one of his relatives' houses, say, or an evening spent in the park), he would get to see what happened to the summer light late at night. In those last long hours of the gradually fading day, the sunlight would turn gold. His shadow, everyone's shadow, would grow longer and longer, and there would be an intense difference between the shady places—under the trees, next to the walls, in his own stretched-out shape on the cobbles or the dirt or the grass—and the increasingly golden areas lit by the last rays of the summer sun. At such times, the dividing line between shadow and light was so strong you almost felt you could touch it as well as see it.

The sounds of the town on a summer night were almost as entrancing: the gulls and other seabirds calling to each other, the soft wind in the trees, the clopping of horses' hooves on the cobbled main street, and sometimes even a bit of music drifting over from the bandstand near the Kursaal. His mother, a talented harpist, loved music, and he felt that because of this he loved music too. She would sing him songs from her own childhood, and when he sang them back to her word for word, she would praise him for his excellent memory.

∎

STUDENT QUESTIONER: It seems to take forty to fifty years to become
  an architect. Why does it need to take that long?
LOUIS KAHN: Why not? You want to die earlier?
STUDENT QUESTIONER: How long did it take you?
LOUIS KAHN: It took me since I was three years old.

He had always felt the strength of his mother's attention. She seemed to
take a special delight in being with him, and even after his little sister
was born, he still felt he was the most important one: the oldest child,
the boy, his mother's dearest companion. Recently, though, he had felt
a slight slackening in her focus on him. She was distracted by many
worries, including all this talk about his father possibly going to America.
He could also see that her stomach was growing larger and larger, and
when he asked about this, she told him he was soon going to have another little sister or brother. This did not strike him as necessarily a
good thing, but he kept this thought to himself. After all, he was getting
to be a big boy now, and he felt he would soon be old enough to take
charge of his own life. He had recently turned three.

It was cold out still, so the fire in the hearth was kept burning at all
hours. The stacks of wood that had been piled up outside in the summer
months kept it fed, day after day. Whenever the fire burned low, someone would bring in more logs to keep it going. Somehow, though, the
fire had been allowed to burn very low. It was down to a few smoldering
embers now. And those coals, licked by a few tiny flames, were not the
usual red or orange or even blue color. For some reason, the color they
gave off was a strange, entrancing blue-green.

The little boy was used to seeing fire: it was a daily presence in his
life, especially in the winter. But he had never seen a fire burn this
color before. The individual coals were like something that had grown
outdoors in the ground—a fresh green shoot, a startling blue flower—
except that this blue-green was a much more intense color than anything he had ever seen in nature. It was as if the coals were lit from
within, as if they were creating a magical new form of light that began
at their center and glowed outward. If the color that showed through on
the surface was this bright, this beautiful, what must the inside be like?

He sat himself down next to the hearth to get a closer look. Normally he was not permitted to sit this near the fire, but no grown-up

was nearby to bother him this time. He stared for a while, and then he adjusted the apron of his pinafore so that it made a little cloth basket in his lap. Just looking at the green-glowing coals was not enough. He wanted to capture them, to play with them. He wanted to make them his own.

He leaned forward and quickly scooped a few of the embers into his lap. Before he even had a chance to examine them, they burst into sudden flame. He saw the fire leap upward toward his face, and instinctively, though the pain itself had not yet had time to reach him, he put up his hands to cover his eyes.

EPILOGUE

"Louis I. Kahn, whose strong forms of brick and concrete influenced a generation of architects and made him, in the opinion of most architectural scholars, America's foremost living architect, died Sunday evening, apparently of a heart attack, in Pennsylvania Station," began the front-page obituary by Paul Goldberger that appeared in *The New York Times* on Wednesday, March 20, 1974. Goldberger briefly recounted the strange circumstances surrounding the death—the body picked up by the New York police and tentatively identified on the basis of Kahn's passport (which showed that he had just returned from London and Bombay), the teletype sent to the Philadelphia police, their failure to notify the widow, her search for her missing husband—but soon moved on to six columns largely devoted to Kahn's buildings, philosophical theories, and personal characteristics. Like the calmly smiling picture that accompanied it, the text presented an *eminence grise* of the architectural world, "a small man whose white hair and bow tie were often in disarray, but whose modest physical appearance was in sharp contrast to the vastness of his influence on architects both in America and abroad." The person described here was someone who clearly knew his own mind and had made his respectable mark upon the world—a solid, revered, if perhaps slightly mystical figure with a strong list of tangible achievements to show for his seventy-three years on earth.

And while this was true, it was far from the whole story. Even as this prominent and fully laudatory obituary reached the newsstands, the hidden difficulties and conflicts were beginning to surface privately.

For decades Lou had managed to hold things together by the sheer force of his magnetic personality, but soon after he died, they started to fall apart.

Esther Kahn, worried about the half-million-dollar debt he had left, felt pressed on all sides, and when David Zoob, Lou's lawyer, went to her and asked her to make some provision for Lou's other two children, she vehemently refused. "She became angry," said the architect Peter Arfaa, to whom Zoob had appealed for help in overcoming' Esther's recalcitrance. Her response, according to Arfaa, was "They're bastards. They're not entitled to anything of Lou's." And when, a month after Kahn's death, the Philadelphia AIA organized a memorial service for him at Trinity Church in Rittenhouse Square, Esther told Peter Arfaa not to invite the other mothers and children. "She didn't want them—she was adamant," recalled Arfaa, who, in his capacity as head of the local chapter, politely informed the widow that the organization could not and would not prevent them from coming.

For Esther, it was as if all those years of tolerating Lou's bad behavior had come to nothing in the end. Her patience had finally been exhausted, and since Lou was no longer there to stanch her anger, she gave in to it. And Philadelphia, or at least her friends, relations, and acquaintances in Philadelphia, abetted her. The secret which had once been widely known—the fact that Lou had two other families—now became hushed up and covered over. Lou's curious personal life had never been written about or made public in any way, and now it was rarely even mentioned, as Esther began the process of reconstructing her position as the one and only Mrs. Louis I. Kahn.

Meanwhile, though, the currents of familial connection continued to run underground. Alexandra Tyng wrote her undergraduate dissertation on Kahn's work, identifying him clearly as her father, and in 1984 an expanded version of her thesis was published as a book called *Beginnings: Louis I. Kahn's Philosophy of Architecture*. Throughout these years Alex maintained her close relationship with Nathaniel and, in a somewhat more attenuated way, her friendship with Sue. And in 1980, when she was in her mid-twenties, she paid a visit to Lou's relatives out west, who up until then hadn't had a clue about her existence.

"Alex called us on the phone when she was coming out to California," said Lou's niece Rhoda, who despite her surprise was instantly welcoming. She offered to have Alex picked up at the airport, and since the rest of the family was busy at the time, she sent her son, Steven Kantor, as the driver. That's how he and Alex met. A few years later, Lou's daughter and his grandnephew—two strands from opposite ends of the family, as it were—announced that they were getting married.

It was during the wedding celebrations in Philadelphia that Rhoda first encountered Anne Tyng, who impressed her as "very pretty, very friendly, very intelligent." She was also very tiny, Rhoda noted, like her house in Philadelphia's historic district: "Everything went up, nothing was expanded. A kitchen without a stove; she used a toaster oven. It was amazing what she made on it." Rhoda also recalled Anne's "original ideas" about things like the Fibonacci numbers and the golden spiral and how "there was a connection throughout the universe. Her conclusions came from things that she researched. You don't know if she's a little strange or just brilliant," Rhoda said. "And she was adamant about things." During that same visit Rhoda also met Harriet Pattison, who struck her as a very different physical type from Anne—"taller, a little bit heavy, a round face"—but equally sure that she had been "the person behind the man," the true soul mate. "At Alex's and Steve's rehearsal dinner, there was an empty seat beside Harriet, and I went to sit down in it," Rhoda remembered. "And she said, 'That is reserved for Lou.'"

Esther Kahn, though she sent a very thoughtful gift (one of Lou's drawings), declined her invitation to attend Steve and Alex's wedding. This was in 1983, and emotions were perhaps still a bit raw. But a few years later, when Kahn's Salk project was threatened by a plan for new additions to the site, Harriet Pattison, Anne Tyng, and Esther Kahn all banded together to register their protest against the changes. Their objections, though initially successful, ultimately did not prevail, and the eucalyptus grove at the entrance to the plaza was cut down to make room for the new buildings. A similar thing happened several decades later at the Kimbell Art Museum, when Pattison's meticulous landscaping was uprooted to make room for a Renzo Piano addition. There was nothing unusual in the failure of these family protests, even if the makeup of the family itself was rather out of the ordinary. The world does not stand still, even for a great work of architecture, and one learns to consider oneself lucky if the structure itself remains intact.

By the time the Kimbell site revisions were completed, in 2013, Harriet was the only one of the three women still alive. Esther had died in 1996. Anne lived until 2011—long enough to see the restored, newly refurbished Yale University Art Gallery building, which, as she confided to a friend at the opening, looked better than it ever had before. And Anne also got a chance, before her traveling days were over, to make one final visit to the Estonian island that Lou considered his birthplace.

Pärnu may or may not be the actual place of birth, but no official body in that mainland city seems particularly interested in or even aware of Louis Kahn. In contrast, the town of Kuressaare (formerly Arensburg) on the island of Saaremaa (formerly Ösel) proudly claims Lou as a native son. In 2006 a group of Estonian architects chose Kuressaare as the location for a weekend-long symposium in honor of Kahn's life and work. Anne Tyng was invited to give a talk; her daughter, Alexandra, volunteered to paint a portrait of Lou and bring it to the symposium; and *her* daughter, Rebecca Tyng Kantor, had already found her way to Estonia on a Fulbright fellowship. So all three generations congregated on Saaremaa for the October 2006 festivities. Nathaniel Kahn, whose 2003 film about Lou, *My Architect*, had first ignited the Estonians' interest in doing the conference—and had also, not incidentally, broken the long public silence about Kahn's additional families—came along as well.

"The only thing missing is that I wish my sister Sue Ann was there," said Nathaniel. "If she had played a piece of Bach on the flute, which my father loved so much, it would certainly have made the celebration complete. It would have been nice if the three of us could have walked through the streets together. On some level I think Lou would have liked that."

Alex agreed that "it would have been really neat if my sister had gone. But she was there in spirit."

Sue Ann had very much wanted to be there, but her full-time administrative job at the Mannes College of Music kept her in New York that whole fall. As part of her contribution-in-absentia, she had given her sister a necktie of Lou's to use in the posthumous painting of their father. Alex persuaded her husband, Steven, and her son, Julian, to serve as living models wearing the necktie and, drawing on her own childhood memories as well as old photos, she painted a portrait that placed Lou in front of the finished Assembly Building in Dhaka—a fantasy of sorts, since the project wasn't actually completed until nine years after his death. But for Alex, this backdrop made perfect sense. "There's a dramatic contrast between Bangladesh and Estonia, and I was thinking how, as a boy, he had no idea how far he would travel and how far his influence would reach," she said. "I also wanted to avoid putting him in a specific time frame. The capital complex wasn't finished when he died, so in reality he could never have stood there. So the portrait represents a whole range of time from his childhood to the end of his life and beyond."

Alex also felt that there was a visual connection between the two places. "The massive forms of the mosque and capital building at Dhaka are to me like a modern castle, square and stark with corner towers, very much like the medieval castle at Kuressaare," she pointed out. "I wanted to establish this link to his origins, since the portrait was to hang in Kuressaare."

It hangs there still, prominently displayed in a public room of the Kuressaare Town Hall. It is Alexandra Tyng's gift to the city of Kahn's childhood, and it is also her gift to Lou himself: placing him forever beyond time, giving him a kind of ghostly afterlife. And as you stand in front of it, looking at the bow-tied, dark-suited, white-haired man who holds his spectacles in his hand so that his slanting eyes can stare directly back at you—their blue color noticeably picked up in the watery lake and the unclouded sky that surround the oddly geometrical buildings behind him—you may find yourself mimicking, without even trying to, the enigmatic smile he wears on his face.

There was the man, who no longer exists, and there are the buildings, which endure. As with any artist, a question arises regarding the relationship between the two. How do the finished works, which are what draw our interest in the first place, connect to the daily life that happened to be going on in the background? The danger in any biographical examination lies in pressing too hard on the connection, for even if we intuitively sense that there must be one, our ponderous insistence may cause the fragile bridge to crumble beneath our weight. And when the artist is an architect—a collaborator, a negotiator in a commercial context, a central figure directing vast and not entirely controllable movements of people and materials—that link between the personal life and the work produced will seem even more tenuous, less visible, less necessary.

With Louis Kahn, there were also other factors that contributed to the dissociation: People around him had grown used to protecting him from any publicity that did not contribute directly to his reputation. They felt that his secrets, however widely or informally known, were his own affair, and this wish to protect grew even fiercer after his death. Kahn may have run his office like an artist's atelier, but architecture is not, after all, like painting or sculpture, either in the public mind or in its own. It views itself as one of the "learned professions," akin to medicine and the law. It has its standards—of behavior and ethics as well as of education and qualification—and it has its own regulatory societies charged with maintaining them. Architects are deemed to be "pillars of the community," in Ibsen's ironic phrase, and even when their personal lives are messy (as they have been from Borromini onward), their outward presentation is expected to be august and businesslike.

Lou's behavior, with its prolonged love affairs leading to illegitimate yet acknowledged children, did not conform to the agreed-upon professional image. His colleagues, to the extent they knew about his private life, found it mildly unnerving if not downright embarrassing, and the passage of forty years has not eroded their desire to sweep this personal material under the carpet. "Not under the carpet, and not that it didn't exist," protested Richard Saul Wurman, but he still felt there was something unseemly about exposing Lou's quirks to the public eye. He pointed out that the Philadelphia of that period "was still a Puritanical society," and even though "we all knew it was odd" for Lou to be living in the way he did, people still felt he needed and deserved their protection. "He had a battle, being Jewish and going to Penn," and any criticism or even hint of personal exposure could have offered ammunition, Wurman felt, to the profession's genteel anti-Semites, among whom he counted G. Holmes Perkins and Ed Bacon. But was Bacon's opposition to Kahn *really* because he was Jewish? "Because he was Jewish," Wurman insisted, "and because he spoke his truth. Bacon did not want the truth."

Yet even Lou's manifest allegiance to the truth, one of his most noteworthy characteristics as an architect, risked being tarnished by the existence of his secret life. Jack MacAllister, among many others, commended Lou for "always looking for the fundamental underlying truth of anything." Yet MacAllister was forced to acknowledge that this did not necessarily apply to his personal life. "His behavior in life was not socially acceptable, so he had to cover it over," Jack offered as an excuse.

Shamsul Wares put it even more strongly. "He was a mental case. He was influenced by his phallus. He had certain problems with his sexuality—a psychology based on the phallic foundation," said this noted admirer of Lou's humane and powerful National Assembly Building. For Wares, the flawed man who had affairs and the generous architect who gave Bangladesh the centerpiece of its new democracy were easily separable figures. "His illicit connections with women have nothing to do with his creativity," Wares said.

The landscape architect Lois Sherr Dubin loosely echoed this last idea when she observed, "His personal life was like an appendage." Work, she seemed to think, was the only thing that really mattered to Kahn. And yet Dubin herself drew a connection between the public figure and the private one when she said, "I think he was a lusty, sensual man and all that implies. He wasn't a dried-up ascetic." This was not only what made *him* attractive, as a colleague, a teacher, a friend; it was also what made his whole architectural approach so alluring. Dubin emphasized how powerfully his vision appealed to design students, especially against the gray background of Fifties blandness and Philadelphia restraint. "In this uptight time and campus, *the* most exciting place was our architecture school," she recalled. "Why? Because of Lou Kahn, and the people that came from all over the place to work with him. It was simply the most vital, alive place. And in that kind of place there are simply no boundaries. Anything goes."

Such freedoms, of course, invariably lead to problems. "Desire is irresponsible," Lou himself commented. "You can't say that desire is a sense of purity. It has its own purity, but in the making of things great impurities can happen."

He saw the danger, but he did not disown it. And this respect, if that is the right word, for desire, for the original impulse that motivates all making and taking, was essential to Kahn's views, governing his sense not only of how life might be lived but also of how architecture might be practiced. "I do not believe that beauty can be deliberately created," he wrote in his notebooks. "Beauty evolves out of a will that may have its first expression in the archaic. Compare Paestum with the Parthenon. Archaic Paestum is the beginning. It is the time when walls parted and the columns became and Music entered architecture. Paestum inspired the Parthenon. The Parthenon is considered more beautiful, but Paestum is still more beautiful to me. It presents a beginning within which is contained all the wonder that may follow in its wake."

To insist on a perpetual sense of wonder—or to argue, as Kahn did, that a great building "must begin with the unmeasurable, must go through measurable means when it is being designed and in the end must be unmeasurable"—is to resort continually to the same impulses that fuel desire. One must be constantly acting on one's own feelings, one's own responses: Is this what I really wanted to do? Does this or that element need to be altered to accomplish what I envisioned? How about this unexpected factor—can I use it to get back to my original idea, but in a new way? The process is all about beginnings, for Kahn. And it is in the beginning, of course, that every desire burns with its most searing intensity. Kahn's wish to return there, repeatedly, was perhaps his most salient characteristic as both an architect and a man.

The two were, in any case, probably not separable. Anne Tyng, who knew him as both lover and colleague, felt that "he really lived for his work" but also that "his work expressed his life." Speaking for a video camera nearly twenty years after his death, she mused, "I think he was really in touch with the unconscious, the creative principle, which is usually viewed as feminine . . . As though you were open to all the processes of space and time, and out of that you would find order."

Anne and Lou's daughter carried this same idea even further when she said about her father that he "strongly believed in principles which were similarly applied to both his work and personal life. This may seem a very strange thing to say, since many people who knew him would say that he was a very unconventional person who did great architecture but did not handle his personal life very well. But he had a sort of philosophy according to which things would simply arrange themselves in the most appropriate way, and, if one let them happen, they would turn out." Alex Tyng did not mean that Kahn made no effort, or had no artistic intentions—"Certainly he did not just let his buildings happen"—but she felt he was focused mainly on how various elements came together to produce the right form. "If instead one tries to fit the parts together and they do not fit," she went on, "then it is the wrong expression of the form. That was the same kind of sense that he had about his personal life; I mean, if the elements—meaning circumstances and people and feelings—were right they would fit together."

While admitting that this was not always easy on the other "elements" in the human equation, Alex hesitated to place all the blame on Lou. "I think you should look at the characters of the women he was with (I'm talking about his major relationships)—they're all very strong women, and good people," she observed. "He was very ambitious, but it wasn't a power thing. He just wanted to create. You could say he used people, but he was also respectful of them." If there was anger sometimes on the part of the women and children—and Alex acknowledged that there was—it was never a bitter or vindictive anger. "He was a very loving person," she said of Lou, echoing what both of the other children (and not just the children) had said of him.

"He had an enormous amount of love. He loved everybody," Shamsul Wares told Nathaniel Kahn when the filmmaker came to Bangladesh in search of his long-dead father. Wares was stressing the way in which the National Assembly Building in Dhaka—"his biggest project, in the poorest country in the world"—was itself a sign of that expansive love. "And sometimes when you love everybody, you do not see the closest ones," he added.

But love is not the only human expression that made its way into Kahn's work. What Lou's architecture recognizes, and what it took from his own physical sense of himself, is the fact that we are all bodies moving through space, viscerally sensing ourselves as individuals in relation to that space. Louis Kahn, you might say, inhabited his own body more viscerally than most, and perhaps that gave him special access to the way buildings could respond to the human body, at rest and particularly in motion.

"Motion—movement—is such an important part of our dreams," he wrote in 1961. "I don't know anybody who doesn't dream of flying through space (you've got to move your arms a bit) and this is speed to equal any kind of speed—or to swim marvellously, without much effort at all. From this, I feel that the making of a positive architecture of movement, which I like to call a viaduct architecture—which takes into account all the aspects of movement and separates them into identities which don't inhibit—has free exercise . . . So, therefore, the architecture of movement." For Kahn, this emphasis on movement necessarily meant making provision for stoppage and rest; and that was true whether he was talking about cities, with their arterial streets and traffic-halted interchanges, or monasteries, with their ambulatories and secluded places of contemplation.

This awareness of the body in motion is something that transmits itself to you whenever you enter a structure he designed. It is there from the very first moment, when you go into the building and discover a space you could not have imagined from the outside, and it is there as you move around from room to room, from floor to floor, always coming upon new enticements of light, shape, and texture that lead you further in. It is there, most of all, in your sense of yourself as being tenderly enclosed, or borne upward, or crowned with grandeur—all in the context of a weighty structure whose mass exists, not to intimidate the human-sized body, but to offer it protection and reassurance.

Vincent Scully highlighted the connection between Lou's own physical nature and the buildings he designed in a compelling description he gave of the man himself. "The other thing about Kahn that one felt right away was the vitality, the love of life that came out of him," Scully remarked. "He had a kind of physical generosity; he gave off life. He was a wrestler, you know—a very muscular person who walked on the balls of his feet. His hands were very big, fleshy, strong, and he gave off a sense of power." Scully knew of a woman who had once spotted Lou in New Haven and had followed him down the street because "he looked so vital, so strange, so alive, so full of life in contrast to the death of most things and people." And this quality, insisted Scully, was intimately connected to his work: "Kahn had that, and he gave it in his buildings. This was one of the greatest things about him: to make people realize that the arts—the physical arts—are physical; they are experienced in physical, empathetic ways. That's why I dislike the things that are written about Kahn that are all cerebral, philosophical, sociological . . . He was physical; Lou had the physical perception of form, and that is what made him a great architect."

There is an old photograph of Lou, taken during a 1936 summer vacation at the Brookwood Labor College in Katonah, that gives a sense of the man Scully was describing. In it, Lou stands with his back to us, dressed in an old-fashioned archery outfit and aiming off to his left with a huge bow and arrow. The skimpy costume clings tightly to his narrow hips and slender waist, and the revealing cutouts around the torso show off the taut muscles of his strong back and wide shoulders. Kahn is thirty-five years old here, but he still has a full head of ungrayed hair, and he radiates both the animal vitality and the athletic self-confidence of a very young man.

His head is turned slightly to the side, so that one catches a glimpse of the profile, recognizably Lou's. But either because the photograph is taken at some distance, or because the heavily muscled left arm blocks the lower half of his face, the scars are hardly visible. In this respect, it is a bit like a self-portrait he sketched in pencil during his Grand Tour in 1928–29, a graceful drawing which portrays him in half-face as the dinner-jacketed dandy smoking a pipe, with nary a scar in sight.

He may have succeeded in ignoring them, but in some people's eyes the scars were definitive. "I think there's a lot in his architecture related to his personal life," said Jack MacAllister. "One is the imperfections of the material." For MacAllister, the building processes Kahn favored because they showed how something had been made—the pocked concrete, the die-marked extruded steel—were directly linked to his facial scars. And even the colleagues who took a somewhat less reductive approach included the scars when listing the obstacles in Lou's path. "Lou had a lot of things to overcome," Richard Wurman pointed out. "He had a terrible voice, he was scarred, he was short, he was poor, he couldn't drive. And I think he did whatever he could, maybe not consciously, to overcome these things. I am not a shrink—I do not know that it is so—but it could be one of the interpretations." Wurman was explicitly referring to all the involvements with women, but he also thought this theory applied to Lou's architecture career. "He was overcoming whatever insecurities he had—from his poor background, from not being one of the guys. Comfort is not your friend," Wurman stressed. "What's your friend is what you learn by overcoming that. Lou had a battle."

Nathaniel Kahn imagined a battle, too, but in a very different way. For him, Lou's whole approach to both life and work was like something out of King Arthur. He noticed his father's scars, but thought of them as part of Lou's chivalric ferocity: "There was something of the warrior about him. Definitely." And this need to wage war on the conventions of architecture, not to mention the conventions in general, influenced the rest of Lou's appearance as well. Nathaniel pictured him as a kind of matador, flirting with the traffic as he dashed across the street, wearing his coat over his shoulders like a cape, flamboyantly aware of how he looked. "Even his outfit: he's dressing up," said Nathaniel. "He took great pride in his clothes. He had very fine shoes. He liked black wingtip shoes, and he had a pair of beautiful brown shoes—cordovans, I think. It was a role; he put on his architect's outfit to do battle in the world."

Alex Tyng (who, like her sister, had virtually no awareness of the scars and always thought of her father as "handsome") also noticed the elegant clothing. "He just had to find the perfect thing all the time, and he was not satisfied with second-best," she pointed out. "His clothes were carefully picked out, and I always laugh when I hear people say he had baggy pants and shoes that didn't match and a crooked tie. His tie was crooked because it was hand-tied, and his pants were specially tailored. He always wore subtle colors and very fine materials with certain textures and only black socks. He had a very definite sense of what he wore, a sense of taste. I suppose people liked to see him as a character and wanted to be able to make a caricature of him, but I never saw him as such."

Jack MacAllister could have been one of the people she was referring to. "He had a kind of peasant quality about him," said Jack, "the way he would sit and say that a boiled potato was the best meal he'd ever had, and really and truly enjoy simple things. I mean Lou didn't really like sophisticated personal things, as far as his own lifestyle. And in a way," he acknowledged, "that's humility." But MacAllister was also arguing against the idea of a humble Lou, suggesting that what he really had was "peasant charm," not humility in the ordinary sense. "I don't think Lou was humble at all," Jack insisted. "And I don't even think of that as derogatory. I think he knew he was goddamn good."

It's true; he did know that, from quite an early age, at least in regard to his artistic talents. When he took the boat over to America from Europe at the age of five, he was proud that the captain valued his drawings enough to reward him with oranges. It did not occur to Lou that anything like pity could have entered into the transaction. And the same was true of the preferential treatment he received from his family, and particularly from his "noble," "unselfish" mother. The fact that all the scarce family resources were centered on him—the way his mother always rooted for him and supported him, even at the expense of the other children—was something he attributed to his own manifest abilities. An outside observer might have imagined that at least part of Bertha's motive was a sense of guilt and overprotectiveness in regard to this damaged, somewhat sickly child. But one of the things she protected him from, it seems, was any suspicion that this could have been her attitude. Where others might have seen pity, he saw only admiration and faith. "My mother held true to the absolute confidence in me," he remarked toward the end of his life.

And perhaps this affected him in another way as well. Pity was simply not a part of his vocabulary. He did not see himself as its recipient, and nor did he have the capacity—or the need, or the wish—to feel it for others. He could be empathetic, especially on the grand scale, as he was in Bangladesh and India; and he could be loving and warm and appealing and companionable, to lovers and children along with colleagues and friends. But when his desires came into conflict with someone else's, he had an inherent ruthlessness that enabled him to see his own choices as the only possible ones. Pity did not come into it, because pity might have stopped him, and he needed above all to keep going—or rather to keep beginning, again and again.

In the course of his half-century as a practicing architect, Louis Kahn produced an estimated 235 designs. Of these, 182 were commissions; the other 53 were speculative drawings, planning-related projects, designs for objects, or competition entries, none of which resulted in lasting structures. Out of the commissioned plans, 81 ended up being constructed, but that included a number of office remodels, home interiors, and small alterations or additions done mainly in the years before his reputation began to solidify. Of the forty or so projects completed after 1952, a mere handful account for Kahn's huge and continuing reputation. The indisputable masterpieces are the Salk Institute, the Kimbell Art Museum, the Phillips Exeter Library, the Indian Institute of Management, the Yale Center for British Art, and the National Assembly Building of Bangladesh. To this select list many people would be inclined to add the Richards Medical Building, the Rochester Unitarian Church, the Yale Art Gallery, and, as of 2012, the FDR Four Freedoms Monument. Kahn himself might have appended the Trenton Bath House to the list. But even granting all of these, as well as generously including, say, three of the nine private houses, you still come up with only fourteen major buildings out of a lifetime of very hard work.

"Success . . ." mused I. M. Pei when Nathaniel Kahn went to interview him for *My Architect* and pointedly contrasted Pei's successful record of construction with Lou's small output. "Three or four masterpieces more important than fifty, sixty buildings."

· Among well-known architects, Pei was not alone in finding Kahn's work inspirational. "My first works came out of my reverence for him," Frank Gehry confided. "As time goes by," said Moshe Safdie, "Kahn somehow stands out as *the measure*, the standard, something to compare to, to evaluate by, to give sustenance to." Calling Lou "the most beloved architect of our time," Philip Johnson went through a list of the other greats (Frank Lloyd Wright, Mies, Le Corbusier), pointing out how mean or difficult each one was, then added, "Lou—there was a man." What made his achievement even more remarkable, Johnson felt, was how inveterately he ignored the business side of the business: "How he ever got any clients is a mystery . . . Lou did it by being an artist."

Renzo Piano, who as a young man worked with Kahn for a year or so on the Olivetti-Underwood factory, had an even fuller sense of indebtedness. "Magic," he said, when asked what he had learned from Louis Kahn. "Or searching for magic. I started to learn that there's a magic in architecture. There's a little red line that connects the art of building, putting things together, with the art of creating marvel, stupor, amazement." And the other thing he had learned, he felt, was the importance of obstinacy. "Louis Kahn was an incredibly obstinate man. I remember I found him many, many times in the morning, eight o'clock in the morning, still asleep in the office, because he was working so late he was just sleeping in the office on a table. When you work together with somebody like that," Piano observed, "you understand that sublime persistence is the only way to get to the center of things. For Kahn everything became architecture in some way. Even music. The entire experience of life becomes architecture."

In speaking about what Lou brought to the profession as a whole, many of his former employees emphasized the ageless universality of his work. His buildings "aren't tied to the fashions of the time," argued MacAllister. "It's the making of space. It's timelessness," suggested Wurman, pointing out that "his influence is not stylistic." "The idea of not having style, it had depth to it," Anne Tyng elaborated. "He was really going beyond styles, beyond any particular historical forms, to the beginnings of form—the most basic idea of form, which is geometry." Rafael Villamil, who eventually left architecture to become a painter, expressed a similar view in his own terms: "He was influenced by others, but he made those ideas his own. He was an artist finding his voice. You could not put his work under any style, like Internationalist or Brutalist or Postmodern. His work was Kahn." Whereas Villamil considered most modern architecture to be "frivolous, arbitrary, contemporary, and loud," he characterized Kahn's buildings as "profound, mysterious, ageless, and silent."

Yet at least one of Lou's admirers, rather than stressing the agelessness or timelessness of his work, pointed instead to Kahn's unique relationship to time. "Mies, Corbu were all forward-looking architects, interested in the formation of a new world order. Louis Kahn was the only one who was also a backward-looking architect," said Shamsul Wares. "He was the only one who could understand the value of looking backward." This did not mean he was like the postmodernists, merely quoting historical forms. According to Wares, "He didn't copy anything. He developed ideas from the past." Nor did this approach subtract one whit from his impeccable modernist credentials. "The first thing about Kahn is that he is a modernist," insisted Wares. "Because of his understanding of the development, he understood that modernism is necessary, but he also understood the problems of modernism. At one point modern architecture became very lightweight architecture. Other architects didn't care for heaviness; they disliked it. They thought modern architecture is floating things. Kahn understood that heaviness gives stability. He didn't like the instability of modernity."

Shamsul Wares was also interested in the painstaking method Kahn used to arrive at his finished work. "He is a hard worker. He is unlike many architects who instantly conceive what they want to do. None of Kahn's design was achieved from his first idea," Wares commented. "The grand idea cannot come in a single sitting. He's someone who can put up his ideas through his drawings—not through his brain, but through his drawings. He cannot come to the final version at the beginning."

This slow pace may account, in part, for why Kahn was able to finish relatively few buildings. But it also explains some of the special appeal of working for Lou on those seemingly endless projects. It was the process, not just the goal, that those who learned the most from him remembered long afterward. "The standout in the office, and what you do miss, is the search: trying to find an answer and coming up with it, and then you keep going," remarked Henry Wilcots, who spent ten years working under Kahn and another nine helping to finish the Dhaka project after his death. "The finished building is just a bump in the road, just another detail."

But to reach that bump was still an achievement, especially in the absence of the original maker. Of the major projects left unfinished when Kahn died in 1974, only three ultimately reached completion in a form that was recognizably his: the Dhaka Assembly Building, the Yale Center for British Art, and the FDR Four Freedoms monument and park. Probably what accounts for these three successes is not just how far the projects had proceeded before he died, but also who was responsible for their completion. In each case the fidelity to Lou's vision rested in the hands of his long-term employees and friends—people who intimately understood not only what Lou was trying to do, but also how he might have gone about doing it.

The easiest project to complete, because it was the furthest along when he died, was the Yale Center for British Art. By March of 1974, the basic structure was nearly finished: the first three floors were in place, the fourth-floor concrete columns had been poured, and the precast "V" beams for the roof had been selected by Kahn though not yet installed. He had also chosen the stainless steel that would make up the exterior panels of the building. Marshall Meyers, whose firm Pellecchia & Meyers was assigned to finish the Yale Center, estimated that completing the job would take about a year and a half. Instead it took three full years. There were three hundred additional drawings that had to be made, plus cartloads of correspondence to be dealt with, and every action had to be judged against what were presumed to be Lou's original intentions.

Meyers, commenting on the difficulty of the assignment, compared it to "restoring a building that hadn't been built yet. What attitude do you take? . . . Sometimes there was a document or drawing Lou had done that showed his intent. In other cases one could only rely on recent precedent. If a circumstance in construction occurred that required a change to his original intent or no documentation existed, then you had to reflect on his attitudes and architectural principles."

Luckily for the project, Meyers had worked for Kahn in responsible positions over the course of many years, both as his employee and as an independent colleague. In fact, Marshall Meyers had already left Lou's office to found his own architectural firm when he was brought in as the "project representative" at Yale, around the time the museum's first-floor columns were being poured. So their collaboration on this building as two independent architects began while Kahn was still alive.

It was typical of Lou to maintain good relations with the talented colleagues who had left the firm of Louis I. Kahn. Kahn recognized that there was only so far ambitious young architects could rise at his essentially one-man office, and he understood their wish for independence—even if, as David Slovic pointed out, the change meant deciding "to quit a job that's doing the capital of a country and do someone's kitchen." When his staff architects made the decision to leave, Kahn generously stood behind them, often sending jobs their way. After the Salk project was over, for instance, Jack MacAllister went to Lou and told him he wanted to start his own practice. And Lou said, "Let me help you. I had a man come in last week who wants a complete remodel of a Philadelphia house and I can't do it. Let's see if he'll let you do it."

Even if someone was leaving to become something other than an architect, Lou would support his decision. Richard Saul Wurman, who became widely known as a conference organizer, writer, and all-round intellectual guru, remembered asking Lou early on, "Am I making a mistake by doing all these other things I'm interested in?" What he was really wondering was whether he should try instead to concentrate on architecture alone, as Kahn had. Lou's answer epitomized, for Wurman, the way Kahn encouraged you to become yourself. "Ricky," he said, "even when I get a haircut I'm an architect. Do what interests you."

Once they had left, Kahn stayed in touch with his younger colleagues and used their talents whenever he could. Fred Langford was brought in as Lou's concrete consultant on the Kimbell after he had departed to found his own specialized firm. Dave Rothstein, who had done the models for both the Trenton Bath House and the Richards Building while he was still working in Kahn's office, was called back over the years whenever a new model was needed. In 1973, even though he had his own thriving practice by then, he did the model for the Roosevelt Island monument—in exchange, as he recalled, for Kahn's involvement in the early stages of Rothstein's Bishop Field Estate project in Massachusetts. Time and distance never seemed to dim Lou's connection with his protégés. "He would look at you and say something from five or six years ago," Rothstein noted. "He kept track of where you were, not just architecturally, but in life."

Still, there were a small number of employees who never left, and these—most notably David Wisdom and Henry Wilcots—were the ones who took on the responsibility for finishing the massive Dhaka project. Gary Moye, who was part of that group, recalled the makeup of the surviving practice. "David Wisdom & Associates had seven partners—David Wisdom, Henry Wilcots, Gary Moye, Al Comly Jr., John Haaf, Gus Langford, and Reyhan Tansal Larimer," said Moye. "We probably all assisted at one time or another on Dhaka. I think it's important to note that the yeoman's effort goes to David Wisdom and Henry Wilcots. Not enough can be said about that type of dedication and effort, particularly Henry's."

It took them nine years, from 1974 to 1983, to complete the Bangladesh Parliament, known as Sher-e-Bangla Nagar by the people for whom it was made. That meant the entire project, counting Lou's part and theirs, took twenty years from start to finish. As with the Yale Center, there were numerous small decisions to be made after Kahn's death, infinite complexities caused by new and unexpected local conditions, numberless times when the partners had to ask themselves, and each other, what Lou would have done. He had lived to see the walls rising five feet at a time to nearly their full height, and on his last trip he had even managed to see the eight-sided roof of the Assembly Hall set in its place. But after his death, the intense and all-consuming "determination to finish the capital" that he had mentioned in his dream-report needed to be transmitted to other minds and other hands if it was ever to be carried through. This, miraculously, took place, and perhaps no building of Kahn's is as singularly his as this project he never lived to finish.

Even as they were struggling with the immense Dhaka job, David Wisdom & Associates were also involved in another assignment, which they shared with Kahn's friend Aldo Giurgola and his firm, Mitchell/Giurgola. This was the construction, from scratch, of the FDR Four Freedoms Park. At the time of his death Lou had left a set of schematic designs for the project, and the site itself, at the southernmost tip of Roosevelt Island, had been put aside for this particular use, so at least two key elements were safely in place. Kahn had also begun to select the materials, including the granite that would form the walls of the "Room." He had even specified in advance that the facing sides of the granite blocks, set approximately one inch apart, should be highly polished, whereas the other four sides of each cube should retain their natural finish. But this still left many design elements to be decided upon—for example, the choice of the trees to be planted in the "Garden," their exact arrangement in the converging allées, the precise ordering of the granite pieces (which varied somewhat in color), the texture of the crushed granite used in the pathways, the nature of the formwork for the outer concrete walls, the relationship of the ha-ha to the rest of the enclosed space, and all sorts of other things, large and small.

Added to these complications were squabbles among the various governmental and private bodies involved in the project, repeated concerns related to funding and sponsors, and changes in environmental and construction laws (including the newly passed Americans with

Disabilities Act's requirement that the gravel pathways be bonded together with resin so as to be traversable by wheelchairs—not an unreasonable regulation, given FDR's own wheelchair-bound state). Decades passed as these issues were addressed and resolved. Dave Wisdom, who died in 1996, never lived to see the project's completion. Neither did John Haaf, the partner from the firm who took lead responsibility on it. After the dissolution of David Wisdom & Associates, the Roosevelt Island commission passed into the hands of Mitchell/Giurgola and their various subcontractors, who let the project lapse due to a lack of financing. Only after former UN ambassador William vanden Heuvel began a new round of concerted fund-raising—which led to the establishment of Four Freedoms Park LLC, under the directorship of Gina Pollara— was the monument finally finished in 2012, almost forty years after Lou had started it.

Harriet Pattison, after attending one meeting in 1993, was essentially excluded from the design process; the landscape architecture was handled instead by Lois Sherr Dubin, who had been hired as an outside consultant by Mitchell/Giurgola in 1974. Certain elements of Pattison's original plan were jettisoned in the course of construction—the European hornbeams she had selected for the allées, for instance, were discarded in favor of linden trees—and at the time of the monument's opening in 2012, Harriet professed herself unhappy with the Garden. But when she saw the Room itself, she felt "amazement. Really astonishment. Going to the Room was wonderful." The approach worked too, she acknowledged: "the arrival and the steps and then suddenly the perspective and walking through trees down to this wonderful thing." And when she finally got to the Room and was left alone there for a while, she was able to feel a long-deferred satisfaction on Lou's behalf as well as her own. "People had disappeared, and I was right there, alone," she said, and in that moment "I thought about him. There was nobody there then. And I felt wonderful. *He did it.*"

In describing that moment of simultaneous solitude and communion, Harriet Pattison captured something essential about the way Four Freedoms Park affects its visitors. Even if you know nothing about Lou or his history, or for that matter nothing about Franklin Delano Roosevelt and *his* history, you still approach the semi-enclosed, semi-concealed, glimpsed-from-a-distance Room with the kind of excited anticipation Pattison mentioned. In the course of your journey, you will have been faced with all sorts of choices: not only whether to travel to Roosevelt Island via air tram, subway, or car, but also how to get from the park entrance (which is defined by the rather lovely ruin of a Renwick-designed smallpox hospital) to the monument itself. Should you follow one of the lower walkways that will keep you close to the lapping water of the East River, or should you ascend the pyramid-like staircase that will lead you up to the grassy park? If the former, should you take the right-hand walk, with its novel, expansive views of Manhattan, or the left, which looks toward Queens and Brooklyn? And if you go via the park, should you stick with one of the two converging pathways that lead forward under the arching trees, or should you wander down the middle of the grassy trapezoidal expanse? Whichever of these options you choose—whichever of your multiple "freedoms" you exercise—you will experience the same sense of grounded satisfaction when you finally arrive at the walled-but-open structure that is your destination.

Once you are inside the Room, those one-inch slivers of space between the twelve-foot-high blocks of granite can function as either shadow joints (if you view them from an angle) or light joints (if you stand directly opposite them), and either way, they possess a kind of magical ability to reveal and conceal at once. They tease you with the offer of a view, but when you approach and put your eye to the crack, you will see only the same severely restricted strip of Manhattan or Queens that you saw from a few feet away; the very thickness of the walls defeats your effort to widen your perspective. The granite blocks themselves are both protective and imprisoning, conjuring up the thick walls of an ancient castle, with its similarly narrow slivers designed for arrow launching. Yet this sense of containment is countered not only by the wide blue sky above you, but also by the completely open end of the Room, where you can look south toward New York Harbor as well as east and west at the surrounding boroughs. Something about the arrangement is reminiscent of the Salk Institute plaza, though the scale is entirely different. There is no space here for a Salk-like central fountain, but then, there is no need of it: the river itself splashes at the edges of the monument, offering its own quiet accompaniment to your thoughts.

A peaceful place, this memorial to a dead president and his humane, politically advanced exhortations is moving but never sentimental. The austerity of the granite is itself soothing, as if to signal that human emotion is important, indeed essential, but can nonetheless be transcended at times. As you sit contemplatively on one of the granite benches, the stone feels cool to the touch, and the sun, on a bright spring or fall day, is warm on your back. You are in the midst of a great city here, and yet you are also removed: not just from the rushing anxieties of everyday life, but also from the pressing sense of life's evanescence that historical monuments often evoke. The shadow your body casts on the pale granite is overlaid at times by those of the other bodies passing to and fro. But even in the presence of other visitors, your own sense of private communion with the place, if you sit still enough, will always return.

These three posthumously completed structures are the rarities. The vast majority of the projects Kahn left unfinished at his death were never built. Sometimes—as with the museum for the Menil Collection in Houston, which ultimately went to Renzo Piano—another architect stepped in and did his own successful version of the building. Sometimes, as with the Hurva Synagogue in Jerusalem, a whole series of replacement architects was brought in over the decades, and *still* no modern structure was ever built. (A reconstruction of the nineteenth-century Hurva, representing no one's idea of a grand architectural solution, finally opened in 2010.) Nobody ever took Kahn's place on the Palazzo dei Congressi in Venice, or the Abbasad commercial development in Tehran, or several of the smaller commissions he had in hand in America and abroad. They simply went undone.

His death may have prevented these projects from being completed, but it is not certain they would have been finished even had he lived longer. Kahn's career, after all, was littered with unbuilt designs. He was, as he said, a terrible businessman: his projects always came in late, and he had little concern for the bottom line, an attitude which would not have endeared him to many clients. Nonetheless, there could be hidden advantages to his financial inefficiency. A person more obsessed with exact accounting might have realized he was going bankrupt and been forced to close up shop. Lou's useful disregard for such matters allowed him to continue with his work in the way he chose to do it, decade after decade. And this method made a lot of sense to some of his employees, despite its effect on their paychecks. Mundane work delivered on schedule could not compare, in their view, with the masterpieces Lou was slowly and inefficiently producing. "Denise Scott Brown once said to me that Lou Kahn didn't have a good track record because he didn't get his work done on time and he ran over the budget," Marshall Meyers once remarked. "My reply to that would be, 'Well, which track have we chosen to run on?'"

And then there was his notorious allegiance to the truth, or at any rate to his idea of truth in architecture. This too made him difficult for some clients to work with. But what determined the difference between the built projects and the unbuilt ones was not just Lou's stubbornness. After all, there were cases when his strenuous resistance to a client's demands—for instance at Exeter, where he refused to chop off the library's top floor—triumphed, and resulted in a better building. So there was no consistent single problem. A different reason, or at least a different combination of factors, seemed to lie behind each incompletion.

Sometimes, of course, the client simply ran out of money. That probably explains why the Meeting House at the Salk Institute, on which Kahn labored for years, was never built: it was a beautiful luxury, and though Lou considered it in many ways the heart of the project, for Salk the laboratories and studies were far more central to the plan. The proposed residential Village, which also had to be set aside for lack of funds, was another matter. It had never been as important to Kahn—nor, perhaps, to Salk—and the architectural designs for it, which were not particularly noteworthy, had barely taken shape before that part of the project was discontinued.

With the Dominican Motherhouse project, on which Louis Kahn and his office worked intensively for three years, money was only part of the problem. The commission began in 1965, when a group of Dominican nuns sought Kahn out and asked him to build a new convent for them in Media, Pennsylvania. His enthusiasm for the project may have stemmed in part from the inspiration he had received from Le Corbusier's monastery at La Tourette. He had, besides, a fondness for the idea of the contemplative life, with its daily divisions into private and communal acts of worship, and he was eager to design a space that fostered and contained that duality. He also got along very well with the prioress, Mother Emmanuel, who was about his own age, as were most of the other nuns on the building committee.

Kahn first met with the committee in April of 1966, and even though the sisters had already decided among themselves on a budget ceiling of $1.5 million for the whole project, money was not discussed at that meeting. Nor did the subject come up in August, when Lou and his designated project architect, David Polk, met again with the nuns to discuss further details of the program. But in October of 1966, when Kahn and Polk presented drawings and a cardboard model to the Dominican sisters, even these relatively inexperienced clients realized that the extensive buildings and gardens, covering about 150,000 square feet, could not be done for the price they had in mind. And when they finally received the cost estimate in November, their fears were confirmed: the estimate priced the project at $3.5 million. The Mother Superior politely wrote to Kahn a few weeks later saying they couldn't afford the plan he had designed; at the end of December she wrote again, suggesting a vastly reduced scheme and setting a maximum budget of $1 million. (Like most Kahn clients, she was learning from the process: having discovered by now that he would inevitably go over budget, she shrewdly gave him a ceiling that was less than what the nuns could actually afford.)

In March of 1967, after Kahn and Polk had produced many sketches, independently and together, in their effort to work out a smaller-scale design, they submitted a new plan that only took up about 50,000 square feet, and Polk soon followed that up with a cost estimate of $1,593,000, promising in an accompanying letter that the project could actually be built for $1.5 million. The nuns duly raised their ceiling back to the original level, and on August 7, 1967—sixteen months after their initial meeting—Louis Kahn and Mother Emmanuel signed a formal contract for architectural services. Kahn's office then worked hard on the plans for a full year, cutting costs to the bone but also retaining the design principles that mattered most to him. The final compressed but cunningly arranged plan included separate areas for sleeping, eating, teaching, reading, worshipping, and encountering the outside world; it left room for an organic but nonetheless distinct relation between private prayer and the communal life; it physically embodied the convent's hierarchical nature, at the same time as it separated "served" and "servant" spaces; and it relied, as always in Kahn's mature work, on the complementary virtues of heavy masonry and natural light. In August of 1968 Lou was able to present the building committee with a design priced at $1,572,093. At a November meeting held in Media, he promised the sisters that he could have working drawings ready by June of the following year, at which point construction could commence, which meant they would be able to move into their new home before the end of 1970.

But though the question of money continued to worry the nuns, additional and possibly more important factors now entered the equation. The number of new Dominican sisters joining the convent had steadily declined in recent years and was likely to dwindle further. This trend came at the same time as the changes that were slowly permeating the entire Catholic Church in the wake of the Second Vatican Council of 1965. Under the new principles, the whole notion of a monastic life had been reenvisioned and reformed, so that nuns as well as priests and monks were now expected to play a more active role in the worldly communities outside their cloisters. The spiritually contemplative life, the very thing which had drawn Lou to the project in the first place, was now largely a thing of the past, and the convent he had designed for the sisters was therefore no longer appropriate. In the end it was global history, and not just finances, that defeated Kahn's Dominican Motherhouse. The project was terminated by mutual consent, and the two sides "parted friends," according to the nuns.

In the case of the Memorial to the Six Million Jewish Martyrs, which was to be located in New York's Battery Park, the problem was the divergence between client tastes and architect tastes. Hired in late 1966 by the memorial's steering committee—which, unfortunately for Lou, actually consisted of *two* committees, the fifty-member Committee for the Six Million and the seventeen-member "arts advisory" committee chaired by art patron David Kreeger—Kahn had been charged with designing a monument that would commemorate the Holocaust dead. In November of 1967 he presented his first plan: a raised stone platform on which were planted three rows of three glass pillars each, all of them identical in size (twice as tall as a man) and shape (thick rectangular blocks). Resisting the pressure to create a literal rendering of the dead martyrs, Lou had opted instead for abstraction, and in a memo accompanying the plan he explained his choice of glass: "The Architect's central thought was the Monument should present a non accusing character, and he thought of glass for its quality of material presence yet the sun could come through and leave a shadow yet filled with light. Not like marble or stone with its defined shadow; the stone could be accusing, the glass could not."

The first objection came from some Talmudic scholars on the Committee for the Six Million, who pointed out that Jewish numerology equated the number nine with gestation, birth, and other happy subjects, so it was completely wrong for a Holocaust memorial. Others felt that the number six should be included as a nod to the Six Million. Still others grumbled at the absence of any figurative elements.

Kahn quickly redid the design so that it now featured seven tall glass blocks: six around the perimeter and a single one, containing an arched doorway and some inscriptions, at the center. (With his typical tendency toward religious ecumenicalism, Lou noted that in this version, "The one—the chapel—speaks; the other six are silent.") The Kreeger Committee unanimously approved the design. But the larger committee, in a heated session that might have called to mind the old Jewish joke about a roomful of twenty Jews yielding twenty-one opinions, ended up rejecting it. The arguments against Kahn's design were various, but they essentially boiled down to the fact that the committee members did not see their sorrow and their pain expressed in these abstract pieces of glass. They did not, in fact, *want* something "non accusing"; they would have preferred a literal rendering that roused the sentiments and assigned blame in the appropriate quarters. The members of the Committee for the Six Million were holding out, as their spokesman explained, for a Holocaust memorial that "fulfilled their longings, represented their thoughts, or relieved their tragic memories." Unsurprisingly, no such structure was ever built. After trying for another year or two to reach some accommodation with his clients, Kahn sent in his final bill for services. But by this time the Committee for the Six Million had run out of money, and the bill went unpaid.

Reading about these projects that Kahn left unfinished and contemplating the drawings, plans, and models he did for them creates an intense longing to see the buildings themselves. But it is a longing that cannot be fulfilled, even with the best of intentions. It's not just that the remaining unbuilt structures can never be built, for reasons that range from the loss of the original site to the absence of sufficient working drawings. It's that they cannot even be fully imagined.

This truth is borne out by an intelligent and beautifully designed book, *Louis I. Kahn: Unbuilt Masterworks*, that was put together by the architect Kent Larson in 2000. Larson's aim is to offer through computer-generated graphics a sense of what the Memorial to the Six Million Jewish Martyrs, the Palazzo dei Congressi, the Salk Meeting House, the Hurva Synagogue, and other doomed projects would have looked like in the flesh. But that is precisely the problem: the flesh is lacking. There are no human beings peopling these empty Kahn buildings (though people, in their rough form, appear in even his earliest sketches for those projects). And the buildings themselves are far too cold and perfect. They are noticeably without the idiosyncratic flaws that characterize the materials of Kahn's finished buildings—the rough textures of the concrete, the tiny cracks in the travertine, the silvery aging of the wood, the softly rounded corners of the brick. They lack the sense that a human hand has made them, and they also lack any sense of mortality. These perfect buildings will never age, as Kahn's own structures have done. And without that sense of mortality, it turns out, the images can never really come to life. There is a deadness to Larson's computer renderings that may be barely detectable now, but that will become clearer and clearer to the trained eye as digital technology matures—much in the way we moviegoers of the twenty-first century, watching the last century's special effects, can now see how creakily fake they look. But the level of graphic technique is not the only problem. However good the visual evocations of Lou's lost buildings become, they will not be able to match the feeling we get from walking through his actual structures. Reality, a sense of presence, was and is essential to his work.

Some people have called Louis Kahn a mystic, and perhaps he was.

He certainly loved to speak in mysterious, sometimes mystifying terms, and he clearly believed in a pre-existing order which he was aiming to discover, or uncover, in his designs. That all sounds very Platonic, at the very least. But set against this philosophical aspect was another side of Kahn that included his solidity, his practicality, his down-to-earthness. Things of the flesh mattered to him; materiality mattered to him. This was part of what it meant to be an architect, in his eyes. "A painter can make doorways smaller than people; a sculptor can make square wheels on a carriage to express the futility of war," he once pointed out. "The architect has to make doors bigger than people and has to use round wheels."

Maybe it is inaccurate to describe his practical qualities as if they were in opposition to his mysticism. As a man and as an architect he was of a piece, thoroughly himself at all times. Still, that self was a complicated one, covered over by or even including a whole series of performed roles—Delphic seer, wise peasant, gallant knight-errant—which had been part of him for so long they had almost become a second skin.

But even a skin, close as it is to the person it contains and much as it may define him in the eyes of others, is only an outward surface. As Kahn's buildings repeatedly tell us, what you see on the outside is not a true or complete guide to what lies within. In all his best creations, from the Trenton Bath House to the Dhaka Parliament, it's necessary to penetrate to the interior in order to begin learning the building's secrets, though in doing so you will also find that there are additional secrets forever being kept from you. And the same, it is probably safe to say, is true of the man himself.

NOTES

All the passages in this book that are direct quotations are cited in the notes below (along with a small number of details and facts that are not quotations but seemed worthy of citation). The reader who wants to know where a particular quote comes from can simply locate the opening and closing words of the quote, keeping in mind that all quotations appear in the order given and are divided up according to the chapter in which they appear.

Each reference is given in full the first time it appears. For sources that reappear frequently, an abbreviated version is used in every subsequent case.

EPIGRAPH

"I honor beginnings . . . always been": "Lecture at the Pratt Institute," in Robert Twombly (ed.), *Louis Kahn: Essential Texts*, New York: W. W. Norton & Company, 2003, p. 278. [Hereafter cited as *Essential Texts*.]

PROLOGUE

4 *"I'm too . . . religious"*: Susan G. Solomon, *Louis I. Kahn's Jewish Architecture*, Waltham: Brandeis University Press, 2009, p. 124.

5 *"You say to brick . . . an arch"*: John Lobell, *Between Silence and Light: Spirit in the Architecture of Louis I. Kahn*, Boston: Shambhala Publications, 1979, p. 40.

8 *"We know . . . kind of man"*: "Marin City Redevelopment" in Alessandra Latour (ed.), *Louis I. Kahn: Writings, Lectures, Interviews*, New York: Rizzoli, 1991, p. 111. [Hereafter cited as *Writings, Lectures*.]

10 *"frozen music"*: Johann Wolfgang von Goethe, from Johann Peter Eckermann's *Conversations with Goethe in the Last Years of His Life*, translated by Margaret Fuller, Boston: Hilliard, Gray and Company, 1839, p. 282.

ENDING

15 *"indigestion"*: Esther Kahn quoted in Richard Saul Wurman (ed.), *What Will Be Has Always Been: The Words of Louis I. Kahn*, New York: Rizzoli, 1986, p. 282. [Hereafter cited as *What Will Be*.]

16 *"I find . . . two months or so"*: Kent Larson, *Louis I. Kahn: Unbuilt Masterworks*, New York: Monacelli Press, 2000, p. 183.

16 *"Every time he talked . . . the spirit of light"*: Balkrishna V. Doshi quoted in *What Will Be*, pp. 272–73.

17 *"I'm at the airport . . . I was really touched by that"*: Stanley Tigerman quoted in *What Will Be*, p. 299, and in Carter Wiseman, *Louis I. Kahn: Beyond Time and Style*, New York: W. W. Norton & Company, 2007, p. 261.

19 *"Prof. Louis I. Kahn . . . USA"*: Luggage tag on suitcase of Louis I. Kahn, Sue Ann Kahn Collection, The Architectural Archives, University of Pennsylvania. [Hereafter shortened to The Architectural Archives.]

19 *"Is there anything . . . gray"*: Esther Kahn quoted in *What Will Be*, p. 283.

20 *"It was feared . . . too tired to call"*: Kathy Condé event chronology, March 17–19, 1974, Esther Kahn Collection, The Architectural Archives.

21 *"lying face up . . . men's room"*: Police report filed by Officer Joseph K. Folmer of the NYPD on March 17, 1974, supplied to the author by the New York Police Department Legal Bureau on June 6, 2013, in response to F.O.I.L. request #2013-PL-3245.

21 *"Notify Esther Kahn . . . deceased this city"*: Telegram quoted in *The Philadelphia Inquirer*, March 21, 1974, p. 1.

22 *"DOA"*: Masking tape on suitcase of Louis I. Kahn, Sue Ann Kahn Collection, The Architectural Archives.

22 *"Of course . . . rescue squad"*: Esther Kahn's letter to Professore Bruno Zevi, October 15, 1974, Esther Kahn Collection, The Architectural Archives.

23 *"It was quite a shock . . . so vigorous"*: Sue Ann Kahn's interviews with the author on April 4, May 10, September 26, and December 13, 2013, in New York, with additional information supplied in various phone conversations and emails. [Hereafter cited as Sue Ann Kahn interview.]

23 *"Is he dead? . . . ever come again?"*: Nathaniel Kahn's interviews with the author on April 14, 2013, and November 4, 2013, in Philadelphia and on June 13, 2013, via telephone, with additional information supplied via email and telephone on subsequent dates. [Hereafter cited as Nathaniel Kahn interview.]

24 *"You never stop loving someone"*: Louis Kahn's words as told by Anne Tyng to Alexandra Tyng, from Alexandra Tyng's interviews with the author on April 16, 2013, and November 4, 2013, in Philadelphia, with additional information supplied in numerous informal talks, phone conversations, and emails on subsequent dates. [Hereafter cited as Alexandra Tyng interview.]

24 *"My mother called . . . now he's dead"*: Alexandra Tyng interview.

24 *"Kahn, a Blender of Logic . . . strong and subtle"*: *The New York Times*, March 20, 1974, p. 64.

25 *"Police Here . . . Kahn's Death"*: *The Philadelphia Inquirer*, March 21, 1974, p. 1.

25 *"Louis Kahn, Fundamental Genius"*: *The Philadelphia Inquirer*, March 21, 1974, p. 10-A.

25 *"It is with the deepest . . . who all loved him"*: Telegrams to Esther Kahn and the Office of Louis Kahn from Richard Nixon, Teddy Kollek, Isamu Noguchi, Buckminster Fuller, and others, March 20–22, 1974, Esther Kahn Collection, The Architectural Archives.

26 *"There was this group . . . all the students"*: Ed Richards' interview with the author on May 14, 2013, in Philadelphia. [Hereafter cited as Richards interview.]

26 *"I was kind of . . . found out later"*: David Slovic's interview with the author on May 15, 2013, in Philadelphia. [Hereafter cited as Slovic interview.]

26 *"I was asked to go . . . other members there"*: Jack MacAllister's interview with the author on June 18, 2013, in Tiburon. [Hereafter cited as MacAllister interview.]

27 *"in her line of sight"*: Anne Meyers quoted in Carter Wiseman, *Louis I. Kahn: Beyond Time and Style*, New York: W. W. Norton & Company, 2007, p. 266.

27 *"I remember . . . having him taken away"*: Nathaniel Kahn interview.

28 *"The funeral was actually . . . in the office for years"*: Alexandra Tyng interview.

28 *"When my sister . . . side chapel"*: Sue Ann Kahn interview.

28 *"Alex said . . . my mother"*: Nathaniel Kahn interview.

28 *"He felt . . . I didn't"*: Alexandra Tyng interview.

29 *"Rabbi Caine . . . friends and relatives"*: *The Evening Bulletin*, March 22, 1974, p. C-3.

29 *"Esther was there . . . Academy Award"*: Richards interview.

29 *"I remember . . . on their shoulders"*: Nathaniel Kahn interview.

29 *"Immediately . . . Volkswagen bus"*: *The Evening Bulletin*, March 22, 1974, p. C-3.

29 *"I remember Sue . . . did it together"*: Alexandra Tyng interview.

29 *"My mother . . . wishing that I had"*: Nathaniel Kahn interview.

30 *"I wish I had . . . at first"*: Sue Ann Kahn interview.

30 *"1974 – Dies . . . to Philadelphia"*: *Toledo Blade*, December 26, 1993.

31 *"a nice myth"*: Dialogue quoted from Nathaniel Kahn's documentary film *My Architect*, 2003. [Hereafter cited as *My Architect*.]

31 *"There is no doubt . . . has disappeared"*: Alexandra Tyng interview.

33 *"Out of the mind . . . could do in five"*: Salk poem quoted in Romaldo Giurgola, *Louis I. Kahn: Works and Projects*, Barcelona: Editorial Gustavo Gili, 1993, pp. 9–12.

IN SITU: SALK INSTITUTE FOR BIOLOGICAL STUDIES

40 *"interstitial"*: Kendall Mower, in his public tour of the Salk Institute's architecture at noon on August 6, 2013.

40 *"This is the cat's meow . . . daylight harvesting"*: Tim Ball, giving a private tour of the Salk Institute to the author on August 6, 2013.

42 *"Salk . . . jaded"*: Anonymous staff and researchers encountered in the plaza of the Salk Institute, August 6, 2013.

42 *"Kahn didn't know . . . like it a lot"*: Greg Lemke's interview with the author on August 6, 2013, at the Salk Institute.

PREPARING

47 *"I remember . . . very proud"*: Louis Kahn quoted in *What Will Be*, p. 225.

48 *"alien passengers"*: Ship's manifest for Bertha and children's passage from Liverpool in 1906, National Archives at Washington, D.C.; Series Title: *Passenger Lists of Vessels Arriving at Philadelphia, Pennsylvania*; NAI Number: 4492386; Record Group Title: *Records of the Immigration and Naturalization Service, 1787–2004*; Record Group Number: 85; Series: T840; Roll: 052.

48 *"Leib . . . Hebrew"*: Ship's manifest for Leopold's passage in 1904, National Archives at Washington, D.C.; Series Title: *Passenger Lists of Vessels Arriving at Philadelphia, Pennsylvania*; NAI Number: 4492386; Record Group Title: *Records of the Immigration and Naturalization Service, 1787–2004*; Record Group Number: 85; Series: T840; Roll: 046.

49 *"We lived in poverty . . . to some extent"*: Architects' Personal History and Field Interview File for Louis Kahn, including interviews and test results from the creativity study conducted under the auspices of the Institute of Personality Assessment and Research, University of California, Berkeley, December 12–14, 1958, with follow-up by mail. [Hereafter cited as Berkeley creativity study.]

50 *"scarface"*: Nathaniel Kahn speaking in *My Architect*.

50 *"I was born . . . was in everyone's life"*: Louis Kahn quoted in *What Will Be*, p. 10.

50 *"One day . . . your drawing, not mine"*: Louis Kahn quoted in *What Will Be*, p. 124.

51 *"Louis, I'm afraid . . . good idea"*: Louis Kahn quoted in *What Will Be*, pp. 120–21.

52 *"Sawtooth Houses"*: Harry Kyriakodis, *Northern Liberties: The Story of a Philadelphia Ward*, Charleston: History Press, 2012, p. 143.

52 *"A city should . . . someday like to be"*: Louis Kahn quoted in Alexandra Tyng, *Beginnings: Louis I. Kahn's Philosophy of Architecture*, New York: John Wiley & Sons, 1984, pp. 127–28. [Hereafter cited as *Beginnings*.]

52 *"My son is a genius!"*: Sue Ann Kahn interview.

52 *"I was always . . . just made drawings"*: Louis Kahn quoted in *What Will Be*, p. 224.

53 *"natural education"*: Joseph A. Burton, "The Aesthetic Education of Louis I. Kahn, 1912–1924," *Perspecta*, Volume 28 (1977), p. 205. [Hereafter cited as Burton.] This extremely helpful article by Joseph A. Burton is the source of most of my information about Kahn's three teachers, J. Liberty Tadd, William Gray, and Paul Cret. In particular, my section on Tadd is completely dependent on Burton's account, pp. 205–10.

54 *"creative . . . better it works"*; *"conviction"*: Videotape of Anne Tyng interviewed by Peter Kirby on May 26, 1992, The Architectural Archives.

54 *"speaking through the finger tips . . . steel bar"*: Tadd quoted in Burton, p. 208.

54 *"box with spaces . . . visions 'sans situ' "*: Undated notebook with unnumbered pages, Louis I. Kahn Collection, University of Pennsylvania and the Pennsylvania Historical and Museum Commission, catalog number 030.VII.4. [Hereafter cited as Louis I. Kahn Collection.]

54 *"Drawing and manual training . . . designing and creative work"*: Tadd quoted in Burton, p. 208.

55 *"Form encompasses . . . belongs to the designer"*: "Form and Design" in *Essential Writings*, p. 64.

55 *"One who accurately . . . any other way"*: Tadd quoted in Burton, p. 208.

56 *"renounce forever . . . All the Russias"*: National Archives and Records Administration (NARA), Washington, D.C.; Naturalization Petitions for the Eastern District of Pennsylvania, 1795–1930; NARA Series: M1522; Reference: (Roll 106) Petition Numbers 13876–14100.

56 *"Studying was . . . through to me"*: Louis Kahn quoted in *What Will Be*, p. 226.

56 *"very poorly academically . . . Alexander Dumas"*: Berkeley creativity study.

56 *"He was always . . . flunked"*: Norman Rice quoted in *What Will Be*, p. 288.

56 *"I was to be . . . door is opened"*: Louis Kahn quoted in *Beginnings*, p. 128.

56 *"I wouldn't have . . . Central High School"*: Louis Kahn quoted in *What Will Be*, p. 224.

56 *"My art teacher . . . intensely dedicated"*: Berkeley creativity study.

57 *"the skyscraper . . . is wrong"*: Gray quoted in Burton, p. 211.

57 *"was a matter . . . very nice guy"*: Louis Kahn quoted in *What Will Be*, p. 224.

57 *"I was given . . . be selected too"*: Louis Kahn quoted in *Beginnings*, p. 127.

58 *"Every year . . . credit was very good"*: Louis Kahn quoted in *What Will Be*, p. 121.

58 *"The family . . . with her hands"*: Esther Kahn quoted in Alessandra Latour, *Louis I. Kahn: l'uomo, il maestro*, Rome: Edizioni Kappa, 1986, p. 19. [Hereafter cited as Latour.]

59 *"my sister had . . . was fine, unselfish"*: Berkeley creativity study.

59 *"worked very hard . . . and teacher"*: Norman Rice quoted in *What Will Be*, p. 294.

60 *"modernized classicism . . . each floor, etc."*: Burton, p. 214.

60 *"the thoughtful making of spaces"*: *Writings, Lectures*, pp. 75, 88, 101, 106.

61 *"For beginning . . . seen a library"*: Louis Kahn quoted in Thomas Leslie, *Louis I. Kahn: Building Art, Building Science*, New York: George Braziller, 2005, pp. 18–19. [Hereafter cited as Leslie.] Thomas Leslie's book is an invaluable source for everything to do with Kahn's technical achievements. Even in sections where he is not quoted directly—for instance, in the descriptions of the processes that lay behind the Yale University Art Gallery and Kimbell Art Museum ceilings—I have relied heavily on Leslie's accounts.

61 *"superior excellence"*: Arthur Spayd Brooke Memorial Prize, Louis I. Kahn Collection.

62 *"He quickly . . . especially for Lou"*: Norman Rice quoted in *What Will Be*, p. 294.

63 *"Russian intelligentsia. . . . it was Lou"*: Videotape of Esther Kahn interviewed by David Brownlee on April 27, 1990, The Architectural Archives. [Hereafter cited as Brownlee video.]

63 *"Being an impatient person . . . spellbinder"*: Esther Kahn quoted in Latour, p. 23, and speaking in Brownlee video.

64 *"The next Friday . . . not even you are going to keep me back"*: Esther Kahn quoted in Latour, p. 23.

64 *"scars on face"*: Louis Kahn's 1928 passport, displayed in the Vitra exhibition *Louis Kahn: The Power of Architecture*, London Design Museum, 2014, and other venues.

65 *"She made . . . I felt incompetent"*: Berkeley creativity study.

65 *"A very interesting . . . helpful"*; *"Dear Mom & Pop . . . Love, Lou"*: Unsent postcards, Collection of Sue Ann Kahn. Most of the material about Kahn's Grand Tour comes directly from William Whitaker, who has compiled a detailed itinerary

of the 1928–29 trip, complete with quotations from the postcards. It was Whitaker, too, who pointed out to me the gap between the modernist buildings Kahn visited for architectural purposes and the ancient ruins he nonetheless found himself attracted to.

66 *"I went to visit . . . taken everything away . . . daughters and sons . . . much moved by it . . . used to speak of"*: Louis Kahn quoted in *What Will Be*, p. 225.

66 *His name does not appear*: An email from Olavi Pesti of the Saaremaa Museum, dated March 3, 2016, informs the author: "There was no regular passenger shipping traffic between Riga and Kuressaare in the end of 1920s, but the steamships 'Vasa' and 'Kalevipoeg' of the regular line Riga-Pärnu sometimes in the summer season steamed also through port Roomassaare (Kuressaare) when a lot of passengers wanted to travel here to the resort." Another email, from Heie Treier, dated March 2, 2016, adds: "People of the Louis Kahn Estonia Foundation have searched for Kahn's name in the lists of passengers of the ships that traveled between Riga and Kuressaare. Kahn's name was not found in these lists."

68 *"Typical mountain . . . avalanches"; "Compared to other countries . . . source of"*: Unsent postcards, Collection of Sue Ann Kahn.

70 *"The Value and Aim of Sketching"*: The text (though without Kahn's sketches) is reproduced in *Writings, Lectures*, pp. 10–12.

70 *"The article . . . own handiwork"*: Letter from Bertha Kahn to Louis Kahn, July 17, 1931, Collection of Sue Ann Kahn.

70 *"He didn't write . . . I got nothing . . . you bore me . . . different from ours"*: Esther Kahn quoted in Latour, p. 23, and speaking in Brownlee video.

70 *"very little English . . . from Russia . . . When you came to my family . . . someone they could control"*: Esther Kahn in Brownlee video.

71 *"I saw Lou . . . magnificent performance . . . three months later"*: Esther Kahn quoted in Latour, p. 23.

72 *"secondary, completely routine"*: Berkeley creativity study.

72 *"This is the first . . . in a respectful way"*: From the unpublished journal of Esther Kahn, quoted with permission, Collection of Sue Ann Kahn. [Hereafter cited as Esther Kahn's journal.]

73 *"lovely honeymoon"*: Esther Kahn's journal.

73 *"After we got . . . bother anyone"*: Esther Kahn quoted in *What Will Be*, p. 282.

74 *"Lou came home . . . walked out"*: Esther Kahn quoted in Latour, p. 23.

74 *"allowances"*: Esther Kahn's journal.

74 *"I could go . . . done for me"*: Esther Kahn quoted in Latour, p. 23.

75 *"I say there were . . . and myself . . . thought he was great"*: Esther Kahn quoted in *What Will Be*, p. 280.

75 *"We are just this Thursday . . . palm trees . . . a bit much for her eyes . . . wonderfully illuminated . . . don't write!"*: Undated postcards and letters in German from Bertha and Leopold Kahn to Louis and Esther Kahn, 1930–31, translated from the German by Martin and Barbara Bauer, Collection of Sue Ann Kahn.

76 *"You refer . . . quite worried"*: Letter from Bertha Kahn to Louis Kahn, June 17, 1931, Collection of Sue Ann Kahn.

76 *"with great regret"*: Zantzinger as quoted in the Chronology compiled by William Whitaker for the Vitra exhibition catalogue, *Louis Kahn: The Power of Architecture*, Karlsruhe: Vitra Design Museum, 2012, p. 23. [Hereafter cited as Vitra Chronology.]

77 "In the 2 years . . . still working . . . things we want . . . a better life": Esther Kahn's journal.

78 "Dearestest . . . Regards to Kit . . . It turned out to be . . . love and kisses, Lou": Undated letters from Louis Kahn to Esther Kahn, Collection of Sue Ann Kahn. (Note that in these letters, as throughout this book, Louis Kahn's eccentric spelling and syntax have been preserved without correction.)

79 "Louis I. Kahn . . . Philadelphia Penna": Printed heading on handwritten undated letter from Louis Kahn to Esther Kahn, Collection of Sue Ann Kahn.

79 "nothing to be ashamed of": Vincent Scully, Louis I. Kahn. New York: George Braziller, 1962, p. 14. [Hereafter cited as Scully.]

79 "assistant principal architect": Vitra Chronology, p.24.

81 "both cried like Babies . . . very much": Letter from Leopold and Bertha Kahn to Louis Kahn, February 28, 1936, Collection of Sue Ann Kahn.

81 "So much has . . . ill all the time": Esther Kahn's journal.

81 "She forgets . . . she doesn't . . . Aunt Katie": Undated letter from Esther Kahn to Louis Kahn, Collection of Sue Ann Kahn.

82 "adult children . . . Responsible Relative": Letter from County of Los Angeles Department of Charities (Bureau of Indigent Relief) to Louis Kahn, September 26, 1938, Collection of Sue Ann Kahn.

82 "Lou is not . . . will be soon": Esther Kahn's journal.

86 "the baby's room": Sue Ann Kahn interview.

IN SITU: KIMBELL ART MUSEUM

91 "The building does dictate . . . on that wall": Eric Lee's interview with the author on January 17, 2014, in Fort Worth.

92 "It has that . . . down the middle": Nancy Edwards' interview with the author on January 17, 2014, in Fort Worth.

94 "I think . . . I don't know . . . painting out there": Eric Lee's interview with the author on January 17, 2014, in Fort Worth.

95 "One thing . . . other museums . . . sweet spot": Claire Barry's interview with the author on January 17, 2014, in Fort Worth.

96 roughly five foot six: Kahn variously reported his own height as five foot seven (on his 1928 passport), five foot six (in the anecdote told by Louise Badgley about dangling his feet in a roomette), and five foot six and a half (in the Personal Data Blank he filled out for the Berkeley creativity study).

98 "It is no mean feat . . . limits of a place": T. J. Clark, Picasso and Truth, Princeton: Princeton University Press, 2013, pp. 108–9, 281.

99 "This building feels . . . a premise constructed . . . There's something . . . truth to begin with": Louis Kahn quoted in What Will Be, pp. 177, 27–28.

BECOMING

104 "Lou felt . . . adored him": Esther Kahn quoted in Latour, p. 25.

105 "The Prince": Nick Gianopulos's interview with the author on October 19, 2015, in Gladwyne. [Hereafter cited as Gianopulos interview.]

105 *"Oscar was . . . a kisser"*: Peter Arfaa's interview with the author on November 4, 2013, in Philadelphia.

106 *"they were both . . . primadonna"*: Esther Kahn quoted in Latour, p. 25.

106 *1941 income figures*: All income and expenditures figures for this and other years, including itemized deductions and other specifics, derive from the Kahn tax returns—both business and personal—archived in the Louis I. Kahn Collection.

107 *"Well, in those days . . . in great form"*: Peter Blake quoted in *What Will Be*, p. 303.

108 *"All of us . . . in the suburbs"*: Oscar Stonorov and Louis Kahn, *Why City Planning Is Your Responsibility*, New York: Revere Copper and Brass, 1943.

109 *"in terms that . . . to finish it"*: Oscar Stonorov and Louis Kahn, *You and Your Neighborhood: A Primer*, New York: Revere Copper and Brass, 1944.

110 *"Monumentality in architecture . . . intentionally created"*: "Monumentality," in *Essential Texts*, pp. 21, 27, 30, 23, 22.

111 *"Whenever he came home . . . as a hugger"*: Sue Ann Kahn interview.

112 *"longingness . . . write soon"*: Letter from Leopold and Bertha Kahn to Louis, Esther, and Sue Ann Kahn, January 7, 1942, Collection of Sue Ann Kahn.

112 *"Your letter was . . . heard from him"*: Letter from Bertha and Leopold Kahn to Esther, Louis, and Sue Ann Kahn, January 20, 1942, Collection of Sue Ann Kahn.

113 *"I have never . . . often to you"*: Letter from Louis Kahn to Anne Tyng, December 24, 1953, published in Anne Tyng (ed.), *Louis Kahn to Anne Tyng: The Rome Letters, 1953–1954*, New York: Rizzoli, 1997, p. 80. [Hereafter cited as *The Rome Letters*.]

114 *"Advertising Ideas . . . Dear Lou . . . Much Love, Oscar"*: Letter from Oscar Kahn to Louis Kahn, undated but postmarked April 9, 1945, Louis I. Kahn Collection, catalog number 030.II.A.60.38. (Note that all misspellings in this and other Kahn family letters, diaries, and notebook entries have been left uncorrected and appear in precisely that form in the originals.)

117 *"Oscar was . . . shiny things"*: Ona Russell's interview with the author on August 7, 2013, in La Jolla. [Hereafter cited as Ona Russell interview.]

117 *"Oscar was naturally . . . bases in life"*: Alan Kahn's interview with the author on August 3, 2013, in Whittier, California, with a follow-up phone conversation on September 20, 2014. [Hereafter cited as Alan Kahn interview.]

117 *"When my father died . . . Kahn that became famous"*: Rhoda Kantor's interview with the author on August 3, 2013, in Whittier, with follow-up phone conversations on August 13, 2013, and September 20, 2014. [Hereafter cited as Rhoda Kantor interview.]

118 *"He never talked . . . not Oscar"*: Sue Ann Kahn interview.

118 *"is unable to make . . . two brothers . . . subsiding into material"*: Louis Kahn delivering the lecture "Architecture and Human Agreement," as filmed by Duncan White, 1971, The Architectural Archives.

119 *"likened the emergence . . . spent light"*: "I Love Beginnings," in *Writings, Lectures*, pp. 285–86.

119 *"By chance . . . I promptly accepted"*: *The Rome Letters*, p. 28.

120 *"The more established . . . women architects"*: *The Rome Letters*, p. 27.

120 *"My first impression . . . aspect of him"*: Anne Tyng quoted in Latour, p. 41.

120 *"I found it . . . drew and talked"*: *The Rome Letters*, p. 31.

121 *"The space . . . think like a man"*: *The Rome Letters*, p. 28.

122 *"Stonorov was very . . . things clarified"*: Anne Tyng quoted in Latour, p. 41.

122 *"The office was . . . live together"*: Galen Schlosser quoted in Latour, p. 111.

123 *"We were both . . . life of its own"*: *The Rome Letters*, pp. 34, 37.

124 *"shadow joint . . . wood and stone"*: Anne Tyng quoted in Latour, p. 43.

124 *"the joint is the beginning of ornament"*: *Writings, Interviews*, p. 295; Latour, p. 43.

124 *"concept of a 'giant pointillism'"*: Anne Tyng quoted in Latour, p. 43.

124 *"inglenooks"*: George H. Marcus and William Whitaker, *The Houses of Louis Kahn*, New Haven: Yale University Press, 2013, pp. 62, 144, 197.

125 *"Communist sympathies"*: David B. Brownlee and David G. De Long, *Louis I. Kahn: In the Realm of Architecture*, New York: Rizzoli, 1991, p. 45.

125 *American Society of Planners and Architects*: All of my information about Kahn's involvement in the ASPA comes from Andrew M. Shanken's informative article "Between Brotherhood and Bureaucracy: Joseph Hudnut, Louis I. Kahn and the American Society of Planners and Architects," *Planning Perspectives* 20 (April 2005), pp. 147–75.

126 *"talked a good deal . . . Harpo Marx"*: Scully, p. 16.

126 *"On ways . . . conditions . . . to the designer"*: Undated notebook with unnumbered pages, Louis I. Kahn Collection, catalog number 030.VII.4.

.127 *"When I finished . . . blind all together"*: Undated letter to Louis Kahn from Leopold Kahn, Collection of Sue Ann Kahn.

128 *"My dearest children . . . a little improved"*: Undated letter to Louis and Esther Kahn written jointly by Leopold and Bertha Kahn, Collection of Sue Ann Kahn.

128 *"They were a . . . whatever I was playing"*: Sue Ann Kahn interview.

128 *"She appreciated . . . songs in German"*: Rhoda Kantor interview.

128 *"singing . . . diffused it around her . . . tea with her"*: Alan Kahn interview.

128 *"She was like a guru . . . I foresee"*: Rhoda Kantor interview.

129 *"make-shift"*: Berkeley creativity study.

130 *"I knew . . . discussion about it"*: Rhoda Kantor interview.

130 *"They sort of . . . lot of languages"*: Alan Kahn interview.

130 *"Grandpop . . . closer to her father . . . below her"*: Rhoda Kantor interview.

130 *"She spoke . . . like an aristocrat"*: Alan Kahn interview.

131 *"Esther was not . . . have to work"*: Rhoda Kantor interview.

131 *"Dearest Esther . . . Europe unfolded itself"*: Undated letter from Louis Kahn to Esther Kahn, on stationery printed in English and Hebrew with the heading "Hotel Ben-Yehuda, 000 Western Carmel," Collection of Sue Ann Kahn.

132 *"She always made . . . about Lou's"*: Sue Ann Kahn interview.

132 *"Louis is . . . make money"*: Letter from Annie Israeli to Esther Kahn, undated but postmarked August 14, 1949, Collection of Sue Ann Kahn.

133 *"He got the prize . . . a lot then"*: Sue Ann Kahn interview.

134 *"overwhelmingly . . . monumental impact . . . and better"*: Vitra Chronology, p. 25.

134 *"Roman architects . . . the choreography . . . ripple of columns . . . alcoves or windows"*: Frank E. Brown, *Roman Architecture*, New York: George Braziller, 1965, pp. 19–23.

135 *"Dearest Esther . . . love to all, Lou"*: Postcard from Louis Kahn to Esther Kahn et al., undated but postmarked February 26, 1951, Collection of Sue Ann Kahn.

136 *"greenways"*: *The Rome Letters*, p. 45.

137 *"gifted designer . . . claim that title"*: Gregory L. Heller, *Ed Bacon: Planning, Politics, and the Building of Modern Philadelphia*, Philadelphia: University of Pennsylvania Press, 2013, p. 99.

137 *"I never once . . . with kindness"*: Gianopulos interview.

138 *"triangulated geometry . . . innovative structure?"*: *The Rome Letters*, p. 47.

139 *"It could fail . . . canted joists"*: Gianopulos interview (including Lou's comment about visiting the Major, as reported by Nick).

139 *allowing the pour to proceed*: See Leslie, pp. 65–68, for a detailed account of the manner in which the construction contractor, George Macomber, tested the design of the Yale Art Gallery ceiling.

139 *"I do not like . . . destroy it"*: Louis Kahn quoted in *Beginnings*, p. 67.

140 *"The Pyramids try . . . I was made"*: Louis Kahn quoted in *What Will Be*, p. 1.

140 *"I believe in frank . . . acknowledge this"*: Patricia Loud, *The Art Museums of Louis I. Kahn*, Durham: Duke University Press, 1989, p. 84.

140 *"honesty, reality . . . could have done"*: Scully, p. 21.

140 *"Architecture is the thoughtful making of spaces"*: *Writings, Lectures*, pp. 75, 88. See also the Personal Data Blank in the Berkeley creativity study, where Kahn responds to the command "List those things which you have done which you consider innovations in the field of architecture or design" with three underlined items: *The distinction in the planning of spaces between "the spaces which serve" and "the spaces served"*; *Architecture is the thoughtfull making of spaces*; and *The integration of the mechanical and electrical service with the construction to give form to the building*.

140 *"These stairs, now . . . use them"*: Patricia Loud, *The Art Museums of Louis I. Kahn*, Durham: Duke University Press, 1989, p. 84.

141 *"Only Lou and the doctor . . . love child"*: *The Rome Letters*, p. 58.

141 *"Dearest Anne . . . By-By Honey . . . Lou"*: *The Rome Letters*, pp. 66–67.

142 *"My best . . . positively hate them"*: *The Rome Letters*, pp. 69–70.

142 *"Don't fail . . . least worry"*: *The Rome Letters*, p. 84.

142 *"ALL MY LOVE TO BOTH OF YOU—LOU"*: *The Rome Letters*, p. 120.

142 *"Dearest Anny . . . Synagogue to design"*: *The Rome Letters*, p. 121.

143 *"Nature of Space . . . Design"*: *The Rome Letters*, p. 72.

143 *"Now that I . . . give or take"*: *The Rome Letters*, p. 107.

143 *"She is a . . . so loving"*: *The Rome Letters*, p. 138.

144 *"WILL MEET BOAT . . . LOVE LOU"*: *The Rome Letters*, p. 188.

145 *"sweet . . . like a ballerina"*: MacAllister interview.

145 *"gentle, kind . . . lovely, gentle woman"*: Lois Sherr Dubin's interview with the author on May 21, 2013, in New York. [Hereafter cited as Dubin interview.]

145 *"almost British . . . she was so 'right'"*: Joseph Kuo's interview with the author on September 28, 2014, in Philadelphia.

146 *Anne heard Marie speaking in Chinese*: All information in this paragraph comes from Alexandra Tyng interview.

146 *"baffled entrances . . . over a year"*: *The Rome Letters*, p. 192.

147 *"June 7 . . . symbolic of religion . . . satisfied with his work"*: Undated notebook with unnumbered pages, Louis I. Kahn Collection, catalog number 030.VII.4.

148 *"Alex time"*: Richards interview.

148 *"She would say . . . courthouse or something"*: Alexandra Tyng interview.

149 *"He really adored . . . to anybody"*: Esther Kahn quoted in Latour, p. 25.

149 *"squeaky . . . was an epiphany . . . going to be famous"*: Richard Saul Wurman's interview with the author on October 9, 2014, in New York. [Hereafter cited as Wurman interview.]

150 *"And it came to me . . . sure it happened . . . seeing another woman . . . her own thing"*: Sue Ann Kahn interview. All of the information about Esther's affair comes from Sue Ann Kahn, who relayed to the author the information she derived from a telephone conversation with the daughter of Esther's lover.

152 *"I saw the toe . . . when she saw me"*: Ona Russell interview.

152 *"I came down . . . saw him cry"*: Alan Kahn interview.

153 *"She was a compelling . . . awe and idealization"*: Berkeley creativity study.

154 *"often from abroad to this country"*: Donald W. MacKinnon, "Some Critical Issues for Future Research in Creativity," collected in the volume *Frontiers of Creativity Research*, ed. Scott G. Isaksen, Buffalo: Bearly, 1987, pp. 127–28; see also Donald W. MacKinnon, "Architects, Personality Types, and Creativity," collected in *The Creativity Question*, ed. Albert Rothenberg and Carl R. Haussman, Durham: Duke University Press, 1976, pp. 175–89.

155 *"character sketch . . . I suffered severe burning . . . Constant disagreements . . . became water"*: Berkeley creativity study.

160 *"Bob Venturi . . . all of us combined"*: Kahn colleague quoted in Nathaniel Kahn interview.

160 *"Bob Venturi's girlfriend"*: Sue Ann Kahn interview.

160 *"Dearest Best . . . her faith in him . . . a great great work"*: Undated letter from Louis Kahn to Harriet Pattison, Collection of Harriet Pattison; displayed in Vitra exhibition *The Power of Architecture*, London Design Museum, July 2014.

161 *"The building is . . . desire for creation . . . a new image"*: Letter from Louis Kahn to Harriet Pattison, September 15, 1959, Collection of Harriet Pattison; quoted in George H. Marcus and William Whitaker, *The Houses of Louis Kahn*, New Haven: Yale University Press, 2013, p. 63.

162 *"Tout le monde . . . tres importante"*: Undated postcard (postmarked 1959) from Louis Kahn to Esther Kahn, Collection of Sue Ann Kahn. The English translation, omitting Lou's ever-present solecisms, is roughly: "Everybody, all of France, is beautiful and agreeable. Carcassonne is very important architecture."

162 *"I suggested to Lou . . . someone else"*: *The Rome Letters*, p. 202.

162 *"When I was about five . . . cover up the truth"*: Alexandra Tyng interview.

163 *"If you could . . . special moment . . . come in tomorrow?"*: Wurman interview.

164 *"I remember . . . in time for dinner"*: Emails from Edward Abelson and Sandra Abelson forwarded to the author by Sue Ann Kahn.

164 *"He spent more . . . not with his family"*: MacAllister interview.

165 *"Everyone had a different Lou . . . I had no funding . . . all sounding boards"*: Wurman interview.

165 *"He ran the office . . . he would choose"*: Sue Ann Kahn interview.

166 *"Everyone remarked . . . maybe he did"*: Sue Ann Kahn interview.

166 *"Early in my . . . I pay Gabor"*: Gary Moye's interview with the author, conducted via email starting on May 25, 2014, with numerous exchanges extending into 2015. [Hereafter cited as Moye interview.]

167 *"About a month ago . . . not just little things"*: *Writings, Lectures*, pp. 155–56.

167 *"Gabor was bizarre . . . talking to him"*: Wurman interview.

168 *"The distinction . . . minor lack"*: Berkeley creativity study.

168 *"Yes . . . love-hate affair . . . cope with him"*: Gianopulos interview.

172 *"Kaddish/kiddush"*: Susan Solomon, *Louis I. Kahn's Jewish Architecture: Mikveh Israel and the Midcentury American Synagogue*, Waltham: Brandeis University Press, 2009, p. 106. My debt to Solomon's book extends far beyond this single quotation; in fact, just about everything in my description of the Mikveh Israel process stems from her extraordinarily detailed and well-researched work.

172 *the money changers out of the temple*: This is the one fact about Mikveh Israel that does not come from Solomon. It comes instead from the author's interview with Fred Langford on April 3, 2014, in Cape May Courthouse. [Hereafter cited as Langford interview.]

173 *"probably the single . . . since the war"*: MoMA catalog for the Richards Building exhibition, New York, 1961, p. 3.

173 *"Why is . . . waiting for you"*: Anne Tyng's account as told to her daughter, quoted in Alexandra Tyng interview.

174 *"If the world . . . bath house in Trenton"*: Louis Kahn quoted in Robert McCarter, *Louis I. Kahn*, London: Phaidon Press, 2005, p. 122. Again, as with Solomon, my debt to McCarter's excellent book is far larger than a few individual citations can suggest.

IN SITU: PHILLIPS EXETER LIBRARY

180 *chamfered edges*: As Nathaniel Kahn demonstrates in *My Architect*, this design—a brick building with four chamfered edges—is reminiscent of one of the industrial buildings that Louis Kahn would have seen during his childhood in the Northern Liberties. It's never easy to track the influences on Kahn, but in this case, just as with his Indian Institute of Management, Philadelphia probably belongs in there with Rome.

180 *"Will my coat . . . be okay"*: Author's conversation with anonymous Exeter students on October 24, 2013.

180 *"Need is so many . . . know what it is"*: Louis Kahn quoted in *What Will Be*, p. 29.

181 *"Because it is not . . . on the stairway"*: Louis Kahn quoted in *What Will Be*, p. 79.

185 *"He loved used . . . what the book's about"*: MacAllister interview.

186 *"I like English history . . . Volume Zero"*: Louis Kahn quoted in *Beginnings*, pp. 177–78.

186 *"What would happen . . . all over again"*: Berkeley creativity study.

186 *"You plan a library . . . could be the beginning"*: Louis Kahn quoted in Robert McCarter, *Louis I. Kahn*, London: Phaidon Press, 2005, pp. 305–6, 318.

186 *"I see a library . . . go to the light"*: Louis Kahn quoted in David B. Brownlee and David G. De Long, *Louis I. Kahn: In the Realm of Architecture*, New York: Rizzoli, 1991, p. 390.

187 *"It was eerie . . . what's outside"*: Gail Scanlon's interview with the author on October 24, 2013, in Exeter.

188 *"I really think . . . rather than artistic"*: Drew Gatto's interview with the author on October 24, 2013, in Exeter.

189 *"so-called beauty"*: Louis Kahn quoted in *What Will Be*, p. 79.

189 *"No space . . . how it was made . . . the wall does not . . . opening, it cries"*: "Law and Rule in Architecture," in *Essential Texts*, pp. 130–31.

189 *"those open circles . . . It's impossible . . . overall feeling . . . lightness below us"*: Drew Gatto's interview with the author on October 24, 2013, in Exeter.

ACHIEVING

193 *"Dr. Salk to office, 1501 Walnut"*: 1962 office calendar, Louis I. Kahn Collection, Box 121.

193 *"He lived . . . from there . . . I remember . . . windowsill"*: Alexandra Tyng interview.

194 *"There's a picture . . . businessman"*: Langford interview.

195 *"I found . . . warms my heart"*: Jonas Salk quoted in *What Will Be*, p. 296.

195 *"I have to say . . . many difficulties"*: Jonas Salk speaking in *Signature Against the Sky*, a documentary film made for WCAU-TV Philadelphia, directed by Bob Olander, c. 1967, The Architectural Archives. [Hereafter cited as *Signature Against the Sky*.]

196 *"When you ask . . . as myself"*: Louis Kahn quoted in *What Will Be*, p. 131.

196 *"folded plate scheme"*: Leslie, p. 138.

197 *"It was twilight . . . two alleys . . . greater building"*: Jonas Salk quoted in *What Will Be*, p. 296.

198 *"When the folded . . . Vierendeel truss . . . drunken sailor . . . Jack is quick . . . man can draw . . . be tough . . . makes two of us . . . it becomes powder . . . color Lou loved . . . old castles . . . in repose"*: Langford interview.

199 *"Lou loved ruins . . . it will look like"*: MacAllister interview.

200 *"Precast is . . . more machine-like . . . bleeds . . . becomes a scar . . . reuse out of it"*: Langford interview.

201 *"He was very interested . . . vision of concrete"*: MacAllister interview.

201 *"The main thing . . . logic to it"*: Langford interview.

201 *"The fact . . . related to his face"*: MacAllister interview.

201 *"When I first . . . his personality"*: Langford interview.

202 *"I think it was . . . three-digit IQs"*: MacAllister interview.

202 *"I think he was . . . such a life themselves"*: Slovic interview.

203 *"Not again!"*: Harriet Pattison quoting Louis Kahn in *My Architect*.

203 *"outsiders"*: For details about the Noguchi playground and the reasons it was never built, see Hayden Herrera, *Listening to Stone: The Art and Life of Isamu Noguchi*, New York: Farrar, Straus and Giroux, 2015, pp. 378–84.

203 *"There is no meeting . . . get some antiques . . . if he heard me . . . Who shall I say . . . supported him all her life"*: Sue Ann Kahn interview.

205 *"Mrs. Kahn . . . No calls"*: 1962 office calendar, Louis I. Kahn Collection, Box 121.

208 *"There were two . . . in the office then,"*: Wurman interview.

209 *"They had these . . . own pace"*: Slovic interview.

209 *"we did work . . . a week"*: Langford interview.

209 *"He could really . . . he didn't care"*: Richards interview.

210 *"Lou brought . . . talked about things"*: Dubin interview.

210 *"The biggest lesson . . . the right answer"*: MacAllister interview.

210 *"Lou was very . . . his Penn class"*: Langford interview.

210 *"It's very hard . . . it's fabulous"*: Richards interview.

211 *"universal elements . . . the column became"*: Charles Dagit, *Louis I. Kahn Architect*, New Brunswick: Transaction Publishers, 2013, p. 40.

211 *"If he owed you . . . it's a process"*: Richards interview.

211 *"He didn't . . . wonderful spaces"*: Dubin interview.

211 *"Lou would walk . . . Whose is it?"*: Charles Dagit, *Louis I. Kahn Architect*, New Brunswick: Transaction Publishers, 2013, p. 38.

212 *"He came in . . . say it was crap"*: Richards interview.

212 *"The time that Lou . . . towards the end . . . pull it off"*: Slovic interview.

213 *"He went . . . he saw too much"*: Richards interview.

213 *"easy to work with . . . Mr. Magoo . . . am on the site"*: Langford interview.

213 *"He was just . . . scream about it"*: MacAllister interview.

213 *"broker's pencil . . . embedded in the drawings"*: Slovic interview.

213 *"When I was a student . . . freer with charcoal"*: Richards interview.

214 *"I think he . . . want to change it"*: Langford interview.

214 *"I will help you realize your dream"*: Balkrishna V. Doshi's interview with the author on March 3, 2014, in Ahmedabad. [Hereafter cited as Doshi interview.]

214 *"he started talking . . . the embassy plan"*: Balkrishna V. Doshi, *Le Corbusier and Louis I. Kahn: The Acrobat and the Yogi of Architecture*, Ahmedabad: Vastu-Shilpa Foundation for Studies and Research in Environmental Design, 2012, p. 38–39. [Hereafter cited as *Acrobat and Yogi*.]

214 *"I came back . . . ruins around buildings"*: *Writings, Lectures*, pp. 118, 123.

215 *"the new idiom . . . haunt me . . . their pursuits"*: *Acrobat and Yogi*, p. 40.

215 *"He was very worried . . . rather than compromise"*: Wurman interview.

216 *"the grand old . . . patron of architects"*: *Acrobat and Yogi*, p. 43.

216 *"I said . . . good as Corbusier"*: Doshi interview.

216 *"to promote . . . universalism"*: Mission Statement of the Tagore Society of Philadelphia, Louis I. Kahn Collection, File 030.II.A.64.18.

218 *"dislikes irrationality . . . formal religion"*: Berkeley creativity study.

218 *"He is the one . . . are hard . . . be proud"*: Scully, pp. 10, 43.

220 *"First of all . . . make an arch"*: Doshi interview.

221 *"Why don't . . . what people have"*: Moshe Safdie's interview with the author on April 25, 2014, in Cambridge.

221 *"From 2:30 . . . very organized"*: Doshi interview.

221 *"Tell him . . . Nothing, nothing"*: Yatin Pandya's interview with the author on March 5, 2014, in Ahmedabad.

221 *"It was Kasturbhai's . . . turning corridor"*: Doshi interview.

222 *"He is a man . . . made of good stuff"*: Jules David Prown and Karen E. Denavit, *Louis I. Kahn in Conversation: Interviews with John W. Cook and Heinrich Klotz, 1969–70*, New Haven: Yale University Press, 2014, pp. 225, 233, 234.

222 *"This is like . . . another century"*: Doshi interview.

222 *"duplicate the work . . . worth living for"*: Louis Kahn in *Signature Against the Sky*.

223 *"ill health . . . When you look at . . . whispering in Kahn's ear"*: Nurur Rahman Khan's interview with the author on March 10, 2014, in Dhaka.

224 *"I was asked . . . it's okay . . . He liked going . . . had run out"*: Henry Wilcots' interview with the author on November 4, 2013, in Philadelphia, supplemented by many additional email exchanges. [Hereafter cited as Wilcots interview.]

225 *"a no man's land . . . give the meaning it lacked"*: Letter from Louis Kahn to Harriet Pattison, January 1963, Collection of Harriet Pattison; published in Vitra Chronology, p. 27.

226 *"In Dacca . . . five times a day"*: Louis Kahn quoted in *What Will Be*, pp. 24–25.

227 *"Spirituality . . . truth is obscure"*: Shamsul Wares's interview with the author on March 10, 2014, in Dhaka. [Hereafter cited as Wares interview.]

227 *"didn't have . . . that once"*: Wurman interview.

228 *"Leopold was never . . . came by bus"*: Leonard Traines's telephone interview with the author on October 27, 2015.

228 *"He demanded . . . my grandmother"*: Rhoda Kantor interview.

228 *"He was the noise . . . like a bandbox"*: Alan Kahn interview.

228 *"I remember Leopold . . . incoherent or anything"*: Ona Russell interview.

229 *"He was seeing bugs . . . system breakdown"*: Alan Kahn interview.

229 *"babysit"*: Langford interview.

229 *"I remember him . . . in that setting"*: Ona Russell interview.

229 *"Brooks Brothers . . . was Lou saying?"*: Jeff Kahn's interview with the author on June 17, 2013, in Oakland.

230 *"When he talked . . . he was saying"*: Lauren Kahn's interview with the author on June 17, 2013, in Oakland.

230 *"It was hysterical . . . feel his equal"*: Rhoda Kantor interview.

230 *"There was a mystique . . . Lou is coming!"*: Ona Russell interview.

230 *"Your father is . . . How was your day?"*: Alexandra Tyng interview.

230 *"In 1964 . . . giving me work"*: The Rome Letters, p. 210.

231 *"Anne would . . . crazy-making"*: MacAllister interview.

231 *"Lou would never . . . talking about"*: Richards interview.

231 *"One day . . . Anne was a brilliant . . . something in her"*: Moshe Safdie's interview with the author on April 25, 2014, in Cambridge.

232 *"Anne made the decision . . . little terror"*: Richards interview.

232 *"I think he just . . . when I was ten"*: Alexandra Tyng interview.

232 *"He always . . . the same intensity"*: Alexandra Tyng quoted in Latour, p. 57.

233 *"He was on the fifth . . . we all knew . . . Lou about something"*: Slovic interview.

233 *"It was humiliating in some ways"*: Harriet Pattison in *My Architect*.

233 *"We always used to . . . he was smiling . . . had mistresses"*: Richards interview.

234 *"It was the age . . . giant free-for-all"*: MacAllister interview.

234 *"The only one . . . a boy involved"*: Langford interview.

235 *"I was an outsider . . . what he was talking about"*: Doshi interview.

235 *"I called him . . . went to Philadelphia . . . We met on the telephone . . . Wonderful woman . . . His house was filled . . . got along"*: Wilcots interview.

236 *"the well-named Quaker"*: MacAllister interview.

237 *"Dave was different . . . packing case together"*: Wurman interview.

237 *"Dave was the office . . . Do such and such"; "Dave's details were all very practical . . . go storming out"*: Henry Wilcots quoted in Michael Borowski, "The Ultimate Manager: The Role of Wisdom in Louis Kahn's Office," published in Andrew Pressman, *Professional Practice 101: Business Strategies and Case Studies in Architecture*, New York: Wiley, 2006, p. 164.

237 *"Dave was not a rah-rah man . . . lot of those"*: Wilcots interview.

237 *"We brought this matter . . . willingness to speak up to Lou"*: Moye interview.

238 *"old-time friends . . . didn't get upset"*: Wilcots interview.

238 *"Dave Wisdom . . . not individually strong"*: Slovic interview.

238 *"Dave Wisdom . . . like everyone else"*: Richards interview.

238 *"a real nice person . . . antagonistic brothers"*: Langford interview.

238 *"Day or night . . . as a professional business"*: Moye interview.

238 *"He was there in the morning . . . everyone else did"*: Langford interview.

239 *"Right . . . because of your religion?"*: Wilcots interview.

239 *"To the end . . . working on Sunday"*: David Wisdom quoted in *Louis I. Kahn: Conception and Meaning*, an extra edition of *Architecture and Urbanism*, Tokyo: A+U Publishing, 1983, p. 222.

239 *"He would come to your . . . cheap tracing paper"*: Langford interview.

240 *"The beauty of . . . you had to follow that"*: Wilcots interview.

240 *"Never having . . . top this one"*: Louise Badgley quoted in *What Will Be*, p. 266.

240 *"Once during one of . . . key to Kahn's architecture"*: Vitra Chronology, p. 27.

241 *"a disgracefully . . . a terrible square"*: Vincent Scully quoted in *What Will Be*, p. 297.

241 *"It was busy . . . was ever fired"*: Wilcots interview.

241 *"At the end of . . . run out of money"*: Richards interview.

241 *"the mother hen, a very jolly kind of person"*: Wilcots interview.

241 *"He turned on the charm . . . helped Lou in this way"*: Moye interview.

242 *"They were very open . . . paying proposition"*: Slovic interview.

242 *"President Khan . . . Why didn't I think of that?"*: MacAllister interview.

243 *"I introduced myself . . . some of his architect friends"; "Okay, you win . . . painting the walls"*: Rafael Villamil's interview with the author on November 3, 2013, in Philadelphia, with follow-up telephone conversation on November 5, 2013.

243 *"I also feel . . . ways of nature"*: Letter from Louis Kahn to Luis Barragán, January 20, 1965, Collection of the Barragan Foundation, Basel, Switzerland; displayed at the Vitra exhibition *The Power of Architecture*, London Design Museum, July 2014.

244 *"There should be no . . . the Pacific"*: Louis Kahn quoted in *What Will Be*, p. 3.

244 *"Lou liked it . . . the United States"*: MacAllister interview.

247 *"Standard Western reinforcing . . . make up for it"*: Langford interview.

247 *"because Lou owed . . . conventional honor"*: Gianopulos interview.

248 *"A disaster . . . not so heavy . . . Favorite uncle"*: Langford interview.

249 *"I would also . . . will always treasure"*: Fred Langford, "A Report on Concrete and Formwork: The National Assembly Building Second Capital Project," submitted on behalf of Louis I. Kahn Architect to the Pakistan Public Works Department, June 30, 1966, p. 95, The Architectural Archives.

IN SITU: NATIONAL ASSEMBLY BUILDING OF BANGLADESH

253 *Raymond Meier's color pictures*: These are to be found in his gorgeous book *Louis Kahn Dhaka*, published in Switzerland by Editions Dino Simonett in 2004.

254 *"I have a book of castles . . . thoroughly at this book"*: "Law and Rule of Architecture II," in *Essential Texts*, p. 147.

254 *"They've destroyed . . . only in photographs"*: Wares interview.

255 *"he brought us democracy"*: Shamsul Wares in *My Architect*.

255 *"This is the process . . . disorientation"*: Wares interview.

255 *"Yes, yes . . . lose your way . . . within a serene context . . . people moving together"*: Dr. Shirin Sharmin Chaudhury's interview with the author on March 12, 2014, in Dhaka.

258 *"may never have been said before"*: "The Room, the Street, and Human Agreement," in *Essential Texts*, p. 253.

259 *"What is assembly . . . more mysterious"*: Wares interview.

ARRIVING

264 *Kahn's plan for Exeter*: See Jay Wickersham, "The Making of Exeter Library," *Harvard Architecture Review*, 1989, pp. 139–49 for the fullest and most accurate description of the design and construction process.

265 *"without surrendering . . . to make adjustments"*: Letter from Louis Kahn to Rodney Armstrong, April 17, 1968, Phillips Exeter Academy Archives; copy supplied to the author by the Academy archivist, Edouard L. Desrochers.

266 *"It's my favorite . . . the human spirit"*: Sue Ann Kahn interview.

266 *"The Kimbell . . . conception of architecture"*: Robert McCarter, *Louis I. Kahn*, London: Phaidon Press, 2005, p. 340.

266 *"If you liked . . . love Kimbell"*: Wurman interview.

266 *"This building feels . . . other hand did it"*: Nell E. Johnson and Eric Lee (eds.), *Light Is the Theme: Louis I. Kahn and the Kimbell Art Museum*, New Haven: Yale University Press, 2011, p. 73.

267 *disappeared silently and completely*: So it seemed, at any rate, to C. K. Williams, a poet who spent many hours of his youth hanging around Kahn's office, where his college friends Wurman and Rothstein worked. Citing a poem Czeslaw Milosz wrote about a painting in the Kimbell Museum, Williams remarked on this juxtaposition of his two "masters": "It pleases me to think of Czeslaw making his way through those serenely elegant, luminous spaces Lou had devised: Milosz hushed in the inspiration of his experience of it, the other embodied in the very hush." (C. K. Williams, "Kahn," in *All at Once*, New York: Farrar, Straus and Giroux, 2014, p. 35.)

267 *"all-embracing . . . ought to be"*: Leslie, p. 181.

267 *"The average size . . . up to 30 feet"*: Leslie, p. 187.

268 *"Marshall would leave . . . lead person"*: Wilcots interview.

269 *"gentle collaboration"*: Marshall Meyers quoted in Latour, p. 81.

269 *"He never worked . . . from on high"*: Marshall Meyers quoted in *Louis I. Kahn: Conception and Meaning*, an extra edition of *Architecture and Urbanism*. Tokyo: A+U Publishing, 1983, p. 223.

269 *"worked best with . . . a discourse"*: Marshall Meyers quoted in Latour, p. 79.

269 *"wings," "beam-splitter"*: Leslie, pp. 192, 189.

270 *"Komendant is very . . . analyzing it"*: Louis Kahn quoted in *What Will Be*, p. 27.

272 *"office boy"*: Wilcots interview.

272 *"Lou didn't drive . . . end of the driveway"*: Slovic interview.

273 *"He had very . . . meatball to go around"*: Nathaniel Kahn interview.

273 *"Since we moved . . . came second"*: Esther Kahn quoted in Latour, p. 25.

273 *"his mission . . . being done"*: Nathaniel Kahn interview.

274 *"that you were . . . all of those things"*: Dialogue between Nathaniel Kahn and Harriet Pattison in *My Architect*.

274 *"He was devastated . . . in distress"*: Nathaniel Kahn interview.

274 *"She said Jamie was going to be her creation"*: Morton Paterson's interview with the author on September 28, 2014, in Philadelphia.

275 *"Lou cried . . . Marie Kuo died"*: Sue Ann Kahn interview.

276 *"If something fell . . . of his life, I think"*: Sue Ann Kahn interview.

277 *"Who's going to . . . your work in Venice?"*: Wilcots interview.

279 *"Picasso said . . . harsh word, ugly"*: Louis Kahn quoted in *What Will Be*, p. 19.

280 *"Hi, Mr. Kahn . . . were not quite right . . . three families . . . I told my mother . . . Like, why didn't he . . . a people person . . . really good cook"*: Alexandra Tyng interview.

281 *"The meals she served . . . kind of light . . . Anne was . . . or an old person"*: Nathaniel Kahn interview.

282 *"I just decided . . . inject some normality . . . started to notice . . . over his head"*: Alexandra Tyng interview.

283 *"To be fair . . . going to go?"*: Nathaniel Kahn interview.

283 *"I think she . . . I mean that literally"*: Peter Arfaa's interview with the author on November 4, 2013, in Philadelphia.

284 *"in a kind of innocently . . . to be with her"*: Slovic interview.

284 *"I think his loyalty . . . us as people"*: Alexandra Tyng interview.

284 *"He was a man . . . grab things"*: Wares interview.

285 *"He never talked . . . That takes confidence"*: Langford interview.

286 *"Ricky, look at this!"*: Wurman interview.

286 *"the beginning of . . . street is a community room . . . belong to him alone . . . are on trial"*: "The Room, the Street, and Human Agreement," *in Essential Texts*, pp. 253, 254, 255, 257, 256.

290 *"The burnt wood figure . . . constructive criticism"*: Handwritten notes made by Louis Kahn on the back of a BOAC receipt for a London–Tel Aviv flight, Collection of Sue Ann Kahn.

292 *"He said no . . . with politics"*: Sue Ann Kahn interview.

292 *"I would say Lou was completely apolitical"*: Esther Kahn in Brownlee video.

293 *"as ruinous as . . . our sense of democracy . . . the Roosevelt Memorial . . . reason for living"*: "Lecture at Pratt Institute," in *Essential Texts*, pp. 279, 268.

293 *"four essential . . . in the world"*: Franklin Delano Roosevelt's words as engraved on the wall of the FDR Four Freedoms monument, Roosevelt Island.

294 *"He was trying to make . . . and feel safe"*: Lauren Kahn's interview with the author on June 17, 2013, in Oakland.

294 *"My dearest ones . . . all in stone"*: Undated letter from Louis Kahn to Harriet Pattison, Collection of Harriet Pattison; displayed in the Vitra exhibition *The Power of Architecture*, London Design Museum, July 2014.

295 *"How far apart . . . bring out for him"*: Samuel Hughes, "Constructing a New Kahn," in *The Pennsylvania Gazette*, March/April 2013, pp. 36–49.

295 *"He turned me down . . . places that will scare me . . . comfortable in his relationships"*: Steve Korman's interview with the author on November 3, 2013, at Korman House.

296 *"When Lou brought her . . . the love of his life . . . It was kind of fun . . . resented this whole situation"*: Norma Shapiro's interview with the author on November 3, 2013, at Shapiro House.

297 *"Philadelphia was . . . about the affairs"*: Sue Ann Kahn interview.

297 *"I spent . . . he didn't want to"*, *"blacked out . . . care about you"*: Steve Korman's interview with the author on November 3, 2013, at Korman House.

298 *"It was one . . . but an hour?"*: Toby Korman Davidov's telephone interview with the author on November 9, 2013.

IN SITU: INDIAN INSTITUTE OF MANAGEMENT AHMEDABAD

304 *"I don't think . . . sacred space"*: Doshi interview.

305 *"began with . . . were students"*: "Form and Design," in *Essential Texts*, p. 64.

305 *"Economy has . . . can buy"*: Louis Kahn delivering the lecture "Architecture and Human Agreement," as filmed by Duncan White, 1971, The Architectural Archives.

309 *"What slice . . . side of a building"*: Louis Kahn's annotated sketch in Robert McCarter, *Louis I. Kahn*, London: Phaidon Press, 2005, p. 225. No Wallace Stevens work contains anything like this exact line, though a number of his poems (including one titled "Architecture") allude to the sun. But Harriet Pattison, who often read poems aloud to Lou, has found a slip of yellow trace paper marking the poem "The Bouquet" in her copy of *The Auroras of Autumn*, and she is fairly certain the line that struck Lou was the middle one in the stanza:

A pack of cards is falling towards the floor.
The sun is secretly shining on a wall.
One remembers a woman standing in such a dress.

(Quoted from *The Collected Poems of Wallace Stevens*. New York: Alfred A. Knopf, 1954, p. 450.)

309 *"He wanted a thin joint . . . It's like an offering . . . you don't think of memory"*: Doshi interview.

BEGINNING

315 *"I like English . . . Minus-One"*: *Writings, Lectures*, p. 329.

317 *"constant residence"*: This and other information about the Mendelowitsch family in Latvia and Estonia comes from a 2006 archival reference report addressed to Ingrid Mald-Villand from Latvijas Valsts Vesturs Arhivs, 09.2006, Nr. 3-M-2305. Information about Leiser-Itze Schmulovsky's birth and circumcision comes from the actual birth records in Hebrew and Russian (available online through ancestry.com at www.lvva-raduraksti.lv/en/menu/lv/7/ig/7/ie/3417/book /28766.html). The Arensburg addresses and business types for the Mendelowitsches, as well as other details about the early years of the twentieth century in Arensburg, come from Olavi Pesti's "Kuressaare of a Century Ago," originally published in Estonian in *Ehitukunst*, no. 47/48, 2006, and translated into English by Peeter Tammisto (available online at http://ehituskunst.ee/olavi-pesti-kuressaare -of-a-century-ago/?lang=en).

·317 *"hotel"*: Louis Kahn quoted in *What Will Be*, p. 225.

319 *"A building . . . was made"*: "The Room, the Street, and Human Agreement," in *Essential Texts*, p. 258.

322 *One of his very earliest memories*: Berkeley creativity study.

323 *"It seems to take . . . three years old"*: Dialogue between Louis Kahn and an unidentified student from the question-and-answer period after the lecture "Architecture and Human Agreement," as filmed by Duncan White, 1971, The Architectural Archives. ,

323 *a strange, entrancing blue-green*: There are many accounts of the burning from Lou and others, most of which include the same details. Here is Esther's version, which takes advantage of her chemistry background: "sometimes, when there is something wrong with the oxygen, the coal burns green, which was exactly how the coal was one day. Lou was three years old and he loved the green colour. Many times he said that for all his life he would never forget that colour green. That day he wore a little pinafore, and put his hands in the fireplace to pick up the coal, save the colour and put it into his pinafore, which went up in flames. He immediately covered his eyes" (Esther Kahn quoted in Latour, p. 17).

EPILOGUE

327 *"Louis I. Kahn . . . America and abroad"*: Paul Goldberger's obituary of Louis Kahn, *The New York Times*, March 20, 1974, pp. 1, 64.

328 *"They're bastards . . . she was adamant"*: Peter Arfaa's interview with the author on November 4, 2013, in Philadelphia.

328 *"Alex called us . . . reserved for Lou"*: Rhoda Kantor interview.

330 *"The only thing . . . would have liked that"*: Nathaniel Kahn quoted in Samuel Hughes, "Journey to Estonia," *The Pennsylvania Gazette*, January/February 2007, pp. 36–43.

330 *"it would have . . . hang in Kuressaare"*: Alexandra Tyng quoted in Samuel Hughes, "Journey to Estonia," *The Pennsylvania Gazette*, January/February 2007, pp. 36–43.

332 *"Not under the . . . did not want the truth"*: Wurman interview.

333 *"always looking . . . cover it over"*: MacAllister interview.

333 *"He was a mental . . . his creativity"*: Wares interview.

333 *"His personal life . . . Anything goes"*: Dubin interview.

333 *"Desire is . . . impurities can happen"*: Louis Kahn quoted in *What Will Be*, p. 43.

334 *"I do not believe . . . in its wake"*: Louis Kahn quoted in *Beginnings*, p. 108.

334 *"must begin with . . . be unmeasurable"*: Louis Kahn quoted in *Beginnings*, p. 71.

334 *"he really lived . . . would find order"*: Videotape of Anne Tyng interviewed by Peter Kirby on May 26, 1992, The Architectural Archives.

334 *"strongly believed . . . fit together"*: Alexandra Tyng quoted in Latour, p. 59.

335 *"I think you . . . loving person"*: Alexandra Tyng interview.

335 *"He had an enormous . . . closest ones"*: Shamsul Wares in *My Architect*.

336 *"Motion—movement . . . architecture of movement"*: Louis Kahn quoted in *Beginnings*, p. 112.

336 *"The other thing . . . a great architect"*: Vincent Scully quoted in Latour, p. 147.

337 *"I think there's . . . imperfections of the material"*: MacAllister interview.

337 *"Lou had a lot . . . had a battle"*: Wurman interview.

338 *"There was something . . . do battle in the world"*: Nathaniel Kahn interview.

338 *"handsome"*: Sue Ann Kahn and Alexandra Tyng interviews.

338 *"He just had . . . saw him as such"*: Alexandra Tyng quoted in Latour, p. 63.

338 *"He had a kind . . . goddamn good"*: Jack MacAllister quoted in *What Will Be*, p. 291.

339 *"My mother . . . confidence in me"*: Louis Kahn quoted in *What Will Be*, p. 233.

339 *an estimated 235 designs*: The figures about Kahn's built and unbuilt projects come directly from William Whitaker or from his List of Projects in the Vitra catalogue, *Louis Kahn: The Power of Architecture*, Karlsruhe: Vitra Design Museum, 2012.

340 *"Success . . . sixty buildings"*: I. M. Pei in *My Architect*.

340 *"My first works . . . reverence for him"*: Frank Gehry in *My Architect*.

340 *"As time goes . . . sustenance to"*: Moshe Safdie quoted in *What Will Be*, p. 295.

340 *"the most beloved . . . being an artist"*: Philip Johnson in *My Architect*.

340 *"Magic . . . becomes architecture"*: Renzo Piano quoted in the Vitra catalogue, *Louis Kahn: The Power of Architecture*, Karlsruhe: Vitra Design Museum, 2012, p. 259.

341 *"aren't tied to the fashions of the time"*: MacAllister interview.

341 *"It's the making . . . not stylistic"*: Wurman interview.

341 *"The idea of not having . . . which is geometry"*: Videotape of Anne Tyng interviewed by Peter Kirby on May 26, 1992, The Architectural Archives.

341 *"He was influenced . . . and silent"*: Rafael Villamil's interview with the author on November 3, 2013, in Philadelphia, with follow-up telephone conversation on November 5, 2013.

341 *"Mies, Corbu . . . version at the beginning"*: Wares interview.

342 *"The standout in the office . . . just another detail"*: Wilcots interview.

343 *"restoring a building . . . architectural principles"*: Marshall Meyers quoted in Latour, pp. 85–87.

343 *"to quit a job . . . someone's kitchen"*: Slovic interview.

343 *"Let me help . . . let you do it"*: MacAllister interview.

344 *"Am I making . . . what interests you"*: Wurman interview.

344 *"He would look at you . . . but in life"*: David Rothstein's telephone interview with the author on March 12, 2015.

344 *"David Wisdom . . . particularly Henry's"*: Moye interview.

346 *"amazement . . . He did it"*: Harriet Pattison quoted in Samuel Hughes, "Constructing a New Kahn," in *The Pennsylvania Gazette*, March/April 2013, pp. 36–49.

349 *"Denise Scott Brown . . . to run on?"*: Marshall Meyers quoted in *Louis I. Kahn: Conception and Meaning*, an extra edition of *Architecture and Urbanism*, Tokyo: A+U Publishing, 1983. p. 227.

349 *With the Dominican Motherhouse project*: The entire description of the design process given here derives from two excellent works by Michael Merrill, *Louis Kahn: On the Thoughtful Making of Spaces: The Dominican Motherhouse and a Modern Culture of Space* and *Louis Kahn: Drawing to Find Out: The Dominican Motherhouse and the Patient Search for Architecture*, Baden: Lars Müller Publishers, 2010.

351 *"parted friends"*: David B. Brownlee and David G. De Long, *Louis I. Kahn: In the Realm of Architecture*, New York: Rizzoli, 1991, p. 388.

351 *"arts advisory . . . The Architect's central . . . glass could not"*: Kent Larson, *Louis I. Kahn: Unbuilt Masterworks*, New York: Monacelli Press, 2000, p. 115. Larson's helpful book is the source of most of the information given here about the Memorial to the Six Million Jewish Martyrs.

352 *"The one—the chapel . . . are silent"*: Museum of Modern Art press release No. 102, for an exhibition of the scale model of Kahn's design, October 17, 1968.

352 *"fulfilled their . . . tragic memories"*: Kent Larson, *Louis I. Kahn: Unbuilt Masterworks*, New York: Monacelli Press, 2000, p. 119.

354 *"A painter can . . . use round wheels"*: "Law and Rule in Architecture II," in *Essential Texts*, p. 150.

FURTHER READING

Because this book is a biography, dealing with both the man and his work, it leaves out a great deal of known information about the architecture in order to touch on all the other dimensions of Kahn's life and still keep within a reasonable length. There are dozens of other books (not to mention hundreds if not thousands of articles) written exclusively about Louis Kahn's architecture, and for those who have become interested in the subject, here is a brief list of recommended reading. All of these books have proven enormously instructive to me, and all can be usefully read by someone without architectural training.

Brownlee, David B., and David G. De Long, *Louis I. Kahn: In the Realm of Architecture*. New York: Rizzoli, 1991.

Goldhagen, Sarah Williams, *Louis Kahn's Situated Modernism*. New Haven: Yale University Press, 2001.

Larson, Kent, *Louis I. Kahn: Unbuilt Masterworks*. New York: Monacelli Press, 2000.

Leslie, Thomas, *Louis I. Kahn: Building Art, Building Science*. New York: George Braziller, 2005.

Loud, Patricia Cummings, *The Art Museums of Louis I. Kahn*. Durham: Duke University Press, 1989.

Marcus, George H., and William Whitaker, *The Houses of Louis Kahn*. New Haven: Yale University Press, 2013.

McCarter, Robert, *Louis I. Kahn*. London: Phaidon Press, 2005.

Merrill, Michael, *Louis Kahn: On the Thoughtful Making of Spaces:*

The Dominican Motherhouse and a Modern Culture of Space and *Louis Kahn: Drawing to Find Out: The Dominican Motherhouse and the Patient Search for Architecture*. Baden: Lars Müller Publishers, 2010.

Scully, Vincent, *Louis I. Kahn*. New York: George Braziller, 1962.

Solomon, Susan, *Louis I. Kahn's Trenton Jewish Community Center*. Princeton: Princeton Architectural Press, 2000; and *Louis I. Kahn's Jewish Architecture: Mikveh Israel and the Midcentury American Synagogue*. Waltham: Brandeis University Press, 2009.

Twombly, Robert (ed.), *Louis Kahn: Essential Texts*. New York: W. W. Norton, 2003.

Additionally, for those who might want to learn more about Kahn's paintings and sketches, here are two good books on that subject:

Hochstim, Jan, *The Paintings and Sketches of Louis I. Kahn*. New York: Rizzoli, 1991.

Johnson, Eugene J., and Michael J. Lewis, *Drawn from the Source: The Travel Sketches of Louis I. Kahn*. Cambridge: MIT Press, 1996.

ACKNOWLEDGMENTS

Financial support for this project was provided by Joan K. Davidson and Furthermore Grants in Publishing, a program of the J. M. Kaplan Fund, and by the NEH Public Scholar Program, whose generous award enabled me to finish writing the book.

I would like to thank Sue Ann Kahn for permission to quote from the letters and unpublished writings of Esther I. Kahn and Louis I. Kahn. Additional permissions were granted by Nathaniel Kahn, Alexandra Tyng, Rhoda Kantor, and The Architectural Archives at the University of Pennsylvania. The Archives, home of the Louis I. Kahn Collection, are an essential resource for anyone writing about Kahn, and I am especially grateful to their curator, Bill Whitaker, for all the help he gave me with this book. Not only did he dig up everything I asked about, from architectural sketches to calendars and tax returns, from videotaped interviews to notebooks and letters; he also selflessly shared with me the results of his detailed research into the events of Louis Kahn's life.

Pictorial assistance for this book came, to begin with, from the family members who shared with me their old family photographs—in particular Alex Tyng, Sue Ann Kahn, Nathaniel Kahn, Ona Russell, Rhoda Kantor, and Lauren Kahn. I want to thank them for allowing me to reproduce some of these pictures, and also to thank Sue Ann for permission to use four portraits done by Louis Kahn. Special thanks to Raymond Meier for generously allowing me to reproduce three of his terrific color photos of the Dhaka building's interior, which I regretfully had to render in black-and-white. Thanks also to the Phillips Exeter Academy, which granted me permission to use two archival photos of the library; to the Kimbell Art Museum, which helpfully commissioned a new shot of the galleries; to the Keith de Lellis Gallery, which allowed me to reproduce their John Ebstel photos of the Trenton Bath House; and to Mort Paterson, who kindly supplied the snapshots of Marie Kuo. Finally, I must once again mention my gratitude to The Architectural Archives, which provided me with the scans for about a third of the photos, both personal and architectural, that appear in this book.

Other institutional assistance was supplied by the Institute of Personality and Social Research, University of California at Berkeley, which—through the kind assistance of Elizabeth Peele—gave me access to the results of the 1958 psychological study in which Kahn participated. The Museum of Modern Art in New York shared archival information about the 1961 show celebrating the Richards Building and the party that preceded it. The Jews in Latvia Museum in Riga, in the person of its director, Ilya Lensky, provided useful contextual information about Kahn's birth and family background. And the New York Institute for the Humanities offered me, as always, both library privileges at NYU and enlightening conversations with knowledgeable colleagues.

Whoever attempts at the present time to write about Louis Kahn owes an enormous debt to the people who began documenting his life and work soon after his death. These include, first of all, Richard Saul Wurman, whose 1986 book *What Will Be Has Always Been: The Words of Louis I. Kahn* contains extensive quotations from Kahn's notebooks and talks as well as a variety of interviews with those who knew him. Equally important for my purposes were Alessandra Latour's two books, *Louis I. Kahn: l'uomo, il maestro*, in which she collects a crucial set of interviews she conducted in 1982 and 1983, and *Louis I. Kahn: Writings, Lectures, Interviews*, which reveals Kahn through his own words. David Brownlee and David De Long's 1991 book *Louis I. Kahn: In the Realm of Architecture* remains a central text, significantly amplified by Brownlee's lengthy and detailed interviews with Esther Kahn, which are preserved on videotape at The Architectural Archives. Two books by family members, Alexandra Tyng's *Beginnings: Louis I. Kahn's Philosophy of Architecture* and Anne Griswold Tyng's *Louis Kahn to Anne Tyng: The Rome Letters, 1953–54*, provided essential material for my project.

Nathaniel Kahn's marvelous film *My Architect* was both a beginning and an endpoint for me: I must have watched it at least six times since it first came out in 2003, and I have repeatedly drawn from it and tested my own ideas against it. The recent Vitra Design catalogue, *Louis Kahn: The Power of Architecture,* is noteworthy for William Whitaker's Chronology and List of Projects, both of which were crucial to my work. My predecessors in the work of biography, including Carter Wiseman and Charles Dagit, provided helpful information that was no longer available to me directly, and I owe a special debt to Joseph Burton for his seminal article on Louis Kahn's aesthetic education.

Nothing can replace direct communication, though, and I am especially grateful to the people who talked to me about Louis Kahn. My greatest thanks go to his three children—Nathaniel Kahn, Alex Tyng, and Sue Ann Kahn—who spoke to me for untold hours and were generously willing to explore, with unremitting affection and occasional pain, the personality and achievements of their father. Other Kahn relatives whose conversation helped me a great deal include Rhoda Kantor, Alan Kahn, Marvin Kantor, Jeff Kahn, Lauren Kahn, Ona Russell, Leonard Traines, and Rebecca Tyng Kantor. Edward Abelson and Sandra Abelson, Esther Kahn's nephew and niece, transmitted useful memories to me through their cousin Sue Ann. Harriet Pattison gave me advice and information in a series of friendly emails.

Just as Louis Kahn's buildings could not have been built without the help of the people who worked with him, this book could not have been written without their essential aid. My heartfelt thanks go out to his former colleagues and employees—namely, Henry Wilcots, Fred Langford, David Slovic, Nick Gianopulos, Jack MacAllister, Richard Wurman, Gary Moye, Moshe Safdie, Ed Richards, David Rothstein, Rafael Villamil, Harry Palmbaum, and David Zuckerkandel. I will never forget, in particular, the fascinating day I spent talking about concrete with Fred, nor the precision of detail about architectural projects and office practices that emerged from Henry's prodigiously well-stocked memory in response to my incessant questions.

Around the world, in every place I visited, people put themselves out to help me in my researches. In Ahmedabad, these essential helpers included the celebrated architect Balkrishna V. Doshi and his colleague Yatin Pandya. In Dhaka, James Timberlake and Jacob Mans kindly allowed me to join their Penn travel group; Shamsul Wares and Nurur Rahman Khan took time off from their architectural practices to speak with me in detail about Kahn; Dr. Shirin Sharman Chaudhury, Speaker of the Bangladesh Assembly, interrupted her busy day to talk with me about the Parliament Building; and Julfikar Ali Manik, journalist extraordinaire, devoted several days of his life to making my whole trip a success. In Estonia, I received the generous assistance of Heie Treier, who came down from Tallinn to show me Lou's castle; Hannes Hanso, the hospitable mayor of Kuressaare; Olavi Pesti, Kuressaare's chief historian; and Philippe Hache, a historically knowledgeable resident of Saaremaa. At Exeter, I was bountifully aided by librarians Gail Scanlon and Drew Gatto, archivists Edouard L. Desrochers and Thomas Wharton, and faculty member Todd Hearon. In Fort Worth, my trip to the Kimbell was enormously enhanced by conversations with local architect and Kahn scholar Mark Gunderson, as well as discussions about the building with museum director Eric Lee and curator Nancy Edwards. At the Salk Institute in La Jolla, I was the lucky recipient of Tim Ball's detailed practical knowledge and Greg Lemke's friendly openness; I also benefited from the kindness of Robert Redford, who loaned me a copy of his Salk Institute film—one segment of the six-part Cathedrals of Culture series—before its general release. At First Unitarian Church in Rochester, Carol Anne Teague made me feel welcome during my day-long visit and Bill Fugate answered my subsequent questions. In New York, Lois Sherr Dubin spoke with me about FDR Four Freedoms Park, Kahn's early teaching years at Penn, and a variety of other subjects. In the Philadelphia area, Peter Arfaa, Morton Paterson, Joseph and Marianne Kuo, Larry Korman, Steve Korman, Toby Korman Davidov, John Andrew Gallery, and Norma Shapiro all gave generously of their time to fill me in about Lou's life and work; Dr. Bill Tasman advised me about cataract surgery in 1962; David Livewell directed me to Harry Kyriakodis's history of the Northern Liberties ward; and Susan Solomon gave me a revelatory tour of the Trenton Bath House.

Many other people helped with this project in ways both large and small, and I want to single out a few of them. Martin and Barbara Bauer not only translated the Kahn family letters from German to English, but also offered me accommodation in their wonderful Katzbach Academy, where I was able to complete a first draft of the book. Katharine

Michaels, Susan Solomon, and Laura Hartman each read the manuscript and commented on it with great delicacy and piercing practicality. Arthur Lubow, whose steadfast advice helped guide the whole process, lent crucial finishing touches to the final draft. Tom Laqueur, Jean Strouse, Stephen Greenblatt, and Mark Stevens wrote me letters of reference and listened to endless musings on the subject of Louis Kahn. Additional semi-captive listeners included Joe Lelyveld, Janny Scott, Alida Becker, Tim Clark, Anne Wagner, Nick Rizzo, Charlie Haas, BK Moran, Simone Di Piero, Toni Martin, David Hollander, Patty Unterman, Tim Savinar, Mimi Chubb, James Lasdun, Brenda Wineapple, and, above all, my husband, Richard Rizzo, who accompanied me on many of the site visits and formulated several astute observations that I shamelessly stole for the book.

Farrar, Straus and Giroux is the kind of publishing house that makes it a pleasure to be a writer. From Jonathan Galassi and Jeff Seroy, both longtime friends of mine, to the many production, editorial, design, and publicity people—Tyler Comrie, Brian Gittis, Debra Helfand, John Knight, Jonathan Lippincott, Rob Sternitzky, and others—who brought my manuscript to its finished state and beyond, the people at FSG have jointly steered this book into its best possible shape. None of them shares responsibility for any of its faults, but they all deserve praise for its virtues. Of no one is this more true than Ileene Smith, my cherished editor of three books so far and many more to come, I hope.

INDEX